# Vegetable Verbiage

**Warm-season vegetables:** Frost-sensitive plants that grow best in the heat of summer. Plant warm-season vegetables in spring after the threat of frost has passed, or in summer in warm areas for a fall harvest. Warm-season vegetables include

- Beans
- Corn
- Cucumbers
- Eggplant
- Melons
- Peppers
- Pumpkins
- Squash
- Tomatoes

**Cool-season vegetables:** These vegetables can withstand frost. They grow best in the cool months of early spring and fall. Plant cool-season vegetables six to eight weeks prior to the last spring frost to mature in late spring or summer, or plant them in late summer or early fall to mature in fall. If allowed to grow too long into warm weather, many cool-season vegetables will *bolt* (flower and set seed) and become bitter tasting. Cool-season vegetables include

- Beets
- Broccoli
- Cabbage
- Carrots
- Cauliflower
- Lettuce and other salad greens
- Onions
- Peas
- Potatoes
- Radishes
- Spinach
- Turnips

**Thinning:** The process of pulling out young seedlings so that plants are appropriately spaced and not overcrowded. You most commonly thin vegetables — such as carrots, beets, lettuce, and radishes — whose seeds you *broadcast* (scatter) randomly over a planting bed.

# Keys to a Productive Vegetable Garden

- Plant at the right time of the year.
- Plant in full sun.
- Grow varieties that are well adapted to your area.
- Prepare the soil before planting, working in organic matter and appropriate nutrients.
- Space plants appropriately and make sure to thin vegetables planted from seed.
- Fertilize young plants on a regular basis.
- Water regularly so that your plants never completely dry out, but not so often that the soil is constantly saturated.
- Harvest on a regular basis to keep plants producing.

# Vegetable Gardening For Dummies®

Cheat Sheet

## Easiest Ways to Grow Common Vegetables

The best way to grow some vegetables — such as, tomatoes and peppers — is to plant seedlings in your garden; you can purchase these seedlings, or transplants, at a nursery or start them indoors from seed. The best way to grow other vegetables — such as, cucumbers and peas — is to sow seed directly in your garden. You can plant some vegetables either way.

The following table lists the best planting techniques for common vegetables as well as the recommended spacing between plants (you usually plant vegetables that are started from seeds closer together and then thin them to this distance after the seeds germinate).

| Vegetable | Best Planting Method | Spacing |
| --- | --- | --- |
| Beans, bush | Direct seed | 3 to 4 inches apart |
| Beans, pole | Direct seed | 4 to 6 inches apart |
| Beets | Direct seed | 2 inches apart |
| Broccoli | Easy from seed or transplant | 14 to 24 inches apart |
| Cabbage | Easy from seed or transplant | 14 to 24 inches apart |
| Carrots | Direct seed | 2 inches apart |
| Cauliflower | Easy from seed or transplant | 14 to 24 inches apart |
| Celery | Transplants | 6 inches apart |
| Corn | Direct seed | 12 to 18 inches apart |
| Cucumbers | Direct seed | 24 to 48 inches apart |
| Eggplant | Transplant | 18 to 24 inches apart |
| Lettuce | Easy from seed or transplant | 6 to 10 inches part |
| Melons | Direct seed | At least 24 to 36 inches apart |
| Onions | Easy from seed or transplant | 3 to 4 inches part |
| Peas | Direct seed | 2 to 4 inches part |
| Peppers | Transplant | 18 to 24 inches apart |
| Potatoes | Eyes (pieces or root) | 8 to 10 inches apart |
| Pumpkins | Direct seed | 36 to 48 inches apart |
| Radishes | Direct seed | 1 to 2 inches apart |
| Spinach | Direct seed | 3 to 4 inches apart |
| Squash, summer | Direct seed | 18 to 36 inches part |
| Squash, winter | Direct seed | 24 to 48 inches apart |
| Tomatoes | Transplant | 18 to 36 inches apart |
| Turnips | Direct seed | 2 to 3 inches apart |

## ...For Dummies: Bestselling Book Series for Beginners

# Praise for Gardening For Dummies, 2nd Edition

"Despite the humorous title, *Gardening For Dummies* is a valuable book full of down-to-earth garden advice. I've been gardening most of my life and I still found something new to learn in this well-organized book."
— Larry Sombke, public radio's *Natural Gardener*

"Creating a successful garden just got easier with the 2nd edition of *Gardening For Dummies*. It's packed with down-to-earth gardening advice that both novice and experienced gardeners will find useful."
— Doug Jimerson, VP Editor-in-Chief of garden.com

"*Gardening For Dummies* offers the perfect map for a new generation of gardeners…with this book and a little time practicing in the garden, you won't be a 'dummy' for long!"
— Willliam Raap, President, Gardener's Supply Co.
— Celia Ng, New York, New York

# Praise for Vegetable Gardening For Dummies

"This book contains all the basic requirements for the average American to plan and maintain a healthy and hardy vegetable garden. The chapters are comprehensive, witty, and easy-to-read. Planting and culture descriptions of individual vegetables are excellent with colorful descriptions and scrumptious recipes."
— Michael D. Orzolek, Prof. of Vegetable Crops, Pennsylvania State University

# Praise for Flowering Bulbs For Dummies

"What a joy it is to have this book available to all gardeners. Bulb gardening has now been reduced to a simple pleasure."
— Dan Davids, President, Davids & Royston Bulb Co., Leading Flowering Bulb Wholesaler

"Flower bulbs are one of nature's close to perfect perennial plants. This book, with its easy, well-written style, covers just about every aspect of bulb gardening that the home gardener might encounter and should assure gardening successes with bulbs for all who read it!"
— Brent & Becky Heath, authors of *Daffodils for American Gardens*

# Praise for Houseplants For Dummies

"Indoor gardening, quite an intimidating prospect for the brown-thumbed novice, comes alive under the user-friendly guidance of *Houseplants For Dummies*. Larry Hodgson has succeeded in making interior plantscaping accessible for both the novice and the seasoned professional."
— Matthew Gardner, President, California Interior Platscape Association

"Finally a book that takes the mystery out of how to keep houseplants alive! Even a veteran black-thumber will turn a shade of green after reading this concise, clearly presented houseplant primer. Following the right-on information presented in this book on how to take care of your houseplants when you're gone more than pays for the price of the book in saved plants."

— Steve Frowine, President, The Great Plant Company

"In my experience, the greatest success with plants comes with confidence. Larry Hodgson starts us off with a bang by demystifying common versus scientific names in a way that will make it easy for the gardener to feel at home. The analysis of home and self-analysis of the gardener in Chapter 2 are brilliant, and he goes on to simplify many of the other areas in which the beginner may fear to tread. The straightforward explanations, presented with a light touch, draw the reader in without taking away the pride of achievement that will come from filling the home with perfect plants."

— Derek Burch, Ph.D., Botanical and Horticultural Consultant

# Praise for Lawn Care For Dummies

"I would recommend this book to anyone starting a new lawn or improving an existing one."

— Kevin N. Norris, Director, National Turfgrass Evaluation Program

"This is the one book you should have, keep handy, and use often!"

— Doug Fender, Executive Director, Turf Resource Center, Rolling Meadows, IL.

# Praise for Decks & Patios For Dummies

"Thorough and thoughtful, with plenty of solid, 'on the ground' advice. Bob Beckstrom will have you thinking like a landscape architect, a carpenter, a mason, an artist. If you're considering finally living to the limits of your lot line, this book is required reading: it's the guidebook to turning your yard into your favorite getaway destination."

— Bill Crosby, Editorial Director, ImproveNet

"This is an exceptionally complete guide. It treats decks and patios not as isolated projects but as features that should fit with the entire property, and it helps homeowners avoid later disappointments by covering details often overlooked in the eagerness to enjoy outdoor living. You know the book is thorough when it goes so far as to recommend that, before digging post holes by hand, you do some physical workouts!"

— Huck DeVenzio, Advertising Manager, Wolmanized wood

 ™

# References for the Rest of Us!™

## BESTSELLING BOOK SERIES FROM IDG

Do you find that traditional reference books are overloaded with technical details and advice you'll never use? Do you postpone important life decisions because you just don't want to deal with them? Then our ...*For Dummies*® business and general reference book series is for you.

...*For Dummies* business and general reference books are written for those frustrated and hard-working souls who know they aren't dumb, but find that the myriad of personal and business issues and the accompanying horror stories make them feel helpless. ...*For Dummies* books use a lighthearted approach, a down-to-earth style, and even cartoons and humorous icons to diffuse fears and build confidence. Lighthearted but not lightweight, these books are perfect survival guides to solve your everyday personal and business problems.

> "More than a publishing phenomenon, 'Dummies' is a sign of the times."
>
> — The New York Times

> "A world of detailed and authoritative information is packed into them..."
>
> — U.S. News and World Report

> "...you won't go wrong buying them."
>
> — Walter Mossberg, Wall Street Journal, on IDG Books' ...For Dummies books

Already, millions of satisfied readers agree. They have made ...*For Dummies* the #1 introductory level computer book series and a best-selling business book series. They have written asking for more. So, if you're looking for the best and easiest way to learn about business and other general reference topics, look to ...*For Dummies* to give you a helping hand.

IDG BOOKS WORLDWIDE ™

8/98i

# VEGETABLE GARDENING FOR DUMMIES®

by Charlie Nardozzi and the Editors of the
National Gardening Association

IDG Books Worldwide, Inc.
An International Data Group Company

Foster City, CA ♦ Chicago, IL ♦ Indianapolis, IN ♦ New York, NY

## Vegetable Gardening For Dummies®

Published by
**IDG Books Worldwide, Inc.**
An International Data Group Company
919 E. Hillsdale Blvd.
Suite 400
Foster City, CA 94404
www.idgbooks.com (IDG Books Worldwide Web site)
www.dummies.com (Dummies Press Web site)

Library of Congress Catalog Card No.: 98-89728

ISBN: 0-76485-5129-9

Printed in the United States of America

10 9 8 7 6 5 4 3 2 1

1B/RR/QR/ZZ/IN

Distributed in the United States by IDG Books Worldwide, Inc.

Distributed by Macmillan Canada for Canada; by Transworld Publishers Limited in the United Kingdom; by IDG Norge Books for Norway; by IDG Sweden Books for Sweden; by Woodslane Pty. Ltd. for Australia; by Woodslane (NZ) Ltd. for New Zealand; by Addison Wesley Longman Singapore Pte Ltd. for Singapore, Malaysia, Thailand, and Indonesia; by Norma Comunicaciones S.A. for Colombia; by Intersoft for South Africa; by International Thomson Publishing for Germany, Austria and Switzerland; by Distribuidora Cuspide for Argentina; by Livraria Cultura for Brazil; by Ediciencia S.A. for Ecuador; by Ediciones ZETA S.C.R. Ltda. for Peru; by WS Computer Publishing Corporation, Inc., for the Philippines; by Contemporanea de Ediciones for Venezuela; by Express Computer Distributors for the Caribbean and West Indies; by Micronesia Media Distributor, Inc. for Micronesia; by Grupo Editorial Norma S.A. for Guatemala; by Chips Computadoras S.A. de C.V. for Mexico; by Editorial Norma de Panama S.A. for Panama; by Wouters Import for Belgium; by American Bookshops for Finland. Authorized Sales Agent: Anthony Rudkin Associates for the Middle East and North Africa.

For general information on IDG Books Worldwide's books in the U.S., please call our Consumer Customer Service department at 800-762-2974. For reseller information, including discounts and premium sales, please call our Reseller Customer Service department at 800-434-3422.

For information on where to purchase IDG Books Worldwide's books outside the U.S., please contact our International Sales department at 317-596-5530 or fax 317-596-5692.

For information on foreign language translations, please contact our Foreign & Subsidiary Rights department at 650-655-3021 or fax 650-655-3281.

For sales inquiries and special prices for bulk quantities, please contact our Sales department at 650-655-3200 or write to the address above.

For information on using IDG Books Worldwide's books in the classroom or for ordering examination copies, please contact our Educational Sales department at 800-434-2086 or fax 317-596-5499.

For press review copies, author interviews, or other publicity information, please contact our Public Relations department at 650-655-3000 or fax 650-655-3299.

For authorization to photocopy items for corporate, personal, or educational use, please contact Copyright Clearance Center, 222 Rosewood Drive, Danvers, MA 01923, or fax 978-750-4470.

is a trademark under exclusive license to IDG Books Worldwide, Inc., from International Data Group, Inc.

# About the Authors

**Charlie Nardozzi** has been around vegetable gardens ever since he was old enough to follow his grandfather around the potato patch. After spending his young years in the shadow of his Italian grandfather's farm in Connecticut, helping to bail hay, feed pigs, pick apples, and weed potatoes, he moved to Vermont to go to school.

He graduated from the University of Vermont in 1981 with a degree in Plant & Soil Science. The next step was to see the world, and Charlie spent nearly three years in the Peace Corps in Thailand, helping farmers grow everything from rice (not that Charlie felt he really could tell *them* how to grow rice) to garlic, chili peppers, and mangoes. He returned to the United States and received a Master's degree in Education, again from the University of Vermont. After working as a landscaper, at local nurseries, and at the County Cooperative Extension Service office, he ended up as horticulturist at the National Gardening Association and has been there for the past 10 years.

Not only does Charlie write for *National Gardening* magazine and contribute to many of the *...For Dummies* series gardening books, he has a local call-in gardening question-and-answer radio show, is often seen on TV as the gardening expert on such shows as HGTV's *Today at Home,* and gives talks to gardening groups across the country. Heck, you'll even see him on the National Gardening Association Web site, answering questions there too! At home, he tends demonstration gardens with his herbalist wife Barbara, stepson Zander, daughter Elena, and Toby the cat.

**The National Gardening Association** is the largest member-based, nonprofit organization of home gardeners in the United States. Founded in 1972 (as "Gardens for All") to spearhead the community garden movement, today's National Gardening Association is best known for its bimonthly publication, *National Gardening* magazine ($18 per year). Reporting on all aspects of home gardening, each issue is read by some half-million gardeners worldwide. These publishing activities are supplemented by online efforts, such those on their World Wide Web site (www.garden.org) and on America Online (at keyword HouseNet). Other NGA activities include:

- **Growing Science Inquiry and GrowLab** (funded in part by the National Science Foundation) provides science-based curricula for students in kindergarten through Grade 8.

- 1972, the ***National Gardening Survey*** (conducted by the Gallup Company) collects the most detailed research about gardeners and gardening in North America.

- **Youth Garden Grants.** Every year the NGA awards grants, each of which includes more than $500 worth of gardening tools and seeds, to schools, youth groups, and community organizations.

For more information about the National Gardening Association, write to 180 Flynn Ave., Burlington, VT 05401 USA.

# ABOUT IDG BOOKS WORLDWIDE

Welcome to the world of IDG Books Worldwide.

IDG Books Worldwide, Inc., is a subsidiary of International Data Group, the world's largest publisher of computer-related information and the leading global provider of information services on information technology. IDG was founded more than 30 years ago by Patrick J. McGovern and now employs more than 9,000 people worldwide. IDG publishes more than 290 computer publications in over 75 countries. More than 90 million people read one or more IDG publications each month.

Launched in 1990, IDG Books Worldwide is today the #1 publisher of best-selling computer books in the United States. We are proud to have received eight awards from the Computer Press Association in recognition of editorial excellence and three from Computer Currents' First Annual Readers' Choice Awards. Our best-selling ...*For Dummies*® series has more than 50 million copies in print with translations in 31 languages. IDG Books Worldwide, through a joint venture with IDG's Hi-Tech Beijing, became the first U.S. publisher to publish a computer book in the People's Republic of China. In record time, IDG Books Worldwide has become the first choice for millions of readers around the world who want to learn how to better manage their businesses.

Our mission is simple: Every one of our books is designed to bring extra value and skill-building instructions to the reader. Our books are written by experts who understand and care about our readers. The knowledge base of our editorial staff comes from years of experience in publishing, education, and journalism — experience we use to produce books to carry us into the new millennium. In short, we care about books, so we attract the best people. We devote special attention to details such as audience, interior design, use of icons, and illustrations. And because we use an efficient process of authoring, editing, and desktop publishing our books electronically, we can spend more time ensuring superior content and less time on the technicalities of making books.

You can count on our commitment to deliver high-quality books at competitive prices on topics you want to read about. At IDG Books Worldwide, we continue in the IDG tradition of delivering quality for more than 30 years. You'll find no better book on a subject than one from IDG Books Worldwide.

**IDG BOOKS WORLDWIDE**

*John J. Kilcullen*
John Kilcullen
Chairman and CEO
IDG Books Worldwide, Inc.

*Steven Berkowitz*
Steven Berkowitz
President and Publisher
IDG Books Worldwide, Inc.

*Eighth Annual Computer Press Awards ➤ 1992*

**IX WINNER**

*Ninth Annual Computer Press Awards ➤ 1993*

**X WINNER**

*Tenth Annual Computer Press Awards ➤ 1994*

*Eleventh Annual Computer Press Awards ➤ 1995*

IDG is the world's leading IT media, research and exposition company. Founded, in 1964, IDG had 1997 revenues of $2.05 billion and has more than 9,000 employees worldwide. IDG offers the widest range of media options that reach IT buyers in 75 countries representing 95% of worldwide IT spending. IDG's diverse product and services portfolio spans six key areas including print publishing, online publishing, expositions and conferences, market research, education and training, and global marketing services. More than 90 million people read one or more of IDG's 290 magazines and newspapers, including IDG's leading global brands — Computerworld, PC World, Network World, Macworld and the Channel World family of publications. IDG Books Worldwide is one of the fastest-growing computer book publishers in the world, with more than 700 titles in 36 languages. The "...For Dummies®" series alone has more than 50 million copies in print. IDG offers online users the largest network of technology-specific Web sites around the world through IDG.net (http://www.idg.net), which comprises more than 225 targeted Web sites in 55 countries worldwide. International Data Corporation (IDC) is the world's largest provider of information technology data, analysis and consulting, with research centers in over 41 countries and more than 400 research analysts worldwide. IDG World Expo is a leading producer of more than 168 globally branded conferences and expositions in 35 countries including E3 (Electronic Entertainment Expo), Macworld Expo, ComNet, Windows World Expo, ICE (Internet Commerce Expo), Agenda, DEMO, and Spotlight. IDG's training subsidiary, ExecuTrain, is the world's largest computer training company, with more than 230 locations worldwide and 785 training courses. IDG Marketing Services helps industry-leading IT companies build international brand recognition by developing global integrated marketing programs via IDG's print, online and exposition products worldwide. Further information about the company can be found at www.idg.com.                                                                10/8/98

# Dedication

To the long line of vegetable gardeners and lovers in my family — from my grandparents Rocco and Lucia, to my mother Angela, to my wife Barbara, and finally the future gardener, my daughter Elena. They've all been an inspiration.

# Author's Acknowledgments

If I've learned anything in my years growing and studying about vegetable gardening, it's that no one person can know everything about vegetables. This book came together due to the efforts of many individuals. First and foremost, a big thank you goes to Lance Walheim, author of *Roses For Dummies* and *Lawn Care For Dummies,* for writing many of the chapters in this book and supplying valuable feedback on the other chapters. This book wouldn't have happened without you, Lance.

At NGA, thanks to Mike MacCaskey for giving me his faith as well as time to write this book while also helping with photo selection, outline fine-tuning, and general "how do you write a ...*For Dummies* book" questions. To David Els, NGA's President, and Larry Sommers, NGA's Vice President, for their support. Also, thanks to the rest of the editorial staff at NGA; Shila Patel, Managing Editor; Linda Provost, Art Director; Kim Mitchell, Assistant Editor; and Suzanne DeJohn, Barbara Richardson, and Kathy Bond Borie, Staff Horticulturists, for their periodic input, patience, and understanding while I "closed the door" and cranked through writing these chapters.

To Bill Marken, ...*For Dummies* Series Editor for getting us off on the right foot with his input on the outline. To Technical Editors Steve Reiners and Sam Cotner for their valuable feedback on growing vegetables in their regions of the country.

At IDG Books Worldwide, Inc., thanks to Project Editor Kathy Cox for her organization and encouragement, and to Copy Editors Kim Darosett, Wendy Hatch, and Gwenette Gaddis for their help making *Vegetable Gardening For Dummies* a good read. To Sarah Kennedy, former Executive Editor; Holly McGuire, Acquisitions Editor; and Kathy Welton, Vice President and Publisher, for their belief in gardening as a good thing.

And finally thanks to you, the reader, for growing your own vegetables and wanting to know more.

# Publisher's Acknowledgments

We're proud of this book; please register your comments through our IDG Books Worldwide Online Registration Form located at http://my2cents.dummies.com.

Some of the people who helped bring this book to market include the following:

*Acquisitions and Editorial*

**Project Editor:** Kathleen M. Cox

**Acquisitions Editor:** Holly McGuire

**Copy Editors:** Kim Darosett, Gwennette Gaddis, Wendy Hatch

**Technical Editors:** Samuel D. Cotner, Ph.D., Texas A&M University; Stephen Reiners, New York State Agricultural Experiment Station

**Editorial Manager:** Rev Mengle

**Editorial Coordinator:** Maureen F. Kelly

**Acquisitions Coordinator:** Jon Malysiak

**Editorial Assistants:** Jamila Pree, Paul Kuzmic

*Production*

**Project Coordinator:** Karen York

**Layout and Graphics:** Daniel Alexander, Lou Boudreau, J. Tyler Connor, Brian Drumm, Maridee V. Ennis, Angela F. Hunckler, Brent Savage, Jacque Schneider, Brian Torwelle

**Proofreaders:** Christine Berman, Kelli Botta, Michelle Croninger, Nancy Price, Nancy L. Reinhardt, Rebecca Senninger, Ethel M. Winslow, Janet M. Withers

**Indexer:** Anne Leach

**Illustrator:** Katherine Hanley

**Color Photographs:** D. Cavagnaro; Crandall & Crandall; Dargan/Crandall; Dency Kane; Dwight Kuhn; Positive Images: Jerry Howard, Pam Spaulding, Lee Lockwood, Margaret Hensel; Michael S. Thompson

---

*General and Administrative*

**IDG Books Worldwide, Inc.:** John Kilcullen, CEO; Steven Berkowitz, President and Publisher

**IDG Books Technology Publishing:** Brenda McLaughlin, Senior Vice President and Group Publisher

**Dummies Technology Press and Dummies Editorial:** Diane Graves Steele, Vice President and Associate Publisher; Mary Bednarek, Director of Acquisitions and Product Development; Kristin A. Cocks, Editorial Director

**Dummies Trade Press:** Kathleen A. Welton, Vice President and Publisher; Kevin Thornton, Acquisitions Manager

**IDG Books Production for Dummies Press:** Michael R. Britton, Vice President of Production and Creative Services; Cindy L. Phipps, Manager of Project Coordination, Production Proofreading, and Indexing; Kathie S. Schutte, Supervisor of Page Layout; Shelley Lea, Supervisor of Graphics and Design; Debbie J. Gates, Production Systems Specialist; Robert Springer, Supervisor of Proofreading; Debbie Stailey, Special Projects Coordinator; Tony Augsburger, Supervisor of Reprints and Bluelines

**Dummies Packaging and Book Design:** Patty Page, Manager, Promotions Marketing

♦

The publisher would like to give special thanks to Patrick J. McGovern, without whom this book would not have been possible.

♦

# Contents at a Glance

# Cartoons at a Glance

## By Rich Tennant

page 303

page 195

page 7

page 258

page 39

Fax: 978-546-7747 • E-mail: the5wave@tiac.net

# Table of Contents

· · · · · · · · · · · · · · · · · · · · · · · · · · · · · · · · · · · · · · · · · · · · · · · · · · · · · · · · · · · ·

# Introduction

• • • • • • • • • • • • • • • • • • • • • • • • • • • • • • • • • • • • • • • • • • • • • •

*T*here's something very special about vegetable gardening. Growing your own fresh food is nutritious, delicious, beautious (it's a word now), exciting, fulfilling (or just filling), economical, ecological, artistic, colorful, easy, educational, and just downright fun. And I'm not making this up just to get you to buy this book.

Vegetables are everywhere! They're in the news as scientists uncover yet another vegetable that has great cancer-fighting properties. They're in restaurants as vegetable juice bars overtake cappuccino bars in the fancier sections of New York City. And heck, I wouldn't be surprised to see a TV show about vegetables before long. How about *The Eggplant Files*?

Most importantly, vegetables are on our plates at breakfast, lunch, and dinner more and more. As we become more food conscious, vegetables are gaining in importance as a major part of a healthful diet. You've heard it on TV, in the newspaper, and maybe from your doctor: Eating fresh vegetables — and eating them often — is good for your health. In fact, it may be the single best thing that you can do to ensure long-term health and fight off disease. So, you're thinking, sure vegetables are good for me, but why do I want to *grow* them?

My answer can be summed up in three words: *safe, fresh,* and *delicious.* Consider these facts:

✔ **Fresh garden vegetables are more nutritious than store-bought:** Supermarket vegetables are often picked early, before they reach full maturity and have usually been in storage, reducing their nutrient content. Storage can also result in decay and possible contamination.

✔ **You control what goes on your garden vegetables.** Because store-bought vegetables are often shipped in from thousands of miles away (and sometimes from foreign countries), you have no control over what chemicals farmers use to grow the vegetables and no control over any biological contaminants that hitchhike along with the produce. You can decide for yourself if you consider that a health threat. But if you grow your own vegetables, you decide what gets sprayed on them, and you know exactly what you're eating. (In this book, I lean towards an organic gardening style, which is the process of growing vegetables without dependence on chemical fertilizers.)

✔ **Vegetables are ornamental as well as edible:** You can combine them with flowers and herbs — red lettuce in a mixed bed of blue pansies and bright green parsley, Swiss chard with yellow daffodils and Johnny-jump-up violas, scarlet runner beans clinging to towering stalks of sunflowers — in endless combinations. Vegetables can be just as beautiful as any ornamental garden flower.

✔ **Vegetable gardening is educational for kids:** The idea of watching a plant grow from seed to flower to fruit and then eating it is a good way to keep a short attention span focused — especially when the ultimate goal of the exercise is eating. For kids especially, vegetable gardening builds confidence and a feeling of accomplishment while encouraging kids to eat more vegetables.

✔ **Vegetable gardening is good for the soul:** Vegetable gardening is a good way to feed your stomach and your soul with needed time for reflection, relaxation, and rejuvenation. In a world where we're so dependent on machines like computers and cars but have little under-standing of them, vegetable gardening is simple and doesn't require the help of a specialized technician. That sense of independence is some-thing that's getting harder and harder to find.

Once you start vegetable gardening, not only do you feel a sense of satisfac-tion and pride that you can grow some of your own food, but you also notice a strange thing happening: You start seeing your hobby not as a chore but as a rewarding activity. You look forward to checking your garden to see what's ready to harvest and giving yourself a chance to slow down and relax. I often come home from work and immediately go into my garden to check the status of my pumpkin plants, snack on a few cherry tomatoes, and pull a few errant weeds before I even enter my house.

In your garden, you'll have no surprises and lots of peace of mind. And best of all, after eating fresh, home-grown juicy tomatoes, sweet melons, and crisp beans, you'll be hard pressed to buy week-old produce (most likely bred for increased storage life, ease of harvest, and disease resistance rather than flavor) in the grocery store again.

Face it: Garden-grown vegetables just taste better. In fact, some garden varieties, like 'Brandywine' tomatoes or 'Silver Queen' corn, have developed almost cultlike followings because they taste so good — a taste you can only get home-grown.

## About This Book

The best part about vegetable gardening is that you don't have to be a rocket scientist (or a farmer) to grow this stuff. Many vegetables are easy to grow as long as you take the proper steps. That's where I come in. In this book, I and other editors from the National Gardening Association take you by the hand down the vegetable gardening path through a process that helps ensure that you create an attractive garden and yield a bountiful harvest, without having to spend from dawn to dusk in your vegetable patch (even though it is a nice place to hang out).

Ever since I was a little boy helping my grandfather weed and harvest his potatoes, I've been around vegetable gardens, growing and eating fresh vegetables. I believe that all types of gardening are wonderful, but vegetable gardening is close to my heart — and stomach. Being from an Italian family, food is important to me. Meals are social events, and food is one of the main topics of conversation. In addition, being a vegetarian, I'm particularly conscious of the health benefits of foods and, as you might guess, I eat a *lot* of vegetables.

This book is designed to help you find out more about aspects of vegetable gardening that you're interested in; it's not meant to be read from cover to cover. Flip around to topics that interest you — you're in the driver's seat. And if there's a concept that you need to know from earlier in the book, I explain it again or refer you to the chapter where you can find that information.

We've arranged this book in several parts to make finding the information you need easier, even if you aren't sure just what you need to know. The parts are divided into chapters so that all the text doesn't run together in one large, incomprehensible, scary lump. Remember, the Table of Contents and the Index can help you get to where you need to be in the book, and headings within each chapter get you to the precise information.

# Part I: The Creative Part

I know you're already interested in vegetables. You wouldn't be looking at this book if you weren't. But in case you need a little more convincing about why you should grow your own veggies, I lay it out for you here. After you've screamed "enough convincing," I tell you more about the location, design, and growing schedule for making your vegetable garden a unique part of your home landscape. And if you like weather and dates (we've all had some!), I give you weather information just for gardeners as well as planting dates for various regions of the country.

# Part II: Vegging Out

At this point in the book, I could get into more on planting, soil building, watering, fertilizing, and so on . . . but because this is a *vegetable* gardening book, you probably want to know something about which vegetables to grow. So in this part, you find out about a wide range of vegetables from asparagus to zucchini and many more vegetables in between. I tell you how to grow them, what the best varieties are, how to control pests, and even offer some recipes and health tips. Interested in growing a specific vegetable? Flip through this part, find your veggie (or fruit or herb) of choice, and read on.

## Part III: Green Acres . . . or Yards . . . or Feet: The Get-Down-and-Dirty Part

Now for the nuts and bolts. The success of any garden often begins and ends with your soil. So this part starts off with basic soil-building techniques. Then after your soil's ready, you can find out about planting, watering, fertilizing, and weeding your garden. But don't forget the best part of vegetable gardening: harvesting and eating all the fresh produce — and storing some for later.

## Part IV: The Part of Tens

One of this book's messages is to keep vegetable gardening simple. To help you do just that, in this part, I give you lists of which vegetables to grow in almost any situation, plus some ideas for what to do with those pesky zucchinis that just keep coming. You also find out about special tools that make weeding and planting a lot easier, and if you just can't get enough of that great produce, I discuss ways to extend your growing season beyond the limits of Jack Frost.

## Appendix

After finding out about all the great vegetable varieties and the basics of planning and caring for a vegetable garden, you may want to run out today and start growing. In this appendix, you'll find more growing information as well as names and addresses of companies that sell all kinds of vegetable seeds, plants, and gardening equipment. In addition, you find Web sites that you can contact for more vegetable growing information.

# Icons Used in This Book

As you read this book, you'll notice icons (little symbols) in the margin of the text. These icons are meant to highlight key bits of information. Here's a list of the icons used in this book and what they mean.

How does your garden grow better? This icon highlights tips that expert gardeners have discovered. This information may save you some trial and error.

 Sometimes it helps to speak the language. This icon points out terms you should know, if only to be clear about what you want at the local nursery.

 This icon highlights veggies that work well in containers.

 This icon highlights information about potential dangers to you or your plants.

 This icon highlights activities that are friendly to the environment so that all your gardens will be safe and fresh for years to come.

 I feel strongly that gardening, especially vegetable gardening, should be a family experience, so I include many kid-friendly tips throughout this book to help you get children involved, from how to grow a fortlike bean teepee to how to combine vegetables with different cultural importance to create ethnic gardens.

 Sometimes you want to know why and how something happens. This icon highlights information you don't need to know but may want to know to enrich your gardening know-how.

 This icon highlights veggies and techniques that work well in small gardens.

 This icon points to other materials you may want to check out for more information about a particular vegetable or growing technique.

# Silencing the Excuses

I've heard it before: "But I don't have enough room for a vegetable garden," or "I don't have time to take care of vegetables," or "This seems awfully complicated." Well, if you just don't want to grow vegetables, I can't help you, but if these are your excuses, put them aside. In this book, I show you how to grow vegetables in the smallest spaces. In fact, if all you have is a small patio and no open soil, you can still harvest a bumper crop by planting in containers.

I also show you that with planning and care, vegetable gardening doesn't take much time at all. While your neighbors slave away trying to save their gardens from weeds and pests, you'll spend most of your time harvesting and eating your veggies and then sitting on your front porch sipping lemonade and admiring your work. This is not to say that vegetable gardening doesn't take time and work. If you want a quality harvest, you have to put some effort into it. But you can simplify things and save time: You can mulch to reduce watering and weeds, plant in raised beds so that you don't have to bend over, and automate your irrigation system so that it waters even while you're on vacation. (I explain how to do all these things throughout this book.)

And you don't have to be a farmer to grow vegetables. Heck, I've seen the most neglected patches of beans and tomatoes produce fruit. The job of vegetable plants is to grow and produce. All you have to do is help them along.

This vegetable gardening stuff is looking easier isn't it? Let's get growing before you change your mind.

# Part I
## The Creative Part

The 5th Wave                    By Rich Tennant

# In this part . . .

**1** In this part, I whet your appetite for home-grown veggies and provide the basics of location, design, and growing schedule so you can make your vegetable garden a unique part of your home landscape. And if you like weather and dates (we all have had some!), I give you climate information geared to gardeners and planting dates for various regions of the country so you can work with Mother Nature to get the best from your garden.

# Chapter 1

# Beauty and a Feast

● ● ● ● ● ● ● ● ● ● ● ● ● ● ● ● ● ● ● ● ● ● ● ● ● ● ● ● ● ● ● ● ● ● ● ● ● ● ● ● ● ● ● ● ● ● ● ●

## In This Chapter

▶ Choosing vegetables

▶ Planning plots with pizzazz

▶ Gardening to prevent pests

● ● ● ● ● ● ● ● ● ● ● ● ● ● ● ● ● ● ● ● ● ● ● ● ● ● ● ● ● ● ● ● ● ● ● ● ● ● ● ● ● ● ● ● ● ● ● ●

*H*ere's a great experience that I guarantee will happen when you start growing your own vegetables. You'll invite some friends over for lunch or dinner who have never eaten much fresh garden corn, tomatoes, beans, or whatever. They'll kind of roll their eyes when they see hearty portions of vegetables on their plates. They'll dig in out of politeness, and then they'll be silent. Then, you're likely to hear, "Umm, I can't believe vegetables can taste this good."

Believe it or not, vegetables are *supposed* to taste good. Picked at perfect maturity and brought to the table as fresh as a newborn, garden-grown vegetables always taste great. They aren't picked before they reach full maturity, and then stored in a truck for a week on their way to the supermarket (I'll be lucky if they ever let me in a supermarket again). Fresh means flavor. And growing your own vegetables is the way to ensure that you get them fresh.

Vegetable gardening — preparing the soil, planting seeds, nurturing plants until maturity, and then bringing a delicious harvest to the family table — is part of an age-old cycle that goes back to ancient peoples. The process is rewarding and fulfilling in a way that connects to our very roots (no pun intended) as human beings. I love growing the food that I eat, and in this chapter, I explain why that is. In addition, you find out about selecting vegetable varieties, creating an appealing garden, and staving off pests. And along the way, I hope to inspire you to get a little dirt under your fingernails and start your own garden. Dig in!

# Planting Plots with Personality

A lot of planning goes into your vegetable garden (see Chapter 2), but that doesn't mean it should resemble a miniature farm, with perfectly-spaced rows of typical vegetables that leave no room for ingenuity. Looking for some alternatives to a traditional vegetable garden? Here are some suggestions for distinctive gardens to get your mouth watering and your creative juices flowing.

## Ornamental edible gardens

Figure 1-1 shows a plan for a summer vegetable-flower garden that could be tucked into any sunny corner of a front or back yard. You can find out more about creating a plan for your garden in Chapter 2.

Here are some tips to make this kind of planting work:

- **Match the bloom seasons of flowers with the growth cycles of vegetables.** In other words, mix flowers that grow in cool weather with vegetables that like similar conditions. Chapter 3 gives you all the information about vegetable planting times. You can find out more about flower planting times in *Perennials For Dummies* by Marcia Tatroe and the Editors of the National Gardening Association and *Annuals For Dummies* by Bill Marken and the Editors of the National Gardening Association ( both published by IDG Books Worldwide, Inc.). You should also consider mixing in some herbs like parsley, chives, and thyme (described in Chapter 12) — most are great ornamentals in their own right.

- **Match cultural needs.** Most vegetables need a constant supply of water. Don't combine these with flowers that like it on the dry side.

- **Give vegetables enough room.** Use the spacing recommendations in Chapter 2. Try to leave at least that much room between flowers and vegetable plants. You may be able to push them a little closer, but don't go too far. If the flowers have a spreading habit, you may even plant things farther apart.

- **Put short plants in front, tall plants in back.** Make a smooth transition in sizes from the front of the bed to the back. That way, you'll be able to see everything — smaller plants won't be blocked or shaded by taller ones.

- **Leave room to harvest.** Use stepping stones or paths so that you can harvest vegetables without damaging flowers.

- **Have a color theme.** Use colors that blend well: pink pansies planted at the base of ruby-colored rhubarb, white alyssum planted with green chard, red leaf lettuce planted with purple Johnny-jump ups, or red petunias planted at the base of pepper plants.

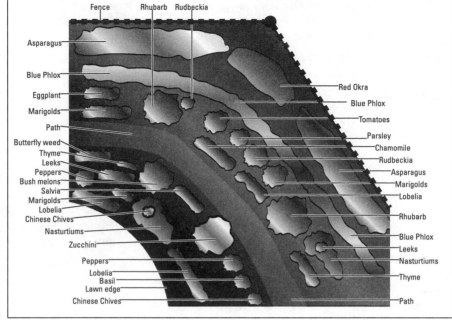

**Figure 1-1:**
Sample
ornamental
edible
garden
using
flowers and
vegetables.

✔ **Plant foliage vegetables and herbs.** Vegetables and herbs with colorful or bold textures combine well with flowers. Use a lot of basil, chard, kale, lettuce, cabbage, chives, parsley, and other leafy vegetables.

## Theme vegetable gardens

You can get creative and group vegetables by their special uses. This is where vegetable gardening gets really fun. You can grow special gardens that are historic, such as the Three Sisters Garden; or you can grow gardens based on food themes, such as the Mexican Salsa Garden. Theme gardens don't have to take over your entire garden. All that's required is a corner or one raised bed. Just remember the spacing requirements for vegetables.

The following list describes several popular garden themes:

✔ **Greens Garden:** Do you love lettuce and other salad greens? Grow a colorful greens garden filled with different colors and textures of lettuce, endive, spinach, Swiss chard, and parsley.

✔ **Mexican Salsa Garden:** Are you addicted to salsa? Create a special nook for your own salsa garden, complete with different varieties of tomatoes, tomatillos, cilantro, peppers, and onions.

- ✔ **Oriental Stir Fry Garden:** Do you love to wok it up? Grow all the ingredients you need for a stir fry by planting pac choi, Chinese cabbage, snow peas, garlic, and scallions.

- ✔ **Pizza Garden:** This one's for the kids. Design a circular garden, and in triangular sections (like pizza slices), grow favorite pizza toppings such as peppers, onions, and tomatoes.

- ✔ **Three Sisters Garden:** Add an historic flair to your vegetable garden by growing corn, pole beans, and squash in a traditional Native American garden (see Figure 1-2).

You can also creat a small-space block garden. Often called the "square-foot garden," this square bed is only 3 feet wide but still packs a lot of punch for a petite plot: The bed is divided into 9 one-foot squares, each planted with a different vegetable. Space-saving vegetable varieties (see Chapter 17) for smaller vegetables like lettuce and carrots work best. Containerized vegetable gardens are a good idea if all you have is a small patio or roof top.

# *Choosing Your Vegetables*

Part of the fun of planning a vegetable garden is perusing mail-order seed catalogs and retail seed racks to select which varieties of a particular vegetable you want to grow. If you select your veggie types before you design your garden, you'll be better able to make sure that you have the right amount of room and the best growing conditions.

A *variety* is a selection of a particular type of vegetable that has certain predictable, desirable traits. These traits may include:

- ✔ **Adaptation:** Some varieties are particularly well adapted to certain areas. For example, tomato varieties exist that produce good-tasting fruit in cool, foggy coastal climates where few other varieties thrive. There are also bean varieties, grown for centuries by American Indians, that grow better in the hot, dry deserts of the American southwest.

- ✔ **Appearance:** Red, yellow, orange, purple, and white tomatoes; rainbow-colored chard, peppers, and even melons; a kaleidoscope of lettuce leaf colors — you ask for it, you can probably get it. And the more beautiful the vegetables, the more beautiful the vegetable garden and the more stunning the food.

- ✔ **Cooking and storage characteristics:** Certain varieties of beans and peas, for example, freeze better than others. Some squash varieties may be stored for months, but others need to be eaten immediately.

- ✔ **Days to maturity (or days to harvest):** *Days to maturity* refers to the number of days it will take (under normal conditions) for a vegetable planted from seed (or from transplants — such as tomatoes and peppers) to mature and produce a crop. Knowing this number has more

**Figure 1-2:**
A Native
American
Three
Sisters
Garden.

significance than just letting you extend your season or ensuring that
your pepper varieties ripen with your tomatoes so that you can make
salsa. It's also an important number for vegetable gardeners who live in
short-summer climates. Average days to maturity are listed for each
type of vegetable in the appendix. You can find specific variety information on individual vegetables in Part II of this book.

✔ **Extended harvest season:** A certain variety of corn, for example, may be
early or late ripening. By mixing varieties that ripen at different times,
you can start harvesting as early as 60 days after seeding and continue
for five or six weeks. Seed catalogs and packages often describe varieties
as early season, midseason, or late season in relationship to other
varieties of the same vegetable. You can get an even better idea of how
varieties relate to each other, and to other vegetables by comparing the
days from seed to harvest (see the preceding bullet), which are also
listed in catalogs and on seed packages.

✔ **Pest resistance:** Many varieties are resistant to specific diseases or pests — a very important trait in many areas. Tomatoes in particular have outstanding pest resistance, with varieties labeled as resistant to verticillium wilt (V), fusarium (F), and nematodes (N). See Chapter 18 for more on pest control.

✔ **Plant size:** Many excellent, compact-growing vegetable varieties are ideal for small spaces or for growing in containers. Even the most vigorous, space-eating vegetables, such as melons and squash, now come in smaller varieties perfect for places where space is limited.

✔ **Taste:** There are fruity tomatoes, super sweet varieties of corn, and spicy, hot peppers. There are flavors for every taste bud.

To realize the scope of your vegetable variety possibilities, see the individual vegetable descriptions in Part II of this book.

## Hybrids: Arranged marriages

As you look through seed catalogs or read seed packets, you may notice the phrase *F-1 hybrid* (or simply *hybrid*) before or after the names of some varieties. Generally, these seeds are more expensive than others.

*Hybrid seeds* are the result of a *cross* (pollen from one flower fertilizing a flower from another similar plant, resulting in seed) of selected groups of plants of the same kind, called *inbred lines.*

To produce an inbred line, a variety is bred to itself for ten or twelve generations. The seeds from theses crosses result in a group of plants that are almost genetically identical. In other words, they're like twins. Different inbred lines are then crossed to produce hybrids, or the F-1 generation. If the breeder hits upon the right combination of inbred lines, the resulting F-1 plants show what's called *hybrid vigor* — a significant increase in qualities such as early and uniform maturity and increased disease resistance. The increased vigor makes hybrids worth the extra cost. The added expense is mainly a product of the space and labor required to maintain the inbred lines that serve as the parents of the hybrid. Also, to make the cross, the flowers of one inbred line must actually be hand pollinated from the other inbred line.

If you choose hybrid seeds, you need to buy a new batch every season, rather than saving your own. When hybrid plants cross with themselves and form seeds, these seeds lose the specific combination of genetic information that gave the hybrid its predictable qualities. If you plant seed from hybrids, you end up with a very mixed bag of plants.

Good examples of hybrid varieties of many vegetables are discussed in Part II.

# Open pollination: A plant free-for-all

In addition to hybrid varieties, there are also *open-pollinated* varieties. These are basically inbred lines that are allowed to pollinate each other in open fields. The resulting seeds are pretty predictable but don't provide the consistency of F-1 hybrids.

Open-pollinated varieties are subject to the whims of nature, and some plants may be a little different than you expect. However, if you want to save your own seeds as a seed collector, open-pollinated varieties are the only plants that you can replant seed from and have most of the plants turn out very similar to the parent.

# Heirlooms: Like granny used to grow

Heirloom vegetables resemble the varieties your grandparents grew in that they have been open pollinated for years. Any open-pollinated variety that is at least 50 years old is generally considered an *heirloom*. Heirlooms are enjoying quite a revival because of the variety of fruit colors, tastes, and forms that are available.

Heirloom vegetables are worth trying, but remember that some varieties may not have the disease resistance and wide adaptability that the hybrids generally have. You can find good examples of heirloom varieties of a number of vegetables in Part II.

# Altered genes: The next generation

Another phrase you'll run across concerning vegetable varieties is *genetically modified varieties*. These are plants that have a gene from a totally unrelated species inserted into the variety of vegetable so that the vegetable exhibits a certain trait. For example, geneticists have inserted a gene of the biological pesticide *Bt* (see Chapter 18 for more on this pesticide) into potatoes so that when the Colorado Potato beetle (their biggest enemy) eats the potato leaves, it also eats the pesticide and dies. Bt, however, is safe for humans to consume.

Genetically modified varieties of a number of vegetables are just now becoming available to home gardeners, but many unanswered questions remain about whether this new type of vegetable will be better or worse for people and the environment in the long run.

# Gardening to Prevent Pest Problems

Preventing a problem is always easier than dealing with a problem later. With a little foresight, you can keep pests at bay in your garden. Here's a list of some common-sense pest-prevention measures:

- **Plant your vegetables in the right location.** Many pests become more troublesome when plants are grown in conditions that are less than ideal. For example, if you grow sun-loving vegetables in the shade, mildew problems are often more severe.

- **Grow healthy plants.** I said it once, and I'll say it again: Healthy plants are less likely to have problems. Water and fertilize regularly so that your plants grow strong and more pest resistant.

- **Choose resistant plants.** If you know that a certain disease is common in your area, choose plants that aren't susceptible to that disease or that resist infection. Some vegetable varieties are resistant to specific diseases. For example, some tomato varieties resist verticillium, fusarium, and nematodes. You can find out about these resistant varieties in the vegetable descriptions in Part II of this book.

- **Encourage and use beneficial insects.** Beneficial insects are the good bugs in your garden — the insects that feed on the bugs that bother your vegetables. You probably have a bunch of different kinds of beneficial insects in your garden already, but you can also purchase them to release in your garden. In addition, you can plant flowers that attract these insects. For more on beneficial insects, see Chapter 18.

- **Keep your garden clean.** By cleaning up spent plants, weeds, and other garden debris, you eliminate hiding places for many pests and diseases.

- **Rotate your plants.** Avoid planting the same plants in the same location year after year, especially if you grow vegetables in raised beds. Rotation prevents pests and diseases that are specific to certain plants from building up in your garden. You can find out more about crop rotation in Chapter 16.

- **Know the enemy.** The more that you know about specific pests and diseases common to your area — when they occur and how they spread — the more easily you can avoid them. For example, some diseases run rampant on wet foliage. You can reduce the occurrence of these diseases simply by adjusting your watering so that you don't wet the plants' leaves, or by watering early in the day so that the plants dry out quickly.

If an insect or disease does get out of hand, treat it effectively without disrupting the other life in your garden, which includes everything from good bugs to birds. Control measures may be as simple as handpicking and squashing snails, or knocking off aphids with a strong jet of water from a hose. You can find other physical control measures in Chapter 18.

# Chapter 2

# Choosing Your Spot and Using It Well

So you've decided to plant a vegetable garden. You have visions of spectacular spinach, tantalizing tomatoes, and prize-winning pumpkins dancing through your head. But don't start writing your Golden Trowel (the academy award of gardening) acceptance speech just yet. You have lots of planning to do if you want a beautiful, bountiful harvest, and it all starts with answering some basic questions.

Where are you going to put your garden? How big will it be? What will it look like? Can you provide the full sun, good soil, and frequent watering that most vegetables require?

A vegetable garden should be conveniently located, and it helps if the garden is visible (and looks good, too) so you can easily remember to water, weed, feed, and harvest. (If your garden's out of sight, it's probably out of mind.) In most climates, taking advantage of warm or cool spots in your yard can extend your harvest. You also want to plant enough vegetables to feed your family.

Although an average vegetable garden is about 600 square feet, or about 20 by 30 feet, your garden can be as large or as small as your space and time allow. Consider how much of each crop you want to end up with, and then consult the planting guide in Appendix A for space requirements for vegetables you want to grow. If you're a first-timer, 600 square feet is plenty of space to take care of. If you're a busy person, you may want a smaller garden that's approximately 200 square feet or even a small bed near your house that's 50 or 100 square feet. The key is to start small.

If the soil is in good condition, a novice gardener can keep up with a 400-square-foot garden by devoting about half an hour to it each day at the beginning of the season. In late spring through summer, a good half an hour of work every two to three days should keep the garden productive and looking good. Thirty minutes isn't so bad, and by using some of the time-saving tips I provide throughout this book, such as automatic irrigation controllers and mulching, you may be able to cut down the time commitment even more.

You have a lot to consider when deciding where and how to plant your vegetable garden, and that's the ground I cover in this chapter: where to place your plot and how to get the most out of it.

# Spotting the Best Plot

Choosing a site is the important first step in planning a vegetable garden. It may sound like a tough choice to make, but a lot of the decision is based on good old common sense. For example:

- ✔ Try to locate your garden close to a water source (like an outdoor faucet) and close to your house (you don't want to have to run three miles to get one more perfectly ripe tomato for a dinner salad).

- ✔ If you plan to bring in truckloads of soil amendments (compost and other improvements to your soil), put your garden where it can be reached by a vehicle.

- ✔ A vegetable garden can be a very social place where your family gets together to harvest for dinner and discuss the day's happenings. Locate your garden in a spot that's easy to get to.

A bit of science is also involved in choosing the right spot. In this section, I help you get familiar with the microclimates and conditions that exist in your yard. (In Chapter 3, I show you how the overall climate of your area affects your garden.)

*Microclimates* are small areas of your yard whose temperatures and related growing conditions are slightly different from the overall climate of your neighborhood or town. These differences are usually caused by large objects, such as your house or a tree. For example, the south side of your house may be hotter than the rest of your yard because the sun reflects off the walls. Or an area under a tree may be cooler than the rest of the yard because of the shade provided by the tree's canopy. Microclimates can also be caused by wind or sloping ground.

The following sections describe some things to think about when surveying your yard. (Figure 2-1 puts some of these ideas in visual perspective.) Don't be discouraged if you lack the ideal garden spot — few gardeners have one. Just try to make the most of what you have.

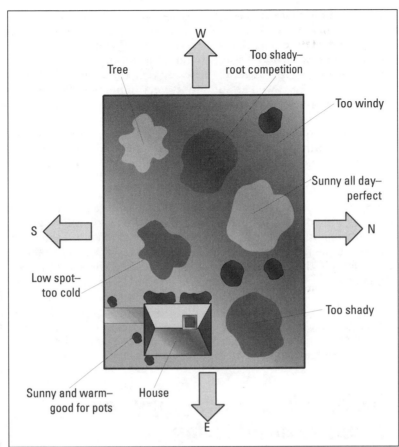

**Figure 2-1:**
A sample
yard with
possible
(and
impossible)
sites for a
vegetable
garden.

## *Catching some rays*

Your garden will do best if it gets full sun — six hours of direct sun is the
minimum needed by most vegetable plants for optimum growth. However, if
your only spot for a garden gets less than this, don't give up:

- ✔ Some crops, especially leafy ones, like lettuce and spinach, produce
  reasonably well in a partially shaded location where the sun shines
  directly on the plants for four hours.

- ✔ Root crops, such as carrots and beets, need more light than leafy
  vegetables, but they may do well in a garden that gets only morning sun
  for four to six hours.

Fruiting plants such as peppers, tomatoes, and beans are sun worshippers
and yield poorly, if at all, with less than six hours of direct sun. If you're
stuck with a shady garden location, start small and experiment with more
shade-tolerant plants to see which do best.

Keep in mind that sun and shade patterns change with the seasons. A site that's sunny in midsummer may later be shaded by trees, buildings, and the longer shadows of late fall and early spring. If you live in a mild-winter climate like parts of the southeastern and southwestern United States where it's possible to grow vegetables nearly year-round, choosing a spot that's sunny in winter as well as summer is very important. In general, sites that have clear southern exposure are sunniest in winter (refer to Figure 2-1).

You don't have to plant all your vegetables in one plot. If your only sunny spot is in the front yard, plant a border of peppers and tomatoes along the front walk and set lettuce plants in a shadier spot out back. Or garden in one spot in summer and another in early spring or fall.

If shade in your garden comes from nearby trees and shrubs, your vegetable plants will compete for water and nutrients as well as for light. Tree roots extend slightly beyond the *drip line,* the outer foliage reach of the tree. If possible, keep your garden out of the *root zones* (the areas that extend from the drip lines to the trunks) of surrounding trees and shrubs. If this isn't possible, give the vegetables more water and give fertilizer to compensate.

Black walnut trees pose a particular problem because their roots give off a substance called *juglone* that inhibits the growth of some plants, including tomatoes. Plants growing in the root zones of black walnuts often wilt and die. Try to leave at least 50 feet between your garden and any walnut trees.

## Rain, rain, go away; my soil needs to drain today

Plant roots need air as well as water. Water-logged soils are low in air content, which is why soil drainage is an important consideration when choosing a garden site. Soils made primarily of clay tend to be considered *heavy.* Heavy soils usually aren't as well drained as sandy soils. Puddles of water on the soil surface after a rain indicate poor drainage.

One way to check your soil's drainage is to dig a hole about 10 inches deep and fill it with water. Let the water drain and then fill the hole again the following day, and time how long it takes for the water to drain away. If water remains in the hole more than 8 to 10 hours after the second filling, your soil drainage needs improvement.

Adding lots of organic matter to your soil can improve soil drainage (I tell you a lot more about how to do that in Chapter 14). Or you can build raised beds on a poorly drained site (see "Deciding on rows, hills, or raised beds," later in this chapter). If your soil is really soggy, due perhaps to a high water table or an impenetrable layer of compacted soil far below ground level (a soil condition called *hardpan*), plastic drain pipes buried in the ground may be your only solution. Consult a landscape contractor for more information on this fairly expensive option.

Soil can also be *too* well drained. Very sandy soil dries out quickly and needs frequent watering during dry spells. Adding lots of organic matter to sandy soil increases the amount of water it can hold (see Chapter 14 for more information).

If you have a really tough time digging that 10-inch hole — if you encounter a lot of big rocks, for example — you may want to look for another spot or go the raised-bed route. You can improve soils that are too clayey or sandy, but very rocky soil can be a real headache, if not impossible to garden in.

Don't plant your garden near the leach lines of a septic system. I think you know why. And keep away from underground utilities. If you have questions, call your local utility company to locate underground lines.

High winds can wreak havoc on tall crops like corn and pole beans and can make any vegetable dry out rapidly. If wind is a problem in your area, protect your garden with a *windbreak* (a fence or several rows of taller plants). You provide maximum protection for your crops if you plant them downwind at a distance that's three to five times the height of the windbreak.

## Getting the scoop on slopes

Ground with a gentle slope to the south makes for an ideal planting site, especially in cold climates. South-sloping soil warms up faster in the spring, diminishing the likelihood of frosts affecting plants. Because cold air is like water (it runs downhill and settles in low spots), frosty air moves past plants on slopes without doing damage. In hot climates, a north-facing slope may help keep plants cooler during midsummer heat.

Too great a slope can be a serious problem, causing erosion and making it very difficult to water plants. On any sloping ground, it's a good idea to plant rows across rather than down the slope so that the plants catch water runoff. You may need to build terraces on very steep slopes to hold soil in place. Drip irrigation, which applies water slowly, can also help reduce runoff and erosion (see Chapter 15 for more on drip irrigation).

## Mapping Out Your Garden

Designing a vegetable garden is both a practical and a creative process. Practically speaking, plants must be arranged so that they have room to grow and so that taller vegetables don't shade lower-growing types. Different planting techniques fit the growth habits of different kinds of vegetables. And you should also think about access: How will you get to your plants to harvest, weed, or water them? On the other hand, creativity is important to the design process. After all, vegetables can be good-looking as well as practical. Consider mixing them with flowers or growing them in containers.

In the following sections, I encourage you to think like a vegetable gardener. I give you the basics so that you can start to sketch out a garden plan of what to plant and where to put it. (See Chapter 1 for more about garden plants.) I also provide some sample garden designs to get your juices flowing. Before you know it, you'll be a vegetable gardening wizard!

*Note:* These sections give you the nuts and bolts information you need to create a final vegetable garden design. If you want a garden that's good rather than just good enough, you have some more reading to do. The descriptions of individual vegetables in Part II suggest ways to grow various types of vegetables — information that will probably influence your design. And the information on planting times in Chapter 3, the scoop on succession planting in Chapter 16, and the lowdown on watering techniques in Chapter 15 will probably change the way you arrange and plant your garden.

## Deciding on rows, hills, or raised beds

Before you sketch a garden plan, you need to decide how to arrange the plants in your garden and how you'll water them (for more information about watering, see Chapter 15). You can use three basic planting arrangements:

- ✔ **In rows:** Any vegetable can be planted in rows, but this arrangement works best with types that need quite a bit of room, such as tomatoes, beans, cabbages, corn, potatoes, peppers, and summer squash.

- ✔ **In hills:** Hills are best for vining crops such as cucumbers, melons, and winter squash. You can create a 1-foot-wide, flat-topped mound for heavy soil, or you can create a circle at ground level for sandy soil. You then surround the soil with a moatlike ring for watering. Two or three evenly spaced plants are grown on each hill. Space the hills the recommended distance for between rows of the vegetable you're planting.

- ✔ **In raised beds:** Raised beds are kind of like wide, flat-topped rows. They're usually at least 2 feet wide and raised at least 6 inches high. Raised beds are best for smaller vegetables that can be planted close together, such as lettuce, carrots, onions, spinach, radishes, and turnips. Vegetables in raised beds can be planted in random patterns or in closely spaced rows.

Any planting area that's raised above the surrounding ground level is a *raised bed*. It can simply be a normal bed with the soil piled 5 or 6 inches high, or it can be a bed located in a large container with wood, stone, or masonry sides, as shown in Figure 2-2.

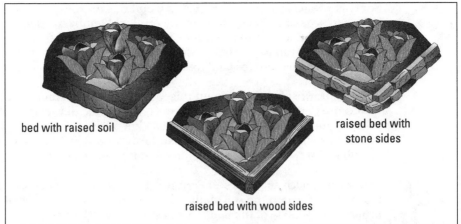

**Figure 2-2:**
Raised beds can be made with soil alone, or with wood, stone, or masonry sides.

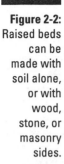

bed with raised soil

raised bed with stone sides

raised bed with wood sides

Raised beds have several advantages:

- ✔ **Raised beds rise above soil problems.** If you have bad soil or poor drainage, raised beds are for you. You can amend the garden soil in the raised bed with the same sterile potting soil you use for containers (see Chapter 17). And because you don't step on the beds as you work, the soil is more likely to stay light and fluffy — providing the perfect conditions for root growth.

- ✔ **Raised beds warm early.** Because more of the soil in raised beds is exposed to the sun, the soil warms early, allowing for early planting and extended harvest seasons.

- ✔ **Raised beds consolidate your work.** By growing your vegetables in raised beds, you can maximize your fertilizing and watering so that more nutrients and water are actually used by the plants rather than being wasted in the pathways.

- ✔ **Raised beds are easy on your back.** If you design the beds properly (about 18- to 24-inches high and no wider than 4 feet), raised beds can make vegetable gardening a lot more comfortable. You can sit on the edge (you can even cap the edge to make it more bench-like) and easily reach into the bed to weed or harvest.

- ✔ **Raised beds are attractive.** Raised beds add a wonderful organized formality to the vegetable garden. They can be made from materials that match your house, patio, or deck. A series of raised beds can create an attractive focal point in your yard.

Wooden raised beds should be made of rot-resistant woods like redwood or cedar, or recycled plastic timbers. I like to use two 2-by-10 for the sides, anchored (with lag screws) at the corners with short 4-by-4 posts buried a foot deep. However, you don't need the posts. If you plant several raised beds, leave at least 3- to 4-foot-wide paths between them for access.

Some gardeners use pressure-treated wood or creosote-treated railroad ties to construct raised beds; check with your local lumberyard for these materials. I prefer not to use woods treated with chemicals. The research still hasn't proven to me that these materials won't get into my soil and food. But it's your choice, and treated timbers do last a lot longer.

The one downside of permanent raised beds is that it's difficult to get a tiller inside the bed to work the soil. However, with some of the newer lightweight tillers, maneuvering a tiller inside a raised bed is getting easier (see Chapter 21 for more information). You can also turn the soil by hand with an iron fork; it's more work than using a tiller, but it's effective.

In dry areas such as the desert Southwest, the traditional bed is not raised — it's sunken. Dig into the soil about 6 inches and make a small wall of soil around the outside of the bed. This design allows the bed to catch any summer rains, protects young plants from drying winds, and concentrates water where the vegetables grow.

## *Planning your planting*

As you plan your garden, you need to pay attention to these columns in Table 2-1:

- ✔ **Seeds/Plants per 100 ft. of row:** How many plants and seed to purchase.

- ✔ **Spacing between rows:** The ideal distance you should leave between rows of different vegetables. This is usually a little more than the distance you should leave between plants.

- ✔ **Spacing between plants:** The ideal distance you should allow between individual vegetable plants within a row or planting bed.

- ✔ **Average yield per 10 ft. of row:** How much you can expect to harvest.

Table 2-1 is adapted from Table A-1 in the appendix, which provides a wealth of information about planting vegetables.

| Table 2-1 | | Spacing and Yield Guide | | |
|---|---|---|---|---|
| *Crop* | *Seed/ Plants per 100 ft. of Row* | *Spacing Between Rows (Inches)* | *Spacing Between Plants (Inches)* | *Average Yield per 10 ft. of Row* |
| Asparagus | 65 pl./1 oz. | 36 - 48 | 18 | 3 lbs. |
| Beans, snap (bush) | ½ lb. | 24 - 36 | 3 - 4 | 12 lbs. |

| Crop | Seed/ Plants per 100 ft. of Row | Spacing Between Rows (Inches) | Spacing Between Plants (Inches) | Average Yield per 10 ft. of Row |
|---|---|---|---|---|
| RowBeans, snap (pole) | $\frac{1}{2}$ lb. | 36 - 48 | 4 - 6 | 15 lbs. |
| Beans, lima (bush) | $\frac{1}{2}$ lb. | 30 - 36 | 3 - 4 | 2.5 lbs., shelled |
| Beans, lima (pole) | $\frac{1}{4}$ lb. | 36 - 48 | 12 - 18 | 5 lbs., shelled |
| Beets | 1 oz. | 15 - 24 | 2 | 15 lbs. |
| Broccoli | 45 pl./ $\frac{1}{4}$ oz. | 24 - 36 | 14 - 24 | 10 lbs. |
| Brussels sprouts | 55 pl./ $\frac{1}{4}$ oz. | 24 - 36 | 14 - 24 | 7.5 lbs. |
| Cabbage | 55 pl./ $\frac{1}{4}$ oz. | 24 - 36 | 14 - 24 | 15 lbs. |
| Carrots | 1/2 oz. | 15 - 24 | 2 | 10 lbs. |
| Cauliflower | 55 pl./ $\frac{1}{4}$ oz. | 24 - 36 | 14 - 24 | 10 lbs. |
| Celery | 200 pl. | 30 - 36 | 6 | 18 stalks |
| Chinese cabbage | 65 pl./ $\frac{1}{4}$ oz. | 18 - 30 | 8 -12 | 8 heads |
| Corn | 3 - 4 oz. | 24 - 36 | 12 - 18 | 1 dozen |
| Cucumbers | $\frac{1}{2}$ oz. | 48 - 72 | 24 - 48 | 12 lbs. |
| Eggplant | $\frac{1}{8}$ oz. | 24 - 36 | 18 - 24 | 10 lbs. |
| Leeks | $\frac{1}{2}$ oz. | 12 - 18 | 2 - 4 | 12 lbs. |
| Lettuce, heading | $\frac{1}{4}$ oz. | 18 - 24 | 6 - 10 | 10 heads |
| Lettuce, leaf | $\frac{1}{4}$ oz. | 15 - 18 | 2 - 3 | 5 lbs. |
| Muskmelon | 50 pl./ $\frac{1}{2}$ oz. | 60 - 96 | 24 - 36 | 5 fruits |
| Okra | 2 oz. | 36 - 42 | 12 - 24 | 10 lbs. |
| Onion, seed | 1 oz. | 15 - 24 | 3 - 4 | 10 lbs. |
| Onion, sets | 400 - 600 pl. | 15 - 24 | 3 - 4 | 10 lbs. |
| Parsley | $\frac{1}{4}$ oz. | 15 - 24 | 6 - 8 | 4 lbs. |
| Parsnips | $\frac{1}{2}$ oz. | 18 - 30 | 3 - 4 | 10 lbs. |
| Peas | 1 lb. | 18 - 36 | 1 | 2 lbs. |

*(continued)*

### Table 2-1 *(continued)*

| Crop | Seed/ Plants per 100 ft. of Row | Spacing Between Rows (Inches) | Spacing Between Plants (Inches) | Average Yield per 10 ft. of Row |
|------|------|------|------|------|
| Peppers | 1/8 oz. | 24 - 36 | 18 - 24 | 6 lbs. |
| Potatoes, Irish | 6 - 10 lbs. seed potatoes | 30 - 36 | 10 - 15 | 10 lbs. |
| Pumpkins | 1/2 oz. | 60 - 96 | 36 - 48 | 10 lbs. |
| Radishes | 1 oz. | 14 - 24 | 1 | 10 bunches |
| Rhubarb | 20 pl. | 36 - 48 | 48 | 7 lbs. |
| Southern peas | 1/2 lb. | 24 - 36 | 4 - 6 | 4 lbs. |
| Spinach | 1 oz. | 14 - 24 | 3 - 4 | 4-5 lbs. |
| Squash, summer | 1 oz. | 36 - 60 | 18 - 36 | 15 lbs. |
| Squash winter | 1/2 oz. | 60 - 96 | 24 - 48 | 10 lbs. |
| Sweet potatoes | 75 - 100 pl. | 36-48 | 12-16 | 10 lbs. |
| Tomatoes | 50 pl./ 1/8 oz. | 24 - 48 | 18 - 36 | 10 lbs. |
| Turnips | 1/2 oz. | 14 - 24 | 2 - 3 | 5-10 lbs. |
| Watermelon | 1 oz. | 72 - 96 | 36 - 72 | 4 fruits |

Vegetable spacings are just guidelines, most likely derived from agricultural recommendations for maximum yield per acre. With close attention to soil preparation, watering, and fertilizing, you can plant closer and still get a good harvest. You can also find compact, small-space varieties of many of the vegetables described in Part II.

Although closer planting is possible, if you plant so close that plants have to compete with each other for food, water, and light, you'll eventually get smaller harvests or lower quality vegetables.

## *Penciling it in*

Drawing a garden plan doesn't require any landscaping expertise. Once you determine the location and dimensions of your garden, you just need a piece of graph paper and a pencil, a list of vegetables you want to grow, and maybe a seed catalog or two. Then, grab your pencil and graph paper and start drawing. Fill in spaces for your favorite crops, taking into account the space requirements of the crops you want to grow (refer to Table 2-1); whether you want to plant in rows, beds, or hills; and how much of each vegetable you want to harvest. Garden design has any number of possibilities. Just keep in mind a few things:

- ✔ **You can't plant everything.** Choose your crops carefully.

- ✔ **Not all plants have it made in the shade.** Tall crops such as corn should be placed where they won't shade other vegetables. The north end of the garden is usually best.

- ✔ **These roots aren't made for walking.** Plan your garden with walkways (at least 2- to 3-feet wide, wider if you need to use a wheelbarrow or garden cart) so you can get to plants easily without damaging roots. For more about walkways, see "Gliding down the Garden Paths" later in this chapter.

Planning on paper helps you purchase the right amount of seeds or transplants and use space more efficiently. It's a good way to see the possibilities for *succession planting* (following one crop with another) and *interplanting* (planting a quick maturing crop next to a slower-maturing one and harvesting the former before it competes for space). For example, you may see that you can follow your late peas with a crop of late broccoli, and you'll be ready with transplants in July. Or you may see that there's space to tuck a few lettuce plants among your tomatoes while the vines are still small. You find out more about all that in Chapter 16. Figure 2-3 shows a sample of what your garden plan might look like. Chapter 1 contains information about other garden designs.

# Gliding down the Garden Paths

You don't want to stand in the mud while you water or harvest, so you need more than bare ground under your feet. Make garden paths wide enough for a garden cart to pass through. And use mulching materials that will keep weeds at bay. The last thing you want to do is *weed* your garden paths! Soft materials, such as straw and bark mulch, are easy on your knees and keep weeds from germinating. Many materials can be used, each unique in appearance, texture, and cleanliness. Here are some choices:

- ✔ **Grass:** Grass makes an attractive, soft-textured garden path, but you must water, fertilize, and mow it to keep it looking good — and that requires extra work. Vigilance and edging, such as rubber edging, help keep the grass where it should be. If you live in an area with frequent summer rain, maintenance will be easier; if you live where it's hot and dry, try a different material for your garden path.

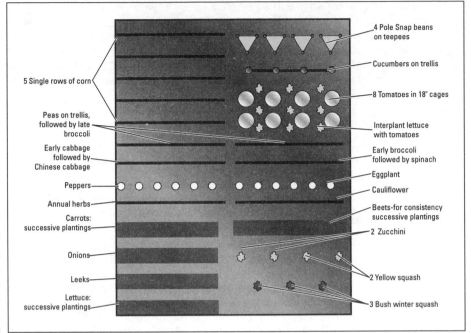

**Figure 2-3:**
A sample
vegetable
garden
plan.

Labels on the figure:

5 Single rows of corn

Peas on trellis, followed by late broccoli

Early cabbage followed by Chinese cabbage

Peppers

Annual herbs

Carrots: successive plantings

Onions

Leeks

Lettuce: successive plantings

4 Pole Snap beans on teepees

Cucumbers on trellis

8 Tomatoes in 18" cages

Interplant lettuce with tomatoes

Early broccoli followed by spinach

Eggplant

Cauliflower

Beets-for consistency successive plantings

2 Zucchini

2 Yellow squash

3 Bush winter squash

✔ **Gravel:** Gravel or more powderlike decomposed granite looks good and water drains through it quickly (and neither gets soggy or messy). However, the material is pretty tough on bare feet and can be difficult to clean if a lot of dirt falls on top of it.

✔ **Masonry:** Brick, cement, flagstone, and the like look great and are easy to keep clean with a garden hose. They are, however, relatively expensive, permanent, and uncomfortable to kneel on (although kneeling cushions can help).

✔ **Organic matter:** Organic matter includes everything from ground bark to straw to sawdust. Organic materials look good and are relatively cheap, but they have to be replaced as they break down. On the other hand, the fact that they do break down means that you can till them right into the soil at the end of the season, improving the soil in the process. Bark lasts the longest but is unpleasant to walk on when you're barefoot. Straw and sawdust are soft on the feet, but they break down quickly and can become soggy if there's a lot of water around.

Most gardeners tend to use whatever materials are cheap and widely available. Pine straw in the South, hay in the North, and gravel in the arid West are all possibilities for garden paths. I prefer organic materials because they add organic matter to the soil, helping my garden prosper.

# Chapter 3
# Working with Mother Nature

● ● ● ● ● ● ● ● ● ● ● ● ● ● ● ● ● ● ● ● ● ● ● ● ● ● ● ● ● ● ● ● ● ● ● ● ● ●

## In This Chapter

▶ The difference between warm-season and cool-season vegetables

▶ The importance of average frost dates

▶ What temperature extremes can do to vegetables

▶ Planting guides by climates

● ● ● ● ● ● ● ● ● ● ● ● ● ● ● ● ● ● ● ● ● ● ● ● ● ● ● ● ● ● ● ● ● ● ● ● ● ●

**M**y dad used to tell me, "Timing is everything." Well, that's especially true for vegetable gardening.

File that axiom where you can't forget it. It will save you lots of heartache and disappointment. For example, if you plant tomatoes too early, the plants will sit there like bumps on a log, not growing, and possibly rotting in cold, wet soil, or worse, turning a mushy black after they've been zapped by a frost. Plant lettuce too late and it will produce more flowers than leaves, and the leaves that you harvest will be tough and bitter. I could give you examples like this for every vegetable, but I'll spare you. Just know that planting at the wrong time of year is a recipe for disaster.

But if you follow the rhythms of nature and plant when conditions are perfect for proper growth, growing vegetables is a breeze. Tomatoes grow like weeds and lettuce is always sweet and tender. But how are you supposed to know about these rhythms? Well, start tapping your foot because this chapter will have you moving like Fred Astaire.

## Some Like It Cool, Some Like It Hot

Vegetables can be divided into two categories based on the conditions in which they grow best:

  ✔ **Cool-season vegetables** such as lettuce, peas, potatoes, broccoli, and cabbage grow best in the cool weather of spring and fall. As vegetables go, they are fairly hardy and survive despite freezing temperatures. However, if the weather stays too cold or too wet, they grow slowly — if at all — and sometimes die. In most areas, cool-season vegetables are usually planted in early spring so that they mature before the onset of hot weather, or in late summer to early fall for maturation in the cool months of fall or early winter. However, there are exceptions. In areas where summers are very cool and winters are mild, such as in coastal areas of the western United States, cool season vegetables can be grown year-round. Where summers are very short and cool, such as many northern and high-elevation areas, cool-season vegetables are grown all summer and are sometimes the only vegetables that will succeed.

In spring, as the weather gets warmer and the days longer, many cool-season vegetables will suffer. Some, such as lettuce, will *bolt,* meaning they start to flower before you get a chance to harvest them. In other words, instead of producing tender crisp leaves, lettuce will send out a tall flower spike. And any leaves that are left will be bitter-tasting and tough. Others, such as broccoli, will form loose clusters of yellow flowers, instead of forming nice tight heads. Some, such as peas, will not fill out their pods properly with sweet, succulent peas.

✔ **Warm-season vegetables,** such as beans, tomatoes, peppers, cucumbers, melons, and corn, like it hot and grow best in the warm months of summer. Because freezing temperatures kill these vegetables, they are usually planted after the threat of frost in spring. Or they are protected in some way to get them through cold weather (see Chapter 22 for ways to protect vegetables and extend your growing season). In warm areas, they also can be planted in late summer for a fall harvest. Many warm-season vegetables, such as peppers and corn, will grow only when soil temperatures reach a certain point. Consequently, it's often best to wait until you are sure that the soil is warm enough before planting or to use some type of season extender that traps heat around the plants. Season extenders also help in cool summer climates such as the Pacific Northwest, where the weather rarely gets warm enough even in summer to ripen heat-loving vegetables such as melons.

# Frost Dates and the Length of the Growing Season

You should know two very important dates for your area if you want to grow vegetables successfully:

✔ The average date of the last frost in spring

✔ The average date of the first frost in fall

Frost dates tell you several important things:

✔ **When to plant:** Cool-season vegetables are generally planted 4 to 6 weeks before the last spring frost. (Fall planting of cool-season vegetables is less dependant on frost dates, but is usually done 8 to 12 weeks before the first fall frost.) Warm-season vegetables are planted after the last spring frost or in late summer in warm areas for a fall harvest.

✔ **When to protect warm-season vegetables:** Frosts kill warm-season vegetables. The closer you plant to the last frost of spring, the more important it is to protect plants. And as the fall frost gets closer, so does the end of your summer vegetable season — unless, of course, you protect your plants. I show you how to provide frost protection in Chapter 22.

✔ **The length of your growing season:** This is the number of days between the average date of the last frost in spring and the average date of the first frost in fall. The length of the growing season can range from less than 100 days in northern or cold winter climates to 365 days in frost-free southern climates. Many warm-season vegetables need long, warm growing seasons to properly mature and are difficult, if not impossible, to grow where growing seasons are short. But how are you to know if your growing season is long enough?

With warm-season vegetables, that's pretty easy. If you check mail-order seed catalogs or even individual seed packets, each variety will have the number of *days to harvest* or *days to maturity* (usually posted in parentheses next to the variety name). This is the number of days it takes for that vegetable to grow from seed (or transplant) to harvest. If your growing season is only 100 days long and you want to grow a melon or other warm-season vegetable that takes 120 frost-free days to mature, you have a problem. The plant will probably be killed by frost before the fruit is mature. In areas with short growing seasons, it's usually best to go with early ripening varieties (shortest number of days to harvest). You can find many effective ways to extend your growing season, such as starting seeds indoors or planting under floating row covers (blanketlike materials that drape over plants, creating warm, greenhouselike conditions underneath). Various methods of extending growing seasons are covered in Chapter 22.

There you have it — frost dates are important. But how do you find out dates for your area? Easy. Ask a local nursery person or contact your local cooperative extension office (look in the phone book under *county government*). You can also look in Appendix A, which lists frost dates for major cities around the country.

Frost dates are very important, but you also have to take them with a grain of salt. After all, these dates are averages, meaning that half the time the frost will actually come earlier than the average date and half the time it will occur later. You should also know that frost dates are usually given for large areas, such as your city or county. If you live in a cold spot in the bottom of a valley, frosts may come days earlier in fall and days later in spring. If you live in a warm spot, your frost may come later in fall and stop earlier in spring. But you'll find out all about that as you become a more seasoned vegetable gardener and unearth the nuances of your own yard. (One thing you'll know for sure is that you can't predict the weather.) Chapter 2 has more information on how to tell whether you live in an unusually warm or cool area or whether you have a microclimate that will influence your vegetable gardening.

Listening to your evening weather forecast is one of the best ways to find out whether frosts are expected in your area. But you can also do a little predicting yourself by going outside late in the evening and checking conditions. If the fall or early spring sky is clear and full of stars, and the wind is still, conditions are right for a frost. If you need to protect plants, do so at that time. Frost-protection techniques are covered in Chapter 22.

# If It's Not Too Cold, It's Too Hot

After all this talk of frost dates, you may be thinking about moving south, to a place where frosts are uncommon, or at least where the growing seasons are very long. That's vegetable paradise, right? Actually, in many cases it is. That's why many vegetable farmers choose such climates to grow their crops. But such climates can have some downsides, too. In many mild-summer climates, such as the southwestern United States, summer temperatures can get too high for some vegetables, and the plants tend to have more pest problems as well. For example, tomatoes, peppers, and eggplants will fail to set fruit (and if they don't set fruit, no fruit happens!) if daytime temperatures stay above 90°F and nighttime temperatures stay above 75°F — not to mention what the intense sunlight does to the fruit. In such areas, many vegetable gardeners do most of their growing in spring and fall to avoid the hottest times of year. They also grow their plants in partial shade to escape the hottest sun.

High temperatures combined with high humidity can also cause disease problems. In the southeastern United States, fungal diseases such as southern blight can run rampant, making it very difficult to grow certain vegetables, unless you plant disease-resistant varieties or use control measures.

So vegetable gardening is not always as simple as you may think. Every area has its vegetable opportunities, as well as its pitfalls.

# Planting Guides Just for You

All right, you say. It can get too hot or too cold. Just tell me when to plant. I can do that. First, I take a little tour around the United States and give you specific planting dates for four different areas, so you can see just how much climate affects planting times.

You'll notice throughout this book that I talk about planting schedules for cold and mild winter areas of the United States. To give you a better sense of what category your location falls under, here are some definitions:

- **Cold winter:** Temperatures get consistently below 0°F in winter. Usually, snow is on the ground for most of the winter.

- **Mild (warm) winter:** Temperatures rarely get below 0°F and, if so, only for short periods. Usually, little if any snow is on the ground in winter, and the snow that falls tends to melt quickly.

Saddle up — the vegetable planting tour begins here.

## In the sultry south

Growing seasons are long in the southeast. Note that many warm-season vegetables are planted in midsummer for fall harvest. Table 3-1 shows recommended spring and fall planting dates for Georgia:

| Table 3-1 | Planting Guidelines for Southern Regions (Georgia) | |
| --- | --- | --- |
| **Vegetable** | **Spring Planting** | **Fall Planting** |
| Asparagus | January 15 to March 15 | November and December |
| Beans | April 1 to June 1 | July 1 to August 1 |
| Beets | February 15 to April 1 | August 1 to September 20 |
| Broccoli | February 15 to March 15 | August 1 to September 1 |
| Cabbage | January 15 to March 15 | August 1 to October 1 |
| Cantaloupe | March 20 to April 1 | July 10 to July 30 |
| Carrots | January 15 to March 20 | August 20 to September 15 |
| Cauliflower | March 1 to April 1 | July 15 to August 15 |
| Collards | February 1 to March 15 | August 1 to September 1 |
| Corn | March 15 to June 1 | NR |
| Cucumbers | April 1 to May 15 | July 15 to August 15 |
| Eggplant | April 1 to May 15 | July 10 to July 30 |
| Kale | February 1 to March 10 | August 1 to September 1 |
| Lettuce | January 15 to March 1 | September 1 to October 1 |
| Okra | April 1 to June 1 | June 15 to July 10 |
| Onion, dry bulb | January 1 to March 15 | October 10 to November 10 |
| Onion, green | January 1 to March 15 | September 1 to December 31 |

*(continued)*

### Table 3-1 *(continued)*

| Vegetable | Spring Planting | Fall Planting |
|---|---|---|
| Peas, garden and edible pod | January 15 to February 15 | NR |
| Peas, southern | April to August 10 | NR |
| Peppers, bell | April 1 to June 1 | July 25 to August 10 |
| Peppers, hot | April 1 to June 1 | July 25 to August 10 |
| Potatoes, Irish | January 15 to March 1 | NR |
| Potatoes, sweet | April 15 to June 15 | NR |
| Radishes | January 15 to April 1 | September 1 to October 15 |
| Spinach | January 15 to March 15 | September 1 to October 15 |
| Squash, summer | April 1 to May 15 | August 1 to August 25 |
| Squash, winter | April 1 to July 1 | NR |
| Tomatoes | March 25 to May 1 | June 15 to July 15 |
| Turnips | January 15 to April 1 | August 10 to September 15 |
| Watermelon | March 20 to May 1 | NR |

*NR = Not reliable in all areas*

## And a little farther north in Michigan

Growing seasons are much shorter up north, running anywhere from 120 to 180 days long. (The dates listed in Table 3-2 are for Lansing, Michigan.) Many cool-season crops can be grown all season long in northern areas.

### Table 3-2    Planting Guidelines for Northern Regions (Michigan)

| Vegetable | Spring Planting | Fall Planting |
|---|---|---|
| Asparagus | April | NR |
| Beans | May 20 to July 15 | NR |
| Beets | April 1 to July 15 | NR |
| Broccoli | April 20 to June 1 | July 1 to 15 |
| Brussels sprouts | April 20 to May 15 | June 20 to June 30 |
| Cabbage | April 20 to July 15 | NR |
| Cantaloupe | May 20 to June 1 | NR |
| Celery | April 1 to May 30 | NR |
| Collards | April 1 to August 1 | NR |

| Vegetable | Spring Planting | Fall Planting |
|---|---|---|
| Corn | May 20 to June 1 | NR |
| Eggplant | May 20 to June 1 | NR |
| Kale | June 20 to July 20 | NR |
| Kohlrabi | April 1 to June 30 | NR |
| Lettuce | April 1 to June 1 | August 1 to August 15 |
| Okra | June 20 to May 1 | NR |
| Onions | April 1 to May 1 | NR |
| Peas | April 1 to April 30 | July 15 to 30 |
| Peppers | May 20 to June 1 | NR |
| Potatoes, Irish | April 20 to June 1 | NR |
| Potatoes, sweet | May 20 to June 1 | NR |
| Pumpkins | May 20 to June 15 | NR |
| Radishes | April 1 to July 1 | August 1 to September 1 |
| Spinach | April 1 to July 30 | NR |
| Tomatoes | May 20 to June 1 | NR |
| Turnips | April 1 to July 1 | August 1 to September 1 |
| Watermelons | May 20 to June 1 | NR |

*NR = Not reliable in all areas*

# In foggy San Francisco

Along the coast of California in San Francisco, many cool-season vegetables can be grown year-round if they don't rot in cool, wet soil (see Table 3-3). However, to be successful with warm-season vegetables, you have plant specifically adapted varieties (such as the 'San Francisco Fog' tomato) and plant in warm locations or use season extenders (see Chapter 22). Even then, sun and warmth may be insufficient to ripen heat-lovers such as melons and peppers. As you move inland to warmer climes, warm-season vegetables are more successful.

| Table 3-3 | Planting Guidelines for Coastal Regions (California) | |
|---|---|---|
| **Vegetable** | **Spring Planting** | **Fall Planting** |
| Artichokes | February to May | NR |
| Asparagus | January to March | NR |

*(continued)*

## Table 3-3 (continued)

| Vegetable | Spring Planting | Fall Planting |
|---|---|---|
| Beets | Year-round | NR |
| Broccoli | February to April | August to September* |
| Brussels sprouts | April to July | NR |
| Cabbage | February to April | August to September* |
| Carrots | March to October* | NR |
| Cauliflower | February to April | August to September* |
| Celery | February to August* | NR |
| Chard | Year-round | NR |
| Corn | April to July | NR |
| Cucumbers | May to mid-July | NR |
| Eggplant | May | NR |
| Kohlrabi | February to May | July to August* |
| Lettuce | Year-round | NR |
| Melons | May | NR |
| Okra | NR | NR |
| Onions | January to March | September to October |
| Peanuts | NR | NR |
| Peas | February to April | August to November* |
| Peppers | May | NR |
| Potatoes, Irish | March to June | August |
| Potatoes, sweet | NR | NR |
| Pumpkins | May to June | NR |
| Radishes | Year-round | NR |
| Spinach | February to April | July to September* |
| Squash, summer | April to July | NR |
| Squash, winter | May to June | NR |
| Tomatoes | April to June | NR |
| Turnips | January to August* | NR |

NR = Not reliable in all areas        * May not mature if planted late

# *Baking in Phoenix*

Summers can be brutally hot in the desert southwest. Warm-season vegetables are planted early and late to miss the hottest time of the year. Most cool-season vegetables are planted in fall to mature in winter (see Table 3-4).

## Table 3-4 Planting Guidelines for Southwestern Regions (Arizona)

| Vegetable | Spring Planting | Fall Planting |
|---|---|---|
| Artichokes | Mid-February to mid-May | September |
| Asparagus | October to March | NR |
| Beans | March to mid-April | Mid-August to September |
| Beets | February | October to mid-December |
| Broccoli | September to November | NR |
| Brussels sprouts | September to November | NR |
| Cabbage | September to November | NR |
| Cantaloupe | February to March | Mid-July to August |
| Carrots | September to January | NR |
| Cauliflower | August to November | NR |
| Celery | Mid-September to mid-October | NR |
| Chard | January to March | October to November |
| Corn | February to mid-April | Late August to mid-September |
| Cucumbers | February to mid-April | Mid-August to mid-September |
| Eggplant | March to April | NR |
| Kohlrabi | Mid-September to November | NR |
| Lettuce | Mid-January to mid-February | September to mid-November |
| Okra | April to June | NR |
| Onions | Mid-September to October | NR |

*(continued)*

### Table 3-4 *(continued)*

| Vegetable | Spring Planting | Fall Planting |
| --- | --- | --- |
| Peanuts | April | NR |
| Peas | Mid-September to November | NR |
| Peppers | Mid-March to April | NR |
| Potatoes, Irish | January to February | NR |
| Potatoes, sweet | April to mid-June | NR |
| Pumpkins | May to early July | NR |
| Radishes | October to mid-February | NR |
| Spinach | October to January | NR |
| Squash, summer | Mid-February to April | August |
| Squash, winter | July | NR |
| Tomatoes | Mid-February to mid-March | August |
| Turnips | October to November | NR |
| Watermelon | February to March | NR |

*NR = Not reliable in all areas*

So you see that, whether you live in the North, South, East, or West, you have a perfect time to plant your veggies. In the next part, I tell you about specific veggies you may want to plant. So, on to the veggies!

# Part II
# Vegging Out

The 5th Wave    By Rich Tennant

@RICHTENNANT

"That's a cross between a winter squash and a rutabaga. It's called a winnebaga."

# In this part . . .

At this point in the book, I could have gotten into
more on planting, soil building, watering, fertilizing,
and stuff, but this is a vegetable gardening book and I'm
sure you really want to know which *vegetables* to grow
(and eat!).  So here they are: Vegetables from asparagus to
zucchini and many, many in between. I tell you how to
grow them, the best varieties, and how to avoid pest and
disease damage. I even offer some recipes and health tips.
Interested in a specific vegetable you'd like to grow? Flip
through this section, find your veggie (or berry and herb,
too) of choice, and read on.

# Chapter 4

# And the Winner Is . . . Tomatoes

*T*omatoes are hands-down the most popular vegetables in the garden. Almost 90 percent of home gardeners who grow vegetables grow tomatoes. After you've picked and tasted a juicy, vine-ripened fresh tomato, you'll understand why. You can't even compare the bland supermarket tennis balls that most people make do with to the taste and texture explosion of the homegrown tomato — and tomatoes are even easy to grow! Just give them a good start and a little attention during the growing season, and you'll be rewarded with more delicious ripe fruits than you can eat.

Tomatoes also are no longer just the round red fruits we're accustomed to seeing. Through breeding and the rediscovery of heirloom varieties, tomatoes now come in almost every color of the rainbow and in a variety of sizes, from black to white, and from as tiny as a blueberry to as large as a grapefruit. Modern breeding practices have created varieties adapted to the heat, cold, and even containers. Great taste, disease resistance, and ease of growing make tomatoes the most rewarding to grow of all the vegetables.

Is the tomato a fruit or a vegetable? Although we all call the tomato a vegetable, botanically, it's a fruit. Any edible plant part that develops from the ovary (found behind the flower) of the plant after fertilization is considered a fruit, so tomatoes, cucumbers, squash, peppers, and eggplant are considered fruits; lettuce, carrots, onions, and spinach are technically considered vegetables. Of course, this is all a moot point because we categorize our fruits and vegetables by their uses, not by their botany. (Case in point: A Supreme Court ruling in 1893 declared the tomato a vegetable.) So be it. Besides, my wife's fruit cake wouldn't taste half as good with tomatoes, peppers, and cucumbers in it.

## Tomato's sordid past

Tomato *(Lycopersicum esculentum)* history starts in the Andean mountains of Peru. A sprawling, low-growing plant with small, red, cherry tomato-like fruits is the wild ancestor of the modern tomato, but this forefather was basically ignored by the native peoples of the Andes. Tomatoes didn't meet with much acclaim until their seeds were dispersed thousands of miles north of their native region to present-day Mexico and were cultivated by native peoples. The Aztecs treasured not the red-fruited varieties but the gold-colored ones. When Spanish explorers came to the Western hemisphere in the fifteenth century, it was the "golden apple" that they found and took back with them to Europe.

However, like the people of the Andes, Europeans didn't warm up to this New World fruit at first. In fact, it took a few hundred years before the tomato was grown as more than an ornamental in Italian, Portuguese, and Spanish gardens. Because of the tomato's resemblance to other nightshade, or solanaceous (from the family name *Solanaceae*) crops, many thought that the fruit was poisonous. The red varieties became more popular than the original golden ones and names associated with this flame-red, attractive fruit circulated throughout Europe until the "love apple" (from the Italian *pomum amoris*) caught on, partly because of the fruit's color, and partly due to rumors of tomatoes' aphrodisiac properties.

By the seventeenth century, tomatoes were becoming more trusted and popular as a food. They made their reappearance in the Americas in Thomas Jefferson's garden in 1782 and slowly gained popularity and notoriety as specialty vegetables in Europe and America. By the 1860s, commercial seedsmen were breeding and selecting for the best varieties so that by the turn of the century, there was a variety of shapes, sizes, and colors of tomatoes. The development of modern agricultural practice after World War II dictated the breeding of tomato varieties that were firm enough to be harvested by machines and shipped thousands of miles to market without spoiling. These hard, less-than-bright-red-colored fruits became the norm in grocery stores, but they also became the inspiration for home gardeners to grow their own.

The pendulum has swung full circle, with consumers demanding better-tasting and better-textured vegetables. Older heirloom varieties, open-pollinated varieties, and modern hybrid varieties (see definitions of heirloom, open-pollinated, and hybrid in Chapter 1) are being bred to yield softer, juicier, more flavorful tomatoes. And that's where I start looking at tomatoes, with the varieties.

# Tomato Varieties

Before deciding which tomato variety to grow, consider the different types of tomatoes. Tomatoes may be classified in many different ways — by fruit color, shape, or size — but the first consideration should be the growth habits of the plants. Plants can grow into huge monsters or tiny pot plants. Whether a cherry tomato, paste tomato, or red slicing tomato variety, tomatoes all fall into one of these categories:

✓ **Indeterminate:** These tomato plants are like the Energizer Bunny — they keep growing and growing and growing. The side branches and shoots continue to grow even after fruit is set (after the flower has been pollinated and the young tomato fruits begin to grow), and can be stopped only by frost, insects, disease, or an ax. These are the plants you'll see in Sunday newspaper advertisements as growing higher than your house. They do produce a ton of fruit, but the tomatoes tend to mature later in the season than those born by the shorter plant varieties. Varieties such as 'Early Girl' and 'Brandywine' are good examples of indeterminate types.

✓ **Determinate:** Unlike indeterminate varieties, determinate varieties tend to stop growing once the shoots set fruit. Varieties vary in the degree that they're determinate, but these plants generally tend to be shorter and produce less fruit while maturing fruit earlier than indeterminates. (See Figure 4-1.) Varieties such as 'Celebrity' and 'Oregon Spring' are good examples of determinate types.

✓ **Dwarf:** These stronger determinate plants tend to reach only a few feet tall, produce all of their fruit at once, and then stop producing for the season. These plants are excellent as patio or container plants, producing cherry tomato-sized fruits. 'Patio' and 'Tiny Tim' are examples of dwarf tomatoes.

✓ **Dwarf-indeterminate:** The best of both worlds, these plants stay dwarf, only reaching about 3 to 4 feet tall, but continue to produce full-sized tomatoes all season long. They grow well when planted in containers or in the garden. Some dwarf-indeterminate varieties include 'Bush Big Boy' and 'Husky Gold.'

In Figure 4-1, you can see differences between determinate and indeterminate.

When in doubt about a variety's quality, look for the All-America Selections (AAS) winner label in the variety's description. This group evaluates new varieties yearly by conducting trials all across the country for outstanding tomato growth and flavor. A variety with this label will likely perform well in your garden.

Tomato varieties also can be classified as hybrids or open-pollinated. *Open-pollinated* refers to varieties that have the ability to cross-pollinate among themselves naturally and produce plants that resemble the parents. *Hybrid* varieties are the product of a cross between two varieties that would not naturally do so and that are genetically different. Hybrids are an invention of post–World War II plant breeders to make varieties more productive, uniform, and disease resistant. See Chapter 1 for more advantages to growing hybrids and open-pollinated varieties.

**Figure 4-1:**
Determinate plants tend to be shorter and produce less fruit earlier than indeterminate plants.

Determinate                    Indeterminate

## Red, round tomatoes

Red, round tomatoes are the classic, bright red, juicy, meaty tomatoes that we all want to grow. You have hundreds of varieties to choose from, but the following list includes some of my favorites. When in doubt about choosing a variety to grow in your garden, ask your local garden center, farmer's market, or neighbor who's growing tomatoes for suggestions about what grows best in the region:

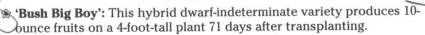

❀ **'Better Boy':** This hybrid indeterminate produces smooth 8- to 12-ounce fruits that are great for slicing and have good disease resistance.

❀ **'Big Beef':** This All-America-Selections-winning, indeterminate hybrid is loaded with disease resistance, producing blemish-free 8- to 10-ounce fruits. It matures 70 days from transplant.

❀ **'Bush Big Boy':** This hybrid dwarf-indeterminate variety produces 10-ounce fruits on a 4-foot-tall plant 71 days after transplanting.

- ❀ **'Celebrity':** A vigorous determinate hybrid and another AAS winner, 'Celebrity' doesn't grow as large as the 'Big Beef' type tomatoes but still produces 7- to 8-ounce fruits about 72 days after transplanting into the garden.

- ❀ **'Delicious':** If you want to grow "the big one," this indeterminate heirloom is for you. Fruits weigh more than 2 pounds each 77 days after transplanting. This variety holds the world record for the largest tomato: 7 pounds, 12 ounces.

- ❀ **'Early Girl':** Despite being an indeterminate hybrid, this plant produces 4- to 6-ounce fruits only 52 days after transplanting.

- ❀ **'Heatwave II':** This determinate hybrid is specially bred to grow and produce fruits in hot, humid conditions. The 7-ounce fruits are produced 68 days after transplanting.

- ❀ **'Oregon Spring':** This determinate, open-pollinated variety is bred to have few seeds in each fruit. The 7- to 8-ounce fruits are produced only 58 days after transplanting.

- ❀ **'Siberia':** This determinate heirloom variety can set fruits in temperatures as low as 38°F. The 2- to 3-ounce fruits are produced only 55 days after transplanting.

- ❀ **'Stupice':** This Czechoslovakian indeterminate heirloom is early and cold tolerant, bearing 1- to 2-ounce fruits 52 days after transplanting.

## *Other-than-red tomatoes*

Tomatoes of a different color (other than red, that is) have become very popular again. The flavor of many of these varieties is comparable to the red varieties, but the colors can be outstanding in salads and casseroles, or just by themselves:

- ❀ **'Big Rainbow':** This unique, indeterminate heirloom produces 2-pound tomatoes with yellow shoulders, orange centers, and red bottoms 95 days after transplanting. A real looker!

- ❀ **'Brandywine':** This Amish indeterminate heirloom has unique potato-leaf foliage and produces 1- to 2-pound pink fruits — reportedly the most flavorful of all varieties — 80 days after transplanting.

- ❀ **'Black Prince':** An indeterminate heirloom from Siberia, this plant produces juicy, deep garnet-colored, 4- to 6-ounce fruits 70 days after transplant. This tomato is something really different!

- ❀ **'Caro Rich':** This determinate, open-pollinated variety produces 5- to 6-ounce, bright orange-colored fruits that have 10 times the amount of vitamin A as other tomatoes 80 days after transplanting.

- ✿ **'Cherokee Purple':** This heirloom indeterminate bears 10-ounce dusky rose/purple colored fruits with thin skins about 80 days after transplanting.

- ✿ **'Husky Gold':** This AAS-winning hybrid, dwarf-indeterminate plant only reaches 4 feet tall, but it produces deep golden-colored, 8-ounce fruits 70 days after transplanting.

- ✿ **'Lemon Boy':** The first lemon-yellow-colored tomato, this hybrid indeterminate produces 7-ounce fruits with lots of disease resistance 72 days after transplanting.

- ✿ **'White Beauty':** This open-pollinated indeterminate produces creamy white 8-ounce fruits 85 days after transplanting.

We've all heard it before: Yellow tomatoes have less acid than reds. But the truth is, growing conditions, the individual genetic traits of varieties, and the amount of sugar in the varieties have more to do with the acidic taste of tomatoes than the skin color. Putting our prejudices to the test, blind taste tests have proven that gardeners can't tell the difference in flavor between red and yellow tomatoes. Try it with your friends!

## Some saucy tomatoes

Eating tomatoes fresh from the garden is pure joy. However, you may want to preserve some of that fresh taste for cooking in the off season. If making tomato sauce, paste, salsa, and juice is for you, these paste tomato varieties are bred to order. Even though any tomato variety can be processed, these pear- or plum-shaped types are meatier and thicker-walled and usually have less juice. The latest trend in paste tomatoes is the *saladette* type. These are bred not only to be good tomatoes for cooking, but also to taste great fresh in salads and sandwiches. Here are some of the best to try:

- ✿ **'Enchantment':** This indeterminate hybrid is a "saladette-type" variety — it tastes good processed as well as eaten fresh. The 3- to 4-ounce egg-shaped fruits are born on disease-resistant plants 70 days after transplanting.

- ✿ **'Italian Gold':** This determinate hybrid is a golden-fruited Roma-type, pear-shaped tomato that adds color to sauces and salsa. It matures 70 days after transplanting.

- ✿ **'Roma':** This is one of the most popular processing tomatoes around. This open-pollinated determinate produces plum-shaped, 3-ounce fruits on compact vines 78 days after transplanting.

- ✿ **'Super Marzano':** A hybrid version of another popular paste tomato, this hybrid indeterminate has 4- to 5-ounce pear-shaped fruits that are more disease resistant and productive than their heirloom cousin. The fruits mature 70 days after transplanting.

❀ **'Viva Italia':** This is another saladette-type that is as good fresh as it is processed. This hybrid, determinate variety produces pear-shaped 3- to 4-ounce fruits with great disease resistance 80 days after transplanting.

Elongated plum- or pear-shaped tomatoes tend to be more susceptible to blossom-end rot (see "Weather-related problems," later in the chapter, for more on this condition). To prevent blossom-end rot, keep the plants well watered, and mulch with a 4- to 6-inch-deep layer of hay or straw to keep the moisture levels constant. Pick off and throw away any affected fruits, and the new ones that develop should be fine.

## Cherry tomatoes

Nothing is more satisfying to me than going into the garden and popping handfuls of cherry tomatoes into my mouth. I swear that my daughter and I eat half my cherry tomato crop before it gets into the kitchen. Cherry tomatoes can be very productive, so often, only one or two plants are enough to keep your family happy all season. If you're growing the dwarf, Patio-type tomatoes, they do best in containers. (See Chapter 17 for more on growing vegetables in containers.) Cherry tomato fruits do tend to crack more easily than larger-sized tomatoes, so make sure that they have plenty of water and mulch (see Chapter 15 for watering and mulching tips). Here are some of my favorite cherry tomato varieties:

❀ **'Micro-Tom':** The world's smallest tomato plant, this dwarf plant reaches only 6 to 8 inches tall and produces pea-sized red fruits 88 days after transplanting. It's great in window boxes and containers.

❀ **'Patio':** This hybrid, dwarf plant produces grape-sized red fruits all at once about 70 days after transplanting.

❀ **'Sweet Million':** This prolific hybrid, indeterminate, 1- to 2-inch-diameter, red-fruited variety has good disease and crack resistance and matures early (60 days after transplanting).

❀ **'Super Sweet 100':** Another prolific hybrid indeterminate, this variety produces strands loaded with sweet-tasting 1-inch-diameter red fruits about 65 days after transplanting.

❀ **'Sun Gold':** This hybrid, indeterminate plant produces fruity tasting 1- to 2-inch-diameter orange-colored fruits 57 days after transplanting.

❀ **'Tiny Tim':** These open-pollinated, dwarf, 18-inch-tall plants are great for containers, producing 1-inch-diameter red fruits 60 days after transplanting.

❀ **'Yellow Pear':** This is an heirloom indeterminate, producing clear yellow, 2-inch-diameter pear-shaped fruits on huge plants about 78 days after transplanting.

## Tomato relatives

Just like in any family, tomatoes have some odd relatives. Following are descriptions of three of the most commonly known tomato relatives. They're all grown similar to tomatoes, but the flavors are much different. If you're in the mood for experimenting, try one of these varieties:

❀ **'Husk Cherry'** *(Physalis peruviana;* **also known as 'Strawberry Tomato' or 'Cape Gooseberry'):** These sprawling plants produce tons of small, papery husks similar to Chinese lanterns. Inside each husk is a cherry-tomato-sized fruit that matures to yellow or gold. The flavor is like a wild berry but sweet. I started growing these tomatoes for my daughter, and she loves them. They mature 75 days after transplant.

❀ **'Tomatillo'** *(Physalis ixocarpa):* The standard ingredient in salsa, these tomato relatives produce papery husks like the 'Husk Cherry,' but the fruits inside are ping-pong-ball size. Varieties come in yellow and purple fruit colors. Fruits mature 65 days after transplant.

❀ **'Tree Tomato'** *(Cyphomandra betacea-amarillo):* Although technically in the tomato family, this tropical plant is as unfamiliar as the uncle you rarely see. It's a small perennial tree native to the Peruvian Andes that produces tons of hen's-egg-sized fruits that range from yellow to red when mature. The flavor isn't like a tomato but more like a tropical fruit. The plants need 18 months of warm weather to mature a crop, so unless you have a greenhouse, growing this variety is limited to gardeners who live in zone 10 areas.

# Jump-Starting Tomatoes

After you get your varieties, it's time to get them growing. Tomatoes require such a long season to mature that they are best bought as transplants through the mail or from local garden centers. You can also start them indoors four to six weeks before your last frost date (see the appendix for average frost dates in your area). I cover starting seeds indoors in detail in Chapter 13. Basically, you want to have a stocky, 6- to 10-inch tall, dark-green-leafed, flowerless transplant ready to go into the garden after all danger of frost has passed.

For gardeners in subtropical areas such as southern Florida, you can plant two crops of tomatoes, one in the spring and another in the fall. Start seedlings indoors in January and February for planting outside in March and harvesting in May and June. For a fall harvest, start seeds in July, or buy transplants for a late August or September planting in the garden. By late fall or winter, you'll be enjoying ripe tomato fruits while colder areas are eating snow.

Tomatoes love to be patted. If you're starting your tomatoes from ~~~ home, keep the plants short and stocky by brushing your hands over the tops of the seedlings 10 strokes daily starting when they are 2 ¹/₂ inches tall. Research has shown this brushing strengthens the stem and causes the seedling to stay short and squat, suffering less transplant shock when planted in the garden.

Tomatoes (and their roots in particular) love heat. To give tomatoes a jump-start, preheat the garden soil by covering it with plastic mulch. Lay the plastic sheet over the garden bed, pull it tight, cover the edges with soil, and let the plastic heat the soil for two weeks before transplanting. While you're waiting for the soil to heat up, *harden off* your transplants (gradually make them accustomed to the outdoor growing environment) by following the guidelines in Chapter 13.

## Planting on and up: Staking, caging, and trellising

Tomatoes are one of the most forgiving vegetables to grow. However, to get the best crop, you need to follow some simple guidelines. Here are the basic steps for planting tomatoes:

1. **Dig a hole twice the diameter and depth of the tomato root ball.**
2. **Place a small handful of all-purpose organic fertilizer or compost into the hole.**
3. **Plant the tomato seedling up to its first set of leaves.**

   Tomatoes have a unique ability to form roots all along their stems. So even if you have a tall, leggy, lanky seedling, just bury the stem either vertically or horizontally in the ground, leaving at least two sets of leaves poking out (see Figure 4-2).

**Figure 4-2:** A lanky tomato planted horizontally in the ground.

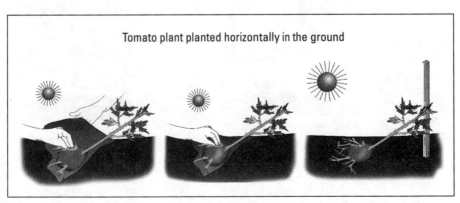

Tomato plant planted horizontally in the ground

If you're using plastic mulch, cut (or burn with a propane torch) a 6-inch-diameter hole in the plastic, and plant your tomato seedlings right through the plastic mulch using the same technique.

Research has shown that red plastic mulch increases tomato yields by 20 percent. In hot-summer areas where high soil temperatures are a problem, however, try using black plastic mulch for spring plantings and white plastic mulch for summer plantings to reflect light and keep the soil cool.

As the weather warms, tomatoes grow quickly. Soon after you transplant, you'll have to decide which trellising method you'll use to keep your tomatoes off the ground. All but the dwarf and dwarf-indeterminate varieties need to be staked, caged, wired, or generally held off the ground to minimize the amount of rot and insect damage on the tomatoes. Figure 4-3 shows two of the basic trellising methods that work well with tomatoes.

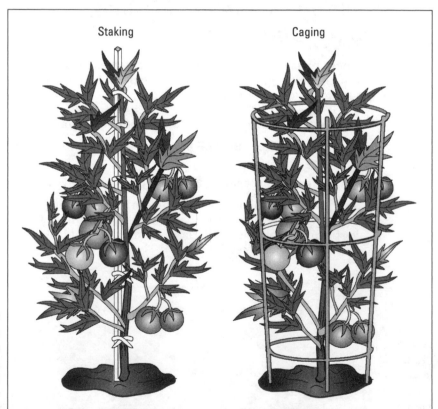

**Figure 4-3:**
The basic staking and caging methods.

Another way to keep vigorous plants (especially indeterminates) in bounds is to prune them. Removing extra side branches called suckers (see Figure 4-4) helps direct more energy to fruit production and less to leaf and stem production. Pruning suckers reduces the overall yield of your tomato plant, but the fruits that you do get will be larger and ripened slightly earlier than if you didn't prune them.

**Figure 4-4:**
Removing
suckers
from tomato
plants.

Sucker

## Fertilizing and maintaining

Tomatoes are generally heavy-feeding plants. They like a soil rich in organic matter and compost, but they also respond well to side-dressing fertilizers during the growing season.

### Side-dressing

Side-dress with a complete fertilizer such as 5-10-10 or an organic fertilizer such as cottonseed meal, sprinkling a small handful around each plant. Apply the first side-dressing when the tomatoes are golf-ball sized, and every three weeks afterward. Try not to get any fertilizer on the foliage, because it may burn the leaves. Scratch the granular fertilizer into the top few inches of soil. (See Chapter 15 for more on fertilizers.)

Use lower rates of nitrogen fertilizers, because higher rates cause tomato plants to sport lots of dark green leaves and produce few tomatoes.

If you prefer to spray your plants, treat your tomatoes to a *foliar feeding* by mixing the fertilizer with water and then spraying it on the plant foliage; this is a quick way to get nutrients to your tomato plants. Using fish emulsion or seaweed mix, dissolve the fertilizers according to the recommendations on the bottle and spray the plants every three weeks. Plants can take up nutrients faster through their leaves than through their roots, but the effects are not as long lasting.

Tomatoes also like Epsom salts. Research has shown that one tablespoon of Epsom salts dissolved in one gallon of water and sprayed on the transplants makes for greener and more productive tomatoes.

### Watering and mulching

Watering is critical for tomatoes to produce the best quality fruits. In general, tomatoes need one inch of water a week, but they may need more in areas with hot, dry summers. Chapter 15 discusses watering strategies.

One of the best things that you can do to conserve moisture is to mulch. Plastic mulch conserves some moisture but is best used in conjunction with soaker hoses or the ditch watering method. The best water-conservation mulch is a 4- to 6-inch layer of hay or straw. You and Mother Nature can still water through this mulch, but the mulch is thick enough to prevent weeds from germinating. Mulching and watering evenly prevents many fruit problems, such as blossom-end rot and fruit cracking. See "Weather-related problems," later in this chapter, for details on these conditions.

## Harvesting tomatoes

After all your hard work comes the fun part: picking and eating! Harvest tomatoes when they are full colored, yet still firm to the touch. Tomatoes will continue to ripen indoors if picked too early, so it's better to err on the early side when harvesting. As long as they show some color when picked, they'll ripen indoors with that vine-ripened flavor.

If you want to push the harvest along, you can prune off some new branches and tiny fruits to redirect the plant's energy to the larger, maturing fruits. Tomatoes don't need direct sun to ripen, just warm temperatures. You can also *root-prune* the plant, cutting 6 inches into the soil in a circle one foot away from the stem of the plant. This severs some of the roots, shocking the plant and forcing it to ripen its fruits faster. It will, however, stop the production of new fruits, so this technique is best used at the end of the season.

If you live in an area with bright sunshine, don't prune off the tomato foliage. Removing too much foliage results in *sunscald,* a condition in which the tomato skin literally gets sunburned. Sunscald itself doesn't ruin the tomato crop, but it opens the door for other rot organisms to attack the fruit.

# Pests and Other Problems

Tomatoes are such vigorous growing plants that they often will outgrow any problems and still give you a harvest. But to get the most out of your plants, look out for the following troubles caused by the insects, diseases, or weather. (For a general description of and a plan of action against the most common insects and diseases, see Chapter 18. Remember that spraying is only a last resort; and many plants can withstand a small infestation of bugs or a few diseased leaves.)

Here are a few insects that are a particular problem with tomatoes:

✔ **Tomato hornworm:** These huge (they sometimes grow to 4 inches long) green caterpillars look like the monster that ate Tokyo (see Figure 4-5). They eat leaves and fruits of tomatoes, and I swear that if you're quiet enough, you can actually hear them chewing. A few hornworms can devastate a tomato plant quickly. The simplest control is to hand-pick the caterpillars off the plants and wrestle them into a can of soapy water to drown. Early morning is the best time to remove these pests from plants — like many people, they're still sluggish.

✔ **Tomato fruitworm:** This green (with white or yellow stripes) 1-inch-long caterpillar also feeds on foliage and fruits. Tomato fruitworms can be hand-picked (as with the hornworm); for severe infestation, spray plants with Bt (see Chapter 18 for more on Bt).

**Figure 4-5:**
A tomato hornworm makes its way to a meal.

✔ **Stinkbug:** A problem mostly in warmer areas, these $1/2$-inch-long gray or green shield-shaped insects primarily feed on the fruits, causing hard, white or yellow spots on the tomato skin. To control stinkbugs, keep the garden weed-free — the pests hide in weeds around the garden — and spray plants with pyrethrin.

## Got a disease?

Leaf diseases can devastate tomatoes. Follow the guidelines in Chapter 18 to reduce the amount of disease in the garden. Many varieties now are resistant to some of the diseases mentioned. The following are some of the most common diseases.

✔ **Blights and leaf spots:** The devastation starts with the lower leaves getting brown spots, turning yellow, and eventually dying. The symptoms of leaf spot look very similar to the symptoms of late and early blight. The disease slowly spreads up the plant, eventually defoliating the whole plant. These fungal diseases are particularly active during warm, wet weather. To control blight and leaf spots:

   1. **Clean up and destroy all diseased foliage in the fall.**

   2. **Rotate crops, as described in Chapter 16.**

   3. **Mulch the seedlings with plastic, hay, or straw after planting to prevent water from splashing the spores from the ground onto the leaves.**

   4. **If nothing else is working and the condition is severe, spray the plants with a preventive fungicide, such as copper, early in the season.**

✔ **Verticillium and fusarium wilt:** These soil-borne fungal diseases cause yellowing, wilting, and early death of tomato plants. Once infected, the plants will likely die. The best prevention is to rotate your plantings and plant wilt-resistant plants (indicated by the letters *V* and *F* after the variety name).

## Weather-related problems

Not all problems with tomatoes are insect- or disease-related. Excess or lack of water, too much fertilizer, cold temperatures, and varietal differences can all contribute to deformed fruits. Here are a few of the more common problems and some solutions:

✔ **Blossom drop:** Your tomatoes are flowering beautifully, but the blossoms all seem to drop without forming any fruit. This condition, called blossom drop, is caused by air temperatures above 90°F or below 55°F. At these temperatures, most tomato flowers will not set fruits. The solution is to grow varieties adapted to the heat ('Heatwave II') or cold ('Siberia'), or to protect the plants during flowering with shade cloths or covers.

✔ **Blossom-end rot:** The bottom, or blossom end, of tomatoes turns brown and rots (see Figure 4-6). Blossom-end rot is caused by fluctuating moisture conditions in the soil, so the best cure is to mulch the plants well, make sure that they're planted in well-drained soil, and keep them evenly watered.

**Figure 4-6:**
Something's
rotten at
the end.

✔ **Fruit cracking:** Many types of fruit cracking affect tomatoes, but all involve fluctuating moisture conditions and exposure to cold temperatures early in the season. To avoid this problem, plant varieties that are less likely to crack (such as 'Big Beef'), reduce nitrogen fertilization, mulch the plants to keep the soil moisture even, and protect flowering plants from cold nights with row covers (see Chapter 22).

✔ **Sunscald:** The top surface of the tomato skin has lightly colored patches caused by direct exposure to the sun. These patches eventually rot. To avoid sunscald, grow indeterminate varieties that have lots of foliage to shade the fruits, avoid pruning the leaves, or provide afternoon shade with shade cloths.

# Health Tips and a Recipe

Ripe tomatoes have almost as much vitamin C as oranges, are packed with vitamin A (some varieties such as 'Caro Rich' have ten times the amount of regular tomato varieties), and contain essential amounts of phosphorous, folic acid, copper, and other minerals. Tomatoes also contain other healthful substances such as *lycopene*. Lycopene, the same substance that gives tomatoes their red color, has been found to reduce the incidence of prostate cancer. If you're looking for ideas on how to prepare your tomatoes, try this sauce recipe.

## Basic Tomato Sauce

**Tools:** *Saucepan, frying pan*

**Preparation time:** *15 minutes*

**Cooking time:** *2 hours*

**Yield:** *8 pints*

| | |
|---|---|
| *12 pounds of fresh tomatoes* | *1 cup chopped green pepper* |
| *2 tablespoons minced parsley* | *1 cup chopped celery* |
| *1 tablespoon finely chopped parsley* | *2 large cloves garlic, minced* |
| *2 tablespoons basil leaves* | *1 tablespoon sugar* |
| *2 tablespoons oregano* | *1 to 2 tablespoons olive oil* |
| *2 cups chopped onions* | *salt and pepper to taste* |

*1* Wash the ripe tomatoes well; peel; and remove the cores, green areas, and blemishes.

*2* Chop the tomatoes and put them in a large saucepan. Add the parsley, basil, and oregano, and simmer the mixture for 2 hours, stirring frequently or until the sauce has reduced by one-half.

*3* In a frying pan, sauté the onions, green pepper, celery, and garlic until they're translucent, and then add them to the tomato sauce. Add all the remaining ingredients (the sugar, olive oil, salt, and pepper), mix them thoroughly, and serve.

You can alter this basic recipe by adding cayenne pepper, wine, meat, or other flavorings that suit your taste buds.

# Chapter 5

# Tomato Cousins: Peppers and Eggplants

• • • • • • • • • • • • • • • • • • • • • • • • • • • • • • • • • • • • • • • • • • • • • • • •

## In This Chapter

▶ The history of the pepper and the eggplant

▶ Sweet, hot, and ornamental pepper varieties

▶ Eggplant varieties for all occasions

▶ Growing peppers and eggplants in your garden

▶ Troubleshooting your crop

▶ Nutritional information and a recipe

• • • • • • • • • • • • • • • • • • • • • • • • • • • • • • • • • • • • • • • • • • • • • • • •

*P*eppers and eggplants — two tomato relatives (they're all in the nightshade, or *Solanaceae,* family) — may not have the popularity of their big red tomato cousins, but their varieties do have a similar diversity of tastes, colors, and shapes. Peppers, in particular, are going through a resurgence of interest, and breeders have responded to that interest by creating new and improved varieties. Whether they be sweet or hot peppers, there are many new varieties to choose from. No longer simply green, yellow, or red, sweet pepper varieties come in a rainbow of colors, including orange, purple, and chocolate. The new varieties adapt better to cold and hot temperatures and have better ornamental qualities. With the popularity of salsa (now the number one condiment in the United States, according to the U.S. government), nachos, and spicy foods in general, hot peppers are really getting attention. From the mildest jalapeño to the hottest 5-alarm habañero, varieties are available for all taste buds and tolerances.

Eggplants (named because some varieties have fruits the shape and color of hens' eggs), though not as popular as peppers, have also gained a lot of attention because of the discovery of varieties other than the traditional dark purple, teardrop shape. Long, thin, Oriental types make excellent grilled snacks, eaten skin and all. (Even my seven-year-old daughter likes them!) Small, round, green, Asian eggplants are great in soups and casseroles. Even unusual round, orange, Turkish types exist that are used in specialty ethnic cooking.

## Well-traveled nightshades

Like tomatoes, peppers *(Capsicum annuum)* are a New World crop. Originating in the region around present-day Bolivia, peppers evidently were used in cooking 8,000 years ago. The pepper slowly spread North, reaching Mexico and the Caribbean in time for Christopher Columbus to "discover" it. Thinking he found the prized black pepper (*piper nigrum* — a different plant entirely), he named these hot fruits *peppers* and brought them back to Europe. Hot peppers became the rage in Europe, and they were spread far and wide by traders. In fact, within 100 years of peppers' arrival in Europe, they were being used for cooking in countries literally around the globe. From humble beginnings in South America, to international star in cooking, hot peppers became the spice rage of the world. Even though most of the commercial pepper production now is for sweet peppers, only relatively recently have sweet peppers, such as the bell peppers you buy in a grocery store, become popular.

Eggplants *(Solanum melongena)* are no less traveled. The origin of this tropical vegetable is India. Eggplants quickly spread throughout Asia and finally into Europe by the 1500s and to America by the 1800s. Today, you can grow varieties from Japan, Italy, Turkey, and India — all having different shapes, colors, and tastes. Historically, eggplants haven't been very popular in the United States. But recently, like with peppers, gardeners and cooks are embracing the variety of shapes, colors, and flavors of eggplants, serving them grilled, pickled, or tossed in salads.

Both peppers and eggplants are beautiful plants to grow in your garden, and they make excellent container plants if you have limited space. Some pepper varieties have purple stems and fruits, while eggplants have beautiful purple flowers, and some have fruits with white and pink stripes. So, reserve a spot in the vegetable or flower garden for these beautiful, edible fruits.

# Peppered with Peppers

An abundance of pepper varieties are available to home gardeners, including many new varieties of hot peppers. In the following sections, I classify peppers into four groups: sweet bell peppers, sweet non–bell peppers, hot peppers, and ornamental peppers. Most plants grow to 2 to 3 feet tall unless otherwise noted.

## Those sweet bells

Bell pepper fruits come in blocky, round, or elongated shapes. Most fruits start out green but mature through a variety of colors before ripening to thier final color. The days to maturity given in the following descriptions represent the time from transplant in the garden to full size. Add two weeks to this number to know when they will mature to their final color. Sweet bells have the sweetest flavor when harvested at the mature color stage but still can be harvested green and taste good. The thick-walled varieties are best for stuffed-pepper recipes. Varieties listed later also offer good disease resistance.

Variety descriptions for sweet peppers frequently use words such as lobes and blocky. No, I'm not talking about ear shapes. When you cut a pepper crosswise near the stem, you'll notice that the walls divide the pepper fruit into sections. Pepper experts call these sections *cells* or *lobes*. Well-defined lobes or cells make peppers *blocky*. Most bell peppers have 3 to 4 lobes. Blocky fruits are best used for stuffing or slicing into pepper rings.

Here are a few of my favorite varieties of sweet bells, all of which offer good disease resistance:

- **'Arianne':** These blocky, Dutch-bred peppers mature early (in 68 days) to a deep orange color.

- **'Bell Boy' hybrid:** These 4-lobed, thick-walled All-America Selections winners (see Chapter 4) yield fruits that turn red on *compact* (smaller than usual) plants. They mature in 70 days.

- **'California Wonder':** These classic, thick-walled, 4-inch by 4-inch blocky bells mature to red in 75 days and are great for stuffing. They also come as a yellow-fruited variety called 'Golden CalWonder.'

- **'Chinese Giant':** These old-fashioned, thick-walled, huge (6 inches by 6 inches) bell peppers mature to red and are very sweet. They're good stuffing peppers and mature in 75 days.

- **'Chocolate Beauty' hybrid:** These 3- to 4- lobe bells mature in 70 days to a rich chocolate color. The fruits are sweet, but no, they don't taste like Hershey bars.

- **'Golden Summer' hybrid:** These blocky, thick-walled, 4-lobe fruits are lime green in color and mature to gold in 67 days.

- **'Jingle Bells' hybrid:** These bells mature in 60 days. Compact plants are loaded with miniature (1 to 2 inches in length and width) bell peppers that mature to red.

- **'Lilac Bell' hybrid:** These 3- to 4-lobe bells have beautiful lilac-purple skin with ivory-white *flesh* (the pepper without its skin or seed cavity). You can harvest the fruits at the lilac stage or allow them to mature to red. They mature in 70 days.

- **'North Star' hybrid:** These bells are some of the earliest bell peppers to mature (in 60 days) to red. This variety matures quickly and can tolerate cool temperatures, making it a great variety for gardeners living in short growing season areas (like the mountains).

- **'Valencia' hybrid:** These plants have good foliage cover and produce large, 5-inch by 5-inch peppers with thick walls and sweet, orange flesh. They mature in 70 days.

❀ **'Vidi' hybrid:** These early French bells mature in 70 days. The plants
     mature into red, 5- to 7-inch-long peppers that withstand less-than-ideal
     growing conditions.

## Beyond bells

Sweet peppers are more than big, blocky bells. Some of the sweetest peppers that I've tasted are long, tapered (or blunt-ended), thin-walled, Italian
frying types. Other great sweet peppers come in round, cherry shapes and
short, fat heart shapes. These pepper plants grow 2 to 3 feet tall, and most
mature to the color red, which is when they're the sweetest. So heat up the
frying pan and dive in!

   ❀ **'Biscayne' hybrid:** These 6-inch-long, 2-inch-wide, Cubanelle-type
     (feature a blunt end) bells mature in 65 days. They're good for frying.

   ❀ **'Corno di Toro':** These bells are original Italian "bull's horn" peppers,
     so-called because the fruits are 8 to 10 inches long and are curved like
     the horn of a bull. Three-foot-tall plants ripen yellow or red fruits in 68
     days. These peppers are great for frying. 'Sweet Toro' is a newer, hybrid
     version.

   ❀ **'Gypsy':** These All-America Selections winners produce 4-inch-long,
     wedge-shaped fruits early in the season. The fruits mature from yellow
     to orange-red in 60 days. This variety is very productive and adapts to
     many growing conditions.

   ❀ **'Large Red Cherry':** These thick-walled, 1-inch-round sweet peppers
     are often available at salad bars. The plants are compact — 1¹/₂ feet
     tall — and are very productive. They mature in 80 days.

   ❀ **'Paprika Supreme' hybrid:** Care to make your own paprika powder?
     Well, here's the pepper for you. These 7-inch-long, flattened, thin-walled
     fruits are perfect for drying after they mature, which takes 100 days.

   ❀ **'Peperoncini':** These 4-inch-long, wrinkled peppers are best known as
     the pickled, light green peppers served in Italian antipasto. They take
     62 days to mature.

   ❀ **'Pimiento L':** These compact 1¹/₂-foot-tall plants produce 4-inch-long,
     heart-shaped fruits, which most people know as canned pimientos or as
     the red peppers inside green olives. They also taste sweet in salads and
     mature in 95 days. A hybrid version is 'Pimiento Elite.'

   ❀ **'Sweet Banana':** Probably the most well-known of the long, tapered
     sweet peppers, these 6-inch-long fruits, which mature from yellow to
     red, are born on compact 1¹/₂-foot-tall plants. They take 72 days to
     mature. 'Banana Supreme' is a hybrid version.

# Turn on the heat

At one time, the only hot peppers you'd see people eat were the dried flakes sprinkled on pasta in Italian restaurants. How times have changed!

With the growing interest in cuisine from around the world — such as Mexican, Korean, Thai, and Indian — hot peppers are enjoying widespread popularity. Trying to generalize about hot peppers is difficult because the flavor and level of hotness varies with each type of pepper. Hot pepper plants generally are easier to grow and produce more peppers than sweet pepper plants. Because some varieties are so hot that they could strip paint (well, maybe not quite *that* hot), you won't need to add very many to your cuisine.

Before getting into hot pepper varieties, you need to understand the heat in hot peppers. The active ingredient that causes all the fire is called *capsaicin* (the tiny, blisterlike sacs on the inner wall of the fruit, as shown in Figure 5-1), which is located on the pepper's *placental wall*. You find fewer sacs at the tips of hot peppers, so you could bite off the tip of a hot pepper and be fooled into thinking it's not that hot. If you cut into the pepper or handle it roughly, however, you break the inner-wall lining, releasing capsaicin throughout the fruit — even to the tip.

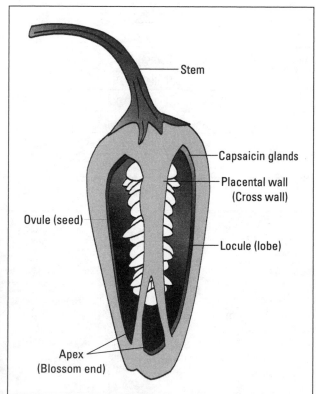

**Figure 5-1:**
The capsaicin is located inside a pepper fruit in the placental wall.

Stem

Capsaicin glands

Placental wall
(Cross wall)

Ovule (seed)

Locule (lobe)

Apex
(Blossom end)

To counteract the hotness of hot peppers, try eating dairy products such as yogurt, ice cream, or milk with your hot dishes.

Beware that some varieties, such a habañero, are so hot that you can get serious burns in your mouth, or, if you get the capsaicin in your eyes or in a wound, you can get burns there also.

### Scoville unit chart: Measuring heat

To help you decide how hot you want to go with hot peppers, the Scoville Heat Scale was developed in 1912 by Wilbur Scoville. The scale ranges from 0 to 350,000 and measures pepper hotness in multiples of 100. Table 5-1 shows some of the most popular hot pepper types and their hotness ratings. The chart gives a range for each rating because weather, growing conditions, and pepper variety can all affect how hot a pepper is. This chart can help you decide how hot you want your peppers to be.

| Table 5-1 | Scoville Heat Scale |
|---|---|
| **Pepper Types** | **Scoville Rating Range** |
| Bell | 0–100 |
| Hot cherry | 100–500 |
| Jalapeño | 400–2500 |
| Anaheim | 500–2500 |
| Ancho/poblano | 1,000–1,500 |
| Serrano | 10,000–25,000 |
| Hot wax | 10,000–40,000 |
| Tabasco | 30,000–50,000 |
| Cayenne | 30,000–50,000 |
| Habañero | 100,000–350,000 |

# Chile, chili, chilli?

What do you call these hot things? The confusion over hot pepper names started in Mexico. The Spanish word for pepper is *chile,* and it's used to describe all peppers, such as Jalapeño chile or Cayenne chile. When translated into English, however, all hot peppers became known as chile, even though a chile pepper in the Southwest may mean a very different variety than a chile pepper in California. So *chile* can mean almost any hot pepper. *Chili,* by the way, is the dish that you eat, while *Chilli* is the spice powder that can be made from any number of different chiles. Confused yet? The key point to remember is whether it says chile, chili, or chilli, it's probably hot.

### Hot peppers to grow

Here are some different hot pepper varieties that you can grow:

❀ **'Anaheim TMR 23':** These moderately pungent, smooth-skinned, 7-inch-long, 2-inch-wide peppers are produced on 3-foot-tall, leafy, disease-resistant plants. They mature in 75 days. You can use the dried pods to make the wreaths or *ristras* (wreaths made of dried peppers) popular in the Southwest.

❀ **'Ancho'(Poblano):** These red, mildly hot, 4-inch-long, wrinkled, heart-shaped peppers often are stuffed and served as chile rellenos. You can dry them and make them into wreaths or powder. They take 75 days to mature.

❀ **'Charleston Hot':** These very hot, 4-inch-long, 1-inch-wide cayenne peppers mature to orange in 72 days. They're known for their insect resistance.

❀ **'Cherry Bomb' hybrid:** These mildly hot, 2-inch-round, thick-walled fruits mature in 65 days to a bright red.

❀ **'Habañero'(Capsicum chinense):** These are some of the hottest peppers known to mankind! These 1-inch by 1-inch, lantern-shaped fruits mature to orange on 3-foot-tall plants. They thrive in the hot weather and take a long season to mature. The hottest variety of this type is a red variety called 'Red Savina,' which tops 300,000 on the Scoville scale. These hot peppers can be dangerous! They take 100 days to mature.

❀ **'Hungarian Hot Wax':** These medium-hot, 7- to 8-inch-long, tapered, peppers mature from yellow to red and are great for pickling. They take 70 days to mature.

❀ **'Jalapeño M':** The classic salsa, nacho, and pizza hot peppers. These moderately hot, 3-inch-long, round-tipped fruits taste great eaten green or red. 'Jalapa' is a more productive hybrid version, and 'Senorita' is a very mild variety, rating only 400 Scoville units. These peppers take 75 days to mature.

❀ **'Serrano':** These candle-flame-shaped, 2$^{1}/_{2}$-inch-long, fiery hot peppers are born abundantly on 3-foot-tall plants. They're great in salsa and often are used in sauces. They mature in 77 days.

❀ **'Super Cayenne II' hybrid:** These 3- to 4-inch-long, fiery hot fruits taste great eaten green or at mature red. The attractive plants are 2 feet tall and look good in containers. A yellow-fruited similar variety called 'Yellow Cayenne' is also available. These peppers take 75 days to mature.

❀ **'Super Chili' hybrid:** These All-America Selections winners produce an abundance of 2-inch-long, cone-shaped, hot fruits that you can dry or eat fresh. These peppers take 75 days to mature.

❀ **'Tabasco'** *(Capsicum frutescens):* These 2- to 3-foot-tall plants produce fiery hot, 2-inch-long, pointed fruits, which mature from yellow to red. Famous for producing Tabasco sauce, this pepper variety needs a long, hot growing season to mature. The peppers take 90 to 100 days to mature.

❀ **'Thai Hot':** These 1-inch-long, fiery hot peppers from Thailand mature in 80 days. Compact 1$\frac{1}{2}$-foot-tall plants bear tons of fruit, making them attractive ornamentals as well. Larger fruit-sized types of this variety include 'Giant Thai Hot.'

## Pretty peppers: The ornamentals

Most peppers are produced on plants that are small enough to grow in containers (see Chapter 17 for more on growing vegetables in containers) or in the flower garden. However, some varieties have been specifically bred for their attractive fruits, stems, and leaf colors as well as their fruit shapes. The ornamentals in the following list are also edible. Here are some of my favorites:

❀ **'Christmas Pepper':** These 8- to 10-inch-tall, bushy plants produce an abundance of missile-shaped fruits that start out yellow, mature to orange, and then finally to red. So on the same plant, you can have peppers at different maturities and therefore different colors. They take 90 days to mature.

❀ **'Mirasol':** These 3- to 4-inch-long, conical-shaped fruits are unique in that the plants hold them erect. They take 100 days to mature. The mature peppers are moderately hot with a slight fruity taste.

❀ **'Pretty Purple':** All parts (leaves, stems, and fruits) of these 2$\frac{1}{2}$-foot-tall plants are dark purple. Upon maturity (which takes 75 days), the 1-inch-long, fiery hot peppers turn red, creating a gorgeous ornamental effect.

❀ **'Poinsettia':** The crown of these plants bears clusters of 3-inch-long red peppers that point upward, reminiscent of the poinsettia flower. The fruits are very hot and mature in 90 days.

❀ **'Sweet Pickle':** Surprise — these aren't hot ornamental peppers, but sweet ones! Two-inch-long, oval, thick-walled fruits mature from yellow to orange, purple, and red, often having all three colors present on one plant. They take 65 days to mature.

❀ **'Thai Hot':** See the section "Turn on the heat," earlier in this chapter, for a description of this pepper.

# Eggplants by Shape

Lest you think peppers are the only international travelers with variety and a zest for life, eggplants also come in a range of shapes, colors, and sizes. I arrange the varieties in the following sections by shape so that you can choose the variety that's right for your tastes. The days to maturity in the following descriptions represent the time from transplant to harvest.

## Large and oval

Large, oval eggplants are the varieties that most people are familiar with. They're the dark purple, teardrop-shaped fruits that you see in grocery stores. The plants grow 3- to 4-feet tall, each producing an average of 8 to 10 fruits. Large, oval eggplants are great in casseroles, such as eggplant parmesan casserole. Here are some of my favorite varieties:

- ❀ **'Black Beauty':** These classic, large, purple-skinned eggplants grow best in areas with long, hot growing seasons. They mature in 75 days.

- ❀ **'Black Bell' hybrid:** This large, oval, purple-skinned variety is widely adapted and early maturing (in about 65 days).

- ❀ **'Ghostbuster' hybrid:** This unique, white-skinned variety turns yellow when mature, which takes 80 days. For the best flavor, pick and eat these eggplants when they're white.

- ❀ **'Purple Rain' hybrid:** These beautiful, white-striped, lavender-skinned eggplants are early and productive. They mature in 66 days.

- ❀ **'Rosa Bianca':** This Italian heirloom features white fruits with lavender streaks across them. They mature in 75 days.

- ❀ **Violette Di Firenze':** These violet-skinned fruits have an unusual oval shape and are ribbed like squash. They take 80 days to mature.

## Cylindrical

Traditionally called Oriental eggplants, these cylindrical fruits are long and thin (2 inches wide and up to 10 inches long). The plants are smaller than the oval-shaped varieties, reaching only 2- to 3-feet tall, and produce about 15 fruits. They're great grilled or used in hors d'oeuvres:

- ❀ **'Asian Bride' hybrid:** These 6-inch-long fruits have tender skin and are white with lavender streaks. They take 70 days to mature.

- ❀ **'Ichiban' hybrid:** These fruits have dark purple skin and grow on plants with purple-tinged leaves. They grow best in hot climates and take 61 days to mature.

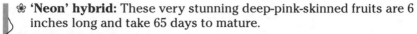

- ❀ **'Neon' hybrid:** These very stunning deep-pink-skinned fruits are 6 inches long and take 65 days to mature.

- ❀ **'Ping Tung Long':** These long, lavender-skinned fruits grow on plants with good heat and disease resistance. They take 65 days to mature.

- ❀ **'Tango' hybrid:** These unique white-skinned fruits are 7 inches long and take 60 days to mature.

- ❀ **'Thai Long':** These compact 1- to 2-foot-tall plants withstand light frosts and produce long, thin fruits with light green skin. They mature in 80 days.

## Small and round

These plants grow only 1- to 2-feet tall, making them great for container culture. Each plant produces 20 to 25, 1- to 3-inch-round fruits. The following eggplants are novelties but also are great for skewering and pickling:

- ❀ **'Bambino' hybrid:** These prolific plants produce an abundance of small, round, dark-purple-skinned fruits. The fruits take 45 days to mature.

- ❀ **'Easter Egg':** These white-skinned, egg-shaped fruits remind you of chicken eggs. They turn yellow at maturity, which takes 65 days, but are best when eaten white; they taste bitter if you allow them to mature to yellow.

- ❀ **'Kermit' hybrid:** These Thai specialty fruits have green skin with white stripes — very unusual. They take 60 days to mature.

- ❀ **'Turkish Orange'** *(Solanum gilo):* These bushy, 2- to 3-foot-tall plants have good insect resistance while producing fruits that mature from green to orange. The fruits are best when eaten green, before their skin turns orange and bitter. They take 80 days to mature.

# How to Grow Your Own

Many of the cultural instructions for growing tomatoes hold true for peppers and eggplants. (See Chapter 4 for more on tomatoes.) They're warm-season crops, so you don't need to rush to plant them until the ground has warmed up sufficiently:

- ✔ In most areas, you need to start peppers and eggplants indoors, usually six to eight weeks before the last frost date for your area (see the appendix for first and last frost dates). You can also purchase them from a local nursery or through the mail as transplants. (See Chapter 13 for seed-starting basics and information on ordering plants through the mail.)

✔ If you live in zone 9 or 10, you can sow the seeds directly into your garden. If you keep the plants healthy and have no frost in your area, peppers and eggplants can actually be *perennials* (plants that grow year-round) and will bear fruit all season.

Even in cold climates, I've dug up plants in fall, placed them in pots in my greenhouse all winter, and then transplanted them back out in spring. Even three years old, these plants remain very attractive and healthy.

Peppers and eggplants are more finicky than are tomatoes about temperatures, fertilization, and general growing conditions and are less forgiving of home gardeners' mistakes. For this reason, I'm extra cautious about starting pepper and eggplant seedlings early indoors; giving them ample light, fertilizer, and water; hardening them off well; and waiting to plant until the soil temperature is at least 60°F (see Figure 5-2), 4 inches deep in the soil. Ideally, you should purchase or have grown a 4- to 6-inch-tall, dark-green-leafed, stocky transplant that is not root-bound (roots growing around container).

**Figure 5-2:**
Wait until the soil is 60°F before planting peppers and eggplants.

Soil Thermometer

One handy product that you may want to purchase is a soil thermometer. Usually costing less than $20, a soil thermometer can help you gauge when to plant warm-season crops such as peppers and eggplants. Place the thermometer in a shady spot and take readings in the morning for accuracy.

If your peppers have flowered or set fruits before you've transplanted them, or when the seedlings still have only four to six leaves each, remove any blossoms or fruits. The plants will then send more energy to grow more leaves and roots to support a larger harvest later, rather than maturing only a few peppers early.

Peppers and eggplants grow best in raised beds (see Chapter 2 for more on raised beds) because the soil warms faster and drains quicker:

- ✔ In cold areas, cover the top of the beds with black plastic mulch (see Chapter 15 for details on how to use mulch in your garden) to preheat the soil before planting.

- ✔ In warm areas, mulching with hay, straw, white plastic, or even aluminum foil in summer helps keep the soil cool.

  Aluminum foil also reflects light back into the sky, confusing some insects that are trying to find your plants.

To plant each transplant, first use a propane torch or scissors to burn or cut holes in the plastic mulch every 1 to 1¹/₂ feet (wider for taller varieties) for peppers and every 2 to 3 feet for eggplants. If you're using mulch other than plastic, use the same guidelines for planting your transplants. Plant eggplant and pepper transplants at the same soil level as they are in their containers; unlike tomatoes, eggplant and pepper transplants can't send out more roots from their stems. Cover the plantings with a floating *row cover* (a lightweight, cheesecloth-like material that lets air, water, and sunlight through to keep the air warm and bugs out). (See Chapter 22 for more about row covers.)

## Fertilizing and watering tips

Peppers and eggplants are sensitive to excessive fertilizer, in particular nitrogen. Plants fertilized with too much nitrogen will grow large but will have few fruits. This doesn't mean you should neglect fertilizing your plants. Simply avoid using high rates of nitrogen fertilizers. Instead, apply a 2- to 3-inch layer of compost over the bed and add one teaspoon of 5-10-10 fertilizer around each transplant. See Chapter 15 for more on fertilizing.

Water your plants well, following the suggestions in Chapter 15. Watering is particularly important during 90°F weather when water stress and high temperatures can cause flowers to drop. For taller varieties such as the 'Corno Di Toro' pepper and the 'Black Beauty' eggplant, stake and cage the plants to help keep them upright. *Side-dress* (add fertilizer around the plants during the growing season) the plants around the drip line of the plant (see Figure 5-3) with a tablespoon of 1-2-2 ratio chemical fertilizer or an organic fertilizer such as 5-10-10.

**Figure 5-3:**
Spread
fertilizer at
the drip line
around a
pepper
plant.

Fertilizer

Peppers love magnesium. To give your peppers a boost, mix 1 tablespoon of Epsom salts in 1 gallon of water and spray the pepper plants at flowering.

## Harvesting tips

Peppers and eggplants are great to grow because you don't have to wait until the fruits are fully mature before you pick them. You can pick and enjoy sweet peppers green or wait until they ripen to orange, yellow, or red for a sweeter taste. Hot peppers vary in their hotness depending on stress. Stressed peppers tend to be hotter yet, so if you withhold water and fertilizer when the hot peppers are ripening, you can increase the heat in the peppers' flavor. Cool, cloudy weather tends to make hot peppers less hot.

You can pick eggplants at almost any stage. The key is not to let them become overmature, or the texture will become soft and mushy. To check eggplant maturity, watch the fruit's skin. A dull-colored skin means it's overmature. Double-check by cutting into the fruit and looking at the seeds. Brown-colored seeds are another sign of overmaturity.

A simple test for maturity is to push the eggplant's skin with your finger nail. If the skin bounces back, then the fruits are ready to harvest. If your nail indents the skin, then the fruits are overmature. If your fruits are really mature and rotting on the vine, just pick them and throw them out; they won't taste very good.

The key to harvesting is to do it often. The more often you harvest, the more peppers and eggplants you get. To harvest, cut peppers and eggplants with a sharp knife just above the top of the green cap on the fruit. The fruits will continue to ripen after you harvest them, so store them in a cool place. If you want to dry your peppers, pick them when they mature and hang them to dry in a warm room with good air circulation. See Chapter 19 for tips on preserving your harvest.

Harvesting hot peppers and eggplants can be tricky. Use gloves when harvesting eggplants or hot peppers. Hot peppers need careful handling because they contain capsaicin, which can easily cause burning, especially in your eyes or in open cuts. (I've known of gardeners having to go to the hospital to be treated for burns from hot peppers.) Some eggplant varieties have spines on their stems. Work around these sharp spines when harvesting the fruits.

## *Pest patrol*

If you see holes in a pepper fruit and find a small, white worm inside the fruit, welcome to the pepper maggot. The adult fly lays eggs on the fruit in midsummer. After the eggs hatch, the larvae tunnel into the fruit. To control these pests, cover young plants with row covers, use reflective aluminum foil mulch to confuse the adult flies, and hang yellow sticky traps to catch the adult flies before they lays their eggs.

Although peppers and eggplants generally have fewer pest problems than their tomato cousins, they share such pests and diseases as Blossom drop, sunscald, blossom-end rot, fruitworms (also called corn earworms), and Verticillium wilt (see Chapter 4 for more on these pests). Flea beetles (see Chapter 18) and Colorado potato beetles (see Chapter 6) also love eggplants. Chapter 18 describes many other common insect and disease problems that affect all vegetables.

# Healthful Tips and a Recipe

Peppers contain many important vitamins and minerals; hot peppers, in particular, are used medicinally to treat a range of ailments from cuts to cancer. One old notion about the health effects of eating peppers was that eating too many hot peppers could cause ulcers. Not only has this idea been discredited, but, in fact, capsaicin (the hot compound in hot peppers) has been proven to stimulate the flow of gastric juices, shielding the stomach lining and helping to *prevent* ulcers. Capsaicin also has been identified as an antioxidant that helps to protect cells from cancer-causing chemicals, an anticoagulant that can possibly prevent heart attacks and strokes caused by blood clots, and an anti-inflammatory salve that's used on the skin and can help treat arthritis.

Peppers are also high in certain vitamins. Green bell peppers have twice the vitamin C as citrus fruits; red sweet peppers have three times as much. Hot peppers have three and a half times as much vitamin C as oranges. Peppers are also relatively high in vitamins A, B, and E.

If you're lost for ways to eat sweet or hot peppers and eggplants, here's a sample recipe that's simple and nutritious. (If you're cooking-impaired, *Cooking For Dummies,* written by Bryan Miller and Marie Rama and published by IDG Books Worldwide, Inc., is a good source of information about basic cooking techniques.)

## Ratatouille

How about a good bowl of ratatouille (pronounced *rat-ta-tooey*) to use up all those tomatoes, peppers, and eggplants? Here's a basic recipe for this seasoned stew, but you can alter it by adding other vegetables, herbs, and spices that suit your taste.

**Tools:** *Knife, sauce pan, frying pan*

**Preparation time:** *30 minutes*

**Cooking time:** *1 hour*

**Yield:** *8 servings*

*6 ripe, medium tomatoes, peeled and quartered*

*1 medium onion, finely chopped*

*2 cloves of garlic, peeled and crushed*

*¼ cup olive oil*

*1 large eggplant (or 2 to 3 long, thin eggplants), cubed, but not peeled*

*2 medium zucchinis, sliced into ½-inch pieces*

*2 medium sweet peppers, cut in strips*

*1 small hot pepper (your choice of variety for hotness), finely chopped (optional)*

*salt and pepper and other herbs (such as basil, oregano, and bay leaves) to taste (optional)*

**1** Drop all the tomatoes into a saucepan of boiling water for 30 to 45 seconds. Then put the tomatoes in cold water and slip off their skins. Place the peeled tomatoes in a bowl and cut them in quarters.

**2** In a large saucepan, sauté (fry in a small amount of oil) the onion and garlic in the olive oil until they're transparent.

**3** Stir in the remaining vegetables (the eggplant and all the peppers) and peeled tomatoes; add the salt and pepper and herbs to taste. Cover and simmer (cook slowly) over low heat for 30 minutes. Uncover and simmer 15 more minutes, or until the liquid is reduced and the mixture is slightly thickened. Serve hot or cold.

# Chapter 6

# The Big Three Root Crops: Carrots, Onions, and Potatoes

- - - - - - - - - - - - - - - - - - - - - - - - - - - - - - - - - - - - - - - - - - - - - - - - - - - - - - - - -

## In This Chapter

▶ Choosing the best carrot, onion, and potato varieties for your garden

▶ Growing, caring for, and harvesting your roots

▶ Controlling root pests

▶ Growing sweet potatoes

- - - - - - - - - - - - - - - - - - - - - - - - - - - - - - - - - - - - - - - - - - - - - - - - - - - - - - - - -

*R*oot-crop vegetables are an example of those good things in life that you can't actually see. Their tops are green, unassuming, and may even be mistaken for weeds — but oh, when you give them a yank! I can still remember the look on my daughter's face when she first helped me dig potatoes and discovered that they grow underground. Digging for potatoes was like a treasure hunt. I think that most gardeners feel that same sense of wonder and excitement when they dig or pull up their root crops. The result is always something marvelous.

You can grow many different root crops, but the big three are carrots, onions, and potatoes. These three root crops aren't botanically related like peppers, eggplant, and tomatoes are; what they do have in common is that they're grown for their underground parts: roots, bulbs, or *modified stems* (underground stems that expand to produce large, edible areas).

You don't eat the roots of all root crops. With carrots, radishes, parsnips, and turnips, you are eating the roots of the plant. But with onions, you're eating the *bulbs* (like daffodil bulbs), and with potatoes, you eat the modified underground stems, called *tubers*.

Carrots, onions, and potatoes are the most popular root crops to grow in your garden. I discuss other root crops such as beets, garlic, radishes, parsnips, and turnips in Chapter 11. I give some growing tips later on in this chapter.

# Carrot Characters

Carrot *(Daucus carota)* varieties are categorized by their shape. There are long, thin carrots; short, stocky carrots; and even little, round, baby carrots. A few varieties are supercharged with vitamins, and some non-orange-colored varieties and many hybrids have added vigor and disease resistance. If you're trying to decide which carrot variety to grow, consider your type of soil as well as the use you plan for the carrots. Loose, sandy soil is good for growing any root crop. If you have heavy, clay soil, consider a variety that's shorter in length, such as 'Short 'n Sweet.' See Chapter 14 for information about soil types.

## Carrot types

Carrots often are described as a certain type, such as Baby. If the carrot type is part of a variety name, you can determine what the carrot will look like when it matures. Table 6-1 shows the common types of carrots and their characteristics. All the types listed, except Baby carrots and Imperators, range in size from 6 to 8 inches. Aside from eating the carrots fresh, you can best use certain carrot varieties for juicing and storing; some even grow well in containers.

## Rooted in history

Carrots, onions, and potatoes have a long, rich history. The first cultivated carrot varieties from Central Asia were actually green and purple in color. Traders brought these and other carrot varieties to Europe, where orange eventually became the carrot color of choice. People loved to eat the tasty roots, and women used the tops as feathery ornaments for their hair. Bugs Bunny would be proud that someone else prized the tops as well as the roots of carrots.

Onions also hail from Central Asia, where they've been used medicinally as well as for food for 5,000 years. Egyptians, Indians, and Romans all touted the benefits of eating onion bulbs and their relatives: leeks, shallots, and garlic (see Chapter 11 for more on these onion-family crops).

Potatoes got their start on the other side of the world. Still grown in the mountains of Peru and Bolivia where they originated, potatoes were brought back to Europe by the Spanish conquistadors. Potatoes were slow to gain popularity because they were identified as a member of the poisonous nightshade family, like tomatoes and eggplants. However, Europeans soon found out that tubers were great to eat and that potato plants were dependable producers. Potatoes soon became the staple food in diets around the world.

| Table 6-1 | Carrot Types | |
|---|---|---|
| *Type* | *Size and Uses* | *Best Soil Type* |
| Baby | Short (3 to 4 inches); early maturing; grows well in containers | Grows best in heavy, clay soil |
| Chantenay | Wide *shoulders* (the top of the carrot root), tapered to a point | Grows well in heavy soil |
| Danvers | Tapered to a point; thinner than Chantenay; good for storing | Grows best in sandy, loose soil |
| Imperator | Similar to Danvers, just longer (10 to 12 inches) | Grows best in sandy soil |
| Nantes | Cylindrical shape with blunt end; good for juicing | Grows well in sandy soil |

Most short varieties that you find in grocery stores are Baby carrots, and the longer carrots may be any of the other types mentioned in Table 6-1. Baby carrots may be varieties that are naturally short or larger varieties harvested at an immature stage. All types are easy to grow and worth trying in your garden.

## Carrot varieties

Knowing what type of carrot a certain variety is can help you when deciding which carrot variety to grow. With some of the most widely known carrot varieties, you can easily identify the carrot type because it's part of the variety's name; some examples include the heirlooms 'Royal *Chantenay*,' 'Scarlet *Nantes*,' and '*Danvers* Half Long.'

The carrot varieties in the following list fall into one of the five types of carrots identified in Table 6-1, but they also have special characteristics that may make them perfect for your garden. I like these varieties because they are flavorful, disease resistant, and easy to grow. All are good for baking. The days to maturity are from seeding in the ground until first harvest, although early season carrot varieties are flavorful even if you harvest them before they fully mature. The following are some of my favorite carrot varieties:

* **'Baby Spike':** This 3- to 4-inch Baby carrot *holds its shape* (stays sweet and small even if you forget to harvest it on time) well past maturity. It matures in 50 days.

* **'Bolero':** This hybrid, Nantes-type carrot has extra disease resistance and stores well. It matures in 72 days.

* **'Fly Away':** This hybrid, Nantes-type variety has more resistance to carrot rust flies (see the section "Avoiding Root Pests," later in this chapter) than other carrot varieties. It matures in 75 days.

* **'Healthmaster':** This hybrid, Danvers-type variety grows up to 10 inches long and contains 30 percent more vitamin A than other carrot varieties. It matures in 110 days.

* **'Imperator':** This Imperator-type variety is long and narrow and has a deep orange color. It matures in 70 days.

* **'Merida':** This Nantes-type carrot often is grown as a fall crop and in mild-winter areas, such as the Pacific Northwest, where it can *overwinter* (live through the winter) and be harvested in spring. It matures in 75 days.

* **'Purple Dragon':** This Chantenay-type carrot has a deep purple exterior and orange-yellow interior, making it unique. It matures in 75 days.

* **'Short 'n Sweet':** This 4-inch Chantenay-type carrot grows well in heavy clay soil. It matures in 68 days.

* **'Sweetness II':** This hybrid, Nantes-type carrot is extra sweet. It matures in 66 days.

* **'Sweet Sunshine':** This Chantenay-type variety has a yellow core and skin and a mild flavor. It matures in 72 days.

* **'Thumbelina':** This unusual Baby-type, All-America Selections winner has a round root that's the length of a silver dollar; it's especially good for baking. It also grows well in containers and in heavy clay or rocky soil. It matures in 65 days.

# Onions of Interest

The two most important factors to consider when choosing onion *(Allium cepa)* varieties are flavor (of the onion) and location (your garden's location, not the onion's location in your garden).

Although most people use taste as their first criterion, the old advice about "location, location, location" has greater relevance when growing onions. Onions are particular about how much sunlight they get, forming bulbs in response to the number of daylight hours. As a result, onion varieties are classified by day length — long day, short day, or intermediate day — as well as by taste — sweet (which are good for fresh eating only) or pungent (which are good for storing). In general, short-day onions grow well in the southern United States, long-day onions grow well in the northern United States, and intermediate-day onions grow well in the in-between regions.

See the sidebar "What a difference a day makes!" if you really want to get into a discussion on day length and onions. If you want to avoid the whole issue, try growing some fun onion relatives such as leeks, garlic, and shallots, which I discuss in Chapter 11.

## Onion varieties

In the following list of my favorite onion varieties, I distinguish between onions that are long day, short day, and intermediate day. Within each group are sweet and pungent varieties. These varieties are the most *widely adapted* (able to grow in a wide variety of geographic regions under various weather conditions) and easiest to grow. Keep in mind that pungent onions are much better for storage than sweet varieties. I also indicate whether you can purchase the variety as a set or plant. (Check out the appendix for a listing of companies that specialize in onion sets and plants.) The days to maturity are from either directly seeding in the garden or *setting out* (placing outdoors) sets or plants. Short-day onions are generally planted in fall to grow through the winter, so the take longer to mature than other types. Long- and intermediate-day onions are usually planted in spring. All the onions in the following list have yellow skin and white flesh unless otherwise noted.

Short-day onions:

- ❀ **'Granex 33'** *(Vidalia):* This classic hybrid sweet onion is a well-known, short-day variety. It also is available as a plant and is popular in the Southeast. It matures in spring 180 days after fall seeding.

- ❀ **'Texas Grano 1015' (Texas Supersweet):** This sweet, short-day variety can grow as large as a baseball and still remain sweet. It's also available as a plant and is popular in Texas and the Southwest. It matures 175 days from fall seeding.

- ❀ **'White Bermuda' (Crystal Wax):** This sweet, short-day variety with white skin and flesh also comes in a red version and is available as a plant. It mature 170 days after seeding.

Intermediate-day onions:

- ❀ **'Candy':** This sweet, hybrid, intermediate-day onion is widely adapted. It's also available as a plant. It matures 85 days after seeding.

- ❀ **'Italian Red Torpedo':** This sweet, Italian heirloom, intermediate-day, red onion forms a bottle-shaped bulb with a mild taste and pink flesh. It matures 110 days after seeding.

# What a difference a day makes!

The long-day, short-day, intermediate-day onion issue can get confusing. Short-day onions form bulbs when they receive 11 to 12 hours of daylight. Long-day onions form with 14 to 16 hours of daylight.

Generally, gardeners north of 35° latitude (a line running from northern North Carolina, through Oklahoma and Arizona to central California) grow long-day onions because their summer days are long enough to initiate bulb formation.

Gardeners south of that line grow short-day onions because they're closer to the equator and their day lengths are pretty steady at 12 hours. Gardeners in the South also have the luxury of planting short-day onions in fall, overwintering them (because of their mild winters), and harvesting in late spring.

Northern gardeners need to plant in spring for a summer harvest. If you were to plant long-day onions such as 'Buffalo' in the South, they'd never receive enough daylight hours to bulb up. Likewise, short-day onions such as the famous 'Vidalia' onions, grown in spring in the North would bulb up quickly while the plants were small because they'd receive the necessary 12 hours of daylight early in the season. The end result would be small bulbs.

Modern plant breeders have made this whole task a bit easier by introducing intermediate-day varieties that aren't as dependent on certain amounts of daylight hours to form bulbs. These varieties like intermediate lengths of daylight (12 to 14 hours) and grow best in hardiness zones 5 through 8 (see the hardiness zone table in the appendix).

The easiest way to grow onions is to buy *sets* (small onions that have been pregrown so that they mature faster) if you're growing long-day onions or plants of short- or long-day onions, which you can find at a local store or through the mail. If you want to try a lot of different varieties, though, starting your own seeds is the way to go.

❀ **'Walla Walla Sweet':** This sweet, intermediate-day variety has light-yellow flesh and good cold tolerance. It's also available as a plant and is popular in the Northwest. It matures 115 days after seeding.

Long-day onions:

❀ **'Buffalo':** You can store this early, hybrid, pungent, long-day onion until January. It matures 88 days after seeding.

❀ **'Copra':** You can store this hybrid, long-day, pungent variety until spring. It matures 104 days after seeding.

❀ **'Red Burgermaster':** This hybrid, red-skinned, pink-fleshed, pungent, long-day onion stores well, and it's the classic onion that tastes so great in sandwiches. It matures 110 days after seeding.

❀ **'Sweet Sandwich':** This hybrid, long-day variety actually gets sweeter in storage and comes in a white-skinned version. Both versions are available as plants. It matures 100 days after seeding.

❈ **'Yellow Stuttgarter':** This standard long-day storage variety often is sold as an onion set. It matures in about 90 days from a set and 120 days after seeding.

What makes onions pungent or sweet? The sulfur, not the sugar. Sweet onions have less sulfur than pungent varieties, so they taste sweeter. Although the sulfur can make the onion more pungent, it also makes those varieties great storage onions. To keep your sweet onions as sweet as they can be, don't apply any sulfur fertilizers and keep the onion plants stress free by controlling weeds and making sure that the plants receive enough water and fertilizer.

## Unusual onions

You may have run across some lesser-known onion types in restaurants or produce markets. *Scallions* (also called bunching onions, spring onions, or green onions) basically are onions that are picked for their delicate, juicy, green tops before they form bulbs, which tend to be quite small. Scallions take up less space in your garden than regular onions because you can plant them closer together, and they can give you a quick crop when planted in spring or fall. Growing scallions is a good way for novice onion growers to start. Any onion variety grown from a seed can be harvested as a scallion, but here a few varieties of onion that are especially widely adapted as scallions:

❈ **'Evergreen Long White'** *(Allium fistulosum):* This hardy variety may even overwinter in the North. It matures 65 days after seeding.

❈ **'Kincho':** This long, slim variety with a snow-white stem is hardy and especially adapted for fall planting. It matures 75 days after seeding.

❈ **'Red Beard'** *(Allium fistulosum):* This tender variety has unique coloring: a red stem with a white tip and green leaves. It matures 75 days after seeding.

Another group of onions are called multiplier, or perennial, onions. These onions come back year after year and reproduce easily. The two main types are Egyptian top-set onions (also known as walking or tree onions) and potato onions.

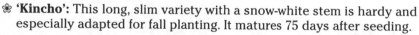
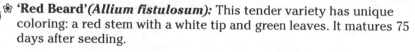

✔ *Egyptian top-set onions* reproduce by forming clusters of onion sets on the tips of their growing stalks, as shown in Figure 6-1. As the weight pulls the stalks down, the clusters root wherever they land, making the onions look like they're walking slowly across your garden. During the winter months, Egyptian top-set onions primarily are eaten as scallions, but the top-sets make good, small, sweet onions when you pick them in summer. They're also very cold hardy.

> ✔ *Potato onions* form a main onion in summer from a fall planting. They're hardy in zone 4 and produce many smaller sets that you can replant after summer harvest to produce more onions the following year.

If you're looking for onions as perennials in your garden, consider trying Egyptian top-set onions and potato onions.

**Figure 6-1:**
An Egyptian
top-set
onion plant.

# One Potato, Two Potato. . . .

If I had to vote on the most underrated vegetable in the world, I would choose the potato *(Solanum tuberosum)*. (See "Growing Sweet Potatoes" later in the chapter for details on sweet potatoes.) Potatoes have a reputation for being common, widely available, inexpensive, and just plain brown and boring. Why bother growing them? Well, first of all, the flavor and texture of fresh potatoes dug from the soil is much better than the bagged spuds sitting in grocery stores for weeks. You also can grow so many different varieties — including novelty potatoes such as purple-, red-, or yellow-fleshed varieties — that you'll astound your family and dinner guests.

Potatoes are one of the most foolproof crops to grow. Start planting early, while the weather is still cool, by placing a piece of the tuber (called a *seed potato*) in a furrow, or trench. After the potatoes start growing, if you *hill* them (push soil around the plants), water them, and keep the bugs away, you're almost guaranteed some great tubers. I explain more about "Planting potatoes" in the section by that name later in this chapter.

# Potatoes classified

Potato varieties usually are classified as early, mid-, and late maturing from the time you plant the seed potato to harvest. If you have a short growing season, grow early maturing plants. If you want to have a constant supply of potatoes all summer, grow a bit of each. Table 6-2 shows the approximate number of days to maturity for each category.

| Table 6-2 | Potato Days |
|---|---|
| *Type* | *Days to Maturity* |
| Early | 65 days |
| Midseason | 75 to 80 days |
| Late | 90+ days |

So many potato varieties are available that narrowing the field is difficult. However, you may want to try some of my top ten favorites, which I describe in the following section. I've included a *fingerling* variety that is the latest rage in restaurants. Fingerling varieties produce an abundance of small, fingerlike tubers that are great roasted, fried, or steamed.

# Favorite potato varieties

Here are my favorite potato varieties in terms of flavor, color, and ease of growing:

❀ **'All Blue':** This midseason spud is guaranteed to turn a head or two. It has blue skin *and flesh*. It has a mealy texture and is best as a mashed potato. Yes, purple mashed potatoes!

❀ **'All Red':** A midseason sister to 'All Blue,' you probably can guess this variety's description: red skin on the outside and pink flesh on the inside. Combined with 'All Blue' and a white variety, you can create a red, white, and blue mashed potato extravaganza!

❀ **'Butte':** This late-season variety is the classic Idaho baking type and one of my favorites. It's a great *russetted* (has rough, brown-colored skin) baking variety that features 20 percent more protein and 58 percent more vitamin C than other varieties. It also is scab and late blight tolerant. (See "Avoiding Root Pests," later in this chapter, for more on these problems.)

❀ **'Caribe':** This early, lavender-skinned, white-fleshed variety produces large tubers. A great masher.

❀ **'Katahdin':** This versatile midseason variety with white skin and flesh is widely adapted and can be fried, baked, boiled, or mashed. It also is drought tolerant, making it a good variety for climates that receive little rainfall.

- ❀ **'Kennebec':** This all-purpose midseason variety with white skin and flesh is dependable. It also resists disease and is a good variety for almost any use.

- ❀ **'Red Norland':** This early variety has red skin and white flesh. Harvested early when plants are just flowering, this variety is commonly sold in markets as a *new red* potato. It tastes best boiled or mashed.

- ❀ **'Rose Finn Apple':** This late-maturing fingerling variety features rose-colored skin and yellow flesh. This fingerling has a firm, moist texture and is great baked or boiled.

- ❀ **'Viking Purple':** This midseason, purple-skinned, white-fleshed variety can endure dry weather and stores well. It tastes great boiled or mashed.

- ❀ **'Yukon Gold':** This very early variety with yellow skin and flesh produces high yields and is drought tolerant, but it's susceptible to diseases. This moist-fleshed potato is best in salads or boiled.

Even though most potatoes are grown from pieces of tubers, called *seed potatoes,* you can grow potatoes from seeds just as you do with tomatoes and peppers. One hybrid, late-maturity, true-seed variety that's currently available is called 'Catalina' (which is very similar to 'Kennebec'). For best results start seeds indoors one month before planting. You grow your crop the same way that you grow other potatoes. Growing potatoes from seeds is a bit trickier but less expensive than planting seed potatoes, and you reduce the chance of passing any tuber-born diseases on to your new crop. (See "Avoiding Root Pests," later in this chapter, for more on potato diseases.)

Don't try to plant potatoes that you purchase from a grocery store. These spuds have been treated with a chemical sprouting inhibitor, so they either won't grow any plants or the plants will be weak and not productive. It's best to purchase seed potatoes from a mail-order catalog or garden center.

# *The Root to Grow and Gather*

The two keys to growing great root crops are preparing the soil bed well and giving the plants room to grow. Root crops need a loose soil bed to grow roots, and they need room to expand. Also, keep them clear of weeds and make sure that they have enough water.

Carrots, onions, and potatoes are root crops that like cool temperatures. They grow best and have the best flavor when temperatures stay below 80°F. Planting onions and potatoes is easy, but carrots are a bit more problematic, as I explain in the "Growing carrots" section later in this chapter.

All root crops like well-drained, loose, fertile soil. And with the exception of potatoes, roots crops grow best in raised beds (see Chapter 2 for more on raised beds). Root crops also can grow if you have a gardening spot that gets only 4 to 6 hours of direct sun a day. Try some carrots and onions in that patch.

To prepare the soil, add a 3- to 4-inch layer of compost or manure at least two to three months before you're ready to plant. If you wait until just before planting to add fresh compost or manure, you're likely to get poor growth. Root crops enjoy phosphorous, which promotes root growth; so perform a soil test (see Chapter 14 for details), and based on the results, add bone meal or rock phosphate fertilizer before planting to keep your roots happy.

Onions in particular like lots of fertilizer and can stand some extra nitrogen, which promotes leaf growth, so add extra fertilizer when the transplants are 6 inches tall and the bulbs begin to swell. Then add a complete fertilizer such as 10-10-10 at 1 pound per 20 feet. (See Chapter 15 for more on fertilizers.)

Another key to root crops, especially carrots and onions, is proper spacing. Thin out the young seedlings by pulling them out or snipping them until they're properly spaced. Onions should be 4 inches apart, scallions 2 inches apart, and carrots 3 inches apart, as shown in Figure 6-2. Thin the seedlings when they're three to four weeks old. I know that thinning sounds cruel, but if you don't thin, the roots won't have enough room to expand, and you'll get lots of plants but few roots — and fewer roots means fewer carrots, onions, and potatoes.

**Figure 6-2:**
Thinning
ensures
good root
formation.

Don't just throw out those onion thinnings. Young onions that have been thinned are great in salads as scallions.

You'll be rewarded with lots of crisp roots in no time if you weed your root crop patch, mulch with hay or straw, and water.

## Growing carrots

Carrot seeds are small and take up to two weeks to germinate, so you run a greater risk of poor germination than with other vegetables. To get your carrots off on the right foot, try these tips:

- ✔ Prepare your carrot bed well by raking and removing soil clumps, rocks, and sticks.

- ✔ Sprinkle carrot seeds on the top of the soil and then cover them with a thin layer of potting soil or sand. Potting soil and sand are lighter than garden soil, enabling tender seedlings to more easily grow through the soil.

- ✔ Keep your soil moist. If it dries, the seedlings can quickly die. (See Chapter 15 for more on watering.)

- ✔ Grow carrots as a fall crop, starting one to two months before your first frost date. They germinate faster in the warmer soil of summer, and their flavor is sweeter when they mature in the cooler fall weather.

For easier germination of small seeds such as carrots, try purchasing pelleted seeds. These seeds are covered with a biodegradable coating, making the size larger and easier to handle but not affecting the seed germination.

If you're really hungry for carrots and can't wait until they fully mature, you can harvest young carrots anytime after the roots have formed. They just won't taste as sweet — unless you grow the baby types.

If carrot tops break off during harvest (and some always do), use a garden fork to dig up their roots. Pull the largest carrot roots first to leave room for the smaller roots to fill out.

## Growing onions

The simplest way to grow onions is from a set or plant. But you can also directly sow onion seeds in spring, two weeks before your last frost date, or start them indoors eight weeks earlier. For a fall planting of onions, start seedlings indoors or buy transplants. Plant the onion plants four to six weeks before the first frost. If you're starting your own seeds for a fall planting, start them indoors eight weeks earlier.

If you start onions indoors, keep the plants stocky and short; whenever they get long and straggly, cut the tops with scissors so that the plants are 3 inches tall. Trimming encourages better root growth and keeps the plants at a manageable size. Keep the seedlings moist and grow them under lights (see Chapter 13 for more on growing seedlings indoors). Then harden off the transplants: gradually introduce them to the outdoor growing environment by bringing them outside for longer amounts of time each day for up to one week; then plant them 4 to 6 inches apart.

You can harvest onions anytime if you want scallions or small, baby onions, but for the largest bulbs, wait until about 80 percent of the tops have naturally started to fall over. Pull the bulbs out on a dry day if possible and then let them dry out in a warm, shady spot. For more on harvesting, see Chapter 19.

## Growing potatoes

Potatoes are mostly grown from seed potatoes, which are either small potatoes or larger ones cut so that each piece has two eyes, as shown in Figure 6-3. *Eyes* are dormant buds, in which roots and shoots grow. Plant seed pieces about 8 to 10 inches apart in rows.

**Figure 6-3:**
Potato eyes are where the shoots and roots of a potato grow.

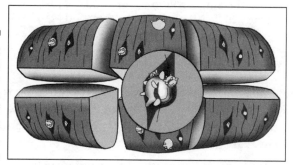

You'll be rewarded with lots of crisp roots in no time if you weed your root crop patch, mulch with hay or straw, and water. Potatoes require one more special technique called hilling. *Hilling* is mounding up the soil around the plants as they grow. For potatoes, hill at least twice during the growing season — about one week after the leaves emerge from the soil and again two to three weeks later (see Figure 6-4). Hilling promotes the production of bigger potatoes and more of them, kills weeds that are growing, and keeps the sun off the tubers.

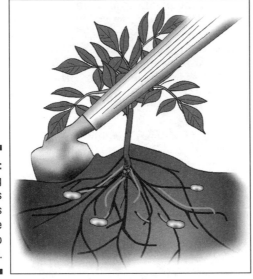

**Figure 6-4:**
Hilling
potatoes
encourages
more
potatoes to
form.

New potatoes are just young potatoes, and with their soft skin and texture, they make a great summer treat. If you can't wait until the main harvest is ready, you can steal a few new potatoes the second time you hill. Just reach into the soil and feel for the small, round tubers. Taking just a few tubers won't kill the plant, and you'll still get some larger spuds later on.

Don't have room but want to grow potatoes? Instead of planting in rows, try growing potatoes vertically in potato towers. Here's how:

1. **Place a 3-foot-diameter chicken wire cage over cultivated soil.**

2. **Add a 2- to 3-inch layer of soil to the bottom of the cage, and line the sides of the cage with hay. Plant four seed potatoes in the bottom of the cage and cover them with soil.**

3. **As the potato plants grow, continue adding soil over them and adding hay around the inside of the cage until you reach the top of the tower. Keep the soil well watered.**

4. **In the fall, open the cage and watch the tubers come rolling out.**

Any direct sun on potatoes causes chlorophyll to form, turning the potato skins green and giving them an off taste. Tubers actually are mildly poisonous at this stage, but you'd have to eat a truck load to really get sick. If you have a small green patch on your potato, just cut if off; the rest of the tuber is fine to eat.

Harvesting potatoes is like going on an archeological dig. After a potato plant dies, use a metal garden fork and dig up the area 1 foot away from the row so that you don't spear the tubers. You'll be amazed at the number of tubers you find — on average, 10 to 20 per plant. Dry the potatoes for an hour or so in the shade, and then store them in a dark, airy, 60°F area for *curing* (the process of letting the skin toughen so the vegetables store better).

# Growing Sweet Potatoes

Sweet potatoes *(Ipomoea batatas)* are a root crop with a reputation for being grown only in the South. In fact, if you choose the right varieties, you can grow sweet potatoes even in cold climates like Minnesota. Sweet potatoes are easy to grow, and they store well indoors in winter. The sweet orange- or yellow-fleshed tubers can be baked, mashed, or sliced and deep fried for a nutritious and delicious snack. Some of the best short-season varieties (90 days) to grow are 'Beauregard,' 'Centennial,' and 'Georgia Jet.' Other varieties that mature one to two weeks later are 'Bush Porto Rico,' Jewel,' and 'Vardaman.'

Many people call sweet potatoes *yams,* but this isn't technically accurate. In the 1930s, growers in Louisiana patented the name "yam" for a new variety of sweet potato, even though that sweet potato wasn't really a yam. Yams are actually a large tropical root crop seldom seen in this country; the "yams" that you see in grocery stores are just different varieties of sweet potatoes.

To grow sweet potatoes, you don't plant seeds. Instead, you buy small plants called *slips.* Slips are available at local garden centers in spring or through the mail. You can start your own at home, but it's better to purchase certified disease-free slips from commercial growers to avoid disease. Sweet potatoes love the heat, so wait until the soil temperature is at least 60°F before planting. To plant:

1. **Create raised beds at least 6 inches tall and amend the soil with compost.**

2. **Plant the slips up to their bottom leaves, 1 foot apart in the raised beds.**

   In cold-winter areas, consider laying black plastic over the beds, punching holes, and planting the slips through the plastic so the soil will heat up faster and the tubers will grow and mature sooner.

3. **Side-dress the plants once, one month after planting, with a 5-10-10 or a mix of blood and bone meal fertilizer; keep the plants well weeded and watered.**

   The vines will create a dense mat-like a groundcover, making this an attractive, as well as edible, plant to grow. Keep the soil on the slightly acidic pH side to avoid some diseases.

4. **Before frost, or about 100 days after planting, dig under the plants and check for roots.**

    Pull plants that have formed good-sized roots and cure (dry) these in a warm (80°F) room for two weeks. The curing process not only helps the skin toughen, but also converts starches to sugars, giving sweet potatoes their characteristic taste.

After curing, eat the tubers or store them in a humid 55°F basement (or in a cool area of your house) all winter.

# Avoiding Root Pests

Many of the same pests that you find on other vegetable crops — such as aphids, flea beetles, thrips, mosaic virus, and nematodes — also occur on root crops. Other potentially damaging pests are animals — such as rabbits, mice, and chipmunks — who enjoy the underground snacks out of sight of predators. I lost most of my potato crop one year due to an overpopulation of chipmunks looking for food. (I discuss insect and animal pests as well as common diseases in more detail in Chapter 18.) Check with the local cooperative extension service or the folks at your local nursery or garden store to find out what specific diseases and insects may be problems in your area, and then as with any vegetable, plant varieties that are resistant to those diseases and insects.

A few pests specifically harm root crops. Here are descriptions of those pests as well as the appropriate controls:

✔ **Blight:** This fungal disease can wreak havoc on potatoes. Late blight, in particular, is the infamous disease that destroyed potatoes in Ireland in the 1840s, causing the Irish potato famine. This disease thrives in cool, humid weather, and infection starts in the form of water-soaked black spots on the leaves. Unfortunately, once blight starts, you can't treat it; plants can die, and any tuber that they produce also may be infected. To avoid this disease, mulch, rotate crops, pull up any *volunteer* potatoes that sprout from old tubers in the ground, and plant certified disease-free seed potatoes.

✔ **Carrot rust fly:** If your carrots' roots have holes bored into them, they may be infected with carrot rust flies. Adult flies lay their eggs on the soil near carrot plants: when the young larvae hatch, they tunnel into the soil to feed on the carrot roots. If your carrots have these holes in them, you can eat the carrots as long as the disease hasn't started rotting the root.

    To avoid this problem, cover the plants with a floating row cover (a cheesecloth-like material that lets air, water, and sun in, but keeps bugs out; see Chapter 22), rotate crops, and grow resistant varieties.

- **Colorado potato beetle:** The most destructive potato pests, these $^1/_2$-inch long, tan- and brown-striped adult beetles lay yellow eggs in clusters on the undersides of potato leaves, starting in early summer. After the eggs hatch, the dark red larvae feed voraciously on the leaves and can quickly destroy your crop. Control these insects by crushing their eggs on sight, handpicking the young beetles, mulching with a thick layer of hay to slow their spread, and spraying the biological spray Bt 'San Diego,' which is specifically designed to kill young potato beetles but doesn't harm other insects, animals, or people.

- **Onion maggot:** This pest's larvae attack the bulbs of developing onions, causing holes and opening the bulb to infection from disease. Onion maggots like cool, wet weather. To control onion maggots, place a floating row over young seedlings, after the weather warms (around 70°F) cover and remix it.

- **Potato scab:** This fungal disease causes a potato's skin to turn brown with a corky texture. Tubers with potato scab are unattractive but still edible. Control this cosmetic disease by lowering the pH of your soil to below 6 (see Chapter 14 for details) and by rotating crops.

- **Wireworm:** These jointed, hard-shelled, tan-colored, 1-inch worms feed on underground tuber roots as well as the bulbs of a number of crops. They're generally a problem with recently sodded soil. Control this pest by setting potato traps before your root crops begin maturing. Spear a potato piece on a stick and bury it 2- to 4-inches in the ground; the wireworms should infest the potato. Dig up the piece after one week and then destroy it.

# Healthy Roots and a Recipe

Carrots and onions contain many nutrients, but potatoes are *the* staple diet in more than 130 countries:

- Carrots are the vegetable vitamin A and beta-carotene kings. Beta-carotene is a provitamin that transforms into vitamin A in your body as you need it. It shows promise in preventing breast, lung, stomach, and cervical cancers.

- Onions add vitamin B and phosphorous to your diet, and recent studies have shown that eating only half an onion a day can lower your risk of developing stomach cancer.

- Potatoes have a full complement of vitamins and minerals especially vitamins B and C, potassium, and iodine, and some varieties such as 'Butte' contain extra protein.

Even though potatoes taste great with sour cream and butter, if you add less of them to your potato dishes, you'll have as close to a perfect vegetable food as you can get. Here's a simple recipe to use up your fresh potatoes and onions:

Refrigerate the onions 30 minutes before preparation to prevent your eyes from tearing up when peeling them.

To keep your blue potatoes blue (not a washed-out gray color), add 1 to 2 tablespoons of vinegar to boiling water while cooking.

### Potato Salad

This basic potato salad recipe is just begging for modifications. To make the dish more visually exciting, I like to use red-, blue-, and yellow-fleshed potatoes and red- and white-fleshed onions. For a spicier potato salad, try adding horseradish, mustard, cayenne peppers, or Tabasco sauce.

**Tools:** *Large bowl*

**Preparation time:** *30 minutes*

**Cooking time:** *Boil until tender (15 minutes)*

**Yield:** *6 servings*

| | |
|---|---|
| *5 or 6 medium boiling potatoes (peeled or unpeeled)* | *¹/₂ cup shredded carrots (optional)* |
| *¹/₂ cup minced onions* | *¹/₂ cup chopped green pepper (optional)* |
| *¹/₂ cup chopped celery* | *3 to 5 hard-boiled eggs, chopped (optional)* |
| *¹/₂ cup mayonnaise* | |
| *salt, pepper, and paprika to taste (optional)* | |

*1* Steam the potatoes until tender and then cut them into cubes. (You can also boil the potatoes, but steaming retains more vitamins.)

*2* In a large bowl, combine all the salad ingredients (the onions, celery, mayonnaise, and salt and pepper) except the paprika. Chill the salad for at least 1 hour to allow the flavors to blend.

*3* Sprinkle the salad with paprika and serve.

# Chapter 7

# Lovely Legumes: Peas and Beans

• • • • • • • • • • • • • • • • • • • • • • • • • • • • • • • • • • • • • • •

• • • • • • • • • • • • • • • • • • • • • • • • • • • • • • • • • • • • • • •

*O*ne vegetable that you can always rely on is the bean. For ensured success in your first garden, plant some bean seeds. When I teach gardening to beginner groups, the first plants that I talk about are bean plants — and for good reason. Bean seeds are large and easy to plant, they grow easily, and they don't require lots of extra fertilizer or care. Within 60 days, you're bound to have some beans to eat. With beans, satisfaction is as guaranteed as it gets in the vegetable gardening world.

Peas are in the same legume family as beans; other crops in this family include clover and alfalfa, but you don't eat them. Peas also have large seeds and don't require lots of care. The only difference between peas and beans is that peas like cool weather to grow and mature, whereas beans like it warm. If you get the timing right for beans and peas, you'll have lots of legumes rolling in your kitchen door. See the appendix for a general planting guide for selected beans and peas.

## A Bevy of Beans

All bush, pole, and dried beans are members of the *Phaseolus vulgaris* family. In this section, I classify beans according to their growth habits and usage (that is, whether you eat them fresh or dried). Home gardeners generally don't have to worry about disease resistance with their bean plants:

✔ **Bush beans** get their name because they grow on a bush. They tend to produce the earliest crops, maturing all at once (within a week or so); you have either feast or famine with these types.

## Ancient beans and peas

People have been eating peas and beans since the beginning of civilization itself. Dried pea seeds were found in Stone Age villages in Switzerland as well as in Egyptian tombs. The pea's place of origin is eastern Europe, and until 1,000 years ago, it was eaten only as a dried vegetable. By the eighteenth century, peas (derived from the Latin name for peas, *Pisum*) were commonly grown for their shelled and dried seeds in English and European gardens, and were introduced to the Americas by the explorers.

Ancient Egyptians worshipped bean relatives, such as cow peas (also called black-eyed peas), and some even dedicated tombs to the humble legumes. The modern bean family that people are most familiar with is a South American native that had moved north into many Native American tribes by the time Christopher Columbus arrived in America. These modern beans were part of the famous "three sisters" of corn, squash, and beans that early settlers found the Native Americans growing. The early explorers brought these beans back to Europe and soon spread them around the world. In America, by the late 1800s, beans had become popular partly because the warm, rainy summer climate in the eastern U.S. was conducive to bean growing.

✔ **Pole beans** need staking and usually grow on poles. They tend to mature their crops later than bush beans, but pole beans continue to produce all season until frost or disease stops them.

✔ **Dried beans** are actually varieties of bush or pole beans. You can eat them fresh, like bush or pole beans, but they're better if you allow them to dry and then just eat the bean seeds. Caring for dried beans is easy: Just plant them, care for them, and harvest them when the pods are dried and the plants are almost dead.

Bush and pole beans actually are the same type of bean, just with different growth habits. Bush and pole beans often are called *snap* beans because they snap when you break their pods in half. Another name for these beans is *string* beans, because early varieties had a stringy texture. Modern varieties don't have this texture, so this name isn't commonly used today. Yellow snap varieties mature to a yellow color and are also called wax beans.

Beans harvested at different stages can be called different names. A bean harvested when it's young, before seeds have formed, is called a *snap* bean. If the bean matures further and you harvest it when it's green in color and the bean seeds are fully formed, it's called a *shell* bean. Finally, if the pod dries on the plant and then you harvest it, it's called a *dried* bean. Some bean varieties can be harvested at all stages. However, most bean varieties are best harvested at one particular stage — snap, shell, or dried — depending on their breeding (see "Keep on pickin': Harvesting your crop" for details). Don't get lost in the snap, string thing. Those are just names people have given to a bean eaten before the seeds inside begin to form.

Just for fun — in addition to the bush, pole, and dried beans — I also list some other bean relatives that are tasty and have novel colors and shapes (they're unique). The *days to maturity* represents the time from when you plant the seeds in the ground to when you harvest them. Bean *appétit!*

# Bush beans

Bush bean plants generally are less than 2 feet tall and produce handfuls of beans at harvest. Depending on the variety, the beans are green, yellow, or purple. Most *pods* (the part of the bean that you eat) are 6 to 8 inches at maturity, but you can harvest beans that are flavorful sooner. If you need lots of beans all at once for canning or preserving, grow bush beans. Here are a few of the most reliable varieties to grow:

- **'Blue Lake 274':** This big, meaty, green bean variety matures high yields (about 12 pounds for every 10 feet of row) in 55 days — even under adverse weather conditions. It also comes in a pole bean version.

- **'Contender':** This green bean is one of the earliest to harvest, only 50 days from seeding.

- **'Derby':** This disease-resistant, All-America Selections winner (see Chapter 4) features extra tender pods and high yields 57 days from seeding.

- **'Kentucky Wonder':** This classic green bean also comes in a pole bean variety. Its round, green pods are produced prolifically on sturdy plants 57 days from seeding.

- **'Jumbo':** This variety is a cross between 'Romano' and 'Kentucky Wonder.' It produces large, flat pods with a stronger flavor than other green beans. It matures 54 days from seeding.

- **'Improved Golden Wax':** This disease-resistant, yellow-bean variety produces broad, flat golden pods only 52 days from seeding.

- **'Provider':** This variety has great disease resistance and can grow in adverse weather conditions. Its green pods mature 50 days from seeding.

- **'Roc D'or Wax':** Long, slender, round, bright yellow pods are produced on sturdy plants in 53 days.

- **'Romano':** This long, flat green bean is an Italian classic and also comes in wax and pole varieties. The pods are known for their strong flavor and ability to stay tender even when they're large. It matures in 60 days.

- **'Sequoia Purple Pod':** This attractive purple-podded bean also has purple-colored stems, leaves, and flowers. It matures in 53 days, and it turns dark green when cooked.

Selecting among the various bean types is really just a matter of color and experimentation. Try one and see if you like it.

## Pole beans

Many pole bean varieties share the names and characteristics of their bush bean counterparts. Pole beans mature more beans overall but start a week or so later than bush beans and produce only a handful of beans per day, which makes them great for small families. Pole beans keep growing and growing, producing beans until frost, in all but the hottest summer areas. You can also plant them in summer for a fall crop in warm areas. In the following list of varieties, I mention the pole beans that also have bush forms, plus some other good producing and attractive pole varieties that you may want to try

- ❀ **'Blue Lake':** See the bush variety in the preceding section "Bush beans."

- ❀ **'Goldmarie':** This early yielding, wax pole bean variety produces 8-inch pods 54 days from seeding.

- ❀ **'Kentucky Wonder':** See the bush variety for a description. 'Kentucky Wonder' also is available in a wax pole bean variety.

- ❀ **'Purple Pod':** This unique purple-colored variety grows on a 6-foot-tall plant. When you cook this bean, its color changes from purple to dark green. It matures 65 days from seeding.

- ❀ **'Romano':** See the bush variety for a description.

- ❀ **'Scarlet Runner':** This beautiful, vigorous pole bean is actually in a different species *(Phaseolus coccineus)*. It produces attractive scarlet red flowers and large hairy pods and bean seeds that are edible 70 days from seeding. The seeds themselves taste okay, but this variety is usually grown as an ornamental for its attractive flowers and colorful red and black bean seeds.

## Dried and shell beans

Dried and shell beans are some of the most versatile beans to grow because you can eat them at the snap, shell, or dried stages. Eaten at the shell (fully matured seeds in the pod, but the pod is still green) or dried stage, you're eating the seed inside the pod. These seeds can be a range of colors from white to red and can even be striped and spotted. Dried beans are great baked and in soups and chowders. Most of the varieties in the following list are grown for their dried beans but also taste good at their shelling stage, too. They're the dried beans that most people are familiar with eating and the tastiest to grow. The days to maturity represent the time from seeding to dried bean harvest. Most of these varieties are bushy plants.

If you're confused about the relationship of shell beans, dried beans, and beans in general, welcome to the wacky world of bean-talk. Although shell and dried are technically stages of beans, many gardeners refer to them as varieties, too. Hence the confusion. Whatever you call them, you won't find a more versatile veggie than the lowly bean:

- ❀ **'Black Turtle':** This small black bean matures 85 days from seeding and grows best in warmer climates. Each pod produces 7 to 8 beans, which are often baked as well as used in soups and casseroles.

- ❀ **'Cannellini':** This famous white, kidney-shaped bean is often used in minestrone soups. Large plants produce beans that are best when eaten at the shelling stage, which is 80 days from seeding.

- ❀ **'French Horticultural':** An old-time favorite, this tan-colored bean matures in 90 days. You can eat this variety earlier as a shelling bean.

- ❀ **'Garbanzo' (chick pea):** This large, tan-colored bean is produced on an upright, bushy plant 100 days from seeding. It's often used in salads and soups and as flour. It grows best in hot, dry climates.

- ❀ **'Navy':** A small, semi-vining plant produces white, oval beans 85 days from seeding. These beans are excellent baked.

- ❀ **'Pinto':** A vining plant produces buff-colored, brown-speckled, dried beans 90 days from seeding; these beans are widely used in Mexican dishes. You also can grow this variety as a pole bean.

- ❀ **'Red Kidney':** This bushy plant produces large, red, kidney-shaped beans 100 days from seeding. These beans are used in many baked dishes. 'Red Kidney' also comes as a white-seeded variety.

- ❀ **'Soldier':** This white, kidney-shaped bean with red markings produces 6 beans per pod 85 days from seeding. This bean is great in stews and baked.

- ❀ **'Green Vegetable Soybean':** Unlike the commercial soybean that's grown for animal feed, oil, and so on, this soybean is meant to be eaten at the green shell stage. It has a buttery, almost lima bean flavor, and kids love popping these beans out of freshly steamed pods. These beans are popular in Japan, eaten as a snack with beer. 'Envy' is the earliest maturing of the 'Green Vegetable Soybean' varieties (75 days from seeding).

- ❀ **'Vermont Cranberry':** This red, brown-speckled, New England classic dried bean is one of the most popular beans to grow. It matures 90 days from seeding and is _widely adapted_ (can grow in a variety of geographic regions under a variety of weather conditions).

## Other beans

Some variations on the common bean are exotic and fun to grow. These beans in the following list are grown similarly to bush or pole beans but come in different shapes and flavors. Some of these beans aren't even in the same family as bush and pole beans, so get ready for a treat. Here are some of the best ones to try:

- **Asparagus bean (*Vigna unguiculata sesquipedalis,* or Yard-Long bean):** This pole bean grows more than 10 feet tall and produces extremely long (3 foot!) beans. This variety is popular in Europe but is rarely grown in the United States because it isn't widely known and requires a long growing season.

- **Fava bean (*Vigna acontifolia,* or English Broad bean or Horse bean):** This popular English bean grows on plants that are 2 to 3 feet tall; unlike other beans, the fava bean likes cold weather. You can harvest the 7-inch pods as snap or shell beans; they mature 85 days from seeding. Fava beans are a good alternative to lima beans in cold climates.

- **French fillet:** This classic bean from France has been bred to be tender and stringless. Compact bush plants produce an abundance of these thin, "melt-in-your-mouth," textured beans when harvested young. Pick them when they're less than $1/4$-inch thick, or they'll have started to mature, leaving the pods tough and stringy. A number of new varieties, such as 'Maxibell' and 'Nickel,' mature about 60 days from seeding.

- **Lima bean (*Phaseolus lunatus,* or Butter bean):** Once you've eaten a fresh lima, you'll never settle for the canned version again. Lima beans come in bush and pole varieties and love a long, warm growing season. Fat pods, which are 4 to 8 inches long, produce 4 to 6 beans each that you harvest at the shell stage. One of the best bush varieties is 'Fordhook 242,' which matures in 75 days. A good pole variety is 'King of the Garden,' maturing 88 days from seeding.

- **Southern pea (*Vigna unguiculata,* or Cow pea):** Although it's called a pea, the southern pea actually is more like a bean in growth and usage. Like limas, southern peas grow best in warm climates. The plants are either bush or semi-vining, and you harvest the pods about 60 days from seeding at the shell or dried stage. Some of the more famous types are Black-Eyed peas such as 'Pink-Eyed Purple Hull,' which is named for the black speck on the seed; Crowders such as 'Mississippi Silver' named for the way the seeds grow jammed in the pod; and Cream peas such as 'Lady,' named for their smooth pod.

So don't be bound by common beans. Try a few different bean varieties to expand your palate of bean flavors and textures.

# More Peas Pleassssse

One vegetable that is truly a treat to grow yourself is the pea, which is *Pisum sativum* botanically. In grocery stores, peas are available for only a short time, and their flavor isn't as sweet and tender as freshly picked pea pods. Some varieties grow to be huge and bushy, needing extra support to stand tall. Others are short and bushy and don't require fencing or support. Viny pea plants produce a grabbing shoot called a *tendril* that holds onto whatever it come in contact with. Some novel types don't even bother growing leaves. In the following sections, I divide peas into three groups: English, snap, and snow.

A pea is described by the type of pods it has. An *English,* or garden, pea has a tough pod with tender peas inside. A *snap* pea has tender peas inside but also has an edible, sweet pod. A *snow* pea is harvested flat (that is, harvested before the pea seeds inside the pod form) mainly for its tender pea pod. Mind your peas and take a look at some excellent varieties.

## English peas

Sometimes called the garden pea, the English pea is the pea that gardeners are most familiar with. In the following list, the days to maturity represent the time from seeding to harvest. Here are some of the most reliable performing varieties of English peas:

* **'Alderman' (Tall Telephone):** This old heirloom matures in about 74 days. Six-foot-tall vines produce a large number of 4- to 5-inch pods.

* **'Daybreak':** This 2-foot-tall, bush-type variety produces good crops early (in 62 days).

* **'Green Arrow':** This high-yielding, 2-foot-tall, widely adapted variety matures in 70 days.

* **'Maestro':** A prolific early variety reaches only 2-feet tall but produces 4- to 5-inch pods on powdery-mildew-resistant plants.

* **'Novella':** This unique 20-inch-tall, leafless variety produces tendrils and lots of peas in 65 days.

* **'Petit Pois':** This novel *baby* pea (the pea seed inside the pod is smaller than the normal pea seed) is extra sweet and tender. The plants are 20 inches tall and produce peas in 58 days.

* **'Wando':** This very productive, warm weather variety grows 3 feet tall and produces peas in 68 days.

## Snap peas

Snap peas are the new peas on the block. Recent breeding has created a pea pod that *fills out* (the pea seed inside the pod forms) like an English pea but has a sweet, tender pod like a snow pea. Upon harvesting snap peas, cut off the cap (stem end) of the pod and take the string (along the seam) out of the pod, as shown in Figure 7-1; these are the only two parts of the pod that are chewy. The plants range from the original 'Super Snap' that grows to 8 feet tall, to the diminutive 'Sugar Bon' that grows to less than 2 feet tall. Kids love snap peas, and they're as easy to grow as English peas.

Try these varieties of sweet and flavorful snap peas:

❀ **'Cascadia':** These 2-foot-tall vines resist the pea enation virus disease (a problem in the Pacific Northwest) and produce 3-inch, dark green peas 58 days after planting.

❀ **'Sugar Ann':** The earliest maturing snap pea, this variety is ready for harvest in 52 days. The plants grow only 2 feet tall, producing sweet, 2 to 3-inch pods. This snap pea is so dwarf that it doesn't need support and can be grown in containers.

❀ **'Sugar Bon':** A 1- to 2-foot-tall snap pea, this sweet snap pea matures in 56 days and resists powdery mildew disease.

❀ **'Sugar Daddy':** These 30-inch-tall vines produce stringless, podded snap peas 75 days after planting.

❀ **'Super Sugar Snap':** These vines grow to 6 feet tall, producing tons of sweet, long pods and peas 65 days after planting. This variety is more disease resistant and shorter than the original 'Sugar Snap,' which is still available.

**Figure 7-1:**
Remove the cap and eat the pod and all in snap pea varieties.

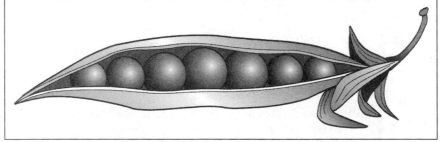

## Snow peas

If you've eaten a vegetable dish in a Chinese restaurant, you've probably tried these sweet-tasting, flat-podded peas. Snow peas are the easiest peas to grow because you don't have to wait for the pea pods to fill out to harvest them. They're tender, stringless, and best when harvested before the peas inside begin to swell. Here are some of the best producing varieties to try:

- ✿ **'Dwarf Gray Sugar':** This viny, 2- to 3-foot-tall plant needs support but produces 3-inch, dark green pods 57 days after planting. The pink flowers are very ornamental.

- ✿ **'Oregon Giant':** These large 4- to 5-inch sweet pods grow on disease-resistant, 3-foot-tall vines 60 days after planting.

- ✿ **'Oregon Sugar Pod II':** Another large-podded, sweet-tasting snow pea, this variety grows to 4 feet tall and matures its pods 68 days after planting. Like 'Oregon Giant,' it's also disease resistant.

# Growing Peas and Beans

Peas and beans are like siblings: They have a lot in common but also have some different preferences. Both peas and beans like moderate moisture throughout the growing season and well-drained soil that isn't heavily amended (nutrient-improved) with fertilizer (see Chapter 15). They're not very demanding at all. The fundamental difference between pea and beans, however, is that peas like cool climates and beans prefer warm ones. If you get the timing right (plant peas when it's cool and beans when it's hot), these two siblings will reward you with a bounty of legumes.

## Planting legumes

When planting legumes, choose a sunny spot with well-drained soil and create a raised bed (see Chapter 2 for information on building raised beds). Raised beds help keep pea seeds from getting soggy while they germinate in cool soil; at the same time, using raised beds warms up the soil for bean seeds, which you plant later.

### Preparing the soil with compost and fertilizer

Plants need nitrogen to grow, and most of the time they get it from the soil. Legumes are unique, however, in that they can use the nitrogen in the air through a special relationship with a type of bacteria called a *rhizobium*. This bacteria naturally occurs in soil and attaches itself to legume roots, living off the plants. In exchange, the bacteria takes the atmospheric nitrogen and changes it into a form that the plants can use. Beans and peas get the nitrogen they need, and the bacteria gets a home. So don't worry about adding more nitrogen fertilizer to legumes; they can take care of themselves. If you see bumps or nodules on the roots of your plants, you know that bacteria is at work.

Books and catalogs often suggest that you buy your own bacteria inoculant powder to add to bean and pea seeds when planting. This powder really isn't necessary. Soil already has bacteria in it, so usually you don't need to add any bacteria to your seeds. The exception, however, is with very sandy or poor soil. These types of soil need a one-time *inoculation* (the mixing of powder with seeds at planting), which peppers the soil with bacteria and gives your plants the boost that they need. After the rhizobium is present in the soil, you don't need to add it yearly.

Even though legumes don't need extra nitrogen, they do benefit from a 2- to 3-inch layer of composted manure worked into the soil before planting. For poor soils with low fertility, add a fertilizer high in phosphorous and potassium, such as 5-10-10. See Chapter 15 for more on fertilizing.

### Determining when to plant

With beans, wait until the soil is at least 60°F before planting. Beans planted in cool soil rot before germinating. Plant bush beans in staggered planting dates, planting small batches of seeds every week or so (see Chapter 16 for more on this succession planting technique). By staggering the plantings, you'll have a continual harvest all summer.

Peas like cool soil and can germinate in 40°F soil. As soon as the soil dries out, build your beds and plant your seeds.

You can determine if your soil is dried out by squeezing a handful of soil; if no water trickles out and the soil clump feels moist and breaks up easily when poked with your finger, the soil is dried out.

You can plant peas three to four weeks before the last frost date in your area if the soil is ready. Pea seeds actually germinate better in 60 to 70°F soils, but if you wait until the soil is warmer, the plants will get off to a late start. By the time the peas would begin flowering, the air temperature would be too warm (above 80°F), and your plants and production would suffer. You also can grow peas as a fall crop, which you start in summer so the plants mature in the cool days of autumn.

To help pea seeds germinate in cold or hot soils, try pregerminating the seeds. Place the pea seeds in a moist paper towel in a dark, warm spot for a few days. Check the seeds daily; when you see a small root begin to grow, plant the peas in the ground. Pregerminating helps the peas get off to a faster start and reduces the chance that they'll rot in cool soil.

### Providing support

How you plant your legumes depends on what varieties you're planting:

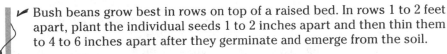

- ✔ Bush beans grow best in rows on top of a raised bed. In rows 1 to 2 feet apart, plant the individual seeds 1 to 2 inches apart and then thin them to 4 to 6 inches apart after they germinate and emerge from the soil.

- ✔ Because you plant peas when the soil is cooler, the germination percentage may be less than with beans. Plant peas less than 1 inch apart in rows 6 inches apart on a raised bed.

Tall vining varieties of beans, such as pole beans, and tall varieties of peas need support to grow their best. The type of support needed depends on the plant (see Figure 7-2).

**Figure 7-2:**
Climbers
versus
twiners.

Climbing pole bean      Twining peas

Pole bean shoots spiral and wrap themselves around objects that they can climb, and peas attach themselves to objects with _tendrils_ (grabbing shoots that hold onto whatever they come in contact with). Generally, beans like to climb poles, and peas like to climb fences. The height of your fence or pole depends on the varieties that you're growing: A 4- to 5-foot fence is good for most peas, and a 6- to 8-foot pole is good for pole beans.

Keep your fences and poles within reach because if the plants grow too tall, you'll need to use a ladder to harvest. For more information on trellises, fences, and teepees (for beans), see Chapter 15.

Plant both pea and bean seeds 1 to 2 inches deep. In between the pea rows, place your trellis — for example, chicken wire — so that the peas can climb up both sides of a fence (or whatever you have available for them to climb on). Plant pole beans around individual poles; plant 4 to 6 pole beans around each pole, about 6 inches away from the pole, as shown in Figure 7-3.

After they start to grow, beans and peas need little attention other than regular watering and weeding. Both benefit from a layer of hay or straw mulch placed around the rows. The hay or straw mulch reduces the need for weeding and keeps the soil moist. (See Chapter 15 for more on mulch.)

**Figure 7-3:**
Plant beans
around a
pole.

Be careful when weeding around peas because they have shallow root systems. Instead of digging in the soil around the roots, pull any weeds by hand or bury young weeds with soil as they germinate. Also, make sure that you use mulch.

## *Keep on pickin': Harvesting your crop*

Here's how to tell when the beans you've planted are ready for harvest:

✔ You can harvest snap beans when the pods are firm and crisp and the seeds inside the pods are undeveloped. (If the pod is smooth and not bumpy, you know that the seeds haven't developed yet.) Carefully hold the bean stem with one hand and pull the individual beans off with your other hand to avoid breaking the plants. (See Figure 7-4.) The more you pick, the more you'll get because the plant wants to produce mature seeds and you keep frustrating it by picking the pods, so harvest even if you're not going to eat all the beans immediately. Remember, you can always share your crop with hungry friends and family.

✔ Harvest shell beans when the pods are full, green, and firm but haven't dried out yet. You can store the beans in a refrigerator for a few days before cooking them.

✔ Dried beans are easy to identify for harvest: Let the pods dry on the plant until they naturally begin to split. Break the bean seeds out of the pods by rubbing the pods in your hands, which shatters them. Store the beans in glass jars in a cool place; you can either eat them or save them to plant next year.

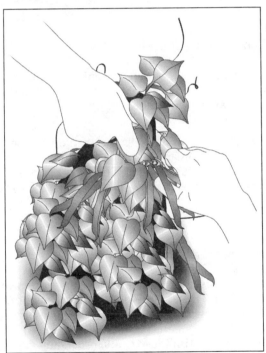

**Figure 7-4:** Picking beans with two hands.

Peas lose quality quickly, so picking them when they're undermature rather than overmature is better. Also, try to cook them the same day because they turn starchy quickly if you keep them for more than one or two days. Here are some guidelines for harvesting peas:

✔ You harvest English and snap peas when the pods are full and before they fade in color. Ask your kids to do test picks. Usually I don't have to ask my kids because they're in the pea patch trying the pods as soon as they can find any plump ones.

> ✔ You can pick snow peas anytime before the pea seeds inside the pods begin to form. After the peas begin to fill out, the pods get tough and stringy.

## Thwarting pests and diseases

One nice thing about beans and peas is that they're susceptible to few serious pests or diseases. Some of the common problems that plague other vegetables such as damping off, fusarium wilt, powdery mildew, and leaf blight can also be problems for peas and beans (see Chapter 18). You can avoid many of these problems in vegetables by rotating crops, tilling in the fall, and growing resistant varieties; see Chapter 16 for details. The following sections describe some problems specific to peas and beans.

### Pesky pea problems

Peas don't have many problems, but here are a few to watch out for:

✔ **Pea aphid:** These pear-shaped, $1/8$-inch, green insects suck the juices from pea leaves and stems and can cause plants to wilt and stunt their growth. If your plants are severely affected by these insects, spray the plants with Safer's insecticidal soap.

✔ **Pea enation virus:** This virus is a particular problem for peas grown in the Pacific Northwest. It's spread by aphids (another reason to control aphids) and causes the plants' leaves and pods to be stunted and deformed. The best solution is to grow disease-resistant varieties such as 'Cascadia.'

### Battles for beans

Here are the most troublesome of the bean problems:

✔ **Mexican bean beetle:** This ladybug relative has an orange-yellow shell with 16 black spots on it. The adult beetles lay masses of orange eggs on the undersides of maturing bean plants. The eggs hatch and then the $1/3$-inch, spiny yellow young that emerge feed on bean leaves, defoliating the plant. To control these pests, crush any egg masses that you see, clean up old bean plant debris where they *overwinter* (live throughout the winter), and spray the adult beetles with *pyrethrin* (a botanical spray made from flowers).

✔ **Rust:** If your beans have red or orange spots on their leaves and then yellow and die, you may have rust disease. This fungal disease overwinters on bean plant debris left in the garden and infects new plants in summer when the weather is right (warm temperatures and high humidity). To prevent rust disease, clean up plant debris in the fall and till your garden. Also, don't work in your garden when the leaves are wet because wet leaves provide the moisture that rust disease spores need to be able to spread.

✔ **Bald heading:** If your bean seedlings emerge from the soil without any leaves, they may have a condition called *bald heading*. Insects can cause this condition, but more likely, you've planted the seeds too deep in the ground or in gravel soil, which causes the leaves to rip off as they try to break through the soil. To prevent this condition, prepare the seed bed by removing rocks, sticks, and clods of soil before planting and don't plant too deep. If you see leafless beans, pull them out and replant. Leafless beans don't produce any crops.

## Cooking without gas

I know, I know, flatulence isn't a glamorous subject, and it may even be embarrassing to mention, but the fact remains, some beans may give you intestinal gas. The biggest culprit is dried beans. If you love beans, but not their side effects, try these preventive measures:

✔ Rinse beans under cold water before cooking.

✔ When soaking beans, add ⅛ teaspoon of baking soda to the water to reduce the sugars in beans that cause gas.

✔ After soaking, rinse beans again in cold water.

✔ Avoid eating other gas-producing vegetables, such as cabbage and broccoli, with beans.

✔ Try adding an enzyme digestive such as Beano to the beans when cooking.

# Health Tips and a Recipe

Beans and peas are great sources of fiber, B vitamins, and minerals such as potassium and iron. Because of their fiber content, beans have been proven to help lower blood cholesterol levels. Beans and peas also are sources of vegetable protein, especially when processed into tofu and other high protein food products. Nutritionally, the best beans and peas are soybeans and dried beans such as pinto and chick peas. These varieties consistently rate high in fiber, protein, folic acid (B vitamin), and minerals. Some varieties, such as soybeans, can provide 50 percent of the recommended daily allowance of minerals such as iron. Soybeans have been proven to reduce the formation of blood clots and even help prevent breast and prostate cancers. All these great health benefits from a humble, easy-to- grow legume! Here's a recipe that enables you to try out your bountiful bean harvest.

## Three Bean Salad

**Tools:** *Large bowl, small bowl*

**Preparation time:** *30 minutes*

**Refrigeration time:** *3 hours*

**Yield:** *8 servings*

| | |
|---|---|
| *2 cups snap green beans, lightly steamed* | *¹/₄ cup parsley, chopped* |
| *2 cups wax beans, lightly steamed* | *1 cup Italian salad dressing* |
| *2 cups kidney beans, cooked and drained* | *2 cloves garlic, crushed* |
| *¹/₂ cup green onions, chopped* | |

*1* In a large bowl, combine all the beans, onions, and parsley.

*2* In a small bowl, mix the salad dressing and garlic together and then pour the mixture over the beans in the large bowl. Combine well.

*3* Cover and refrigerate the salad for at least three hours, allowing the flavors to blend. Stir occasionally.

*4* Drain the salad and serve it over a bed of lettuce.

# Chapter 8

# The Viners: Cucumbers, Melons, Pumpkins, and Squash

• • • • • • • • • • • • • • • • • • • • • • • • • • • • • • • • • • • • • • • • • • •

• • • • • • • • • • • • • • • • • • • • • • • • • • • • • • • • • • • • • • • • • • •

*I*f the heat is on, it's time to grow viners. This group of vegetables is part of the cucumber family *(Cucurbitacea),* and it includes cucumbers, melons, watermelons, squash, and pumpkins. Gourds also are in this family, but I discuss them in Chapter 11.

What all these vegetables have in common is their love of heat, their ability to grow long stems (and *vine* to great lengths), and the fact that they have separate male and female flowers on the same plant. Unlike the other vegetables that I mention in this book (which have both male and female parts in the same flower), the viners need someone to play Cupid and bring pollen from the male flower to the female flower in order to produce fruit. This process is called *pollination,* and usually bees play the Cupid role. Of course, there are exceptions to the Cupid rule, and I discuss them in the sections about the individual vegetables.

This large family of vegetables is known for producing lots of fruits and taking up lots of room in the process. However, modern plant breeders have responded to the need for smaller, space-saving vegetable plants by breeding *bush* (nonvining) varieties of some favorite cucumber-family crops. So now you have one more reason to grow some cucumbers and squash. Actually, if you've ever tasted a vine-ripened melon or cucumber or baked a home-grown winter squash, you're probably hooked. Their flavor and texture are much better than anything you can buy in stores, and if you grow too many vegetables, you can always give them away to hungry neighbors.

## Vining history

Two members of the vining family, pumpkins and squash, are native to America and are well-known when grown together as part of the "Three Sisters:" corn, beans, and squash. (See Chapter 1 for more about a Three Sisters Garden.) The corn provides support for the beans to grow, while the squash fills out around them on the ground. People in North America have grown pumpkins and squash for thousands of years.

Other vegetables in the cucumber family are of Indian and African descent. Cucumbers *(Cucumis sativus)* originally were grown 3,000 years ago in India, and it was said that their growth depended on the virility of the grower. I'm not going to get into that; anyone can grow cucumbers!

Melons *(Cucumis melo)* and watermelons *(Citrullus lanatus)* originally are from West Africa and were first grown 4,000 years ago. All the vegetables in the cucumber family spread throughout the world wherever the ground was fertile and the weather was hot.

# Cool Cukes

Cucumber varieties usually are categorized two ways: as slicers and picklers. Slicing-cucumber varieties (also called slicers) are long, smooth-skinned cucumbers that tend to be larger, a darker shade of green, and have thicker skin with fewer bumps (spines) than pickling varieties, which are short and prickly. Slicing cucumbers are the ones you're probably most familiar with from grocery stores; they're great in salads and other recipes, or just to munch. Of course, you can use pickling varieties the same ways you use slicing varieties, and they're great when eaten fresh, but if you want to make pickles, the pickling varieties have better textures for it.

The easiest cucumber varieties to grow are the hybrid bush types. These newer varieties, such as 'Salad Bush,' are good producers, have good disease resistance, and produce a small vining plant that can grow in a container. Bush types don't produce as many cucumbers as larger vining varieties, nor do they produce them all summer long. But if you have a small family, a few bush varieties is plenty.

To round out the cucumber field, I describe some unusual *heirloom* (old-fashioned) varieties and some modern, seedless cucumber varieties that produce fruit without pollination (see the section "Birds and the bees: Ensuring proper pollination," later in this chapter). If you plant one of these seedless varieties (these varieties actually have seeds, but the seeds are not developed), avoid planting any other cucumber varieties in your garden. If a seedless variety gets pollinated by bees, edible but seedy fruits will result. For that reason, gardeners often grow these varieties in greenhouses, which protect the plants from bees.

And now for a bit of vining vocabulary. When you're reading about cucumber varieties, you may notice some words — such as *gherkin* and *gynoecious* (guy-NEE-shous) — that would challenge even the best Scrabble player. Fortunately, you don't need to memorize these terms to grow good cucumbers, but they do enable you to figure out the type of cucumber that you're buying — as well as impress your friends!

- **Burpless:** This thin-skinned cucumber type has a long, slender shape and a mild, non-bitter flavor. It's said to produce less intestinal gas than other varieties.

- **Gherkin:** Actually, this type is a whole different species of cucumber *(Cucumis anguria)*. It's used commercially as a pickling cucumber. Gherkins have small, oval shapes and prickly skin. As far as the home gardener is concerned, this species difference has no effect.

- **Gynoecious:** This type of cucumber has only female flowers and requires the presence of a male pollinating cucumber variety to produce fruit. Usually, seed companies include seeds of a pollinating variety in packets of gynoecious cucumbers; the seeds are marked with a bright colored coating.

- **Monoecious:** This cucumber type has both male and female flowers on the same plant. Most cucumber varieties are of this type.

- **Oriental cucumbers:** This type of cucumber tends to be a thin, long-fruited variety with ribbing on its skin.

- **Parthenocarpic:** This cucumber type is seedless, producing fruit without pollination. Varieties of this type produce only female flowers and need to be separated from other cucumber varieties. Otherwise, if they're pollinated, they may produce misshapen fruits and form fruits with seeds. (You can still eat them; they'll just look funny.) This cucumber type is often grown in greenhouses.

Now that you know a bit of the language, take a look at some of my favorite cucumber varieties. Most of these varieties vine 4 to 5 feet unless I note otherwise. The days to maturity are from seeding in the ground until first harvest:

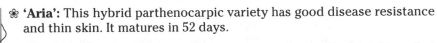

- ❀ **'Aria':** This hybrid parthenocarpic variety has good disease resistance and thin skin. It matures in 52 days.

- ❀ **'Bush Pickle':** This bush, pickling variety produces 4-inch pickles all at once on 2- to 3-foot-diameter plants that mature in 50 days.

- ❀ **'County Fair':** This hybrid pickling variety is best known for its disease resistance, especially to bacterial wilt (see "Controlling pests and diseases," later in this chapter). It matures in 50 days.

❀ **'Fanfare':** This All-America Selections winner is a hybrid slicing cucumber that grows on a semi-bush plant. It vines to 4 feet, has lots of disease resistance, and produces 8-inch fruits. It matures in 63 days.

❀ **'Lemon':** This unique heirloom variety produces yellow, lemon-shaped fruits that are crisp and mild flavored. This slicer matures in 64 days.

❀ **'Marketmore 86':** This widely adapted slicing variety has good disease resistance and produces lots of fruits. It matures in 68 days.

❀ **'Salad Bush':** This All-America Selections winner is a slicing, bush variety that needs only 2 square feet to produce its 8-inch fruits. It matures in 57 days.

❀ **'Suyo Long':** This unusual Oriental-type slicing cucumber is also burpless and produces 15-inch fruits. It matures in 61 days.

❀ **'Sweet Success':** This All-America Selections winner is a slicing, parthenocarpic variety with tender skin and good disease resistance. It matures in 54 days.

❀ **'Wisconsin SMR-18':** This pickling-cucumber variety is highly productive and disease resistant. It matures in 56 days.

Regular production of cucumbers is about 12 pounds per 10-foot row (about 10 cukes per plant). Choose varieties based on disease-resistance, size, productivity, and adaptability.

# Many, Many Melons

Many people think that melons are fruits, but technically they're vegetables. Compared to cucumbers with their various sexual combinations and vine lengths, melons are, well, easy. They all have separate male and female flowers on each plant *(monoecious),* and they all need about 6 to 8 feet of space to vine. Many different types of melons with many unique flavors are available. A number of melons can be harvested on the unripe side and mature off the vine, still producing their sweet flavor. See the harvesting section of this chapter for more on harvesting melons.

Most gardeners are familiar with the two most popular types of melons: muskmelons (also known as cantaloupes) and watermelons. But more and more exotic melon types continue to show up in produce markets and seed catalogs. These exotic types include crenshaw, honeydew, and charentais. They're similar to muskmelons, but they offer a tropical, juicy flavor. Watermelons come in the traditional "let's have a picnic" oblong shape as well as the more compact, round shape (also called an icebox shape). Yellow-fleshed and seedless watermelon varieties also are available. And you thought all melons are alike!

Melons tend to weigh between 2 and 5 pounds, but watermelons can run from 8 pounds to between 20 and 30 pounds.

When is a cantaloupe not a cantaloupe? When it's a *muskmelon.* The round, netted, tan-colored, orange-fleshed fruits that you see in grocery stores usually are sold as "cantaloupes." However, true cantaloupes are tropical fruits that have green flesh and hard skin and are rarely seen in this country. What people from the United States refer to as cantaloupes technically are muskmelons.

Here's a description of some specialty melons:

❀ **Charentais:** This traditional French melon has modern varieties that look like muskmelons. It has deep orange flesh and a honeylike flavor.

❀ **Crenshaw:** This salmon-fleshed, oval-shaped melon with dark green skin turns mottled yellow when ripe. It needs a long season (about four months) to mature.

❀ **Honeydew:** This sweet, juicy melon has smooth tan skin and pale green flesh; unlike other melons, it doesn't continue to ripen off the vine. These melons store longer than muskmelons.

❀ **Mediterranean:** This type of melon is also known as Israeli, Galia, or Middle Eastern. It's part of a large group of tropical melons that generally have yellow skin when mature, and sweet, aromatic, pale green or white flesh.

Like all cucumber-family crops, melons need warmth, water, space, and sun. For those reasons, they grow well in the Southeast and the Southwest United States. But with the right variety selection and some growing tricks (see the "Growing Those Vines" section later in this chapter), cool-climate gardeners can also enjoy these sweet, juicy fruits The days to maturity are from seeding in the garden until first harvest. Here are some popular muskmelon varieties:

❀ **'Alaska':** This early hybrid muskmelon variety grows well in areas with short growing seasons. It produces 4-pound fruits in 70 days.

❀ **'Ambrosia':** This hybrid 5-pound muskmelon has sweet, salmon-colored flesh and has good resistance to powdery mildew disease. It matures in 86 days.

❀ **'Early Crenshaw':** This hybrid early-maturing crenshaw-type melon produces 14-pound fruits with mild-flavored, peach-colored flesh. It matures in 90 days. (I think of it as a delicate-tasting morsel, myself.)

❀ **'Earli-Dew':** This early-maturing hybrid honeydew-type melon has lime green flesh and produces 2- to 4-pound fruits. It matures in 85 days.

❀ **'Earliqueen':** This hybrid 3- to 4-pound muskmelon variety has thick, orange flesh. It matures in 70 days.

❀ **'French Orange':** A cross between the French charentais and a muskmelon, this hybrid 2- to 4-pound melon has aromatic, deep orange flesh and good disease resistance. It matures in 75 days.

❀ **'Passport':** This hybrid Mediterranean-type, 5- to 6-pound melon has light green flesh. It has good disease resistance and is widely adapted. It matures in 73 days.

The following are popular watermelon varieties:

❀ **'Crimson Sweet':** This oval-shaped watermelon variety produces sweet, red-fleshed, 25-pound fruits and has good disease resistance. It matures in 90 days.

❀ **'King of Hearts':** This hybrid, seedless, oval-shaped watermelon variety produces 15-pound, oval-shaped fruits. It matures in 82 days.

❀ **'Moon and Stars':** This heirloom oblong-shaped watermelon features dark green skin with yellow "moon and stars" markings (squint, and you can see them — or what passes for them) and has very sweet, pink flesh. It matures in 95 days.

❀ **'Sugar Baby':** This round, compact watermelon variety produces icebox-size (8- to 10-pound) fruits. It matures in 85 days.

❀ **'Yellow Doll':** This hybrid, oval-shaped, yellow-fleshed watermelon produces 4- to 8-pound fruits. It matures in 70 days.

Seedless watermelon varieties may germinate more slowly than other varieties, especially in cool ( below 65°F) soils.

# Squash Standards

Squash may not be as glamorous as their melon cousins, but boy can they produce. Whether you're growing summer squash or winter squash, they'll produce an abundance of fruit and flowers with seemingly little attention. Just ask any gardener friend who has grown zucchini before, and he or she will attest to how prolific these vegetables are.

One way to slow production is actually to eat the flowers. They taste great sautéed with olive oil and garlic, along with some Italian bread.

The first order of business is to define all the different types of squash:

✔ Summer squash are bush-type plants whose fruits are harvested when they're tender and immature.

Summer squash usually are separated into yellow, straight, or crookneck varieties; green zucchini varieties; or green-, white-, or yellow-skinned, scallop-shaped, "patty-pan" fruits, as shown in Figure 8-1.

**Figure 8-1:**
A scalloped or " patty-pan" summer squash, so named because the fruits look like crimped pie pans.

(They got their names because the fruits resemble the pie shells used in England for baking vegetable, meat, or fish "patties.") Summer squash usually mature within two months of planting and will continue to produce all season long. Summer squash don't store well, however.

✔ Winter squash are mostly vining-type plants whose fruits are harvested when they're fully mature. They mature after three months or more of growing and are best harvested after the cool, fall weather sets in. You can store them for months in a cool basement — hence the name *winter* squash. They are also good for baking.

You can easily get lost in the maze of winter squash types, so here is a quick list of the most popular types. I include the botanical names too, for you Latin buffs.

❀ **Acorn** *(Cucurbita pepo):* This squash type has black, dark green, or white skin and an acorn-shaped, ribbed fruit. It also has pale yellow flesh.

❀ **Buttercup** *(Cucurbita maxima):* This green or orange, turban-shaped type has a "button" on the end of its fruits. It has dry, orange flesh.

❀ **Butternut** *(Cucurbita moschata):* This bottle-shaped squash has smooth, tan-colored skin at maturity and has moist, orange flesh.

❀ **Delicata** *(Cucurbita pepo):* This small, green- and yellow-striped, zucchini-shaped squash has sweet, pale yellow flesh.

❀ **Hubbard** *(Cucurbita maxima):* This large, blue or green, oval-shaped squash has a long neck and dry yellow or orange flesh.

❀ **Kabocha** *(Cucurbita maxima):* This buttercup-like squash has drier and sweeter flesh than other types. It's the latest winter squash craze.

❀ **Spaghetti** *(Cucurbita pepo):* This oblong, tan-colored squash has yellow flesh with a stringy texture.

Keep your squash areas weeded and watered, and you'll be rewarded with super squash. Just remember to give these squash room to grow. Summer squash varieties tend to stay in a bush form, but they still need a few feet to spread out. And even though winter squash do come in bush forms, most of the best-flavored varieties have at least 6-foot vines.

The following lists of summer and winter squash varieties include some of my favorites; they're easy to grow, produce well consistently, and have a sweet flavor. The days to maturity are from seeding in the garden until first harvest.

The following are my favorite summer squash varieties:

❀ **'Black Zucchini':** This standard zucchini-type variety produces tons of dark green, slender fruits on bush plants. Zucchinis also can be yellow-colored such as the 'Butterstick' variety. This variety matures in 53 days.

❀ **'Butterbar':** This hybrid, straightneck, yellow summer squash produces tons of golden-yellow fruits. (Straightneck fruits are shaped straight from beginning to tip.) 'Butterbar' matures in 49 days.

❀ **'Cocozelle':** This Italian heirloom zucchini has green and white stripes and a good flavor.

❀ **'Sunburst':** This hybrid, yellow-skinned, summer squash has tender, scallop-shaped fruits. It takes 50 days to mature.

❀ **'Yellow Crookneck':** This smooth, yellow-skinned, crookneck squash has a delicate texture and flavor. (Crookneck squash have a bent top, or neck.) It takes 50 days to mature.

For an unusual shaped zucchini-type summer squash, try the round, tennis-ball-size 'Roly Poly' or 'Ronde de Nice' squash. You grow these varieties similar to the way you grow other summer squash (which I discuss in the "Growing Those Vines" section of this chapter), and their round fruits are great sautéed, or stuffed and baked.

Good winter squash varieties include:

- ❀ **'Blue Hubbard':** This 12- to 20-pound winter squash has dry, sweet, yellow flesh and a very hard shell. It's especially great for storage and baking and matures in 100 days.

- ❀ **'Burgess Buttercup':** This 3- to 5-pound winter squash has sweet, fiberless, orange flesh. Fiberless flesh is not stringy. This variety is one of my personal favorites. (It's sweet flavor and dry flesh taste great with a little maple syrup mixed in!) It matures in 95 days.

- ❀ **'Cream of the Crop':** This All-America-Selections-winning hybrid acorn squash features 3-pound fruits with white skin and golden flesh on a bush-type plant. It matures in 85 days.

- ❀ **'Delicata':** This 8-inch winter squash has sweet orange flesh and grows on a semi-bush plant (it doesn't vine as far as other squash; the plant is only 4 to 6 feet in diameter). I love to eat this variety baked. It takes 100 days to mature.

- ❀ **'Hokkori':** This hybrid kabocha-type winter squash produces 4-pound fruits with sweet, dry, flaky, deep orange flesh. It takes 95 days to mature.

- ❀ **'Spaghetti':** This ivory-skinned, yellow-fleshed, 4- to 5-pound winter squash has stringy, spaghetti-like flesh. Try this one baked and covered with pasta sauce! It takes 88 days to mature.

- ❀ **'Table King':** This 6-inch-diameter, green-skinned, acorn winter squash grows on a bush plant. It takes 80 days to mature. A similar gold-colored variety is called 'Table Gold.'

- ❀ **'Waltham Butternut':** This variety produces light tan, 5-pound fruits that have smooth-textured orange flesh. It takes 105 days to mature.

# The Great Pumpkins: Squash with Culture

Pumpkins are *the* quintessential fall crop in many areas, and most peoples' favorite winter squash. (Yes, pumpkins are squashes, too. Most pumpkin varieties are in the *Cucurbita pepo* species, directly related to acorn- and spaghetti-type winter squash.) Pumpkins are used in pies and soups and casseroles or carved into ghoulish shapes on Halloween. Even their seeds are edible!

Because people are so interested in pumpkins, modern breeders have created many different varieties. Some varieties are great for carving into jack-o'-lanterns, some are bred for cooking, and still others are known for their tasty seeds. My daughter Elena loves when the family roasts a batch of 'Trick or Treat,' naked-hulled (thin hull) pumpkin seeds because they pop like popcorn. (You can bake any pumpkin seeds, but in my opinion, the hulless types are best for flavor and crunchiness; in case you're wondering, the hull is the coat of the seed.) Other types of pumpkin, like 'Atlantic Giant,' are bred to win awards; they can grow to such huge sizes that they could practically break a truck's suspension. Pumpkins are grown similar to winter squash and require plenty of space to vine. Here are a few of the most popular pumpkin varieties:

❀ **'Atlantic Giant':** This is the pumpkin that sets world records. Technically, it's called a *Cucurbita maxima* (similar to hubbard squash). It requires lots of water, heat, and fertilizer to reach the mammoth 1,000-pound, world-record size. This variety looks like a flat tire when it matures, and even though your pumpkin may not weigh 1,000 pounds, even a few hundred pounds is a lot of pumpkin. 'Atlantic Giant' takes 115 days to mature. This is one large vine.

❀ **'Baby Bear':** This is the smallest pumpkin variety. 'Baby Bear' is an All-America-Selections-winning, 2-pound, minipumpkin that's great for cooking, and its semi-naked (thin-hulled) seeds taste great roasted. This variety matures in 105 days.

❀ **'Connecticut Field':** This 20-pound, flat-bottomed, jack-o'-lantern pumpkin is great for carving and baking. It matures on large vines in 115 days.

❀ **'Lumina':** This unusual, white-skinned, orange-fleshed, 20-pound pumpkin can be made into a ghostly looking jack-o'-lantern. It takes 95 days to mature.

❀ **'Rouge Vif d'Etampes':** (Also known as 'Cinderella.') This attractive, red-skinned, French pumpkin variety is in the *Cucurbita maxima* species. The 10-pound fruits are short and squat (like a wheel of cheese) and are good in pies. It takes 115 days to mature.

❀ **'Small Sugar':** Known as *the* pumpkin for pies, this 4- to 6-pound variety features smooth-textured flesh and a small seed cavity. It takes 95 days to mature.

❀ **'Trick or Treat':** This popular pumpkin is grown especially for its naked seeds, which are great roasted. You also can carve this 8-pound pumpkin and use its flesh in a pie or bake it. The seeds of this all-purpose pumpkin are slower and more finicky about germinating than other pumpkin varieties. (Wait until the soil is 65°F to plant; you may want to start it indoors for three to four weeks before planting outside.) This variety takes 110 days to mature.

To find out how to grow giant pumpkins and details about the yearly competition, contact the World Pumpkin Confederation, 14050 Rt. 62, Collins, New York, 14034. For more on pumpkin-growing, check out this Web site: www.athenet.net/~dang/pumpkins.html#Organizations.

# Growing Those Vines

Warmth, water, and proper pollination are the keys to growing cucumber-family crops. Because these vegetables love the heat, you don't need to rush the season and plant early. Wait until your soil temperature is at least 60°F at seeding depth before planting these vegetables. If you live in zones 3 or 4 and have a very short growing season, you may want to start cucumbers, melons, and squash indoors three to four weeks before your last frost date or buy transplants at a garden center. But if you live in other climate zones, sowing seeds directly in your garden should work fine.

To get a jump on the season in cool areas (zones 3 and 4, though zones 5 and 6 can also benefit), lay black plastic mulch on your soil a week or two before planting to heat up the soil (see Chapter 15 for details). In warm areas such as southern Florida and Texas, you can even start a spring crop of cucumbers or summer squash. Pull out the plants when the summer heat, insects, and diseases become too intense; then plant a fall crop in August to mature three or four months later. (In hot areas, you can have two crops in one year.)

If you don't have a lot of room in your garden (viners require 4 to 6 feet) but really want to grow pumpkins, melons, and vining varieties of squash, try these space-saving techniques:

- ✔ Pinch off the tips of the vines after the fruits have set to keep them from extending too far.
- ✔ Physically pick up the vines and direct them back toward the plant.
- ✔ Plant along the edge of your garden so that the vines run into your lawn. That way you don't have to mow as much lawn, either.
- ✔ Grow cucumbers and melons on an A-frame trellis (see Chapter 15 for trellising options), which helps plants grow straighter and stay cleaner. You may need to support melons with a nylon or fabric sling, shown in Figure 8-2, after they form.

## Planting and feeding

When reading about cucumber-family crops, you may see references to planting in *hills*. This word is really a misnomer. It means planting four or six seeds in a 1-foot-diameter circle. After germination, you thin these seedlings to two plants per hill.

Cucumber-family seeds are large, easy to plant, and quick to germinate, and they grow well in warm soil. Plant seeds about 1 inch deep in the soil, and space them far enough apart so that vining types have room to ramble. For

**Figure 8-2:**
Support
your
trellised
melons with
a sling as
soon as the
fruits form.

vining varieties of cucumbers, melons, squash, and pumpkins, plant the *hills* at least 6 to 10 feet apart. For bush varieties, plant seeds about 2 to 4 feet apart. Follow the spacing guidelines for individual vegetables in the appendix.

This vegetable family responds better than any other family to extra doses of manure and compost. Cucumber-family crops love organic matter, so add a generous 4- to 6-inch-thick layer of compost to each planting bed. Sometimes pumpkin plants vine out of old compost or manure piles, which is evidence of how much this vegetable family loves manure. If you don't have a source for manure or compost, work in a handful of balanced organic or chemical fertilizers, such as 5-10-10, around each plant. Add a side-dressing of the same fertilizer after the plants begin vining to help increase the fruit count and size. See Chapter 15 for details about side-dressing and fertilizer.

You also can plant cucumber-family crops in rows, but the hill method is better with the vining types because it enables you to thin the weakest plants and not throw off the spacing between the remaining plants. If you're using black plastic mulch (necessary in cool areas), your best option is to plant in rows.

## Water, water, water

Cucumber-family crops are like camels; they're almost 95 percent water at maturity. Without a consistent supply of water, your melons won't taste sweet, and your cucumbers will taste bitter. To get the best-sized and best-tasting cucumber, melon, and squash crops, give your plants a consistent supply of water. The general rule is to water so that the soil is wet 6 inches deep. If you're growing your crops with black plastic mulch, consider placing a soaker hose or drip irrigation hose underneath the plastic to ensure that the water gets to the plants. (See Chapter 15 for more watering ideas.) After the soil has warmed, mulch around the plants with a 3- to 4-inch-thick layer of hay or straw to help conserve moisture and keep weeds away. (You don't need to mulch with hay if you're using black plastic.)

If you want the sweetest melons, water consistently until a week or so before maturity and then reduce your frequency of watering; the melon fruits will have less water and taste sweeter.

The great thing about this group of vining crops is that after they start growing and running to their hearts delight, they shade the ground, preventing weeds from germinating and keeping the soil moist. They're their own best friends!

## *The birds and bees: Ensuring proper pollination*

Proper pollination is another key to growing successful cucumber-family crop, which can pose particular problems. Because most cucumber-family vegetables have separate male and female flowers on the same plant, they need Mother Nature's help to pollinate the female flowers and produce fruit.

Most of the problems that I hear from gardeners — like zucchini rotting before it starts growing, too few fruits on squash plants, and misshapen cucumber fruits — are due to poor pollination. Bees are the problem: Honeybees, bumblebees, and many other wild bees carry out pollination, but they're finicky. Bees don't fly if the weather is cloudy or too cool. Also, native bee populations are declining because mites are destroying them. Fewer bees mean fewer chances that your flowers will be pollinated. And each cucumber-family crop flower opens for only one day.

So what's a gardener to do? Either try to attract bees to your garden by growing a variety of flowers and herbs or else pollinate the flowers yourself!

Here's a simple way to pollinate crops if you're having trouble getting fruit. And no, you don't have to buzz around and dress up in a bee costume to fool the plants:

1. **Identify the male and female flowers on your plant (see Figure 8-3).**

   Don't be discouraged if you don't see female flowers at first. Male flowers form about a week ahead of the females. The female flowers will come along; just be patient.

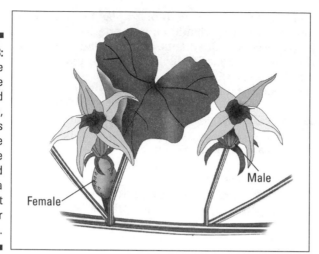

Female

Male

2. **Before noon on the morning that the male flower first opens, pick the male flower and then remove the petals to reveal the sexual parts of the flower (the stamen), which contain the yellow pollen.**

   You use this male flower to pollinate a female flower from the same variety of plant. For example, don't try to use a cucumber flower to pollinate a pumpkin plant.

3. **Choose a female flower that has also just opened and swish the stamen around inside that flower. Repeat this process with other female flowers, using the same male flower for two to three pollinations.**

   Voilà; you've done it. Congratulations, have a cigar!

If your squash and pumpkins are growing close together, and bees cross-pollinate them, will you get a *squakin?* Not this year at least. Cross-pollination happens when the pollen from one variety or type of plant goes to a different variety or type of plant. Only the same species of *Cucurbits* can cross-pollinate each other. For example, a cucumber can't cross-pollinate a pumpkin. However, squash (such as an acorn and zucchini type) and pumpkins in the same species can cross-pollinate each other. (You can tell the species by looking at the second word in the plant's botanical name.) However, this cross-pollination won't affect your crop for this year. Your acorn squash will still look and taste like an acorn squash, even if it was pollinated by a pumpkin flower. However, if you save the squash seed and plant it the following year, you may get an interesting creation. But that's why gardening is fun!

## Harvesting your vining crop

One of the keys to a good cucumber-family crop is harvesting the fruits at the right time:

- Cucumbers are best when harvested small: slicers when they're 6-inches long and picklers when they're 4-inches long.

  If they grow too large and begin to turn yellow, then the seeds inside the cucumber are maturing, and the plant will stop producing flowers and fruits. Pick off and throw away any large fruits that you missed so that you can keep the young ones coming.

- Summer squash should be harvested as small as possible, even if the flower is still attached! This will help you avoid the glut of zucchinis that always happens by midsummer, and you can enjoy the tender flavor of young squash.

- You can harvest winter squash and pumpkins after they change to the expected color of their variety and after their skin is thick enough that your thumbnail can't puncture the fruits when you press on them. If you want to store winter squash and pumpkins through the fall and winter (see Chapter 19 for storage tips), don't let them get nipped by frost, or they'll rot. Leave 2 inches of the stem attached for best storing.

Melons are another matter. Deciding when to harvest muskmelons and watermelons can be tricky. It's frustrating to grow a great crop of melons and then pick them either too soon or too late. With muskmelons, after their skin color turns from green to tan and the netting (the ribbing on the skin that's slightly raised) becomes more pronounced, gently lift the melons up. If they're ripe, the fruits will slip, or easily detach, from the vine. If you're not sure, harvesting early rather than late is better because most melons continue to ripen off the vine.

With watermelons, harvesting is a bit more complicated. Here are some tips to follow:

- **Watch for changing colors:** Two signs that it may be time to harvest watermelons are when the skin color turns from shiny to dull and when the color of the spot where the watermelon rests on the ground turns from white to yellow.

- **Thump the watermelons:** This is definitely one of those techniques that takes practice. I love watching the old-time gardeners thump watermelons with their fingers to figure out when they're ripe. Whether this test is consistently accurate is another story. If you want to become an expert, here's what to look for: Unripe watermelons have a sharp sound, and ripe ones have a muffled sound. The rest is experience. Good luck!

✓ **Look for brown tendrils:** The surest way to tell whether your water-melons are ripe is to look at their tendrils. *Tendrils* are the little curli-cues coming off the stems that attach to whatever weeds and plants are around. When the tendril closest to the ripening watermelon turns brown, it's harvest time.

## Controlling pests and diseases

Keeping a good vine crop down is tough. Once established, vining crops don't have any more pest problems than other vegetables. Modern, disease-resistant varieties help ward off fungi, bacteria, and viruses. However, you still need to watch out for powdery and downy mildew, wilt, and viruses that affect all vegetables (see Chapter 18). Also, stay out of the vine crop patch when the leaves are wet because you can easily spread disease. Common insect pests, such as aphids and cutworms, attack young plants. Here are a few diseases and pests that particularly love vining crops:

✓ **Anthracnose:** This fungus attacks many vegetables, but it especially loves cucumbers, muskmelons, and watermelons. During warm, humid conditions, the leaves develop yellow or black circular spots, and fruits develop sunken spots with dark borders. To slow this disease, space plants a few feet further apart than normal so that the leaves dry quickly in the morning. Also, destroy infected leaves and fruits. Rotate crops yearly to avoid this disease.

✓ **Bacterial wilt:** This devastating bacterial disease is found mainly on cucumbers and muskmelons. Sure signs of the disease are well-watered plants that wilt during the day but recover at night. Eventually, the plants will wilt and die. If you cut open a dead vine, the sap will be sticky and white. To control this disease, control the cucumber beetle, which is the pest that spreads bacterial wilt in your garden. See the following bullet for more on this pesky beetle.

✓ **Cucumber beetle:** This ¹⁄₄-inch-long, yellow- and black-striped (or spotted) adult beetle, shown in Figure 8-4, feeds on all cucumber-family crops. The adults feed on the leaves, and the young larvae feed on the roots.

Cucumber beetles are the chief culprits for spreading bacterial wilt and virus diseases, and they especially devastate young plants. To control cucumber beetles, cover young plants with a floating row cover (a cheesecloth-like material that keeps insects out but lets in air, light, and water; see Chapter 22 for details) as soon as they emerge, and then after flowering, remove it so that bees can pollinate the flowers. Also apply a botanical spray such as pyrethrin on the adult beetles.

✓ **Squash bug:** These ¹⁄₂-inch-long, brown or gray bugs love to attack squash and pumpkins, especially late in the growing season. The adults and smaller-sized young feed on leaves and stems, sucking out the plant juices. These insects move in packs, and their feeding can quickly

**Figure 8-4:**
Cucumber beetles not only feed on cucumbers, but on melon plants, too.

stunt your plants. Squash bugs usually start laying eggs when the plants begin to vine. To control these pests, crush the masses of reddish-brown eggs on the underside of leaves. Also, rotate crops and clean up plant debris in fall where the squash bugs overwinter.

✔ **Squash vine borer:** This pest mostly affects squash and pumpkin plants. In early summer, the adult moths lay their eggs on stems near the plants' bases. After the eggs hatch, white caterpillars with brown heads tunnel into the plants' stems to feed. They can cause well watered vines to wilt during the day and eventually die. Look for entry holes and the sawdustlike droppings at the base of your plants to see if vine borers are present. To control these pests, slit your plant's stem lengthwise from the entry hole toward the tip of the vine with a sharp razor, and physically remove the caterpillar. Then cover the stem with soil; it will reroot itself. Or, you can cover the plants with a floating row cover until they begin to flower, which keeps the moths from laying their eggs. A third option is to inject Bt (*Bacillus thurengiensis;* a naturally-occurring bacterium that attacks only caterpillar-family insects) into the stem with a syringe to kill any caterpillars. Consider growing butternut squash, which is less susceptible to vine borers.

Speaking of desserts, how about some pumpkin pie? This classic pumpkin pie recipe is rich and creamy and loaded with the traditional pumpkin spices of nutmeg, cinnamon, and ginger. Alter the spicing to suit your individual taste.

# Health Tips and a Recipe

Although cucumber-family fruits contain mostly water, they also contain key vitamins and minerals. All the vegetables in this family are high in vitamins A and C and fiber (particularly high in melons and squash), and they add small amounts of calcium and iron to your diet. Melons and cucumbers are the easiest to prepare because they taste best when eaten fresh in salads. You can cook squash and pumpkins as side dishes, main courses, or even desserts.

## Classic Pumpkin Pie

**Tools:** *Measuring cups and spoons, two bowls, pie tin, oven*

**Preparation time:** *30 minutes*

**Baking time:** *60 minutes*

**Yield:** *8 servings*

| | |
|---|---|
| *8 ounces of cream cheese* | *$1/2$ cup sugar* |
| *$1/4$ cup sugar* | *$1^1/4$ teaspoon cinnamon* |
| *$1/2$ teaspoon vanilla* | *$1/3$ teaspoon ginger* |
| *1 egg, beaten* | *$1^1/2$ teaspoon nutmeg* |
| *1 unbaked, premade pie crust* | *1 cup evaporated milk* |
| *$1^1/2$ cups cooked pumpkin* | *2 eggs* |

**1** Preheat the oven to 350°F.

**2** Combine the softened cream cheese, sugar, and vanilla, and then add the beaten egg. Spread this mixture in the bottom of the pie crust.

**3** Mix in the remaining ingredients by hand or with a mixer, whichever you prefer, and then pour the mixture over the cream cheese layer.

**4** Bake for 1 hour. Cool. For an extra treat, try brushing the top with maple syrup and pecans.

# Chapter 9

# King Cole Crops: Cauliflower, Cabbage, Broccoli, and Brussels Sprouts

. . . . . . . . . . . . . . . . . . . . . . . . . . . . . . . . . . . . . . . . . .

### In This Chapter

▶ Tracking the history of cole crops

▶ Selecting cole crop varieties

▶ Caring for your cole crops, from planting to harvesting

▶ Preventing pests

▶ Creating a simple yet sensational slaw

. . . . . . . . . . . . . . . . . . . . . . . . . . . . . . . . . . . . . . . . . .

*C*ole is the German word for cabbage, hence the terms *cole crops* and *cole slaw*. Given this German etymology, it's probably no surprise that the histories of most cole crops are rooted in foreign soil — indeed, wild relatives of cabbage, broccoli, and cauliflower can still be found along the Atlantic and Mediterranean coasts of Europe.

Cabbage, one of the first domesticated crops, is of Western European origin, dating back to the Greeks and Romans. Broccoli and cauliflower hail from the balmier climes of southern Europe; broccoli was brought to Italy in the seventeenth century, and cauliflower made it there in the fifteenth century. Brussels sprouts, developed less than 500 years ago, are mere youngsters in comparison. They're believed to have been discovered in the fourteenth century growing near Brussels, Belgium — hence their name. Most of these European natives were slow to spread around the world, only becoming popular in the United States in the 1920s. However, with the advent of salad bars and a growing interest in eating more fresh vegetables, consumption of two particular cole crops — broccoli and cauliflower — took off.

In this chapter, I discuss several major cole crops, including broccoli, Brussels sprouts, cauliflower, and the king of the cole crops, cabbage. Other related but less popular cole crops such as collards, kale, kohlrabi, and Chinese cabbage are covered in Chapter 11. All fall in the *Brassica oleracea* botanical family.

# Choosing Cole Crops

There's nothing glamorous about cole crops. They aren't as colorful, succulent, or sensuous as tomatoes or melons. Cole crops are simply rugged, tough, good-for-you plants. Just look at variety names such as 'Snow Crown' cauliflower and 'Stonehead' cabbage, and you get the picture.

Cole crops don't appear on the covers of most gardening magazines, but they're reliable staples in any vegetable garden nonetheless. Given cool conditions, fertile soil, and proper watering, these plants produce lots of nutritious and delicious vegetables.

Many people — including a former president — still haven't warmed up to cole crops. I don't understand this aversion. Cole crops are tasty, easy to grow, and capable of producing over long periods of time. Plus, with the exploding interest in eating nutritious foods and the discovery of the great potential health benefits of broccoli and other vegetables in its family (see "Health Tips and a Recipe," later in this chapter), more and more people are dipping, steaming, and stir-frying their way to health with cole crops. (If you need some culinary guidance, try the tasty cole slaw recipe at the end of this chapter.)

## Betting on broccoli

Broccoli is one of the easiest cole crops to grow, and it's one that's close to my heart. Like my ancestors, broccoli hails from Italy. My mother and I still enjoy a good meal of garlic sautéed in olive oil and tossed with broccoli, accompanied by a loaf of fresh Italian bread. She likes the smaller-headed, old-fashioned, sprouting broccoli varieties such as 'DeCicco,' whose stems and leaves are so tender that they're eaten along with the head.

Modern broccoli varieties have been bred to form one large main head. This head is simply a tight cluster of flower buds. Once the main head is cut off, multiple side branches and mini heads form along the plant. In most areas, the side branches and mini heads continue to form until the plant is killed by frost, insects, or disease, so from one plant, you can harvest right through summer, fall, and winter (if your climate is warm enough).

Choosing the right broccoli variety for your garden depends on a number of factors, including where you live and what you plan to do with the crop. Here are a few guidelines to follow when choosing a broccoli variety:

- ✔ If you plan to stock up for the winter by freezing broccoli heads, choose a variety with large heads that mature mostly at the same time. Try 'Green Comet' or 'Premium Crop.'

✔ Broccoli, like all cole crops, likes cool weather. Warm weather makes the heads flower too quickly, resulting in a bitter flavor. Gardeners in warm climates should choose varieties that withstand heat or mature early, before the heat of summer. 'Packman' is a good choice.

✔ If you want a long, steady production of small but tender side shoots, choose an old-fashioned variety with good side-shoot production, such as Mom's favorite, 'DeCicco.'

✔ If you live in a humid climate (such as Dallas) or a coastal area that has lots of fog and mist (such as San Francisco), broccoli heads can rot before maturing. Choose varieties with added disease resistance and tightly clustered flower heads that shed water easily, such as 'Arcadia.'

Here's a list of some of the best broccoli varieties to grow. The days to maturity number listed for each variety refers to the number of days from transplanting a seedling into the garden until the harvest of the main head. If you sow the seeds directly into the garden, add another 20 days to estimate the maturity date. Of course, the actual number of days will vary depending on weather and soil conditions. All plants listed reach about 1- to 2-feet tall:

❀ **'Arcadia':** A large, 8-inch-diameter, blue-green colored head is formed high on stems above the foliage, making this variety easier to harvest than other broccoli varieties. 'Arcadia' is a hybrid variety (see Chapter 1 for more on hybrids), so it's a vigorous grower, producing uniform-sized heads and having excellent disease resistance. It's also tender and tasty. (63 days to maturity)

❀ **'DeCicco':** This heirloom, old-fashioned Italian variety produces a 3-inch-diameter main head and multiple side shoots and has tender leaves and stems. (48 days to maturity)

❀ **'Early Dividend':** This hybrid variety combines early maturity with a large, 8-inch-diameter main head and lots of side shoots. (43 days to maturity)

❀ **'Green Comet':** This early-maturing hybrid broccoli was an All-America Selections winner (see Chapter 4 for a discussion of this award). The plant produces a 6-inch-diameter head and is very tolerant of diseases and weather stress. (58 days to maturity)

❀ **'Minaret Romanesco':** Another heirloom, this broccoli variety produces spiral-shaped clusters of flower buds in a 5-inch-diameter, yellow- to light-green colored main head. The texture of the head is almost nutlike. (85 days to maturity)

❀ **'Packman':** A hybrid, this variety produces a 9-inch-diameter main head earlier than other large-headed varieties such as 'Premium Crop.' It also has excellent side-shoot production. (52 days to maturity)

❀ **'Premium Crop':** An All-America Selections winner, this hybrid broccoli produces a large, 9-inch-diameter head late in the season, but it's slow to flower, so you don't have to rush to pick it. (62 days to maturity)

❀ **'Purple Sprouting':** This Italian heirloom produces a 2-foot-tall plant with multiple small, 3-inch-diameter purple heads late in the season. It's best grown in cool northern areas to mature in late fall, or, in mild-winter climates, you can plant it in fall and grow it through the winter to mature in early spring (see the section "Planting Cole Crops," later in this chapter, for planting tips). The head turns green upon cooking. (125 days to maturity)

Have you ever tasted broccoflower? Brocco what? It's *broccoflower:* a cross between broccoli and cauliflower. You've probably seen this in grocery stores. It looks like cauliflower, but it has a light-green-colored head. The flavor is also a mix, sweeter than broccoli but more tender than cauliflower. It's often called a "green cauliflower" and sold under a variety of names, such as 'Green Goddess,' 'Alverde,' and 'Brocoverde.' You can also grow broccoflower in your garden. The heads are 6 to 8 inches across, with a lime green color, and mature in 80 days. The color intensifies if you don't cover the heads (like a cauliflower) to a darker green color. Harvest broccoflower just as you would cauliflower.

## *Bringing on the Brussels sprouts*

Rows of Brussels sprouts stems standing tall in the garden loaded with sprouts are a sure sign of fall. Although the plants take a whole season for the sprouts to mature, they're relatively maintenance-free, and the sprouts turn a sweet, nutty flavor after they're touched by cold weather.

To the untrained eye, a Brussels sprouts plant can look like a strange life form from another planet. Small, cabbagelike sprouts grow in clusters along the 3-foot-tall stem, and often gardeners remove most of the leaves so that the sprouts grow larger. The plants look like miniature palm trees (see Figure 9-1), with mini-cabbages on the stalk. If fact, if you like cabbage, you'll love the similar flavor of the smaller and more manageable Brussels sprouts.

The key to growing Brussels sprouts is having a long growing season and a cool fall to induce the best flavor. The flavor actually benefits from a light frost. The following varieties are widely adaptable and worth a try in any garden. The days to maturity are from setting out seedlings to first harvest:

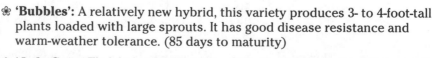

❀ **'Bubbles':** A relatively new hybrid, this variety produces 3- to 4-foot-tall plants loaded with large sprouts. It has good disease resistance and warm-weather tolerance. (85 days to maturity)

❀ **'Jade Cross E':** A hybrid All-America Selections winner, the 2¹/₂-foot-tall plants produce good-sized sprouts all the way up their stalks. (90 days to maturity)

❀ **'Oliver':** This early-maturing hybrid is well adapted to many climates. (90 days to maturity)

**Figure 9-1:**
Sprouts form along the stem of a Brussels sprouts plant.

❀ **'Red Rubine':** Yes, even Brussels sprouts have color variations. This heirloom variety produces very tasty and attractive red sprouts on a hardy, purplish-red-colored plant. The red color remains even after cooking. (95 days to maturity)

## *Counting on cabbage*

When many people think of cole crops, they first think of cabbages. Broccoli and cauliflower may be gaining in popularity, and Brussels sprouts may be novel, but cabbage is a long-time, solid vegetable citizen. It's been an easy-to-grow staple in Europe for hundreds of years and for centuries before that in the Middle East.

Cabbage-growing isn't as popular as it once was, and you rarely find cabbage on the menus of finer restaurants, but the sweet, tender flavor of freshly harvested cabbage makes it worthy of a spot in your garden. With so many varieties to choose from, you can have fresh and delicious cole slaw, sauerkraut, and boiled cabbage almost all season long — from summer into winter.

Cabbage requires the same conditions as other cole crops — cool weather, fertile soil, and proper watering — but the variety that you select is a bit more important to ensure a continuous harvest. You can easily get lost in the dizzying array of cabbage varieties: You can get early-, mid, and late-season varieties; round- and flat-headed varieties; smooth- and savoyed (crinkled)-leafed varieties, and even red-colored varieties. Growing two or three different varieties that mature at different times will allow you to spread out the harvest over the growing season. This avoids the "six heads of cabbage ready all the same week" syndrome. (Even the most ardent cabbage lover would have a hard time eating all that cabbage!)

To get you started on the right foot, I describe ten varieties that represent the universe of cabbages. Cabbage plants can spread to 3 feet in diameter, and all have green leaves and white centers unless otherwise noted. The late-maturing and fall-planted varieties are best for storage (I talk more about storing cabbages in Chapter 19). The days to maturity for each variety are from setting out seedlings in the garden to first harvest. Add 20 days to the maturity date if you directly seed in the garden:

- **'Danish Ballhead':** These 8-inch-diameter, round heads produce late in the season and are great for winter storage. This is a good variety for sauerkraut recipes. (100 days to maturity)

- **'Dynamo':** This new hybrid All-America Selections winner features small, 3- to 4-inch-diameter mini heads on compact plants that mature early in the season. This is a great variety for small families. (65 days to maturity)

- **'Early Jersey Wakefield':** This heirloom early cabbage with a pointed head measures 5 inches in diameter and has compact plants that are slow to split. For more on splitting, see the section "Harvesting cabbage," later in this chapter. (65 days to maturity)

- **'Late Flat Dutch':** This heirloom, late-maturing, 10-inch-diameter variety features a flattened head and is excellent for sauerkraut and storage. (100 days to maturity)

- **'Red Acre':** This early-maturing, 6-inch-diameter, red cabbage with a dense interior and deep color has good disease resistance and is good for storage. (76 days to maturity)

- **'Rio Verde':** A hybrid blue-green colored midseason variety with a 6-inch diameter, slightly flattened head. It's good for storage. (85 days to maturity)

- **'Ruby Perfection':** This midseason hybrid red variety produces attractive 5- to 6-inch-diameter reddish-purple heads. (80 days to maturity)

- **'Savoy Ace':** This early hybrid All-America Selections-winning savoy-leafed variety produces 6- to 8-inch-diameter heads that grow well in summer's heat. (76 days to maturity)

- **'Savoy Chieftain':** This midseason, heavily savoy-leafed variety produces 6- to 8-inch-diameter heads and is best grown as a fall crop. (85 days to maturity)

- **'Stonehead':** This widely grown, early-maturing, hybrid variety produces 5- to 6-inch-diameter solid heads on compact plants. (60 days to maturity)

# Considering cauliflower

Think of cauliflower as broccoli's hard-to-get-along-with brother. Both are from southern Europe, require similar growing conditions, and are closely related botanically. However, cauliflower plants produce only one head and no side shoots, and they have a reputation for being a bit tougher to grow. For example, cauliflower plants are finicky about weather conditions. If the weather gets too cold or too warm when they're forming heads, all you end up with are scraggly, small heads. Temperatures in the 70°F range are ideal, so it's best to avoid growing cauliflower when it will mature in the heat of summer. For that reason, many gardeners like to grow cauliflower as a fall crop started in summer to mature in the cooler, autumn weather.

With the right varieties, proper soil conditions, appropriate watering, and well-timed planting, cauliflower can be a joy to grow in the vegetable garden. It's especially exciting for young gardeners who are amazed to find a beautiful snow-white-colored head hidden under the green leaves. And if you're tired of pure-white heads, purple- and even orange-headed varieties are now available.

Broccoli and cabbage produce *heads,* and Brussels sprouts produce *sprouts,* so what does a cauliflower produce? A *curd.* No, it's not a Middle Eastern ethnic group or something that Little Miss Muffet ate with her whey. Like a broccoli head, a cauliflower curd is comprised of miniature flower heads tightly clustered together. The curds on cauliflowers stay white and tender only if the sun is excluded from them (a phenomenon called *blanching*). If exposed to the sun, the curds turn yellow and develop a mealy texture.

Although botanically related to broccoli, cauliflower is actually grown in much the same way that cabbage is. In fact, Mark Twain once called cauliflower "cabbage with a college education." Like cabbage, cauliflower comes in early-, mid, and late-season varieties. With older cauliflower varieties, you have to wrap the leaves over the head, as shown in Figure 9-2. Many of the newer varieties are *self-blanching* (the leaves naturally grow to cover the head and exclude light) and disease-resistant. However, even these newer varieties benefit from careful inspection to ensure that the leaves are tightly covering the heads once the heads form.

All the varieties in the following list produce 6- to 7-inch-diameter heads. The days to maturity number for each variety is from setting out seedlings in the garden until first harvest. Add 20 days to the maturity date for direct seeding in the garden:

 ❀ **'Fremont':** A self-blanching hybrid variety, 'Fremont' is known for dependable midseason production, even under adverse weather conditions. (70 days to maturity)

**Figure 9-2:**
To ensure that your cauliflower heads stay white, wrap the leaves to blanch the heads.

❀ **'Incline':** This new hybrid Japanese variety produces dense, pure white heads late in the season. It's a vigorous grower that's self-blanching. (76 days to maturity)

❀ **'Orange Bouquet':** Looking for something different? How about a pale orange-headed cauliflower! The orange coloring is from the presence of *carotene* (the same substance that causes carrots to be orange), so this variety is also high in vitamin A and has a sweet flavor. The head actually becomes a brighter orange when exposed to sun, so blanching is not required. (58 days to maturity)

❀ **'Snow Crown':** This is the standard white hybrid variety that's easy to grow, early, widely adaptable, and dependable. (60 days to maturity)

❀ **'Violet Queen':** If you want to grow a purple garden, try 'Violet Queen.' The purple-colored heads on this easy-to-grow plant don't need blanching. The color fades when cooked. (64 days to maturity)

# Planting Cole Crops

The keys to growing all cole crops are cool weather and fertile soil. Cole crops are cool crops: They grow and taste best when temperatures are below 80°F, especially when the crops are maturing. Cole crops grow best in raised beds and are also fairly demanding of nutrients, so be generous with manure and fertilizers (after you've done a soil test as indicated in Chapter 14 and know what nutrient adjustments need to be made), and they'll reward you with plenty of growth and production.

Because cole crops thrive in cool weather, many gardeners can grow all of them to mature as a summer crop and then some as a fall crop. That's two crops in one year! (One caveat: Brussels sprouts may be hard to mature as a fall crop in far northern areas, but are commonly grown in fall in most other areas of the country.)

## *Planting summer cole crops*

Even though you can *direct seed* most summer-maturing cole crops in spring — that is, plant the seed directly in the garden — it's easier to get a jump on the season by starting the plants indoors 4 to 6 weeks before your last frost date (see the appendix for first and last frost dates in your area) and then planting the seedlings in your garden 2 weeks before that date. Spring-planted summer-maturing cole crops can withstand a light frost, and planting them early gives them a jump-start on growing. Once the plants have at least four leaves, cultivate around the plants to kill any weeds and mulch with hay or straw.

Here's a rule-of-green-thumb when it comes to spacing cole crops, especially cabbage: The closer the plants are to one another, the smaller their heads will be (see the appendix for plant spacing guidelines). A dwarfed crop isn't necessarily bad — you may want to produce smaller, more manageable heads of cabbage.

## *Planting fall cole crops*

For gardeners in all but the coldest areas, a fall-maturing crop of broccoli, Brussels sprouts, cabbage, and cauliflower may be easier to manage than a similar summer-maturing crop. Fall weather provides the perfect temperatures to mature cole crops to their sweetest flavor.

For fall cole crops, start seedlings indoors about 3 months before your first frost and then transplant the seedlings to the garden 1 month later. For example, if your first frost is November 1, you should start seeds indoors on August 1 and then transplant them in your garden on September 1. (Starting the seedlings indoors and letting them grow until they're three to four weeks old helps them withstand the shock of being planted in the garden in summer.) To protect the young seedlings from the harsh summer sun, mulch them with hay or straw immediately after planting, and shade them — especially in the afternoon — with blankets or shade cloth (see Chapter 14 for mulching and shading techniques).

In very mild-winter areas such as the U.S. West coast and the Gulf coast, try growing overwintering varieties of broccoli (varieties that can withstand cold temperatures better than other varieties and need a longer season to mature) such as 'Purple Sprouting.' Planted in fall, such varieties slowly grow all winter and mature in spring.

# Nurturing Cole Crops

Cole crops like full sun and well-drained soil that's built into raised beds (see Chapter 2 for information about raised beds). Most importantly, though, cole crops really like fertile soil.

A week or so before planting your seedlings, work a 3- to 4-inch layer of composted manure into the bed. About 1 month after you transplant your cole crop seedlings, apply about 3 to 4 pounds of a complete fertilizer such as 5-10-10 to every 100 square feet of garden (see Chapter 15 for more on fertilizing). Keep the soil moist, and mulch a week or so after transplanting with an organic mulch such as hay or straw. These types of mulches keep weeds at bay and keep the soil cool and moist — just how cole crops like it.

I stress the importance of cool weather for cole crops throughout this chapter, but mild temperatures can be too cool for some cole crops. Even though mature cole crop plants can withstand temperatures into the 20°Fs, young plants may not be so hardy. If broccoli plants are exposed to several days of 40°F temperatures when they're still young, they can form flower heads prematurely when the weather warms. Cauliflower does the same thing (called *buttoning*) when exposed to cold temperatures or other stresses such as crowding when young. In either case, you're left with a small plant and head. To avoid this premature flowering, plant in summer for a fall crop or cover young spring-planted crops with a *row cover* (a plastic or fabric material that lets light through but insulates the plants) to keep them warm (see Chapter 22 for more on row covers).

Keep the plants well watered and mulched so that they grow steadily through the season. Side-dress cole crops with a complete fertilizer such as 5-10-10 about 1 month after transplanting in the garden (see Chapter 15 for more on side-dressing). Keep plants weeded, and they'll reward you with a bountiful harvest.

# Harvesting Cole Crops

If all goes well, cole crops should be ready to eat after a few months (check the days to maturity figures for the variety you choose). In this section, I share some tips to help you get the best harvests.

## Harvesting broccoli

Harvest broccoli by cutting the main head when the flower buds are still tightly clustered together without any signs of blossoming. Even if the head is smaller than you would like it to be, cut it now. After the yellow flowers open, the flavor turns bitter. If you leave a few inches of the main stem on the plant, many broccoli varieties respond by growing side branches that produce little heads (see Figure 9-3). Keep harvesting, and the broccoli keeps producing!

**Figure 9-3:** Side shoots on the broccoli plant keep the harvest coming.

## Harvesting Brussels sprouts

Brussels sprouts taste best after cool weather helps turn some of their carbohydrates into sugars. Following a frost, pick off the marble-sized sprouts from the bottom of the plant first, moving up the stalk. The more sprouts you pick from below, the larger the sprouts above will get. Pull off the lower leaves for easier picking.

To make the sprouts mature faster, snip off the top few inches of the plant once sprouts have formed on the bottom 12 inches of the stalk.

Because Brussels sprouts tolerate temperatures into the 20°Fs, you can harvest right into New Year's in some areas.

## Harvesting cabbage

Harvest cabbage heads when they're firm when squeezed. By periodically squeezing your cabbages through the growing season, you'll be able to tell when they're firm. Don't worry — they won't mind! To harvest, cut the head from the base of the plant with a sharp knife. When harvesting early maturing varieties in summer, don't dig up the plants. Cabbages have the ability to grow smaller side heads on the plant after the main head is harvested; you harvest these side heads the same way that you do the main head.

Sometimes, cabbage heads split before you can harvest them. *Splitting* occurs when the plant takes up too much fertilizer or water, especially around harvest time. This "overdose" causes the inner leaves to grow faster than the outer leaves, splitting the heads. Harvest splitting heads as soon as possible. To stop splitting once it starts, grab the head and give it a one-half turn to break some of the roots (see Figure 9-4). You can also root prune the plant by digging in a circle about 1 foot from the base of the cabbage. Both of these methods slow the uptake of water and fertilizer to preserve the head.

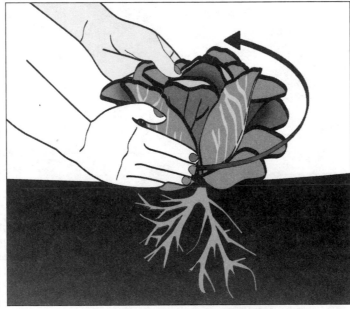

**Figure 9-4:**
Twisting cabbage heads can help prevent or stop cabbage heads from splitting.

## *Harvesting cauliflower*

When heads are anywhere between 6 and 12 inches in diameter and blanched white (for white varieties), pull up the whole plant and cut off the head. Cauliflower, unlike cabbage and broccoli, won't form side heads after the main head is cut.

# Putting a Stop to Pesky Pest Problems

In general, cole crops have only a few problems that home gardeners need to watch out for. Many modern hybrid varieties have added disease resistance, so choose these varieties if diseases are a problem in your garden. General vegetable diseases and pests such as cutworms, aphids, nematodes, flea beetles, and mildews are discussed in Chapter 18, but the following list warns you about some specific cole crop pests:

- **Black rot:** This bacteria is a problem particularly with cabbage and cauliflower. It causes the plant or the head to rot before maturing. The telltale signs are a foul smell, a yellowing of the lower leaves, blackening of the leaf veins, and triangular-shaped yellow areas on the leaf edges. Control this problem by rotating crops (planting other unrelated crops such as tomatoes, beans, or lettuce in that area for 3 years) and removing all old cole crop plant debris.

- **Club root:** If your plants are stunted, pull one up and check the roots. If the roots are gnarled and disfigured, a fungus called club root may be to blame. Rotate crops and raise the soil pH to 7.2 by adding lime (see Chapter 14 for more on acceptable pH ranges for vegetables) to prevent this disease.

- **Imported cabbageworm and cabbage looper:** These two insects are the number one problem with cole crops. A seemingly harmless white butterfly lays single white eggs on the undersides of leaves. The eggs hatch, and green caterpillars crawl out and begin to feed on the leaves. These pests can quickly destroy your crop. As soon as you see signs of feeding — including the caterpillars or their dark green droppings — spray the crop with a biological control called *Bacillus thurengiensis* (Bt). Bt is a very effective bacteria that attacks only caterpillar family insects and is safe to other insects, animals, and humans.

- **Cabbage maggot:** If plants are stunted, pull up one and look at the roots. If you see small white larvae (maggots) feeding there, you probably have cabbage maggots. The adult fly lays eggs on the stems at the soil line. The eggs hatch, and the larvae tunnel into the soil and start feeding on the roots. The maggots are especially dangerous to young seedlings. To control the cabbage maggot, place a floating row cover (a cheesecloth-like material that lets air, water, and sun in but keeps bugs out) over the young seedlings. Once the weather warms, remove the row cover.

# Health Tips and a Recipe

Although most cole crops are good sources of vitamin C, calcium, phosphorous, and potassium broccoli is considered the "Crown Jewel of Nutrition."

One cup contains only 45 calories with all the beta-carotene and vitamin C you need in a day and as much calcium as a cup of milk — without the fat. Broccoli is a good source of iron, phosphorous, and fiber, and it's loaded with cancer-fighting antioxidants such as sulphuraphane. (Actually, all cole crops contain this antioxidant, but broccoli has the highest levels.)

Cole crops can be prepared in many different ways: stir-fried, steamed, dipped, made into soups and sauces, and stuffed. There are many recipes for cole crops, but here, I keep it simple by offering a basic cole slaw recipe. Granted, it isn't glamorous, but fresh cole slaw has a very different and much more appealing flavor compared to what most people get in restaurants.

## Colorful Cole Slaw

**Tools:** *Large bowl, small bowl, blender (optional), shredder*

**Preparation time:** *15 minutes (plus 30 minutes refrigeration)*

**Cooking time:** *None*

**Yield:** *6 servings*

*³/₄ cup plain yogurt*

*1 tablespoon vinegar*

*¹/₂ teaspoon dill weed*

*Salt and pepper to taste*

*4 cups shredded red and green cabbage*

*¹/₂ cup chopped green pepper*

*¹/₂ cup celery*

*1* In a large bowl, toss all the cabbage, green peppers, and celery. Cover and chill.

*2* In a small bowl or blender, mix the yogurt, vinegar, and seasonings (the dill weed and salt and pepper) to create the dressing.

*3* Cover and chill for at least 30 minutes.

At serving time, lightly toss the cabbage mixture with dressing until it's evenly coated.

# Chapter 10

# It's Easy Being Greens: Lettuce, Spinach, Mesclun, and Swiss Chard

. . . . . . . . . . . . . . . . . . . . . . . . . . . . . . . . . . . .

*In This Chapter*

▶ Getting familiar with greens

▶ Leafing through lettuce, spinach, and Swiss chard varieties

▶ Joining the green revolution: mesclun, dandelion, and other unusual greens

▶ Caring for your crops

▶ Preparing a soup that will make your friends green with envy

. . . . . . . . . . . . . . . . . . . . . . . . . . . . . . . . . . . .

*Y*ou'll find no simpler vegetables than greens. Unlike other vegetables that require weeks or even months of nurturing, greens are good things that come even to those who can't wait. Because you don't have to wait for flowering and fruiting to enjoy their green goodness, you can just pick the leaves at any stage, and — voilà! — you have dinner.

In many growing areas, you can have fresh greens year-round from your garden with just a little planning. Sure, it's easy to buy a head of lettuce at the grocery store, but the pure joy of running out to the garden in the evening and plucking a fresh head for dinner gives you a great sense of satisfaction while introducing you to unusual varieties and flavors not readily available from most supermarkets. Plus you don't have to push a shopping cart with a bad wheel or break up any arguments in the cereal aisle just to gather basic salad ingredients.

And speaking of salad, for most people, lettuce and salad are synonymous. Lettuce is definitely the number one green, but in this chapter, I also discuss two other major greens crops: spinach and Swiss chard. I also talk about my favorite unusual greens, including that "mesclun stuff" that's showing up in produce markets and restaurants.

Greens, by nature, are cool, moisture-loving crops. When the weather heats up to above 80°F for several days in a row and the plant is mature enough, annual greens such as lettuce and spinach think the end is near and send up a seed stalk. This process is called *bolting*. Bolting doesn't just mean getting out of the house quickly. It's also a term used to describe a greens crop gone bad. During this process, the flavor of the greens quickly becomes bitter, so plan to plant and harvest your greens while the weather's cool or else grow varieties that are tolerant of the heat.

# *The Love Leaf: Lettuce*

Originally from the Mediterranean area, lettuce *(Latuca sativa)* was eaten at the tables of Persian kings in 550 B.C. and was once thought to be an aphrodisiac. I can't attest to its aphrodisiacal qualities, but I do know that lettuce is considered *the* quintessential salad crop around the world.

The four basic types of lettuce (crisphead, loose head, romaine, and loose leaf) offer a number of tasty varieties to delight the palate. The most common are green-colored leaf varieties, but you can grown many red- and burgundy-colored leaf varieties, too. Some varieties form solid heads, but others do not.

The following list describes the four basic types of lettuce along with their days to maturity and some of my favorite varieties. Just remember that lettuce can be eaten much younger, depending on your needs and appetite:

✔ **Crisphead:** This group is most widely known as the "iceberg" lettuces, so named because when the lettuce was shipped from California (the main lettuce-growing region in the United States) to the East coast in the early 1900s, mounds of ice were used to keep it cool and fresh. This type forms a solid head when mature, with white, crunchy, densely packed inner leaves. Crispheads tend to take at least 70 days to mature from seeding in the garden.

'Iceberg' is the most widely known variety, but many other crispheads are easy to grow. Following are popular varieties of crisphead lettuce:

  ❀ **'Iceberg':** Famous in grocery stores across the country, these compact heads have tightly-packed leaves and white hearts. Best grown in cool conditions (below 70°F) to form solid heads. (Find tips for growing head lettuce in the section "Growing Great Greens," later in this chapter.)

  ❀ **'Sierra':** A French (sometimes called "Batavian") crisphead lettuce with wavy, bright green-and-red tinged leaves, 'Sierra' is a good heat-tolerant lettuce variety. A similar green-leafed version is the variety 'Nevada.'

❀ **'Summertime':** So named for its ability to form solid heads in the heat of summer, 'Summertime' has green leaves and a crisp texture.

✔ **Loose heads (Bibb, Boston, or Butterhead):** This lettuce type features dark or medium green leaves or red leaves and smooth, thick, outer leaves folded around a loosely-formed, yellow-to-white head. The head isn't solid like a crisphead type, but loose heads are easier to grow, especially during the summer heat. This type matures starting at 60 days from seeding.

❀ **'Bibb':** 'Bibb' is an heirloom, dark-green-leafed, loose-head lettuce, that dates back to the 1800s.

❀ **'Buttercrunch':** A bolt-resistant, loose head type, 'Buttercrunch' has thick, juicy leaves; it's best grown as a summer crop.

❀ **'Brune d'Hiver':** Very hardy, with bronzed, light green leaves, this variety is good as a fall or winter lettuce.

❀ **'Deer Tongue':** An heirloom, loose head type lettuce with tongue-shaped green leaves, this plant is slow to bolt.

✔ **Loose leaf:** Loose leaf lettuce doesn't form a solid head and is best harvested by picking off the mature outer leaves, allowing new leaves to continue growing. This type is often cut and allowed to "come again" (see the section "To harvest: Cut and come again," later in this chapter) to provide multiple crops of greens from one head. You can start harvesting this type about 45 days from seeding.

❀ **'Black Seeded Simpson':** This variety is an heirloom lettuce with crinkled, light green leaves.

❀ **'Brunia':** This red-leafed, loose-leaf type features large, unusual pointed, oak-shaped leaves.

❀ **'Oak Leaf':** Green-leafed, this loose-leaf type features unusual, pointed, oak-shaped leaves.

❀ **'Red Sails':** An All-America-Selections–winning (see Chapter 4 for more on this award) red, loose-leaf lettuce, 'Red Sails' is fast-growing, heat-tolerant, and very attractive.

❀ **'Red Salad Bowl':** A red version of the classic 'Salad Bowl' loose-leaf lettuce, which features frilly green leaves and a mild, tender taste. This attractive burgundy-red-leafed version grows and looks best in cooler weather.

✔ **Romaine (Cos):** Romaine was named by the Romans, who believed in the healthful properties of this type of lettuce. Emperor Caesar Augustus even built a statue in praise of romaine lettuce, so it's no surprise that this is the type of lettuce featured in Caesar salad. The alternative name, "cos," comes from the Greek Island Kos, where it is popular. Romaine lettuce grows tall, upright heads and long, thick green

or red leaves with solid *midribs* (the middle vein of the leaf). This type tends to take at least 70 days to mature from seeding and can withstand summer heat.

- ❀ **'Parris Island Cos':** This green-leafed romaine lettuce has 10-inch-tall, thick, green leaves.

- ❀ **'Rosalita':** Red- to purple-colored, this romaine lettuce is well-adapted to various growing regions and has yellow, blanched interior leaves.

- ❀ **'Winter Density':** A green romaine lettuce that's actually a cross between a loose head and a romaine-type lettuce, this 8-inch-tall plant is both heat- and cold-tolerant.

# Popeye's Pal: Spinach

This Middle Eastern vegetable has been cultivated for centuries. The dark green leaves of spinach *(Spinacia oleracea)* are nutritious (just ask Popeye, Olive Oyl, and Brutus of comic book fame) and stronger tasting than lettuces. It's one of the first crops many gardeners plant in spring. In fact, when the heat comes, spinach quickly bolts. If you love spinach and want to eat it throughout the summer, you can grow warm-weather, spinachlike crops that produce all summer, such as New Zealand spinach *(Tetragonia tetragonioides)* and Malabar spinach *(Basella rubra)*.

There are two different leaf types of spinach: smooth and savoy (crinkled). Which is better is a matter of personal preference. The smooth-leaf types are easier to clean, but the savoy-leaf types give you more leaf surface to hold that salad dressing and dip.

Unless otherwise noted, the varieties in the following sections mature in about 30 to 45 days from a spring planting. As with lettuce, you can always harvest the young, tender greens earlier if you just can't wait.

## Some savoy-spinach standouts

The following are popular savoy-type spinach varieties; their leaves are crinkled:

- ✏ **'Bloomsdale Long Standing':** This heirloom variety has thick leaves.

- ✏ **'Indian Summer':** A hybrid variety that features an upright plant habit (it grows more vertical than horizontal), making the thick leaves easier to pick.

- **'Melody':** This hybrid, All-America-Selections–winning spinach features large semi-savoy leaves and good disease resistance.
- **'Tyee':** This hybrid, slightly savoy-type is a vigorous grower. It's a personal favorite because it's easy to grow and slow to bolt.

## Smooth and spinachlike standouts

Following is one smooth spinach variety and a couple of good look-and-taste-alikes that are easy to grow:

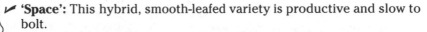
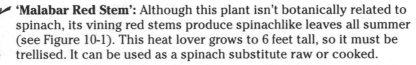
- **'Space':** This hybrid, smooth-leafed variety is productive and slow to bolt.
- **'Malabar Red Stem':** Although this plant isn't botanically related to spinach, its vining red stems produce spinachlike leaves all summer (see Figure 10-1). This heat lover grows to 6 feet tall, so it must be trellised. It can be used as a spinach substitute raw or cooked.
- **'New Zealand tetragonia':** This 1- to 2-foot-tall plant resembles spinach in looks and flavor, but it's able to withstand summer heat. It can be cut repeatedly and still regrow, a method called *cut and come again*. I talk more about it in the section "To harvest: Cut and come again."

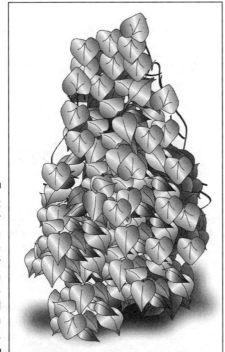

**Figure 10-1:** Malabar spinach is a good hot-weather alternative to traditional spinach varieties.

# The Show Stopper: Swiss Chard

Swiss chard *(Beta vulgaris)* has finally come of age. With the recent introduction of more colorful varieties, this green is now a top specialty treat in many gardens. Swiss chard hails from southern Europe (even Aristotle wrote about the virtues of Swiss chard!) where it grew up next to its close cousin, the beet. In fact, the only differences between the two vegetables are that chard (sometimes known as "spinach beet") doesn't have the bulbous root of the beet, and its greens are more tender and prolific.

I've grown Swiss chard for years because it's so easy to grow; doesn't bolt like spinach; has a consistent flavor, even in the hot summer; and has leaves that keep producing until frost. Now I also grow chard for the gorgeous color of its midribs (the middle part of the leaf). Varieties such as 'Rhubarb' and 'Bright Lights' make this garden green a real show stopper.

The following varieties all mature between 50 and 60 days from direct seeding in the garden, but the baby greens can be harvested as early as 1 month after seeding.

- ✔ **'Bright Lights':** This All-America-Selections hybrid variety features a mix of plants with red, pink, yellow, gold, or orange midribs on leaves that taste as good as they look, with a milder texture than other chard varieties.

- ✔ **'Dorat':** This yellow midrib variety has thick crinkled leaves and a mild flavor.

- ✔ **'Fordhook Giant':** This variety features a thick, celerylike midrib with large, dark green savoy leaves. It's a heavy producer.

- ✔ **'Rhubarb':** An heirloom, burgundy-red midrib variety with dark green leaves, this variety is a bit smaller than other chards, but tasty and good looking.

# A Taste of the Exotic: Specialty Greens

Salad has gone through a revolution in the past 10 years. At one time, salad meant simply lettuce, spinach, and maybe Swiss chard. No longer. With the growing interest in exotic Chinese and European greens, salad palettes have expanded to include many ethnic greens such as arugula and mizuna (see Chapter 11 for more on arugula and mizuna). There's even a growing interest in greens previously thought to be weeds, such as purslane, sorrel, and — the scourge of lawn lovers — dandelions.

Eating these wild greens is not a new idea — when I was a boy, my Italian grandmother picked wild dandelion greens in spring to be sautéed with garlic and olive oil. And my family and I have been eating our lawn each spring for years — my wife, Barbara, loves to cook sorrel soup and marinated dandelions each spring. Such culinary practices are being rediscovered and embraced as the interest in ethnic dishes grows.

For many wild greens, you can just go into your garden or lawn and munch away, but *never* eat greens from lawns treated with pesticides.

You have good reason to cultivate and enjoy these unusual greens. Many are very easy to grow (some can even withstand freezing temperatures), they're more nutritious than traditional lettuce, and their flavors are unique and sometimes quite surprising. Many of the most popular and more mainstream specialty greens like endive are discussed in Chapter 11. But if you're curious about some of the wild ones, try a few of the eyebrow-raising varieties listed here (most are also commercially available). Most can be harvested starting about one month after direct seeding in the garden. (Seeding gives you better varieties and more control than just waiting for the weed to pop up.)

- **Claytonia (miner's lettuce):** Heart-shaped leaves encircle a white-flowered stem. This variety grows best in cool weather and regrows after harvesting. It's good planted in fall as a winter salad green.

- **Cress:** You have different types of cress to choose from. *Watercress* is actually a type of *nasturium* (an annual flower with a large, oval leaf) and likes very moist, cool conditions. *Garden cress* features a curly leaf and hot, peppery taste. It also favors cool weather but is easier to grow than watercress.

- **Dandelion:** Yes, you can plant the same dandelions that dad has spent years pulling out or mowing over. Harvest them young — when the leaves are about 4 to 6 inches long — so that the greens are only slightly bitter. Varieties from France and Italy grow taller and are easier to harvest.

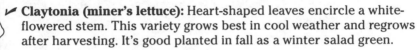

## Mesclun: The salad for the '90s

Mesclun is the buzz word for salad in the 1990s. It has become so popular that 1997 was declared the "Year of the Mesclun" by the National Garden Bureau.

Mesclun isn't actually an individual green but a mix of different greens. The flavors can be mild to piquant, depending on the ingredients in the mix. Traditional mesclun may include a blend of lettuces, endive, arugula, cress, dandelion, and mache. Modern seed companies have expanded the list of possibilities to include herbs, kales, and Chinese greens such as mizuna and pac choi.

The key to a flavorful blend is to harvest the greens when they are small and tender, usually within three weeks of seeding. Because most of these greens are cold-weather tolerant, mesclun is usually the first green harvested from my garden in spring. The greens quickly regrow after cutting for a number of harvests. The greens taste great doused with a balsamic vinegar and olive oil dressing.

- ✔ **Mache (corn salad):** This cool-weather-loving and cold-tolerant green features small, dark green, tender leaves in a rosette shape with a mild, nutty flavor. It rarely turns bitter.

- ✔ **Orach (mountain spinach):** This spinach relative can grow to 4 feet tall, producing arrow-shaped, reddish-purple leaves; it tolerates the heat.

- ✔ **Purslane:** An upright-growing version of the common garden weed (which is a creeper), the varieties have lighter-colored, succulent leaves and are more mildly flavored. Purslane likes sunny, warm weather.

- ✔ **Vegetable amaranth:** This is a variety of the ancient grain amaranth that is harvested young for its oval-shaped, coleuslike leaves. The leaves may be all green or green-and-red colored, depending on the variety. It germinates best in warm weather.

- ✔ **Shungiku:** This Oriental, edible chrysanthemum is harvested when less than 8 inches tall and used in salads, sushi, and pickles. It likes cool weather.

- ✔ **Sorrel:** The 8-inch-long, arrow-shaped greens start growing in early spring and continue until fall. They have a distinct, lemony flavor that's great in salads and soups. This green *perennializes* (comes back each year on its own) well and can grow in light shade.

# Growing Great Greens

Fertile soil and consistent watering are essential to growing great greens. Given those two factors, greens have to be one of the easiest vegetables to grow. The biggest problem gardeners have with greens is too much success.

I remember planting a 10-foot row of lettuce all at once, watching it germinate and grow, and feeling very smug about my success. My satisfaction evaporated when I was inundated one month later with lettuce, lettuce, and more lettuce. I got sick of eating salads, and most of my crop eventually bolted and tasted bitter. I learned my lesson.

Planting small, 2-to-4-foot patches of lettuce every two weeks throughout the growing season (called staggering the planting dates, discussed in Chapter 16) is the best way to ensure a small but manageable supply of lettuce all summer long. In warm areas, you may want to skip planting in midsummer because lettuce will bolt from the heat.

You can squeeze greens into almost any garden. If you don't have room with all those other gorgeous vegetables growing, get creative about where you plant. Because the plants are generally small and fast growing, you can tuck greens in all kinds of empty patches in your garden. For example, you can plant greens in between newly planted tomato, broccoli, or cabbage seedlings; under a pole bean teepee; between rows of corn, or around carrots in the carrot patch. The greens mature and are harvested before the other plants get too large to shade them. In the carrot patch, harvesting the greens gives room for these root crops to enlarge and mature. In summer, after your crop of beans or peas is finished, yank out the exhausted plants and plant a quick crop of lettuce to harvest later in late summer or fall.

The following sections offer additional tips for getting the most out of your greens.

## Exercise your "greens" thumb year-round

In areas with mild summers and winters such as the West coast, greens are easy to grow year-round. For most other areas, spring and fall are the best times to grow greens.

Greens can be direct sown in the garden starting in spring and, in cool areas, planted throughout the summer until August. If you want to get a jump on the season, start seeds four to six weeks before the last frost date in your area (see the appendix for a listing of first and last frost dates) so that they can be planted out two to three weeks later.

Gardeners in mild winter areas such as Arizona, Texas, and Florida may prefer a winter crop of greens because the weather is more favorable. Summer is too hot to germinate the seeds and grow the traditional types of lettuce and greens. For a winter crop, sow seeds indoors in fall to be transplanted into the garden one month later.

If you don't have the right climate for year-round growing but love fresh greens, here are tips for growing your own salad 12 months of the year in spite of cold winters and hot summers:

- ✔ **Choose the right varieties.** To grow a winter greens crop in cold-winter areas (hardiness zone 6 and colder), plant spinach, arugula, claytonia, mizuna, and winter lettuce varieties such as 'Brune D'Hiver.' To grow greens through summer in warm areas (hardiness zone 7 and warmer) choose greens that like the heat, such as purslane, Malabar, or New Zealand spinach.

- ✔ **Time your planting.** Start heat-loving greens in late spring so they mature during summer's heat. For winter greens in the cold areas, start cold-tolerant greens in fall so they mature to full size before the real cold weather of December. The greens don't have to grow during the short winter days and cold temperatures — they just need to stay alive.

- ✔ **Keep the soil fertile.** Successive crops of greens will take nutrients out of the soil, so after every crop you remove, add a 2- to 3-inch layer of compost to the soil and work it in well.

✔ **Protect the plants.** During the summer heat, use shade cloth (cloth material ) to block the afternoon sun. In the North, protect greens through the cold winter by growing them in cold frames (see Chapter 22 for cold frame designs and season-extending ideas).

Growing great crisphead or "iceberg" lettuce can be a challenge for many gardeners. The problem is that crisphead lettuce likes cool temperatures (50°F to 60°F) throughout the growing season, especially when it's trying to form a head. For northern and southern gardeners, fall planting is the key. In warm areas, start seeds indoors in September to be placed in the garden in October or November. In cooler climates, start seeds indoors in July to plant in the garden in August or September. Keep plants well watered and feed them every three weeks with fish emulsion. By the cool days of fall, your iceberg lettuce heads should form.

## Put your greens to bed

Greens are easiest grown in raised beds (see Chapter 2 for more on raised beds). The beds are flat and smooth on top with most of the rocks and debris removed. Raised beds drain water well, which greens love, and are easy to work. Instead of planting in a straight row (which is okay, by the way), you can broadcast the seeds over the top of the entire bed. This *wide row planting* technique (see Figure 10-2) is described in Chapter 2. By using the wide row planting technique, you get more greens per square foot sooner with less weeding and watering.

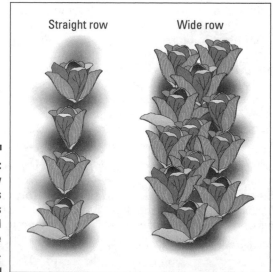

Straight row      Wide row

**Figure 10-2:**
Wide row plantings mean less work and more plants.

## Add fishy fertilizer for needed nitrogen

Greens have simple fertilizing needs. You eat the leaves. Leaves need nitrogen to grow. So the soil needs to be rich in nitrogen. Any questions? That being said, it's important to remember balance in all things, including fertilizer in your lettuce patch. So applying a balanced fertilizer such as 10-10-10 that's high in nitrogen is a good practice. See Chapter 15 for more on balanced fertilizers. I suggest working in a 3- to 4-inch layer of compost and applying soluble nitrogen fertilizer such as fish emulsion every few weeks. The greens stay lush and mature quickly.

## Thin and bare it

Whether you plant in straight rows or wide rows, greens need thinning. Generally, spinach and loose-leaf lettuces need 3 to 4 inches between plants; crisphead and romaine lettuce like 6 to 10 inches.

Thin the seedlings as soon as each plant has four leaves. (Don't throw out those thinnings, though. They make great "baby" greens for salad.) Once the plants are properly spaced, mulching with a 2- to 3-inch layer of hay or straw is a good way to conserve vital moisture, prevent weeds, and keep the leaves clean of splashing soil after rain.

## Water to win the war against wilt

Keeping the soil consistently moist after planting is a good way to avoid a common complaint with lettuces: The seeds never came up.

Greens need moist soil to germinate. Once growing, the plants generally have small root systems, so they're the first vegetable to wilt when the soil is too dry. Water deeply — down to 5 to 6 inches deep — and mulch to keep greens crisp. A simple way to water is to use soaker hoses or drip irrigation (see Chapter 15 for watering techniques).

## To harvest: Cut and come again

Harvesting greens couldn't be easier. After all, you eat the leaves. Except for the crisphead lettuces, harvest greens while they're young and tender to avoid another common complaint of lettuce growers: bitter-tasting lettuce. Bitter taste usually develops in older plants, so start picking when the leaves are 4 inches long. Harvest the outer leaves first to allow the inner leaves to continue to develop. Also, wait until you're almost ready to prepare your meal to harvest. That way, the greens will be fresh and crisp in your salad bowl.

Some lettuces, such as loose-leaf varieties and Swiss chard, are good examples of "cut and come again" greens (see Figure 10-3). You can cut these greens at the ground level — they'll sprout new leaves from their bases — or you can just harvest the mature leaves, leaving the immature leaves to continue growing. This is a great alternative to replanting, and you can cut the plants up to four times.

**Figure 10-3:**
Cut and come again for more lettuce greens.

Crisphead or "iceberg" lettuce can also be harvested young, before heads form. However, to get the solid, blanched heads seen in grocery stores, wait until full maturity when heads are firm when squeezed.

## *Work out the bugs (and other common ailments)*

Greens have some of the problems that plague other vegetables. Insects such as aphids and white flies and diseases such as white mold and viruses can quickly destroy a crop. Because greens tend to have shallow and relatively small root systems, they can succumb easily to damage. Slugs are a threat to young seedlings in moist areas such as the Pacific Northwest, and rabbits and woodchucks are critters that love greens anywhere. All these problems are covered in depth in Chapter 18, but remember that fertile, well-drained soil that's kept moist and fertilized is usually your best bet against any problems with your greens crop. And don't hesitate to yank out an insect infested or animal chewed crop: Greens grow and mature so quickly, it may be better to start over than to nurse a sick crop.

I describe a few specific problems that plague greens in the text that follows:

- **Bottom rot:** This fungus causes lettuce (especially head lettuce) to wilt and rot before maturing. It's mostly seen in poorly drained soil during wet conditions. To avoid this problem, rotate crops, keep your soil well drained, and grow lettuce in raised beds.

- **Spinach leaf miner:** This small fly lays eggs on spinach and Swiss chard leaves. The eggs hatch, and the tiny larvae tunnel in between the leaf layers. Pick off and destroy tunneled leaves, and cover the crop with a floating row cover (a cheesecloth-like material that lets air, water, and sun in but keeps bugs out) after germination to prevent damage.

- **Tip burn:** Tip burn causes the leaves of head lettuce to turn brown at the edges. This condition is seen during hot weather when soil moisture tends to fluctuate, creating a calcium deficiency in plants. Don't bother adding calcium to the soil, but do pick off burned leaves, choose varieties that resist tip burn, and keep the soil evenly moist to control this problem.

# Souping Up Your Body with Greens

Popeye was right about eating his spinach. If there is one crop to eat for the best vitamin punch, it's dark, leafy greens. Spinach, Swiss chard, and other greens are loaded with vitamins A and C and contribute calcium, iron, and fiber to your diet — and they're low in sodium and calories.

Eating greens just in salads can get a bit boring after awhile. If you're starting to feel like Bugs Bunny's relative from eating so many salads, try this simple cream of spinach soup recipe. You can use mostly spinach and Swiss chard, but, to add a little zip to the taste, try including sorrel, dandelion, or other wild greens.

## Cream of Spinach Soup

**Tools:** *Cutting board and knife, measuring cups and spoons, saucepan*

**Preparation time:** *30 minutes*

**Cooking time:** *20 minutes*

**Yield:** *4 servings*

| | |
|---|---|
| *¹/₄ cup chopped onions* | *Salt and pepper to taste* |
| *¹/₄ cup margarine or butter* | *3 cups milk* |
| *3 tablespoons flour* | *3 cups chopped spinach, chard, or a mix of other wild greens* |

**1** Sauté the onions in margarine (or butter) in a heavy saucepan until they're translucent. Stir in the flour, and salt and pepper. Add the milk gradually, stirring constantly. Cook the mixture over low heat until it boils. Then simmer and stir for one minute.

**2** Steam the well-washed chopped spinach and greens until they're tender. Add them to the cream sauce base, heat for 5 to 10 minutes, and serve.

# Chapter 11

# Sweet Corn + 30 Extraordinary Veggies

*T*he preceding seven chapters cover the most popular and widely grown vegetables. But part of the fun of vegetable gardening is trying new and unusual crops. These "experiments" can be as commonplace as corn or as exotic as mizuna.

This chapter starts with one of the most popular vegetables of summer: corn. Corn isn't related to any of the vegetables mentioned in Chapters 4 through 10, so I gave it a special place in this chapter. Although corn is as traditional as apple pie, any vegetable that's closely related to lawn grass has some unique qualities! So I start with a discussion of sweet corn including popcorn and ornamental corn, which are subgroups of the same corn family.

This chapter also includes an alphabetical listing of vegetables to help you decide which vegetables to try and how to grow them. Each listing provides a description of the vegetable, a list of sample varieties to look for, and some basic growing tips. (*Note:* The planting times for each of these vegetables depend on the weather in your area. Refer to seed packages for planting times. See the appendix for information about temperature zones and first and last frost dates.)

As a bonus, I also include cooking tips with many of the vegetables. Like my mom used to say, "You'll never know if you like it unless you try it." Happy gardening, and bon appétit!

# Sweet Corn and Its Relatives

Corn *(Zea mais)* has a reputation of being grown only in large fields, but you can also grow a great crop of corn in a small garden in your backyard. The satisfaction of harvesting your own fresh-picked corn and steaming it for dinner is one of the joys of summer.

## Sweet corn

If all you've ever eaten is sweet corn from the supermarket, you're missing one of summer's true delights. Fresh-picked, steamed sweet corn has a sweet, corny flavor that brings a smile to old and young faces alike. You can also roast corn on an open fire or grill to give it a woodsy flavor.

By selecting the right varieties to grow, you can have sweet corn maturing all summer long. And you don't need a 10-acre field to grow it. Five to six short rows are all you need to get plenty of ears for your family.

### Varieties

The kernels of the sweet corn plant are actually seeds. Most sweet corn varieties come with white, yellow, or bicolor (yellow and white mixed) kernels. Some heirloom varieties that are mostly used for corn flour and roasting feature red and blue kernels. (That's where the red- and blue-colored corn tortilla chips come from.) The color of corn that you choose depends on what flavor you like and what varieties grow well where you live. Varieties mature in 65 to 100 days, so choose a sampling that will mature over time in your garden. Gardeners in cold climates should stick with quick-maturing varieties.

As with many vegetables, there are open-pollinated heirloom varieties as well as many modern hybrids (see Chapter 1 for more about open pollination and hybrids). Two newer hybrid groups that hold their sweetness and tenderness are now commonly found in grocery stores, and their seeds are available in garden centers and seed catalogs:

- **Sugar-enhanced *(se)* varieties** have a special gene in their makeup that increases the tenderness and sweetness of the ears.

- **Supersweet *(sh2)* varieties** have a gene bred into the variety that makes the ears even sweeter than sugar-enhanced, and they can be stored for a week in the refrigerator without loosing their sweetness. However, many feel that what supersweets gain in sweetness, they lose in "real corn" flavor.

Although *se* and especially *sh2* varieties are a bit more finicky about grow-ing, they do allow you to eat your corn over time without worrying about it getting starchy. Still, for best flavor, eat your sweet corn as soon as possible after harvest.

Following are some heirloom, standard, and modern varieties you may want to try:

❀ Some standard heirloom yellow varieties to grow are 'Golden Bantam' and 'Country Gentleman.' Some uniquely colored heirloom varieties include 'Black Mexican' (blue).

❀ A few "standard sugary" hybrids include 'Early Sunglow' (yellow), 'Sugar and Gold' (bicolor), and 'Silver Queen' (white).

❀ For sugar-enhanced *(se)* varieties, try 'Quickie' (bicolor), 'Bodacious' (yellow), and 'Sugar Snow' (white).

❀ For some good supersweet *(sh2)* varieties, grow 'Early Xtra Sweet' (yellow), 'Honey N' Pearl' (bicolor), and 'How Sweet It Is' (white).

Whew, that's a lot of choices! They're actually only the tip of the iceberg, so don't be afraid to try other varieties to see which grow best in your area.

### Growing

Sweet corn is a warm-weather crop, so don't rush to plant it. The soil temperature should be at least 65°F for the best germination.

You may notice that some companies coat their seeds with a brightly colored fungicide to prevent rotting while the seed germinates — rotting during germination is a big problem in wet, cool weather with heavy clay soil. If you're a strict organic gardener, select corn from those companies that sell untreated seed.

Corn is in the grass family, so like your lawn, it needs plenty of nitrogen fertilizer to grow best. Amend the soil before planting with composted manure, and side-dress the patch with a 10-10-10 fertilizer when the plants are "knee-high" and again when *silks* (fine hairs on the ears) appear. Corn was traditionally planted in hills following the Native American technique, but for the best production, plant corn in groups of short rows called blocks. Blocks consist of at least 4 straight rows of corn about 10 to 20 feet long. Rows should be 2 feet apart, with walkways 2 to 4 feet wide between blocks so you're able to easily harvest. Plant the seeds 6 inches apart in a full-sun location in 2-inch-deep furrows. After germination, thin the plants to 12 inches apart.

Each corn kernel needs to be pollinated by pollen from the *tassel* (the antennae-like flower at the top of the corn plant). If corn plants are grouped together, the wind blows the pollen down to the silks on the ears, and the pollen moves along the silks to pollinate the kernels. If you plant one or two long rows, chances are some kernels will not get pollinated, and your ears will look like a mouth that's missing a few teeth. Plant only one variety in each block. This will ensure that the tassels drop pollen when the silks are ready. If you mix varieties within a block, you may not get proper pollination because the pollen may drop when the ears aren't ready. You can stagger the planting dates of your varieties by two weeks or plant other blocks of early-, mid, or late-season varieties to extend the harvest season.

Don't plant supersweet *(sh2)* varieties within 250 feet of any other corn variety. If non-supersweet pollen pollinates the corn, the supersweet corn will lose its extra sweetness.

When the corn plants are about 8 inches tall, hill them (mounding soil up to the lower leaves), as shown in Figure 11-1, to help kill weeds and reduce the likelihood of the tall stalks blowing over when older. Keep the corn well-watered, and watch out for leaf-yellowing. Yellowing leaves are a sign of nitrogen deficiency, so you should add more nitrogen fertilizer, such as fish emulsion, to correct it.

When the husks are bright green and the silks turn brown, your ears are ready to check. Feel the ears and make sure that they feel filled to the tips. You can even pull back the husk at the tip to check the kernels. If you can pinch the kernels and the juice is a milky color, the ear is ready to pick. For the best flavor, right after picking, remove the leaves and the silks and steam or boil the corn in water for about five minutes (for the whole pot); then chomp away for a true taste of summer.

**Figure 11-1:**
Hill sweet corn to help it stand up to high winds and summer storms.

Corn is notorious for attracting certain pests. Caterpillars such as the corn earworm and corn borer can devastate a patch, and animals such as raccoons and birds love sweet corn. Check Chapter 18 for tips on thwarting insects and animals that thrive in the corn patch.

## Ornamental corn

You've probably seen brightly colored ornamental or Indian corn hanging in garden centers in fall. The corn makes great holiday decorations, and birds love the kernels, too. Instead of choosing just from the varieties available locally, you can easily grow your own ornamental corn. The following varieties are purely ornamental; they're not meant to be eaten:

- ❀ **'Wampum,'** a 7-foot-tall plant, has multicolored corn tassels (the top antennae-like, pollen-producing parts of the stalks) that can also be cut and dried.
- ❀ **'Red Stalker'** is an 8- to 10-foot-tall, red-and-purple-colored, stalked corn that makes a great *screening plant* (a tall plant that blocks a view).
- ❀ **'Strawberry'** is a 5-foot-tall plant with miniature 2-inch-long strawberry-colored ears.
- ❀ **'Fiesta'** is a blend of red, purple, white, and yellow kernels on 8-inch-long ears.

Grow ornamental corn as you would sweet corn. Let the ears dry on the corn stalk for best color.

## Popcorn

Popcorn is an educational and tasty vegetable to grow. Sure it's easier to go to the local store and buy popcorn seed (kernels), but with unusual varieties and the opportunity to show your kids where popcorn really comes from, I think it's worth growing. If you can grow sweet corn, you can grow popcorn. Newer varieties have unusual-colored kernels that are good in crafts as well as in your tummy. However, they all still pop into white kernels. Some varieties to try are 'Early Pink,' 'Calico,' and 'Japanese Hulless.' All are 5- to 7-feet tall and need 100 to 120 days to mature.

The only difference between growing sweet corn and popcorn occurs at harvest time. Leave popcorn ears on the stalk until the stalks and husks are brown and dry. Before a frost, harvest and strip away the husks. Hang the ears in mesh bags in a warm, airy, indoor location to continue drying for four to six weeks. Twist the kernels off the cob and store them in glass jars. You can do a sample pop to see if they are dry enough. You pop them as you would store-bought corn — but home-grown popcorn has a fresher taste. Your kids will never look at movie popcorn the same way.

# More Extraordinary Vegetables

Whether you're interested in the tame or the exotic, the following sections give information for growing a cornucopia of other great vegetables in your garden.

## Arugula

Arugula *(Eruca vesicaria)* is also known as roquette or rocket salad. It's one of the main greens found in mesclun mixes (see Chapter 10 for more about mesclun). Arugula is one of the easiest, most cold-tolerant, and quickest-to-mature greens you can grow. The plant is small, with an open habit (it doesn't form a head-like lettuce), and its dark green leaves have a slight peppery and nutty flavor. Arugula adds an interesting zip to everyday salads and is also a nice addition to soups and stir-fries. You can even eat the flowers.

Most gardeners buy arugula without a named variety. However, a few named varieties are now available that are smaller and more cold tolerant, such as 'Sylvetta.' If you want to try these varieties as an experiment, you should be able to find them in catalogs.

Arugula, like most greens, grows best in cool weather. In mild-winter climates, you can plant arugula seeds in fall, winter, and spring. In cold-winter climates, start arugula in spring as soon as you can work the soil; take the summer off and then begin sowing again in fall. Arugula will overwinter in a cold frame very well, even in cold climates. (See Chapter 22 for more on cold frames.)

Seed small patches every two weeks, and in 40 days, you can harvest the 4- to 6-inch-long leaves. In the heat, arugula *bolts* (forms a flower head with bitter leaves) quickly, but you can even eat the flowers if you like a strong, peppery flavor. The only major pest is the flea beetle. See Chapter 18 for tips on controlling this insect.

## Asparagus

One of the joys of spring is picking fresh asparagus *(Asparagus officinalis)* spears from the garden. Unlike most of the vegetables mentioned in this book, asparagus is a perennial plant: It comes back year after year from the crown (the short stem near the roots) and the roots. The crown actually expands with age, producing more spears each year. After the spring harvest, let the spears grow into towering ferns that feed the roots for next year's crop.

### Varieties

Asparagus has male and female plants. Female plants produce spears that eventually grow to produce flowers and seed that not only take extra energy to produce, reducing spear production, but also sow seeds that create a jungle of little asparagus plants. Unfortunately, these young seedlings aren't productive and are mostly just weeds. Male plants don't have flowers and seeds, and are therefore more productive than the female plants.

Older varieties of asparagus such as 'Martha Washington,' which has both male and female spears, were the standards for years. Recently, breeders have developed new varieties that are more productive and better adapted to tough soil conditions. Many are in the "Jersey" series from a breeding program in New Jersey. These are touted as all-male varieties even though they may have a few female plants mixed in. These male varieties are superior for production and growth. Look for varieties such as 'Jersey Giant,' 'Jersey Knight,' and 'Jersey King.' For California and warm-weather gardeners, the University of California has a variety called 'UC 157' that was born and raised in warm soils and performs very well.

### Growing

Asparagus crowns are generally available to purchase in late winter and spring at garden centers or through the mail. Because asparagus is a perennial, you need to pay particular attention to it when planting, and take special care when preparing the planting site. You'll find it easier to amend the soil before planting rather than trying to alter it after you plant the crowns:

1. **Choose a full sun location and pay special attention to removing all the weeds.**

2. **Dig a trench 1-foot deep and as long as you like.**

3. ***Backfill* the trench with 6 to 8 inches of finished compost and soil mixed together.**

4. **Form volcano-like mounds (8 to 10 inches high) every 18 inches and lay the spiderlike crowns and roots of the asparagus on top of the mounds so that the roots drape over the sides of the mounds and the crowns sit on top.**

5. **Cover the crowns with soil and periodically backfill the trench as the asparagus spears grow, until the crowns are about 3 inches below the soil surface.**

Keep the bed well watered, and fertilize each spring with manure or a complete fertilizer such as 5-10-10. Because asparagus is a perennial, you start harvesting in spring when the spears emerge and stop six to eight weeks later:

- ✔ The first year, let all the spears grow into ferns.

- ✔ The second year, harvest only those spears whose diameters are larger than a pencil; your harvest window is about three to four weeks in the spring. Snap off the spears by hand at the soil line when they are 6 to 8 inches tall.

- ✔ The third year, begin harvesting only the pencil-diameter-sized spears for six to eight weeks each spring. Stop after that and let the spears grow into ferns to replenish the crown and roots.

The ferns may be cut down after a hard frost in fall or winter. Weeds are the number one downfall of most asparagus beds. Keep the beds well weeded each year, and you'll lessen the chances of disease and insects reducing your yields.

If you've ever been served white asparagus tips in a restaurant and loved the flavor, you can easily grow your own. All you need to do is *blanch* (block light from the plant, causing no chlorophyll to form and leaving that part of the plant white) the spears by covering the bed with black plastic after the spears begin to break ground. Check them every day or so and harvest as usual. The blanched spears are more tender and have a milder flavor.

# Beets

Beets *(Beta vulgaris)* are best known for their deep-red-colored roots and sweet flavor. However, their leaves (called *greens*) are also very tasty and can be used as a Swiss chard or spinach substitute (see Chapter 10 for more about greens). Try slicing beet roots or greens in salads or cooking the roots in classic beet dishes such as borscht (beet soup). Like most root crops, beets' sweetness improves as the temperatures cool, so leave some in the garden for a late-season harvest.

## Varieties

Beets tend to mature about 50 to 65 days from seeding. Some good varieties to try are 'Red Ace,' 'Detroit Dark Red,' and 'Lutz Green Leaf.' For a long, thin, red root, try 'Cylindra.' These varieties are consistent producers and widely adapted to various growing conditions. If you're interested in beets of different colors, try growing white-fleshed 'Albina Verduna,' which is very sweet, and yellow-fleshed 'Golden' or red-and-white-striped 'Chioggia,' which are sweet, too, but are mostly grown for their looks.

## Growing

Beets grow best in cool, moist conditions. Two weeks before your last frost, prepare a raised bed by working in a 2- to 3-inch layer of composted manure. Then sow seeds $1/2$-inch deep, 2 inches apart. (Even though you eventually thin them to 4 inches apart, it's better to plant close in case the seeds don't geminate uniformly.) Cover the seeds with soil, and keep them well watered. Plant again every two weeks into summer to ensure a continual supply of beets. See Chapter 16 for more on this succession planting technique.

After the seedlings stand 2 to 3 inches tall, thin them to 2 inches apart, eating the tender, thinned greens in salads. Thin the seedlings to 4 inches apart a month later. Harvest the roots when they're golf-ball sized and the most tender. To see whether the beet is large enough to harvest, brush the soil off around the beet root; beets grow right at the surface of the soil, so it's easy to see the top of the roots. But make sure that you leave some beets, especially the 'Lutz Green Leaf' variety, to experience the cool weather that produces the sweetest beets.

Beets seeds are actually tiny dried up fruits with many seeds inside. For this reason, one seed produces many plants. These plants really need to be thinned early. Because many plants grow in the same area, try snipping off the seedlings that you don't want with scissors instead of pulling them out and disturbing the roots. See Chapter 13 for more on thinning seedlings.

Thinning root crops is essential if you want the roots to grow into carrots, beets, onions . . . whatever. If they don't have adequate space, you'll get a small vegetable or no vegetable forming in the roots.

## *Broccoli raab*

Broccoli raab is one vegetable that I had to include in this book. My mother loves it, and of course she's going to read this book, so I better write about it. Actually I love broccoli raab, too, not only for its quick and easy growing habit but also for the mustardy, broccoli taste of the greens. Unlike regular broccoli, you can eat the whole shoot of broccoli raab *(Brassica rapa)*: stems, leaves, head, and all. It matures in about 40 days, so you can grow many crops throughout the year. If you're still not convinced about growing and eating broccoli raab, come visit my momma, and we'll sit down to a plate of cavatelli and broccoli raab.

Varieties of broccoli raab come in two forms: spring raab and fall raab. Choose the variety that corresponds to your planting season. Like broccoli, broccoli raab grows best in cool weather. In mild-winter areas, you can plant it in fall, winter, and spring. In cold-winter areas, plant in spring and fall. Plant every few weeks to ensure a continuous supply of these tasty greens. Direct seed broccoli raab in the garden and grow it as you would broccoli (see Chapter 9). Just before the small head containing flower buds opens, clip the whole plant and sauté away.

# Celeriac

If you like the flavor of celery but have a hard time growing it, try celery's cousin, Celeriac *(Apium graveolens)*. Instead of growing an edible stem, celeriac grows a large, round, white-fleshed root. Once harvested, cleaned, and peeled, it reveals a creamy-white flesh with pure celery flavor. Celeriac tastes great in soups, stir-fries, and salads. Some of the newer varieties that produce consistently good-sized roots include 'Brilliant' and 'Diamant.'

Celeriac likes cool weather and needs a long growing season (100+ days) to mature. In cold-winter climates, start seeds indoors 8 to 12 weeks before your last frost date. In mild-winter climates, start seeds in early summer indoors, and then transplant the seedlings in late summer. Plant the seedlings 8 inches apart in raised beds, and amend them with plenty of compost. Keep the plants mulched with hay or straw and water them well, especially during hot spells. When the roots are about 2 to 3 inches in diameter, you can start harvesting. Pull the whole plant, discard the tops, and peel and chop the root.

The roots develop the best flavor if they're left in the garden until after a few frosts.

# Celery

Celery *(Apium graveolens),* although found in so many dishes, is rarely grown by home gardeners. It can be a challenge to grow because the young plants can die easily or the stems can get stringy. However, growing celery can very rewarding. You can use the leaves and stalks in soups or in raw vegetable dips. If you're growing celery for leaves and stalks, you usually won't get the seeds. Like Celeriac, celery needs a long (120+ days) growing season. It grows best in areas with moderate summers or winters — it doesn't like extremes of heat or cold.

Gardeners may not know that the white stalks of celery are blanched. Home-grown, unblanched celery has a stronger flavor and better nutritional value than store-bought types, but if you like the white stalks, it's easy to blanch your celery, too.

### Varieties

For some widely adapted varieties of celery, try 'Ventura,' 'Utah 52-70 Improved,' and 'Giant Pascal.'

For a unique, semi-self-blanching type, try 'Golden Self-Blanching' or 'Stokes Golden Plume.' These varieties produce golden-yellow color stalks that are naturally semi-blanched. The flavor is milder than unblanched varieties, but it isn't as mild as fully blanched varieties.

There is also a type of celery called "cutting celery" *(Apium graveolens)* that is grown for its leaves and not its stems. This celery isn't common, but it's easier to grow than regular celery.

### Growing

Start celery seed indoors in winter in cold-winter areas and indoors in midsummer in mild-winter areas. Transplant the seedlings outdoors when they're 3 inches tall (about 10 weeks after seeding indoors), spacing them 6 inches apart. Celery requires fertile soil and a constant water supply. Apply plenty of compost or a complete fertilizer, such as 5-10-10, at planting, and mulch the plants well. Side-dress bimonthly with the same fertilizers to ensure good-sized stalks (see Chapter 15 for more on side-dressing). If temperatures get too cold (below 55°F) or too warm (above 80°F) for weeks, celery will suffer, and the stalks will become tough and stringy. After three months or so, begin harvesting your celery stalks, either by pulling up the entire plant or just selecting outer stalks. To blanch, place an empty metal can or milk carton with the ends removed over the stalks ten days before harvesting. You don't need to cover the leaves.

# Chinese cabbage

Chinese cabbage *(Brassica rapa)* combines the best of two worlds. It blends the mild, mustardy flavor of cabbage with the texture of lettuce. Chinese cabbage tastes great in stir-fries, Asian soups, sukiyakis, and salads. It likes cool temperatures and is best grown as a fall or winter crop. Because it takes only 40 to 55 days to mature, it's easy to get a good crop of Chinese cabbage from your fall garden.

Chinese cabbage falls into two categories: heading and non-heading. I discuss the non-heading types, known as pac choi, later in this chapter.

The heading types are tall and torpedo-shaped and called "Michihli," or they're short and barrel-shaped and called "Napa." Some good Chinese cabbage varieties that mature in about 45 days include 'Jade Pagoda' and 'Michihli' (Michihli type) and 'Blues' and 'Nerva' (Napa type).

In cold-winter areas, Chinese cabbage seed of the heading type is best sown indoors in spring for an early summer harvest or indoors in late summer for an early fall harvest. In warm-winter areas, sow the seed in late summer for a fall harvest. Transplant six-week-old seedlings so that they're spaced 1 foot apart, and fertilize them every three weeks with a complete fertilizer. Mulch with hay or straw to keep the soil cool and moist. Start harvesting when the plants are 10 inches tall. The biggest pest of heading-type Chinese cabbage is the flea beetle. See Chapter 18 for more on controlling these insects.

# Collards

This ancient cabbage-family crop is a stalwart in many Southern gardens. Collards *(Brassica oleracea)*, unlike cabbages, don't form heads and can withstand heat and still grow well. The whole plant can be eaten at any stage, and the large, smooth oval leaves, in particular, taste great steamed or mixed in soups. Healthwise, they're one of the best greens you can eat; they're high in vitamin A, iron, and calcium. Some good varieties for production and vigor include 'Champion,' 'Georgia,' and 'Vates.'

Collards like cool weather and mature quickly within 60 to 80 days after seeding. Sow seeds directly in the garden four to six weeks before the last frost date for a spring harvest, and again in mid to late summer for a fall harvest. Thin the seedlings to 10 inches apart. Use these thinnings in soups and casseroles. Fertilize, water, and mulch collards as you would cabbage.

# Endive

This French cool-season green from the chicory family has a reputation for being bitter, but if you grow it yourself, the flavor is mild, and the texture is crunchy. Endive *(Cichorium endivia)* is distinguished from its sister escarole (discussed in the following section) by its deeply cut and curled leaves. You'll find endive in many mesclun seed mixes (see Chapter 10 for more on mesclun) and at restaurant salad bars, blended with lettuce. Some varieties to try are 'Green Curled,' 'Galia,' and 'Tres Fine.'

Growing endive is similar to growing lettuce, and endive matures in the same time frame (see Chapter 10). As an added benefit, if you let the heads get large, the centers naturally blanch, resulting in tender, mild-flavored, creamy-white centers. If the weather is heating up, harvest the greens young (when they're about 6 inches in diameter) before the flavor becomes bitter and the texture becomes tough.

# Escarole

Escarole *(Cichorium endivia)* is endive's sister, with the only true distinguishing feature being the larger heads with broad, thin, smooth leaves of the escarole. It's grown like endive and has the same uses, but it's sweeter and crunchier than endive. Some Italian cooks, like my mom, use escarole in soups, creating a flavorful, sweet, and slightly bitter broth. Escarole also can be blanched by covering the leaves five days before harvest to create an even milder flavor and texture. Some varieties to look for include 'Full Heart Batavian' and 'Broad Leafed Batavian.' For growing instructions, see the previous section, "Endive."

# Florence fennel

Florence fennel *(Foeniculum vulgare)* produces a bulging area at the stem near the soil line called a bulb (technically it isn't a bulb but an enlarged stem). There's also a leaf-type herb called sweet fennel that's grown for its ferny leaves and doesn't produce a bulb. If you like anise flavor, you'll love fennel.

This cool-season crop produces bulbs 80 days after sowing and can be grown as a spring or fall crop. The crunchy bulbs are great sliced in salads, marinated in oil and balsamic vinegar, grilled, or just eaten raw. (My fennel crop never makes it into the house because my daughter Elena likes to pick and eat it while wandering around the yard.)

Even though Florence fennel is grown mostly for its bulbs, you can also use its ferny leaves to add a licorice flavor to salads and casseroles. If you let the plant bolt, the flowers that form produce anise-flavored fennel seeds; you can eat or cook with these great-tasting seeds. The best varieties are the newer ones, which are slower to bolt in the heat and more productive. 'Rudy' and 'Zefa Fino' are good choices.

Fennel likes cool weather to mature the largest and sweetest-tasting bulbs. Prepare the soil, fertilize, and water as you would for lettuce (see Chapter 10). Start fennel indoors in early spring for transplanting outdoors one month later, just before your last frost date. For fall planting, start seeds indoors in late summer. Space transplants 6 to 8 inches apart; harvest a few months later — when the fennel bulbs are 3 to 4 inches in diameter — by pulling the plants out of the ground, cleaning off the soil, and removing the roots and tops.

# Garlic

If any vegetable has experienced a renaissance lately, it has to be garlic *(Allium sativum)*. In recent history, garlic was poo-pooed as a low-class herb that needed to be masked on your breath or you'd risk social embarrassment. Now it's the chic ingredient in many gourmet restaurants and touted as a major medicinal herb to cure everything from earaches to high cholesterol. Garlic is also a key ingredient in some insect repellents and is very effective at repelling vampires (just kidding, I think). These uses come as no surprise to anyone who knows the history of garlic. It has been used medically for centuries, but only recently did we rediscover its benefits. For some unknown reason, many also believe that garlic is difficult to grow. That isn't true.

The key to a good crop of garlic is planting at the right time for your area. Garlic likes cool weather conditions and requires a long time to mature its bulbs.

The beauty of growing your own garlic is sampling the selection of varieties now available. Choosing the variety adapted for your area is the first step, but then you can also try varieties from around the world. The flavors of these different varieties can vary from mild to spicy hot.

## Varieties

Even though you could grow your own garlic from bulbs bought in grocery stores, most of the those varieties are adapted to a California climate. Unless you live in central California where most garlic is commercially grown, it's best to select varieties from catalogs and local garden centers.

Garlic comes in two basic types: soft and hard neck:

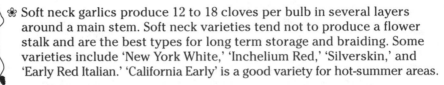

- ❀ Soft neck garlics produce 12 to 18 cloves per bulb in several layers around a main stem. Soft neck varieties tend not to produce a flower stalk and are the best types for long term storage and braiding. Some varieties include 'New York White,' 'Inchelium Red,' 'Silverskin,' and 'Early Red Italian.' 'California Early' is a good variety for hot-summer areas.

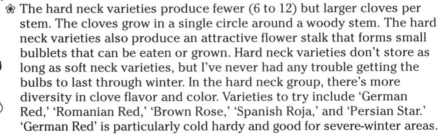

- ❀ The hard neck varieties produce fewer (6 to 12) but larger cloves per stem. The cloves grow in a single circle around a woody stem. The hard neck varieties also produce an attractive flower stalk that forms small bulblets that can be eaten or grown. Hard neck varieties don't store as long as soft neck varieties, but I've never had any trouble getting the bulbs to last through winter. In the hard neck group, there's more diversity in clove flavor and color. Varieties to try include 'German Red,' 'Romanian Red,' 'Brown Rose,' 'Spanish Roja,' and 'Persian Star.' 'German Red' is particularly cold hardy and good for severe-winter areas.

## Growing

For gardeners in cold areas or areas with hot summers, fall is the best time to plant garlic. For gardeners with mild summers and winters, garlic can also be planted in spring.

Prepare the soil as you would for onions, forming raised beds and adding composted manures (see Chapter 14). Garlic needs well-drained soil — if the crop fails, it's usually due to the cloves rotting in wet, cool soil. Fertilize the beds as you would for onions (see Chapter 6).

Plant individual cloves a few inches deep and 3 to 4 inches apart about 4 to 6 weeks before the ground freezes for fall planting or as soon as the ground can be worked for spring planting. For fall planting in cold-winter areas, wait until a few hard freezes and then mulch the beds with a 2- to 4-inch thick layer of hay or straw to protect the cloves over winter. As the cloves start growing in spring, remove the mulch. Once the soil warms, apply a side-dressing of a soluble high-nitrogen fertilizer such as blood meal or fish emulsion (see Chapter 15 for more on side-dressing). In spring- or fall-sown beds, keep the patch well weeded and watered; you may want to mulch in between plants for weed control and moisture retention. Harvest starts when most of the leaves have yellowed, but before the cloves begin to separate away from each other in the bulb.

After harvest, let the bulbs *cure* (toughen their skins) in a warm, dry, airy place for a few weeks. Then braid (just like you do hair) the soft neck varieties or remove the tops of the hard neck bulbs, and store them in a cool, slightly damp basement for use as needed. The bulbs last longest in a slightly damp area, but you can store them in a cool, dry place — they just don't stay hard as long. Garlic flavor is enhanced in storage; cloves often taste best after stored for a few months.

You may come across a third type of garlic that's more related to leeks than garlic. Called 'Elephant' garlic *(Allium ampeloprasum),* it's grown like other garlics but isn't as winter hardy. Elephant garlic plants produce huge white bulbs weighing up to a half pound, with large, easy to peel cloves. The flavor is milder than regular garlic, and you can store the bulbs for up to one year.

## Gourds

Certain vegetables, such as gourds, are grown not for eating — because they taste like cardboard — but for crafts, decorations, and fun.

Gourds come in two general types, small- and large-fruited:

- ✔ The small-fruited gourds *(Cucurbita pepo)* come in a variety of shapes — egg, pear, apple, turban — and are used for decorating and crafts. Unlike large-fruited gourds, you don't have to follow special drying instructions; you can use small-fruited gourds right after harvest.

- ✔ Large-fruited gourds are not only decorative but functional. Some examples of functional gourds are the birdhouse gourd *(Lagenaria siceraria),* dipper gourd *(Lagenaria siceraria),* and luffa gourd *(Luffa aegyptiaca).* Large-fruited gourds require longer growing seasons (140 to 150 days) than the small-fruited gourds, and you must follow special drying instructions before you can use them.

Gourds are great to grow with kids because of all the fanciful creations they can make after the gourds are dried.

Grow gourds as you would winter squash (see Chapter 8). The seeds have particularly thick skins, so nicking them with a file helps water penetrate them and hastens germination.

If you're growing large-fruited gourds in a cold-winter climate, start the plants indoors four weeks before the last frost date to get a jump on the season.

Because gourds love to vine, consider growing them on a trellis or at the edge of your garden to roam the lawn. Wait until the fruit skins are hard and the stems are brown (but before a frost) to harvest. Large-fruited gourds can survive a light frost, but small-fruited ones cannot. When harvesting, cut the vines, leaving 1 inch of stem on the fruit, and wash and clean the skin.

Small-fruited gourds can be used as decorations immediately after harvest, but large-fruited gourds need to dry in a warm, dry, airy room for a few weeks. When you can shake the gourds and hear the seeds rattling around inside, they're ready to carve, paint, and decorate. If you want to accelerate the drying process, try drilling a hole in the bottom of the large-fruited gourd.

## Jerusalem artichoke

If you're looking for a functional, edible plant to screen an area or grow in a far corner of the garden, try the American native Jerusalem artichoke *(Helianthus tuberosa)*. Also known as the sunchoke, these plants grow to 6 feet tall, can spread like a weed, and produce a small, yellow, sunflower-like head late in the season that attracts birds. However, it's what's underground that's edible. About 90 days after planting, each plant produces knobby, potato-like tubers that have a nutty flavor. You can eat them raw in salads or steamed or made into pancakes. A few named varieties are available, such as 'Stampede,' which matures earlier, and 'Fuseau,' which has fewer knobs. Grow Jerusalem artichokes the same way you grow potatoes (see Chapter 6). They tolerate poor soil conditions and even partial sun, although they produce best in full sun.

Once established, Jerusalem artichokes will spread and spread and spread, becoming weeds, even if you mow them down annually. Any tubers left after fall harvest will sprout new plants the next year.

## Kale

If there is one vegetable to grow for purely the health benefits alone, kale *(Brassica oleracea)* is it. Kale offers the highest amount of protein, calcium, iron, vitamin A, and antioxidants (cancer-fighting compounds) of any cultivated vegetable. Luckily, it tastes good too! Lightly steamed or added to soups and casseroles, kale adds a crunch and a mild cabbage flavor to dishes. Like its cousin, collards, it's technically a non-heading cabbage. It's grown like collards, but has smaller and more fringed leaves. Some new varieties with red and purple leaf coloration are now available. Just imagine: a vegetable that tastes good, is good for you, and looks good in the garden:

❀ Some standard curly-leafed varieties are 'Dwarf Green Curled,' 'Siberia,' and 'Vates Dwarf Blue Scotch Curled.' Some of the newer flat-leafed varieties are 'Red Russian,' with oak-shaped, reddish-purple leaves, and 'White Russian,' a white version of 'Red Russian.'

❀ For curly-leafed varieties with different colored leaves, try 'Lacinato' with curly, dark, blue-green leaves or 'Winter Red,' with curly, reddish leaves that have deep purple veins.

Grow kale as you would collards, planting in late summer for a fall harvest. The flavor and sweetness of the leaves improves after exposure to near-freezing temperatures, so I often grow it as a fall crop (by planting in late summer), picking and eating the plants into the winter.

## Kohlrabi

Now here's something different: a vegetable that looks like a flying object from *Star Wars*. It's kohlrabi *(Brassica oleracea),* a cabbage relative that's also called a "stem turnip" because the stem near the soil line forms a round, turniplike globe, which you eat (see Figure 11-2). Once you get over kohlrabi's odd appearance, you may be won over by the taste and crunchiness of kohlrabi. Peeled and sliced, it's excellent in dips and stir-fries. The plant is easy to grow and very hardy. Some standard varieties are 'Early White Vienna' and 'Early Purple Vienna.' (Yes, the latter has attractive purple skin and coloring in the leaves.) If you fall in love with kohlrabi and can't get enough, try growing 'Superschmelz,' a football-sized variety that stays tender and doesn't get woody (tough) even though it's large. The other varieties that I just mentioned get woody if they grow too large, but this is only a problem if you forget to harvest them.

**Figure 11-2:** Kohlrabi are fun to look at and eat.

Like all cabbage-family vegetables, kohlrabi likes cool weather. It's best grown as a spring or fall crop, avoiding the heat of summer that causes the globes to get woody. Start seeds indoors as you would broccoli and cabbage (see Chapter 9), and kohlrabi will mature 50 to 60 days after transplanting in the garden. The fertilizing, watering, and pest control are similar for cabbages. Harvest the globes when they're about 2 to 3 inches in diameter.

## Leeks

Leeks *(Allium ampeloprasum)* haven't received a lot of press in North America, but they're considered a staple in every vegetable garden in England and Europe. I love them because you transplant the seedlings in spring, as you would onions, keep them weed-free and watered, and then forget about the crop until fall. They grow slowly all summer, and by the time cool temperatures arrive, they've formed thick stalks that can be harvested and sautéed in butter or added to potato-leek and other soups. The flavor is milder than that of onions and takes on a slightly sweeter flavor after a few cold nights.

Some leek varieties are very cold-tolerant, so you can harvest right through the winter in many areas. Varieties such as 'Blue Solaise' have attractive blue-green colored foliage that makes leeks a beautiful ornamental as well. Some other good varieties to try are 'King Richard,' 'American Flag,' and the really winter-hardy 'Winter Giant.'

Leeks need a long season to mature — nearly 100 days for many varieties. For cold-winter areas, start seeds in early spring as you would for onions — about 8 to 12 weeks before your last frost date. For mild-winter areas, start seeds in late summer for a fall planting and winter harvest. Transplant the seedlings, 6 inches apart, into 6-inch-deep trenches filled halfway with compost. Fill in the rest of the trench with garden soil as the leeks grow.

Like onions, leeks don't compete well with weeds, so be diligent about weeding. Water and fertilize as you would onions. When the stalks have thickened and after a few cool nights, begin harvesting. Certain hardy varieties such as 'Winter Giant' can withstand temperatures below 20°F and can be harvested and eaten all winter in mild-winter areas. Other varieties can be mulched with hay to allow you to keep harvesting into the winter, even in cold areas.

Hilling the stalks two to three times during the growing season will blanch the bottom of the stems white (see Chapter 6 for more on hilling). The flavor of the blanched stems is milder and the texture is more tender than the green stems.

## Mizuna

Mizuna *(Brassica rapa)* is a leafy-type, Oriental green that is often found in mesclun mixes. Mizuna has a small white stem and deeply cut leaves with a mild, mustardy flavor. Mizuna matures from direct seeding in about 40 days. As with lettuce, you can plant successive crops of mizuna to add a zip to salads and stir-fries. It can also be cut and allowed to regrow many times. Treat it like any green (see Chapter 10) as far as seeding, watering, and fertilizing, and watch out for flea beetles eating the leaves.

## Mustard greens

Another essential Oriental green is mustard *(Brassica juncea)*. When full-sized, mustards have a strong, hot flavor, but if harvested young (6 inches tall), the flavor is much milder. Mustard greens like growing in cool weather, and as with other greens, you can plant successive crops of them. They also regrow from cutting. The mature plants can get a couple feet tall, and some varieties have beautiful coloring on their leaves, making them attractive as well. Some of the most colorful varieties are 'Osaka Purple' and 'Red Giant.' 'Florida Broadleaf' is a standard variety grown in the Southeast. Direct sow seeds in spring or fall in cold-winter areas and late summer in mild-winter areas. Thin plants to 8 inches apart. Water, fertilize, and harvest as you would other greens, which I discuss in Chapter 10.

## Okra

Okra *(Ablemoschus esculentus)* is a classic southern vegetable that loves the heat. In fact, it's one of the few vegetables that keeps producing during the dog days of summer in the South. This tall (4 to 10 feet), stalky plant produces attractive, trumpetlike flowers along the main stem that mature into okra pods. Each flower potentially produces one pod. The pods can be fried, baked, boiled, and eaten on their own or used in soups and stews such as gumbo. Some people don't like the sticky nature of the insides of the pod, but I love them broiled with a little oil.

The standard okra variety is 'Clemson Spineless,' which matures in 60 days, but for gardeners with a short growing season, better choices are 'Annie Oakley II' and 'Cajun Delight,' which mature about 50 days from seeding. For a beautiful and unusual-colored variety, try 'Burgundy.' It has red leaves and pods.

Okra needs heat! Don't direct seed or transplant okra until the soil temperature is at least 65°F. Direct seed in early summer. In cold-winter areas, choose quick-maturing varieties. Thin plants to 1 to 2 feet apart. Fertilize at planting, then when first pods form, and finally in midsummer with compost or a complete fertilizer such as 5-10-10.

Use a knife to harvest the pods just above the *cap* (where the base of the pod attaches to the stem) when pods are 2- to 3-inches long and still tender. Check the plants every few days. The more you harvest, the more the plants will produce. Because okra seed doesn't save well, buy fresh seed every year.

Okra stems and leaves have spines that can irritate your skin. Wear gloves and long-sleeved shirts when working and harvesting in the okra patch.

## Pac choi

No Oriental stir-fry is complete without some juicy, crunchy stalks of pac choi *(Brassica rapa)* tossed in. If you see the words bok choy, pac choi, and pak choi, they're all referring to the same vegetable. These greens feature sturdy white, crunchy stalks and lush, large, green, flat leaves. They produce their vase-shaped, very open heads about 40 to 50 days after transplanting and, like other greens, love cool weather. Judging from their sweet, almost nutty taste, it's hard to imagine that these plants belong to the cabbage family.

Two great varieties are 'Mei Qing Choi,' a "baby"-size head that only reaches 6 to 8 inches tall, and 'Joi Choi,' a standard 12- to 15-inch-tall head that tolerates hot and cold weather without bolting.

See the growing instructions for Chinese cabbage earlier in this chapter. Because it matures so quickly, pac choi can be succession planted in spring, summer, or fall crop in most areas (see Chapter 16 for details). However, avoid summer planting in hot climates.

## Parsnip

Parsnip *(Pastinaca sativa)* is the quintessential fall root crop. I love to grow these white, carrotlike roots because, like gardeners, parsnips get sweeter with age.

As with leeks, you plant these roots in spring and forget about them until fall. Then, after a few hard frosts, start digging. The cold weather helps the carbohydrates in the roots turn to sugar, and boy do they get sweet! But don't yank them all in fall. In all but the extremely cold areas of the United States, parsnips can be harvested all winter right into spring (as long as the ground hasn't frozen) for a sweet spring treat. Some standard varieties to try are 'Andover,' 'Harris Model,' and 'Lancer.'

Parsnips take a long time to germinate and mature. Most varieties take two weeks or more to germinate and 100 to 120 days to produce roots. Luckily, they grow well in cold weather. Grow parsnips as you would carrots, but with one exception: When planting, place pairs of seeds in small holes that are ¹/₂ inch deep and spaced 1 inch apart, then fill the holes with potting soil. Because parsnips may not germinate well, the second seed ensures a better germination rate. When the seedlings are 3 to 4 inches tall, thin them to one seedling per hole.

When growing root crops, especially parsnips, do not spread high-nitrogen fertilizer on the beds before planting. Soils rich in nitrogen produce hairy, forked roots.

## Peanut

Now here's a crop you can grow that will taste good and amaze your kids, who may have thought that peanuts only grew in ball parks and circuses.

The peanut *(Arachis hypogaea)* isn't really a nut but actually a legume similar to peas and beans. Peanuts are a warm-season crop. They grow where okra and sweet potatoes thrive. They like heat and a long growing season. However, even gardeners in cold areas can have some success with peanuts, provided they start early and choose short-season varieties such as 'Early Spanish.' Unless you grow a field of peanuts, you probably won't get enough to make a year's supply of peanut butter, but boiled in salt water, roasted, or eaten green, fresh peanuts are a tasty and healthy snack food. Some other varieties that have bigger pods and more seed per pod include 'Tennessee Red' and 'Virginia Jumbo.' They all need 100 to 120 days of warm weather to mature.

Peanuts like well-drained soil and can tolerate some drought. Plant the seeds, with the shells removed, 1 foot apart in rows 2 to 3 feet apart. The young plant looks like a bush clover plant. Fertilize and water the plants as you would beans (see Chapter 7), but side-dress with 5-10-10 fertilizer when flowers appear to help with the nut formation. Yellow flowers appear within six weeks after planting. Hill the plants to kill weeds, mulch with straw, and then watch in amazement as the fun part begins.

After the flowers wither, stalklike pegs emerge from the flowers and curve downward, eventually drilling 3 inches into the soil (see Figure 11-3). At the ends of these pegs, peanut shells containing the peanuts form. When the plants start yellowing, the peanuts growing underground are mature and ready to harvest. Pull the whole plant up and dry it in a warm, airy place out of direct sun; then crack open the peanut shells for a tasty treat. Most kids are fascinated by things that grow underground, and peanuts are pretty amazing in their own right, so watch your kids get wide-eyed at this underground treasure.

There are actually four different types of peanuts (runner, Virginia, Spanish, and Valencia). The first two are runner types with two large seeds per pod. The second two are bush types with two to six seeds per pod. Growing techniques are the same for each type.

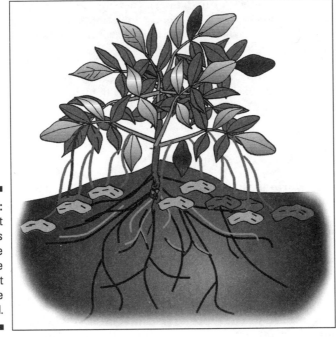

**Figure 11-3:**
Peanut
flowers
produce
stalklike
pegs that
curve
underground.

# *Radicchio*

Radicchio *(Cichorum intybus)* is a type of leaf chicory that can be eaten as a lettuce or allowed to form a small, red, cabbagelike head. It's the latter form that people are most familiar with in salad bars and restaurants. The heads form white veins and grow to the size of grapefruits. Radicchio has a slightly bitter, tart, and tangy flavor and adds culinary and visual pizzazz to salads.

For some home gardeners, radicchio isn't the easiest crop to grow because it often doesn't form heads. Radicchio likes it cool, and it sometimes grows best in spring and sometimes in fall, depending on the variety. The following four modern varieties more consistently form heads than older varieties: 'Rossana' and 'Firebird' (for spring crops) and 'Early Treviso' and 'Inferno' (for fall and winter varieties). If you grow these four varieties at the right time, they should form heads. In cold-winter climates, start it indoors, similar to lettuce transplants, and grow it as spring or a fall crop. In mild-winter climates, it's best grown as a fall crop. Grow radicchio as you would lettuce (see Chapter 10). Most modern varieties, including those previously mentioned, will form heads on their own (without being cut back) 80 to 90 days from seeding. Harvest the heads when they're solid, like small cabbages. The heads are crunchy, colorful, and good in cooking.

If plants don't start forming heads about 50 days after setting them out in the garden, cut the plants back to within 1 inch of the ground and enjoy the lettucelike greens. The new sprouts that grow will form heads.

# Radish

If you're looking for quick satisfaction, grow radishes *(Raphanus sativus)*. The seeds germinate within days of planting, and most varieties mature their tasty roots within a month. When grown in cool weather and not stressed, radishes will have a juicy, slightly hot flavor. Of course, anyone who's grown radishes knows that if radishes *are* stressed by lack of water, too much heat, or competition from weeds or each other, you end up with a fire-breathing dragon that people won't tolerate.

Most gardeners are familiar with the spring-planted red globes or white elongated roots found in grocery stores, but exotic-looking international radishes are showing up in specialty food stores and restaurants. These radishes require a longer season and are often planted to mature in fall or winter:

- Japanese radishes called *daikons* can grow up to 2-foot-long white roots.

- Spicy-hot Spanish black radishes look like round black balls or cylinders and can be kept in a root cellar for six months.

- Chinese radishes look like turnips but are red, green, or white on the inside. They taste similar to the Japanese radishes.

- 'Rat-tail' radishes are grown for the spicy-tasting seed pods that form after flowering.

## Varieties

The following varieties work well for the beginning gardener:

- For the classic red or white round radishes, try 'Cherry Belle,' 'Easter Egg' (a mix of red and white), and 'Scarlet Globe.'

- For the elongated white or red roots, try 'French Breakfast' (a mix of red and white), 'White Icicle,' or 'D'Avignon' (the top of the root is red, and the bottom is white).

- For daikons, try 'Summer Cross #3' and 'April Cross.'

- Black Spanish radishes come as 'Round Black Spanish' or 'Long Black Spanish.'

- Some Chinese varieties are 'Red Meat' (green outside, red inside), 'China Rose' (red outside and red inside), and 'Misato Green' (green all the way through).

### Growing

The round or elongated "traditional" radishes are normally planted in early spring to mature while the temperatures are still cool. Daikons can be planted in spring or summer, depending on the variety. Chinese and black radishes, however, are best planted in late summer or early fall for a fall or winter harvest.

For all types of radishes, form raised beds, fertilize, and sow both spring and fall plantings as you would carrots. The keys to success with any radish crop are loosening the soil well, weeding, thinning the plants to give the roots enough room to expand (usually 6 inches apart), keeping the plants well watered, and growing them when it's cool.

You can harvest spring-planted radish roots as soon as they start to form. Harvest daikon, Chinese, and black radishes when you need them (although they're most tender when eaten on the small side); they can withstand light frosts in the fall. Harvest 'Rat-tail' radish pods once they form.

# Rhubarb

Rhubarb *(Rheum rhubarbarum),* like asparagus, is an exception in the vegetable world. It's a perennial plant (except in zones 8 and warmer where it's treated as an annual), and once established, it will come back faithfully year after year. It will even spread, allowing you to dig, divide, and share plants with friends. Hopefully, you have many friends, because you'll only need a few healthy rhubarb plants to produce plenty for pies, jams, and jellies.

The part of the rhubarb plant you eat is the leaf stalk that grows from the crown of the plant. Don't eat the leaf itself, unless you want an upset stomach. Depending on the variety, the stalks are green or red and taste sour. The most tender varieties have leaf stalks that are red all the way through, such as 'Chipman' and 'Valentine.'

Rhubarb usually isn't eaten raw (even though I have fond memories of eating rhubarb as a child by dipping the stalks in a bowl of sugar!). It's best used as an ingredient in cooking. Can't you just smell that strawberry-rhubarb pie fresh from the oven?

Rhubarb is one of those "plant and forget" crops. If it has full sun, well-drained soil, lots of compost and manure mixed in, and water, it will grow like a weed. Rhubarb does best in cool climates, so gardeners in Florida and Arizona may have to rely on their northern friends for fresh rhubarb.

For best quality, harvest the leaf stalks as soon as the leaves completely unfold to a flat surface. Always leave at least two leaf stalks per plant so the plant can rejuvenate itself. If a seed stalk forms (usually from the center of the plant), cut it off to extend the leaf-stalk harvesting season. The plants die back in fall, but they reemerge in spring from the roots.

Rhubarb is easy to dig and divide. In spring, just as the new shoots are starting to emerge, dig up the whole plant with a sharp spade and divide the main crown into many 3- to 4-inch-diameter sections. Plant these sections; within two to three years, you can harvest from these new plants.

# Rutabaga

Probably the only time anyone thinks of rutabagas *(Brassica napus),* if at all, is Thanksgiving, when they're traditionally served with turkey, stuffing, and all the trimmings. They also can be boiled, mashed, or used in hearty winter soups.

This Old World root crop is easy to grow, and any gardener can have a small patch to satisfy all her fall and winter rutabaga desires (once she knows enough about rutabagas to desire them). The flavor and growth are similar to those of turnips (see the "Turnip" section later in this chapter). In fact, another name for the rutabaga is Swedish turnip, or "Swede" for short. Because the rutabaga is actually a cross between a cabbage and a turnip, if you like either of those vegetables, you may want to give rutabaga a try. The roots have either yellow or white flesh, depending on the variety.

Like turnips, rutabagas love cool weather, and you can eat the lush greens as well as the root. A few varieties to try are 'American Purple Top' (yellow flesh), 'Laurentian' (yellow flesh), and 'Gilfeather' (white flesh).

Grow rutabagas the same way that you grow turnips, except rutabagas need about 100 days to mature from direct sowing; turnips mature in half that time. Rutabagas love the cold, and the roots can get as large as softballs and still remain tender. Leave them in the ground until just before the ground freezes; then harvest them as you need them. The longer rutabagas are in the ground, the sweeter they'll taste.

# Salsify and black salsify

Salsify *(Tragopogon porrifolius)* and black salsify *(Scorzonera hispanica)* are obscure European root crops in the sunflower family. Their flavors remind some gardeners of oysters. They take up to 120 days to mature their long, cylindrical roots with white flesh; they're similar to carrots, but thinner. Scrub the roots, chop them up, and add them to soups or stews.

Growing these root crops is similar to growing celeriac, which is mentioned earlier in this chapter. Salsify and black salsify are direct seeded in spring and harvested in fall after a frost, or in mild areas, you can leave them in the ground all winter for an early spring harvest.

Dig carefully — the long thin roots are brittle and break easily.

# Shallots

If you like the taste of onions or garlic but have a hard time getting them to grow, consider growing shallots *(Allium cepa)*. They look like small onions, but their flavor is milder than any of their *allium* cousins, and growing them is a snap.

Shallots are an indispensable part of many French dishes. Substitute three to four shallots for each onion in recipes. Minced, they can be sautéed in wine and herb butter or used in a béarnaise sauce. A little candlelight, a little champagne, and voilà: Shallots become romantic.

Varieties include the traditional 'Gray' shallots with a yellow/gray skin and white, creamy-colored flesh, and red shallots such as 'Brittany' with red skin and pink flesh. Shallots are usually purchased as sets (similar to onion sets), but recently shallot seeds have become available in many varieties such as 'Pikant' and 'Ambition,' allowing you to grow more shallots at a lower cost.

Plant shallot seed or sets as you would onion seed or sets. They can be grown in spring or fall and will overwinter in all but the coldest winter climates. They require the same fertility and growing conditions as onions (see Chapter 6). About 90 days after planting in the garden, the tops will brown and die. Notice that one bulb sprouts 4 to 5 side bulbs around it. Separate the side bulbs and dry and store these as you would onions. Save some of the largest shallots for a fall or spring planting, and you'll never have to buy shallots again — that is, if you can resist eating them all.

# Sunflower

Sunflowers *(Helianthus annuus)* are all the rage as cut flowers in floral shops, and breeders have created varieties with colored heads ranging from red to white and plants that are 2 feet tall to 10 feet tall to meet the need. Because this book is concerned with things you eat, I focus on the giant snack varieties of sunflowers. Technically, all sunflowers can be eaten, but the snack varieties produce the largest heads containing the meatiest seeds.

Not only are the seeds good human food, but the birds love them, too. You can store some seeds for your feathered friends this winter. Some of the best snacking varieties for both people and birds are 'Mammoth' and 'Grey Striped.'

This may sound obvious, but sunflowers really do like the sun. As a matter of fact, the more sun, the better. Plant seeds in well-drained soil, 10 to 18 inches apart in rows, after all danger of frost has passed. The eating varieties tend to produce a large, yellow-petaled head on a thick stalk with large, hairy leaves. Many of these plants can be huge (sometimes as tall as 15 feet), so the plant needs adequate fertility to grow and produce the best seeds. Amend the soil with plenty of compost or manure, and side-dress monthly with a complete fertilizer such as 5-10-10. In about 80 days, the heads will open.

You'll have to be quick to get the seeds before the birds do. A simple technique is to cover the heads with a paper bag (see Figure 11-4) until the petals naturally wilt and the seeds mature. When you can rub off the seeds with your hand, cut off the head, remove the seeds, and dry them. Lightly roasted, sunflower seeds are a great snack food for kids and grown ups, and you can save some raw seeds for your bird feeder.

Sunflowers don't like company. Their roots exude a chemical into the soil that inhibits the growth of other plants in the area. Therefore, plant sunflowers in their own section, against a fence, or as a background in your garden.

**Figure 11-4:** Cover sunflower heads with a paper bag to prevent the birds from stealing your harvest.

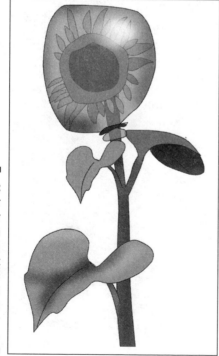

# *Turnip*

All right, turnips *(Brassica rapa)* aren't exactly America's favorite vegetable, but I think they've been given a bad rap. Turnips are easy to grow, and you can eat the greens as well as the roots. If grown in cool weather, they have a slightly sweet flavor.

Like rutabagas, turnips can be eaten boiled, mashed, or added to soups and stews. The white or white-and-purple roots are smaller than rutabagas (tennis ball size) and mature quicker (in less than 50 days from seeding). The greens are great steamed, and they walk hand in hand with collard greens as the favorite Southern leafy crop. Some varieties to try are 'Purple Top White Globe,' 'Shogoin,' and 'Tokyo Cross.' The latter two produce excellent, mild-tasting greens.

Turnips love cool weather. In most areas, you can grow spring and fall crops:

- ✔ Start in spring a few weeks before your last frost date.
- ✔ In early fall, wait until the hot summer weather has passed before planting.

Turnips are best direct seeded in the garden. Prepare the soil and fertilize as you would for any root crop (see Chapter 6). If you want roots, thin the young seedlings to 4 inches apart. If you're growing them for greens only, don't bother thinning them; just start clipping when the greens are 4 to 6 inches tall. Keep the plants well watered and mulched with hay or straw, which, in addition to holding in moisture and controlling weeds, helps prevent the roots from developing a strong flavor. Begin harvesting when the roots are 3 to 4 inches in diameter; then enjoy. Turnips can take a frost, so you can harvest right into winter until the ground freezes.

# Chapter 12

# Herbs, Berries, and More: Not Veggies, but They Sure Taste Good

● ● ● ● ● ● ● ● ● ● ● ● ● ● ● ● ● ● ● ● ● ● ● ● ● ● ● ● ● ● ● ● ● ● ● ● ● ● ● ● ●

*In This Chapter*

▶ Planting, harvesting, and preserving herbs

▶ Growing berries to pair with your vegetables

▶ Discovering flowers that you can eat

▶ Sprouting your own sprouts

● ● ● ● ● ● ● ● ● ● ● ● ● ● ● ● ● ● ● ● ● ● ● ● ● ● ● ● ● ● ● ● ● ● ● ● ● ● ● ● ●

*A* vegetable garden shouldn't be just about vegetables. Your vegetable garden should really be a *food* garden. After all, my mom's tomato sauce recipe would taste like bad tomato soup if not for the fresh herbs that I add. Is it really possible to grow tomatoes without having some fresh herbs like basil and oregano near by? Can you grow pickling cucumbers and not grow dill? Not in my garden. If you truly want to explore the world of culinary delights in your vegetable garden, grow some fresh herbs in it.

But why stop there? You may want to grow other foods as well. How about some fresh fruit? Several types of berries fit neatly into vegetable gardens. How about some edible flowers, too? You can even grow exotic items such as mushrooms and sprouts. That's what this chapter is all about — plants other than vegetables that you may want to grow in your food garden.

## Herbs

Herbs are easy to grow, and they add color, interesting forms, and rich and subtle fragrances to your garden. And fresh herbs can enhance the flavor of food — they turn even the most ordinary recipe into something special. You can add fresh herbs to vinegar and oils, or dry the herbs for future use. Face it, if growing fresh vegetables is about better-tasting food, grow some herbs to add interest and flavor.

Like vegetables, herbs may be annuals (like basil) that you start from seed or transplants each year, biennials (like parsley), or perennials (like chives). Despite their basic differences, most herbs require the same growing conditions: a minimum of six hours of sunlight per day, excellent soil drainage, and moderately rich, loose soil.

All herbs benefit from adding a little fertilizer to the soil. So during soil preparation before planting, use 1½ to 2 pounds of 5-10-10 fertilizer (or its equivalent) per 100 square feet. (See Chapter 15 for more on fertilizer.) Adding more fertilizer than that can cause many herbs to grow too tall and leggy; you want compact bushy plants because these plants usually produce more essential oils for herb flavor.

Plant your herbs where you can get to them for easy harvesting. You can mix them in with your vegetables or plant them in a special show-off bed of their own. If you plant perennial herbs in your vegetable garden, set them off so that you can easily avoid them during spring and fall tilling.

The following sections take an alphabetical look at my favorite herbs.

# Basil

My mother would kick me out of the family if I didn't talk about one of the classic Italian herbs: basil (*Ocimum basilicum* and other species). If you cook any Italian dishes, you should really grow basil. Heck, forget cooking altogether if you want. I like to chop fresh basil and put it on sliced home-grown tomatoes with a little olive oil and balsamic vinegar. Yum.

Although you can't plant basil until after the last frost date, it produces abundantly in the heat of the summer.

You can choose from several types of basil. The one offered by most nurseries or mail-order catalogs is bush or sweet basil — a compact plant that grows up to 18 inches high. Purple basil ('Dark Opal') adds a splendid burgundy color to your garden. You can use it like common basil, though it's a little less sweet. The purple leaves can create a beautiful color when steeped in white vinegar. Recently discovered by many cooks are lemon basil, cinnamon basil, and Thai basil (a strong anise flavor). They add a unique fragrance to both your garden and your kitchen.

Start basil seeds indoors about six weeks before the last frost date or sow the seeds directly in your garden (¼ inch deep) after the last frost date when the soil is warm. In addition to seeds, most nurseries also carry basil transplants. Set transplants or thin seedlings to stand at least 10 to 12 inches apart; more room (16 to 24 inches) is even better because it encourages low, bushy plants to develop. Plant in full sun.

After the plants have grown for six weeks, pinch the center stalks of the basil to force side growth and prevent early flowering — flowers take energy away from the leaves that you eat. If flower stalks do develop, cut or pinch them off early. Mulch the soil and maintain consistent moisture levels. Basil is generally pest-free. As the plants mature, early cold weather can ruin your crop, so be sure to harvest if temperatures dip into the 30s.

Basil is most pungent when it's fresh. The best time to harvest is when the plant starts to form flower buds, but before they open. At this time, snip the leaves and branches and pinch off the flower buds to keep the plant productive. You can also cut the entire plant about 6 to 8 inches above the ground, leaving at least one node (where a leaf was) with two young shoots attached. The plant should produce a second, smaller harvest a few weeks later.

The best way to store fresh basil is to place the stem ends in water like a small bouquet. You can put the leaves in the refrigerator, but they won't last long. Because the leaves lose some of their flavor when dried, freezing is the best method for winter storage. To quick-freeze basil, clean and dry whole *sprigs* (stem pieces with 3 to 4 leaves) and pack them in plastic bags with the air pressed out.

To dry basil, pinch off the leaves at the stem, and dry them in a shady, well-ventilated area. Check the leaves in three or four days, and if they aren't totally dry, finish drying them in an oven; otherwise, the leaves may turn brown and black. Use the lowest heat possible with the oven door slightly open; turn the leaves for even drying and check them frequently until they're dry and crumbly.

I also like to make pesto from the fresh leaves. To make pesto, blend 4 cups of basil leaves with 1/2 cup of olive oil, 1/2 cup of parmesan cheese, and 1/2 cup of pine nuts (you can vary the proportions to your taste buds). Add salt and pepper to taste, and you have a quick dinner. Or you can freeze the pesto to eat in the winter.

# Chives

Chives are one of the easiest plants to grow, period. After you plant chives in your garden, you always have them because they're a hardy perennial — one of the first harvests each year. You can easily dig the plants up, divide them, and move them as your garden evolves over the years. And you need only a few plants to harvest all the chives you'll ever need.

Common chives *(Allium schoenoprasum)* grow to 1 foot tall and have narrow, hollow green leaves and spherical pink or purple flowers; the plants are quite pretty. You can use the leaves in all kinds of sauces and salads to lend a delicate onion flavor. And, of course, what would baked potatoes be without chives? The flowers, when added to white vinegar, impart a lovely pink or purple color.

Garlic chives *(Allium tuberosum)* are close relatives of common chives, but they differ slightly in appearance and flavor. Garlic chives have flat leaves, and their white flowers, which are highly attractive to bees, appear in the summer. Although the seed heads are excellent for decorating wreaths, be careful not to let the seeds fall; garlic chives can become a weedy nuisance. Sometimes called Oriental chives, you can use garlic chives in soups, salads, sauces, and meat dishes to impart their garlicky flavor.

You can start chive plants from seed, or purchase a plant or two, or dig up part of a clump from a neighbor's garden (with her permission, of course). If you're seeding, plant in mid to late spring in a sunny or slightly shady area. Chives prefer rich soil, and after they're established, they'll tolerate either moist or dry conditions. Sow the seeds in clusters that are 1 to 1¹/₂ feet apart. Small clumps of chives planted in pots will grow in a sunny spot indoors. Remove the flower stalks after they bloom. Divide the plants (dig up and separate the small plants) every three to four years.

You can begin harvesting chives six weeks after planting or as soon as the established plants resume growth in the spring. As you need leaves, cut the outer ones near the base. Use the leaves fresh or frozen; they also retain their flavor well when dried.

# Dill

Common dill *(Anethum graveolens)* grows to a height of about 3 to 5 feet. It grows best towards the back of your garden where there is plenty of room. 'Dukat' is an improved new variety with high oil content. 'Fernleaf' is a dwarf variety that reaches only 18 inches tall and is slow to go to seed.

Start from seed sown directly in your garden because dill does poorly when it's transplanted. The plants thrive in rich, loose soil in a sunny location. Plant the seeds one to two weeks before the last spring frost date if you want the crop to mature when you do your first cucumber pickling.

Sow seeds ¹/₄ inch deep in rows that are 18 to 24 inches part, or broadcast seeds over a 2-square-foot bed and gently rake the seeds into the soil. Plants should emerge in 10 to 14 days; let them grow for another 10 to 14 days and then thin them to 12 to 18 inches apart. Make small sowings a few weeks apart in different 2-square-foot areas in your garden until midsummer to get a supply of fresh leaves throughout the season.

The plants get very spindly, so you may have to stake the tallest ones to prevent them from blowing over in a strong wind. Let a few plants mature their seed (let the seed form and drop from the flower naturally); if left undisturbed, they'll provide many new plants next season.

You can start harvesting the fernlike leaves about eight weeks after planting by pinching the outer leaves close to the stem. The leaves have the strongest flavor just when the flower heads are opening. To dry the leaves, place them in a dark place on a window screen; after they're dry, seal them in an airtight jar. Freezing the leaves retains even more of their flavor.

For pickling, cut off the seed heads when they're light brown. Dry them for a few days in paper bags with air holes in the sides, and then shake the seeds loose in the bottom of the bags. You can use then use these seeds for cooking. Dill is great not only in pickles but also on beans and fish.

## French tarragon

French tarragon (*Artemisia dracunculus sativa*) is an essential herb for many cooks, but it can cause some confusion for the first-time grower. You must know exactly what you're buying when you purchase a French tarragon plant because it's often confused with similar-looking Russian tarragon, a weedy plant that has little value in cooking. French tarragon is a hardy perennial that can be grown only from tip cuttings of new growth, root cuttings, or divisions.

 If you find tarragon seed for sale, it's probably Russian tarragon. If you're buying plants at a nursery, rub some of the leaves together and then smell them to determine the variety; the French variety will have the strong licorice scent that you want.

Tarragon does best in full sun or partial shade, and it needs well-drained soil. Purchase plants, or if you have a friend with an established tarragon bed, divide each established plant into two or three plants in early spring, You do this by digging up the entire plant, cutting it evenly into two or three smaller plants, and then replanting one plant and giving away the rest. Space tarragon plants 2 to 3 feet apart and give them room to spread. Divide the plants every two to three years to keep them vigorous and healthy.

Cut back plants to 2 feet when flower buds start to form to prevent flowering and to keep the plants from getting floppy. In cold-winter climates, apply a thick organic mulch — such as straw — over the roots in the winter.

Tarragon leaves have the best flavor if you use them fresh in early summer or freeze them for later use. Tarragon's aniselike flavor makes it a wonderful addition to salads, fish, chicken, sauces, and vinegar. Drying some of the harvest is also an option, but the leaves can lose a lot of their flavor if you let them dry too long. Pack them in an airtight container as soon as they're dry.

# Mint

The mint family offers a tremendous diversity of refreshing scents and tastes for cooking, beverages, and potpourris. However, many types of mint are also very invasive, growing into other garden space, especially in rich, moist soil. So unless you grow them in pots or with some kind of confinement such as metal or plastic (to a depth of 14 inches), they can become a very troublesome weed. I once had mint take over my herb garden in just one year, crowding out all the other herbs. So beware!

Spearmint *(Menthe spicata)* is most commonly used in the kitchen for mint juleps, sauces, jellies, and teas, or to highlight flavor in a fruit salad. It's very fragrant and grows 2 to 3 feet tall with pale violet blooms in mid to late summer. Peppermint *(M. piperita)* is another popular mint with a strong aroma; it grows 3 feet tall with smooth, 1-to-3-inch-long leaves. Another dozen or so mint varieties, including some interesting fruit-scented types such as orange mint and apple mint, are available from garden centers or mail-order herb suppliers (see the appendix for addresses).

Start with one or two plants and set them 2 feet apart in a sunny or shady location. The plants will quickly fill in the open area between them. Use a light mulch to maintain soil moisture and to keep the leaves dry and off the ground. You can easily propagate mint plants by dividing the clumps, so you can share your plants with friends.

Don't let the plants get too thick. Cut them back frequently to promote fresh growth. A rust-fungus infection (small orange-red pustules on the bottom of the leaves) may appear on some leaves; pick and destroy blemished leaves and move roots to a new location.

Pick young or old mint leaves throughout the growing season as you need them. You can easily dry mint leaves on trays or by hanging bunched branches upside down in a dark, warm, well-ventilated area. The leaves are easy to freeze, too.

# Oregano

You can grow several types of oregano. And although I recommend only one for kitchen use, others do have a mild oregano flavor, but they taste like hay; they're best used as attractive border plantings or for wreath making.

The oregano most often used in cooking is *Oreganum heracleoticum,* and it goes by the common names Greek oregano, winter sweet marjoram, and Italian oregano. It's a hardy plant that establishes quickly, getting no taller than 6 to 8 inches. I prefer it over common oregano *(O. vulgare),* which is not as flavorful, though it's covered with ornamental lavender-colored flowers in summer that dry well and are often used in wreaths.

Golden oregano (*O. vulgare* 'Aureum') can be used as a ground cover or in containers.

You can easily start oregano from seed planted after the last spring frost, or you can divide established beds to get new plants. Planting in rich, fertile soil and full sun is best. When the plants are 3 to 4 inches tall and wide, thin them to stand 8 to 10 inches apart. Trim back or prune the plants before they flower (about five to six weeks after planting).

Harvest oregano leaves as you need them, but you'll get the optimal flavor just before flowers bloom. Use the trimmings in your cooking. After trimming, wait for new growth and use as needed. The leaves dry easily and store well, and you can also freeze them.

## Parsley

Parsley deserves recognition for more than just its role as a garnish. It's also a good breath freshener that's rich in iron and vitamin C.

The curly leafed parsley *(Petroselinum crispum),* which comes in many varieties, is the most common type because it makes such an attractive garnish. For cooking, the flat-leafed parsley or Italian parsley *(P. crispum neapolitanum)* is preferable; it's easier to work with and has better flavor than curly leafed parsley.

Although parsley is a biennial (it grows leaves the first year and goes to flower and seed the second), it grows best if you sow seeds every year because the flavor is diminished in the second season. Growing parsley from seed requires patience because the seedlings can take up to four weeks to emerge from the soil.

Soaking seeds overnight in warm water before planting speeds germination.

Sow seeds in individual pots indoors, plant seeds outside in your garden, or purchase transplants (the easiest way to go). Plants do well in sun or partial shade, and they prefer rich, moist soil. Choose a weed-free area when sowing seeds in your garden — you don't want a jungle to grow while you wait for your seeds to germinate. Parsley can handle cold weather, so start seeding three to four weeks before the last spring frost. In mild-winter areas, you can plant seeds in fall for a winter harvest, but plants will go to seed early the next spring. When the plants have four leaf stalks, thin them to stand 6 to 10 inches apart. Provide an even supply of water throughout the summer.

To harvest parsley, cut the outer leaves from the plant as you need them. To dry parsley, cut the plant at the soil level (you can cut as much of the plant as you want to dry; it will grow back from a complete cutting) and hang it in a shady, warm, well-ventilated area. After it's thoroughly dried, crumble the parsley and store it in an airtight container. I like to freeze the leaves to use in the winter, adding them to soups and stews.

To keep parsley fresh as long as possible, store it in the refrigerator, with the leaf stalks in water.

You can dig up a few plants, set them in large pots with extra soil, and bring them indoors to a sunny window for light winter harvests.

## Sage

Sage encompasses a large group of plants, although only a few are really considered good culinary herbs. Most types of sage are perennials in all but the coldest winter areas.

First and foremost among the culinary herbs is garden sage *(Salvia officinalis),* a hardy perennial recognized by its gray-green foliage and beautiful blue flowers in the spring. Plants can get quite tall (over 2 feet) and leggy, so the dwarf type *(S. o.* 'Nana') is a better, more compact form. It has equally good flavor but isn't quite as hardy as its counterpart. Several varieties of garden sage have ornamental leaf color. Purple sage *(S. o.* 'Purpurescens'), golden sage *(S. o.* 'Aurea'), and tricolor sage *(S. o.* 'Tricolor') can add beautiful color to your garden and your dishes.

You can easily start sage plants indoors from seed or in your garden in early spring. However, plants grown from seed may not have the same leaf shape and color as their parent. A better way to grow true-to-form, high quality sage is to grow cuttings from a friend's best-looking plants or purchase plants from a nursery.

Set plants or thin seedlings to stand 24 to 30 inches apart. Sage thrives in full sun and well-drained soil. After the plants are established, they prefer the soil to be on the dry side. Each spring, prune the heavier, woody stems from the plants. The leaf production and vigor of the plants drop off after four or five years, so dig up older plants and replace them with new ones.

Don't harvest sage plants too heavily the first year; leave at least half of each plant intact to give the plants time to get established.

You can harvest the leaves at any time and use them in a variety of meat-based dishes. The leaves keep well dried or frozen.

## Making cuttings

To make cuttings of sage and other herbs, snip 3- to 4-inch-long cuttings from the tip of a nonflowering stem. Dip the cut end in a rooting hormone powder such as Rootone, and place the cuttings in a pot with moistened soilless potting mix. Cover the cutting with a clear plastic bag that has a few holes poked in it for ventilation. Place in a bright, but not directly sunlit, area and keep the soil moist. Check weekly for roots by gently tugging on the cutting. When rooted, transplant into the garden or another pot.

## *Thyme*

The thyme family of herbs is aromatic, versatile, and plentiful — over 50 varieties are grown for culinary or ornamental use. Most of these thymes are perennial and reliably hardy, except in cold-winter areas.

The thyme most often used in cooking is known as English thyme *(Thymus vulgaris)*. Like the other thymes, English thyme has woody stems with small oval leaves. It grows only 8 to 12 inches high (many other thymes are even shorter). Creeping varieties of thyme are good as edging plants and in rock gardens.

Loved for its lemony scent, lemon thyme *('I. citriodorus)* is a delightful plant for both your garden and kitchen. Some varieties have both silver and yellow *variegated* leaves (leaves that sport two or more colors). Lemon thyme is a wonderful ground cover and an excellent container plant.

Caraway thyme *(T. herb-barona)* is a low-growing plant that combines the fragrance of caraway and thyme; it has dark green leaves.

Thyme seeds are troublesome to start because they germinate slowly and unevenly. Buy a plant or two of the variety that you want from a nursery, and plant it in the spring in light, well-drained soil that receives full sun. You can also start plants from cuttings if a friend is willing to part with some. Space plants 9 inches apart. Where winters are cold, mulch the thyme plants after the ground freezes with a light mulch, such as pine needles. Trim the plants back a bit in the spring and summer to contain the plants and prevent the buildup of woody growth.

You can harvest thyme leaves and sprigs all summer. In early fall, cut the sprigs, tie them together, and then hang them upside down in a warm, dark, well-ventilated place to dry. You can also dry stemless leaves on a tray or freeze them. Thyme is used in many dishes including fish and meats.

TIP

## Harvesting and drying herbs

Harvest herbs throughout the growing season because most plants benefit from being cut back. The best time to harvest herb leaves is just as the plants begin to set flower buds — the time when they have their maximum flavor and fragrance.

Cut herbs in the morning when the dew has dried but before the sun is very bright, because many herb oils in the leaves *volatilize* (evaporate) into the air in the heat of the day. After cutting them, wash the herbs, pat them dry, and hang or lay them in a warm, well-ventilated place that's out of direct sunlight until they're dried.

Label and store the herbs in sealed glass or plastic containers out of direct sun.

To freeze herbs, wash and pat them dry. Then chop them by hand or in a food processor. Place the chopped herbs in labeled plastic containers and then freeze them.

A good, quick way to freeze herbs is to add a bit of water to the herbs in the food processor and then pour the herbs into ice-cube trays and freeze them. When you need herbs for stew, soups, or sauces, just pop in an herb cube.

# Fruits and Berries

Growing your own fruits and berries differs quite a bit from growing your own vegetables. Most fruits grow on large trees or shrubs that take up a lot of room and could eventually shade your vegetables. Also, climate adaptation, variety selection, proper pruning, and pest control are critical to successfully growing fruits and berries. In addition, some fruit trees are available that naturally stay dwarf that might fit in your garden. So if you really want to grow fruit with your vegetables, contact your local Cooperative Extension office for specific recommendations on fruits, berries, and dwarf trees for your area.

Like many vegetable gardeners, I enjoy growing some fruit near my vegetable garden; a few berries, which I mention in the following sections, work particularly well. Just remember, you'll need more information than I provide here — this is a book on vegetables, for crying out loud.

## Strawberries

Strawberry plants have a nice compact habit that fits perfectly into a planting bed like you use for vegetables. They're also a fast crop that provides a delicious harvest within a year of planting. And because you should replant the plantings every few years (they develop diseases or become unproductive if you don't), you can move strawberry plants around if you want.

I like to plant through black plastic — just like with tomatoes — with drip irrigation lines under the plastic. (See Chapter 15 for more on drip irrigation.) Space the plants 12 to 18 inches apart in full sun and keep them well watered. Strawberries spread by sending out little runners that end with new baby plants. After these young plants have formed obvious roots, cut the runners and move these young plants around to start new beds. It's important to thin the plants so that the young plants don't fill in around the older plants and crowd them. Make sure to plant varieties adapted to your area, and mulch heavily in cold-winter areas.

## Blueberries

Blueberries grow on handsome shrubs that range in height from 2 to 6 feet, depending on the type that you grow. They have pretty white flowers followed by large clusters of tasty, blue fruit. The pretty green leaves turn bright shades of red, orange, and yellow before dropping in the fall. Blueberries make a nice border or hedge around the outside of a vegetable garden.

Blueberries must be grown in acidic soil (with a pH level between 4.5 and 5.5), so if you don't have that kind of soil, you need to make some adjustments. Amending your soil with a lot of peat moss and some sulfur is one easy way to lower the soil pH; see Chapter 14 for more on soil pH and amending your soil.

Plant at least two different blueberry varieties to ensure good pollination and fruit set, because bees take pollen from one variety and use it to pollinate the other. Again, variety selection is the key to success. Blueberries grow best in areas with cold winters and mild summers. In hot-summer areas, grow blueberry types that are adapted to the heat, such as Southern blueberries or rabbit-eye blueberries. In cooler climates, all other blueberry types are fine to plant.

## Blackberries and raspberries

Both blackberries and raspberries are fast growing and usually thorny. They grow to 6 feet tall and spread wildly from *suckers* (new shoots) off their roots. If you don't watch out, the plants can easily get out of control. However, if you train them to a sturdy trellis and you're diligent about pruning them, blackberries and raspberries can be very productive, hedgelike plantings around the outside of your vegetable garden. Raspberries come in varieties that produce red-, yellow-, and purple-colored fruits. Although most blackberry and raspberry varieties produce only one crop a year, one type of raspberry (called everbearing raspberry) produces two crops in one year. Choose varieties that are adapted to your area and that produce the colored berries you want. Even thornless varieties are available.

# Edible Flowers

One of my fondest memories of my daughter is at an early age (two years old) when she would wander around the garden with my wife, taste testing all the different flowers. Of course, with mom's supervision, she'd eat only the safe ones. That's right, many flowers are edible. Now I'm not saying that all edible flowers pack a huge flavor punch, but putting a few in a salad really adds pizzazz and color, which is why edible flowers are so popular in fancy restaurants. Besides, a vegetable garden should look good, and planting flowers in it certainly helps.

A word of caution, however. Although some flowers are edible, many others are poisonous. Make sure that you know what you're picking before you eat it. And don't let young children eat flowers unattended. The following are some flowers that you should *not* eat:

- Buttercups
- Daffodils
- Four-o'clocks
- Foxgloves
- Hyacinths
- Lantanas
- Lobelias
- Morning glories
- Oleanders
- Sweet peas

Here are some common edible flowers that you *can* munch away on:

- Apples
- Bee balm
- Calendulas
- Borage
- Dandelions
- Daylilies
- Hibiscus
- Lilacs
- Signet marigolds
- Nasturtium
- Pansies
- Red clover
- Roses
- Tulips
- Violets

For more information on edible flowers, check out the book *Edible Flowers: From Garden to Palate* by Cathy Wilkinson Barash, published by Fulcrum.

# Sprouts

Even in the winter when you can't grow anything in your vegetable garden, you can still be eating home-grown fresh vegetables. Sprouts are an easy-to-grow and nutritious alternative to lettuce and other greens. They're just what they sound like — young plants that emerge a few days after seeds have germinated or sprouted. Many of the seed catalogs listed in the appendix offer seed-sprouting kits, but you can easily make your own sprouter. You can experiment with many types of seeds of edible plants, such as beans and broccoli, and even some normally nonedible plants, such as alfalfa and clover. Just remember these two things:

- **Use only untreated seeds.** Many vegetable seeds and other types of seeds are treated with fungicides and other chemicals to aid germination in the soil. You don't want to eat treated seeds.

- **Rinse seeds often and use them as soon as possible.** If you don't rinse sprouts with fresh water often enough, or if you eat them when they're too old, they may develop bacteria that can make you very sick. If you aren't sure whether you should eat the sprouts, dump them out and start over.

Broccoli sprouts have made a lot of news lately because researchers have found that they contain 20 to 50 times the amount of cancer-fighting compounds found in mature broccoli. Here's how I grow broccoli (or any) sprouts:

1. **Start with a clean, pint-size jar topped with a fine screen or cheesecloth.**

   You can secure the top of the jar with a rubber band or a canning-jar lid.

2. **Coat the bottom of the jar with a thin layer of broccoli seeds.**

3. **Add enough lukewarm water to the jar to cover the seeds with a few inches of water, and then let the seeds soak for about 12 hours.**

4. **Rinse the seeds with cold water, drain out all the water, and put the jar in a well-lit location out of direct sun.**

5. **Rinse and drain the seeds three or four times a day to keep them fresh and to prevent bacteria from growing.**

The seeds should sprout in about three to five days. Keep rinsing the sprouts two to three times a day until you're ready to use them, which should be within three to five days of sprouting.

# Part III
# Green Acres . . . or Yards . . . or Feet: The Get-Down-and-Dirty Part

# In this part . . .

**H**ere comes the dirt. The success of any garden often begins and ends in the soil. This part presents basic soil-building techniques. After you prepare the soil, it's time to plant, water, fertilize, and weed your garden. You can also try some farmer-proven growing techniques to increase your yield. Then get ready for the best part: harvesting the fresh produce, eating some now, and storing some for later.

# Chapter 13

# On Your Mark, Get Set . . . Grow!

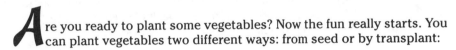

## In This Chapter

▶ Choosing a vegetable planting method: seeds or transplants

▶ Starting seedlings indoors

▶ Caring for your seedlings

▶ Transplanting your seedlings or starter plants in your garden

▶ Planting seeds in your garden

*A*re you ready to plant some vegetables? Now the fun really starts. You can plant vegetables two different ways: from seed or by transplant:

✔ When planting seeds, you either sow the seeds indoors and then transplant the young seedlings in your garden (when the time is right), or you sow the seeds directly in your garden.

✔ To skip the whole seed process altogether, purchase young transplants (seedlings to be transplanted) at your local nursery and then plant them directly in your garden.

Both methods have their advantages, and timing is critical to success.

As I say throughout this book (maybe because my dad used to say it in all situations): Timing is everything when you plant vegetables. If you really want to be successful, you need to find out the planting dates for your area. Each vegetable has its own optimum growing conditions — a right soil temperature, daytime temperature, length of day, and so on — but all these factors vary greatly, depending on where you live. So make sure that you check out Chapter 3 for important climate-specific information. Okay, on to the planting.

You can plant seeds quickly, without much thought. But working deliberately and carefully — whether planting indoors or out — pays off in more sturdy and more vigorous plants. In this chapter, I guide you through the planting process, giving you information about correct seed spacing, planting depth, soil and germinating conditions, and fertilizing so that you produce strong-growing, vigorous plants. I also show you how to plant transplants, whether you grow them yourself or buy them at a nursery.

## Choosing Seeds or Transplants

Whether you choose to grow vegetables from seeds or transplants, each planting method has its own advantages. Here are some advantages to starting from seed:

- **A wider choice of varieties.** Your local garden store or nursery may carry only three or four varieties of tomato transplants but offer a great selection of seeds. And mail-order seed catalogs (see the appendix for addresses) offer *hundreds* of varieties of seeds.

- **Healthy plants.** You don't have to settle for *leggy* (tall, weak, spindly stems), *root-bound* (roots crammed into a small pot) plants that may have been hanging out at a nursery too long. Such plants usually don't get off to a fast start when you plant them in the ground. And when you start from seed, you don't have to worry about introducing any insects or diseases into your garden that may be lurking on nursery-grown transplants.

- **Reduced cost.** Especially if you have a large garden, starting from seed can save you some dough. A six-pack of seedlings may cost you $2.00, whereas 100 seeds may cost only $.79.

- **A lot of fun.** The excitement of seeing those first seedlings push through the soil is something special. Two feet of snow may be on the ground outside, but by sowing seeds indoors, you can enjoy a little spring.

The advantages to growing seeds stack up pretty impressively. But planting nursery-grown transplants has a major benefit as well — convenience. Growing plants from seeds takes time and diligence, but going with nursery transplants gives you an instant garden. If you have problems with transplants, you can always buy more. If you have problems with special seed varieties you started, it's usually too late to start them again indoors, and you're out of luck growing that variety this year.

Growing seeds is like taking care of a new pet. You have to check on seeds everyday, maybe several times a day, to make sure that they're happy. So much for your winter trip to Disney World, unless a reliable neighbor or friend can care for your seedlings. Also, you have to think in advance of what you'll be growing and need to start indoors. In this harried world, it's easier to decide a week or so before planting what vegetable varieties you need and to buy transplants than to plan months in advance to start seeds.

After you consider the advantages of each planting method, you need to make sure that you time your planting for the most productive results.

## Buying small vegetable plants through the mail

A new trend in vegetable gardening is that many mail-order seed companies now offer a wide range of vegetable varieties as small plants or plugs. They offer a wider selection than you can find in garden centers, you don't have to drive around to find the best transplants, and they ship plants to you at the appropriate planting time for your region. But because Mother Nature is never consistent, your plants may show up a little too soon or too late, depending on the conditions of your current growing season. And some mail-order seed companies may require you to purchase a minimum amount of any one type of variety, and the price is generally more expensive than transplants grown at local nurseries. See the appendix for the addresses of various mail-order companies.

## Direct seeding versus seeding indoors

You can start seeds indoors or outdoors. If you plant seeds indoors, you transplant them into your garden later. With *direct seeding,* you skip the indoor step and sow the seeds directly in your garden. Which option should you choose? Probably both, if you're serious about growing vegetables. But consider these points when making your choice:

- ✔ **Starting indoors gives you a jump on the growing season.** If you start at the right time (remember, timing is everything), you can have vigorous seedlings that are ready to go into the ground at the ideal time. In areas with short growing seasons, starting seedlings indoors really gives you a head start.

  The best candidates for an early start are plants that tolerate root disturbance and benefit from a jump on the season. These veggies include broccoli, Brussels sprouts, cabbage, cauliflower, celery, eggplant, leeks, onions, parsley, peppers, and tomatoes. Another group of vegetables that have to be transplanted carefully but do benefit from an early start include cucumbers, melons, and squash.

- ✔ **Seeds are easier to start indoors.** You have more control indoors, enabling you to more easily provide the perfect conditions for hard-to-germinate or very small seeds. You can provide the ideal temperature, moisture, and fertility so that your seedlings grow strong and sturdy.

- ✔ **Some vegetables don't like to be transplanted and are better sown directly in the ground.** These vegetables include many of the root crops, such as carrots, beets, turnips, and parsnips. They're cold-hardy vegetables, so you can direct seed them pretty early anyway. Crops such as corn, beans, and peas are also pretty finicky about transplanting and grow better when you sow them directly in the ground.

# Starting Seeds Indoors

All that you need to start seeds indoors is a container, soil, seeds, moisture, warmth, and light. Oh, if everything in life were only this simple. Check out Chapters 4 through 11 to find out when to start specific vegetables indoors — remember, timing is everything. Here are the basic steps for planting seeds, which I discuss in more detail in the sections that follow:

1. **Sow the seeds in containers filled with sterile soil (which garden centers call a *germinating mix*).**

   Keep the seeds in a warm place until germination.

2. **After the seeds germinate, move the seedlings to a well-lit location (preferably under lights). Keep them moist.**

3. **Thin crowded seedlings.**

   When the seedlings' heights are three times the diameter of your pot, transplant the seedlings to a larger container.

4. **Acclimate the seedlings to outdoor conditions (called *hardening off*).**

5. **Plant the seedlings in your garden.**

Piece of cake; go have a drink. Now on to the details.

## Containing your seeds and seedlings

Just about any container that holds several inches of soil and in which you can punch drainage holes is suitable for growing seedlings. Several low-cost possibilities include milk cartons, paper or Styrofoam cups, cottage-cheese containers, and homemade wooden *flats,* which are shallow, wide, seedling trays.

Garden stores and most mail-order garden catalogs sell a wide variety of plastic, fiber, peat, and Styrofoam flats and containers that satisfy just about any budget. Figure 13-1 shows you some flats that you can buy, along with appropriate lights (which I discuss later in this chapter).

Flats enable you to start many seedlings in a small space, which is helpful when you water or move the plants. Individual peat pots are a good choice for plants like cucumbers, which don't like to have their roots disturbed during transplanting. After you plant the seeds in the flats, the seedlings stay there until planting time.

For gardeners who put a premium on convenience, premade growing cubes are a good idea. But I have to be honest; I'm not a huge fan of peat pots or cubes. The idea behind a peat pot is that once planted (pot and all) in the

Figure 13-1:
Seed-
starting
flats and
lighting.

garden, the plants' roots grow through the sides of the wet pot, and as the season progresses, the peat naturally breaks down and disappears. But sometimes when I've used them, the peat didn't break down. In the fall when I pulled up my plants, the peat pots were still intact and some roots were constricted in the pots.

If you decide to use peat pots or cubes, gently tear the sides of the pots just before planting to create spaces for the roots to grow into the soil. You should plant a peat pot with frayed sides into the garden. But in that case, you may as well use a reusable plastic pot. And the little cubes? These are flat, half-dollar-size peat cubes enclosed in nylon mesh that you place a seed in and then soak in water. As the cubes are soaking, the peat expands to cover the seed and grows into a small peat pot. In my experience, they work okay, but they're hard to wet.

Before you sow any seeds, sterilize your flats and pots (especially ones that you've used before) to prevent *damping off* from killing your seedlings. (See the sidebar "Damping off" for more on this soil-borne disease.) Dip the containers in a solution of 9 parts water to 1 part household bleach and then rinse them in clear water.

## *Adding a little dirtless soil (or is it soilless dirt?)*

The most practical seed-starting mediums for most gardeners are the commercially prepared *soilless* or *peatlite* mixes that are sold in most garden stores as *potting soil* or *germinating mix*. As the name implies, the mix doesn't contain any true soil: It's usually a combination of peat moss, vermiculite or perlite, ground limestone (which brings the pH to proper levels, as I discuss in Chapter 14), and fertilizer, which is good for plant growth. Potting soil is lightweight, it's free of disease organisms that may be present in true garden soil, and it holds moisture well but at the same time offers good aeration and drainage.

Don't use garden soil to start seeds indoors. Garden soil isn't light enough (that is, it doesn't have enough air spaces) and may contain insects or diseases that can kill your tender seedlings.

## *Sowing your seeds in containers*

After choosing the proper container and obtaining soilless soil (also called a *growing medium*), follow these steps to sow your seeds:

1. **Fill a container with moistened growing medium to within ¹/₂ inch of the top of the container.**

   Soilless mixes are dusty and hard to wet initially. Pour the mix into a plastic bag, and then add enough warm water to moisten the mix but not make it into a drippy mud pie. Mix the water and growing medium with your hands or a strong wooden spoon, closing off the opening of the bag as much as possible to keep the dust in. Remove the soil from the bag and place it in the container. Gently firm down the medium with a flat piece of wood (a ruler works fine).

2a. **If you're planting seeds in a flat:**

   Make shallow *furrows* (rowlike impressions) with a blunt stick or by pressing the narrow edge of a ruler into the medium.

   - Sow small seeds such as lettuce at about five to eight seeds per inch if you intend to transplant them soon after they come up. Sow larger seeds such as melons at three to four seeds per inch.

   - Sow seeds more sparingly, at three to four seeds per inch, if you intend to thin, and not transplant them, leaving them in the same container.

   Either method — transplanting the seeds in a new container or leaving them in the same container — works fine; it's just a matter of what pots and room you have. Transplanting into individual pots takes up more room but allows larger plants such as tomatoes more room for their roots to grow. Smaller plants, such as lettuce, grow fine when thinned and left in their original containers.

Seeds can be *broadcast* (randomly spread) instead of planting in rowlike trenches, but row planting and thinning are easier.

**2b. If you're planting seeds in individual containers:**

- Put two to four seeds in each container.

- Later, thin the seedlings, leaving the strongest one.

**3. Sow the seeds at the correct depth (see the appendix), and then cover them with fine potting soil or vermiculite.**

Label each row or container because many seedlings look alike. You can purchase labels from a nursery or through a mail-order catalog, or you can use old ones from nursery transplants that you purchased earlier. Using a waterproof pen, record the type of vegetable, variety, and date that the seed was planted.

**4. Water the seeds gently with a mister or spray bottle.**

A stronger stream of water can wash seeds into one section of the container or move them too deeply into the soil.

**5. Cover the container with a sheet of clear plastic or a plastic bag to hold in the moisture.**

If necessary, use small stakes to prop up the plastic so that it doesn't rest on top of the soil.

**6. Place the planted containers in a warm spot.**

Some warm spots include the top of your refrigerator or near your furnace. But be careful how you water around electrical appliances. You can also buy heating cables or mats that keep the soil warm from below. Follow the package instructions carefully.

The cooler the temperature, the longer it takes for the plants to emerge.

Never put containers in direct sun; the plastic holds in the heat, cooking your seeds to death.

**7. Check the containers periodically to make sure that they're still moist.**

If you see signs of mold, loosen the cover and let air in; the mold should disappear. You can also hook up a small fan to gently blow over the seedlings (without the plastic cover on), keeping the soil on the dry side, but be careful not to dry out the seedlings.

**8. As soon as you see the first green shoots emerge, remove the cover and move your seedlings to a spot that provides plenty of light and proper growing conditions for that vegetable.**

Refer to the chapter covering that vegetable for information about the proper growing conditions.

Until seedlings emerge from the soil, light is unnecessary, with the exception of lettuce and celery seeds. Sow lettuce and celery seeds by lightly pressing them into the soil or covering them very lightly with $1/8$ inch of fine potting soil, and then place the containers in a bright spot or position them under a 40-watt incandescent light.

## How much light and heat?

The light that your young seedlings receive is one of the most important factors in good growth. Placing the seedlings in a south-facing window is one option but not always the best one. Even in a sunny window, plants get only a fraction of the light that they would get outside. Windowsill plants often get tall and spindly because they get too warm in relation to the light that they receive. Try to keep your seedlings on the cool side — 60 to 65°F, 75° maximum — to encourage slower growth; cooler temperatures give you sturdy, stocky plants that transplant well. Although a 10- to 15-degree drop in temperature at night is beneficial, a windowsill can get pretty chilly at night when its wintry outside. Place a blanket between the plants and the glass to keep windowsill seedlings warm on frosty nights, or move plants away from the window at night.

Growing seedlings under fluorescent lights is a good way to keep light-hungry plants happy. If possible, set up your lights near a window so that the plants can receive both natural and artificial light.

Ordinary cool-white, 40-watt fluorescent bulbs are fine for starting seedlings. The more expensive *grow lights* that you can purchase at a nursery or through a mail-order seed catalog produce the broader spectrum light that plants need for flowering and fruiting (although your seedlings will be in the garden before they're ready to flower). Use one set of lights (usually 2 bulbs to a set) for every 1-foot width of seedling-growing area and keep the bulbs 2 to 4 inches from the tops of the seedlings at all times. Keep the lights on for no more than 16 hours per day so that the plants can get their natural rest period. Inexpensive timers that turn the lights on and off automatically are available at nurseries and hardware stores.

Using a soil thermometer, which costs between $10 and $20, check the temperature at plant level under the lights. If the temperature is too warm for good seedling growth, a small electric fan may help keep plants cooler. Check out the appendix for a listing of optimum temperatures and growing requirements for seedlings.

## Making your own soilless mix

You can make up your own soilless mix and perhaps save some money. To germinate seeds before moving them on to more spacious quarters indoors (like a bigger pot), you need to provide a medium that supports the tiny plants and supplies water and air to their roots. The nutrients stored in the seeds nourish the seedlings at this stage of growth. A good germination mix is 2 parts peat moss, 1 part vermiculite, 1 part perlite, and 1 tablespoon of ground limestone per gallon of mix.

Blend the ingredients thoroughly in a garbage can or some other large container.

To grow seedlings to garden-planting size indoors, you need a mix with more nutrients. To the mix described in the previous paragraph, add 2 tablespoons of 20 percent superphosphate and 1 teaspoon of 5-10-5 fertilizer per gallon of mix. (For more on fertilizer and nutrients, refer to Chapter 15.) If this nutrient garbage scares you away, which it should, just buy a bag of potting soil, for peat's sake.

One system that I've used to grow seedlings is to place plant trays on a sheet of plywood supported by sawhorses. The light fixtures, supported from above by rope, are adjustable so that I can raise or lower them to the proper height. If you can't adjust the level of your lights, use pieces of wood to raise the trays closer to the lights when the seedlings are small, and then lower the trays as the plants grow. Because the light is strongest near the center of the bulbs, rotate the trays periodically.

## *Watering your seedlings*

Water fragile seedlings carefully, or you risk uprooting them. Mist them with a gentle spray, or water them from the bottom by setting your container in a pan of water just long enough for the soil surface to wet (sitting them in water longer than this can damage the plants' roots). Then remove the container from the water and let it drain. Keep the soil surface lightly moist but not soggy. Always water with lukewarm water.

As your plants get sturdier, you can water with a sprinkling can that has a *rose,* a nozzle that breaks the water into many fine streams. After the plants grow their first set of true leaves (the first leaves to open as the seed germinates are called *seedling leaves,* and the next set are *true leaves*) and have a bigger root system, let the soil dry out slightly between waterings.

Give the plants enough water at one time so that some of it runs out the drainage holes in the bottom of the container, but never leave the container sitting in water. Overwatering promotes damping-off disease (see the sidebar "Damping off") and decreases the amount of air in the soil, resulting in a weaker root system.

With soilless mixes, you may have a hard time deciding when to water, because the plants look dry on the surface even though plenty of moisture is still present. To check if the soil has moisture, take a small amount of soil off the top $1/2$ inch of mix and squeeze it between your fingers. If you can squeeze out any water, hold off watering. The difference in a container's weight when the soil is moist compared to when it's dry can also indicate when to water. Dry soil is very light. Wilted seedlings are a sure sign that you've waited too long to water, unless your plants have damping off.

Water the seedlings early in the morning, if possible, so that the foliage can dry off quickly during the day to avoid disease problems. Certain types of containers require more frequent watering of their plants than others. Soil in clay pots dries out faster than that in plastic pots. Peat pots dry out fast and are difficult to rewet. Try putting your peat pots or growing-cubes in a tray and packing moist peat moss between them to keep them from drying out too quickly.

## Thinning and transplanting indoors

After seedlings develop their first set of true leaves (or when onions or leeks, which send up a single blade, are two inches tall), you need to thin them or move them from shallow flats to larger quarters. Thinning is an important step, and timing is crucial. If you let your seedlings grow too large in a small container, their growth is stunted. And if you don't space them out at all, you end up with weak plants.

To thin plants that will continue growing in the same container, snip out extra seedlings at the soil line with a pair of scissors, as shown in Figure 13-2. If you try to pull these extras out, you may disturb the roots of the plants that are staying. Snip out any weak or misshapen plants. See the appendix to find out how much space to leave between different types of vegetable seedlings.

**Figure 13-2:**
Thin seedlings at the soil line by using scissors.

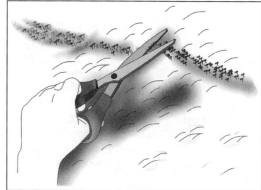

## Damping off

One day you're admiring your strong, healthy seedlings, and the next day you're gaping in dismay at the sight of them toppled over and dying. The attacker is called *damping off,* which is a fungus that infects young seedlings, sometimes even before they have a chance to emerge from the soil. If you examine infected seedlings closely, you usually can see that part of the stem near the soil line is sunken, shriveled, and water soaked. Sometimes a white mold also forms on the stem.

Damping off is one of the most common problems that seed-starters face, but fortunately you can control it with good sanitation and cultural practices (proper watering, fertilizing, and lighting). Sterilizing containers with a bleach solution and using sterile potting soil goes a long way toward preventing problems. Wet potting soil and high nitrogen encourage this fungus, so avoid overwatering, and use a well-drained germinating mix that's low in nitrogen or use fertilizer *after* the seedlings develop their first true leaves. Sowing seeds thinly to allow good air circulation can also help. Many seeds come coated with a fungicide that helps prevent damping off.

If you notice seedlings in one portion of a container beginning to dampen off, cut them off and remove the soil around them as quickly as possible and do what you can to make conditions less favorable for the fungus (basically, let the soil dry more). With luck, you'll be able to save the rest of the batch.

To move seedlings to a new container, first fill a larger container (plastic six-packs, 4-inch pots, or peat pots) with moist potting soil. Poke holes in the soil large enough to put the seedling roots in — the eraser end of a pencil is a good tool for this. Dig around the plants carefully by using the blade of a table knife or a small stick, such as a plant label, and then lift the seedlings out of the soil. Always hold the seedlings by the tips of their leaves; otherwise, you can easily crush their delicate stems or injure their growing tips. Set the plants in the new container, slightly deeper than they were growing before. Firm the soil gently around the roots, water well, and keep the plants out of direct sun for a day or two until they adjust to their new pots.

## *Feeding your seedlings*

Regular fertilizing helps produce strong, healthy plants. After you thin or transplant seedlings, dilute a water-soluble fertilizer to one-third strength (usually something like 1 teaspoon of fertilizer per gallon of water) and use the mixture to water your seedlings. Water with the solution once a week. You can also mix a slow-release fertilizer with your potting soil; the fertilizer releases slowly with every watering. For more on fertilizers, see Chapter 15.

# Transplanting Indoor Seedlings and Starter Plants

After you nurture your seedlings indoors for a good six to eight weeks, and when the weather's right for planting (see Chapter 3 to find out when to plant in your area), you're ready to transplant the seedlings outdoors. Or maybe you haven't grown seedlings at all, but you want to buy some starter plants at a nursery and get them in the ground. I discuss both scenarios in the following sections.

## Buying starter plants

If you don't start your transplants at home, you can buy them at a nursery or garden center. You can find seedlings of almost every type and size around planting time.

Follow these tips when buying starter plants:

- ✔ Whatever starter plants you buy, choose healthy-looking plants. Tomatoes, for example, should have a stocky stem, be about 4- to 6-inches tall, and sport dark-green foliage. Read the chapters that discuss the vegetable you want to try to find out what makes a healthy-looking plant.

- ✔ Avoid crowded, spindly, large plants in small containers because the roots are often bound up and have no room to grow. You can check the roots for yourself by gently removing the transplants from their containers (if you're not sure how to do this, see "Planting roots in the ground," later in this chapter). If you see a dense mat of roots around the outside of the *root ball* (the soil with roots growing in it), the plants probably have been in the pot too long.

- ✔ Buy plants at the optimum size. Plants with four to six leaves and short, stocky stems are usually best. In general, younger plants are better than tall, older plants that most likely were stressed at one point or another.

- ✔ Avoid plants that are already flowering, heaven forbid, and have fruit on them. Plants with fruits never produce well.

You can sometimes buy large tomato plants in 1-gallon or larger pots — sometimes they even have tomatoes on them. In my experience, these large plants rarely grow well after you get them home. I prefer smaller transplants that can get off to a running start.

## Toughening up transplants

Vegetable seedlings that are grown indoors at home or purchased from a greenhouse in spring need to acclimate gradually to the brighter light and cooler temperatures of the outside world. This process, called *hardening off,* slows plant growth, causing the plants to store more food internally and increase the thickness of their outer leaf layers. Basically, hardening off toughens up transplants for the cold, cruel, outside world.

To harden off your transplants:

✔ A week or two before you intend to set plants out in your garden, stop fertilizing and reduce the amount of water you give the plants. Take your plants outside for a half hour of filtered sunlight — setting them under an arbor or open-branched tree — during the warmest part of the day. If the weather is windy, put the plants somewhere where they're sheltered or construct a windbreak out of pieces of wood.

✔ Gradually increase the amount of time that the plants spend outside and the intensity of the light that they're exposed to so that by day seven, they're out all day. Also, make sure that you bring the plants in every night.

Another option is to move your plants to a cold frame (see Chapter 22), opening the cold frame more each day and closing it at night. Plants that are raised in a cold frame from the time that they're young seedlings will need much less hardening off.

Don't overharden your plants. Certain crops, such as cabbage and broccoli, can *bolt* (flower before they're supposed to) quickly if seedlings over three weeks old are repeatedly exposed to temperatures lower than 40°F for a couple of weeks.

## Planting roots in the ground

Before transplanting your seedlings, you need to prepare your soil and sculpt beds or rows (as described in Chapter 14), and your garden must be ready to plant. If you're worried about keeping the rows straight, use string and stakes as described in "Row planting," later in this chapter.

Choose a calm, cloudy day to transplant, if possible. Late afternoon is a good time because plants can recover from the shock of transplanting without sitting in the midday heat and sun. Your garden soil should be moist, not soggy. If the weather has been dry, water the planting area the day before you plant. Moisten the soil in your flats or pots so that it holds together around the plants' roots when you remove the plants from their containers.

When setting out plants in biodegradable peat pots, make slits down the sides of the pots or gently tear the sides to enable the roots to push through. Also, tear off the lip (top) of the pot so that it doesn't stick up above the soil surface and pull moisture out of the soil. With premade growing blocks encased in netting, cut off the netting before planting.

To transplant seedlings:

1. **Use a hoe, spade, or trowel to make a small hole in your garden for each seedling.**

2. *Unpot* **a seedling (unless it's in a peat pot) by turning its pot upside down, cupping the seedling with your hand. Be sure to keep the root mass and soil intact. Potting soil that's on the slightly dry side allows the plants to slip out more easily**

   If the seedling doesn't come out easily, gently tap on the edge of the pot or gently press on the bottom of each cell of the flat with your fingers. Don't yank out a plant by its stem.

3. **Check the root ball's condition.**

   If the roots are wound around the outside of the pot, work them loose with your fingers so that they can grow out into the soil. Unwind larger roots and break smaller ones (this won't hurt them) so that they all point outward. Try to keep as much of the original soil intact as possible.

4. **Mix a diluted liquid starter fertilizer into the soil of the planting hole (see Chapter 15 for more on fertilizers) to help the plants get off to a fast start.**

5. **Put each prepared seedling into the holes that you made.**

   Most young vegetables can be planted up to their first true leaves, as shown in Figure 13-3. If a seedling is tall and lanky, you can sink the seedling a little deeper. Plants — such as tomatoes — grow extra roots along the lower portion of their stems and thrive with this treatment.

6. **With your hands, firm the soil around the roots. Form a shallow soil basin (a moat around the seedling; see Chapter 15) around the base of the transplant to hold water.**

7. **If the weather has been dry or if the soil is sandy, you may want to water the entire bed. If it's rainy or the soil is already very wet, wait until tomorrow to water.**

8. **Keep the bed moist while the seedlings get established and begin to grow strongly.**

   In extreme hot, dry weather, provide temporary shade for transplants with paper tents or wooden shingles pushed into the ground on the south or west side of the plants.

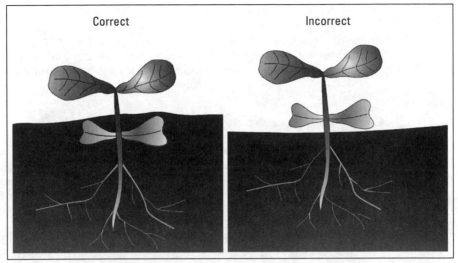

Correct                    Incorrect

**Figure 13-3:**
Plant
vegetable
seedlings
up to their
true leaves.

If you don't get an ideal transplanting day and the weather is hot and sunny, shade the plants until the sun goes down. Don't be alarmed if your plants look a little droopy after you set them out because they'll soon recover. Cabbage seedlings can droop and look almost dead, for example, and be up and growing in a day or two.

# Sowing Seeds Directly in Your Garden

Unless you live in an area where summers are really short, some vegetables are better off sown directly in a garden rather than as transplants. Large-seeded, fast-growing vegetables — such as corn, melons, squash, beans, and peas — usually languish if they're grown in containers for even a day or two too long. Plants sown directly in the ground usually surpass these seedlings if both are planted at the same time. Even if you live in a short-season area, you can help speed new plants along. See Chapter 22 for information on extending your growing season.

If you're direct seeding, make sure that the soil has dried out sufficiently before you work it (see Chapter 14 for more on preparing the soil), and be sure that the soil is warm enough for the seeds that you want to plant. Pea seeds, for example, germinate in soil as cool as 40°F, and you can plant them as soon as you can work the soil in spring. Squash seeds, on the other hand, need warmth. If your soil temperature is much below 65°F, the seeds are likely to rot in the ground before they sprout. (See the appendix for a list of appropriate soil temperatures for different kinds of seeds.) The best way to determine the temperature of your soil is to use a soil thermometer, which you can buy at a garden store.

Chapter 3 gives a general range of planting dates for vegetables in different parts of the United States. But keep in mind that these dates are general guidelines; if your soil is heavy and wet or if your garden slopes to the north, your soil will take longer to warm in the spring than a lighter, well-drained soil or a garden on a south-facing slope; see Chapter 2 for details.

## Choosing a seed-planting method

You can plant seeds in a variety of patterns: single rows, wide rows, beds, raised beds, or hills. The method that you choose depends on your climate, your tools, and your taste. You can find out more about these planting methods in Chapter 2. Whichever method you choose, here are a few basic principles to keep in mind when planting seeds:

- ✔ **Immediately before planting seeds, loosen your garden soil with a hoe or shovel to a depth of 6 inches.** Rake over the area to create a smooth planting surface. Don't walk over areas where you'll be sowing seeds; stay in the pathways. Compacting the soil makes it difficult for seedlings to emerge and send down their roots.

- ✔ **Sow seeds at the proper planting depth.** A seed planted too deeply uses up its supply of stored nutrients before the seedling can push its way to the surface; a seed planted too shallow may dry out. A general rule is to plant seeds to depths that are two to three times their diameters, but the appendix gives recommended planting depths for different kinds of seeds. Also try to sow at a uniform depth because seedlings are more likely to emerge at the same time, enabling you to see where your plants are when you do your first weeding.

- ✔ **Water newly planted seeds carefully.** Use a watering can with a rose (nozzle with multiple holes) or a hose with a *breaker attachment* (a nozzle that breaks the stream into gentle spray). A strong stream of water can wash the seeds out of a bed or too deeply into the ground. Keep the seeds moist but not too soggy until the seeds germinate. Heavy soils often form a crust as they dry out, making it difficult for the seedlings to break through. A moist surface helps prevent crusting, as does covering seeds with vermiculite or a mixture of vermiculite and soil, instead of soil alone. If the weather is dry after you sow the seeds, gently water the seeded area every two days or so.

The following sections explain the basic methods for planting your seeds.

### Row planting

The first step when row planting is to mark the placement of a row within your garden. A planting line, consisting of a simple string and stakes, enables you to easily lay out rows. Make a *furrow,* or trench, at the correct depth along the row. To make a shallow furrow, lay a rake or hoe underneath your string marker, and press the handle into the soil. You can make deeper furrows (ones that can be used for watering, too) by dragging the corner of your hoe across the soil surface, using the string as your guideline.

Sow seeds more thickly than you want the final spacing of the crops to be to ensure an adequate number of plants (see Figure 13-4); some seeds may fail to sprout. Thinning rows is less of a chore if you space seeds as evenly as possible. Large seeds like peas and beans are easy to space at precise intervals, but evenly spacing small seeds can be a real challenge.

**Figure 13-4:**
When row planting, sow seeds thickly in a shallow furrow.

Row planting

Cover the seeds with fine soil and then firm them in with the back of a hoe to make sure that all the seeds are in contact with the soil. Water gently.

If you're planting long rows of corn, beans, or peas that will be furrow-irrigated (see Chapter 15), fill the furrows with water first and then push the large seeds into the top of raised beds.

### Wide row planting

You can plant more seeds in less space by using the wide row planting method. This method not only saves space but also allows you to concentrate watering, weeding, and fertilizing in a smaller area. Follow these steps for wide row planting:

1. **Choose the location and width of your row, usually 10 to 16 inches wide. You may want to run strings along the outside edges of the row to clearly designate the planting area.**

2. **Smooth the soil until it's level.**

3. **Sprinkle seeds over the entire row — with most crops, try to land the seeds about $1/2$ to 1 inch apart (for peas and beans, $1^1/2$ to 2 inches). Pat them down with the back of a hoe.**

4. **Use a rake to lift soil from the side of the row to cover the seeds. Gently smooth the soil covering the seed to the same depth throughout the row.**

   With small seeds like carrots and lettuce, cover the seeds with a thin layer of potting soil. Pat the potting soil down again to bring the added soil into firm contact with the seeds.

5. **Water the seeds.**

### Bed planting

Planting beds is essentially the same as planting wide rows. To prepare your beds, see Chapter 14. If you don't have permanent beds, mark the dimensions and smooth out the soil. You can broadcast (sprinkling by hand), as shown in Figure 13-5, sow in single rows with a few inches between rows, or plant individual seeds at the proper distance apart.

**Figure 13-5:**
Broadcasting
seeds in a
bed.

Broadcasting

### Hill planting

Plant seeds for vining crops that spread out — such as squash, melons, or cucumbers — in hills or circular groups, as shown in Figure 13-6. Loosen the soil in a 1-foot-diameter area, and level the area. Then plant five to six seeds close together. Keep the two strongest seedlings (the ones that are the biggest and sport the most leaves) and thin out the remaining seedlings by cutting them with scissors.

Hilling

**Figure 13-6:** Sow vining crop seeds in hills.

If your soil is heavy, you may want to plant in a raised hill (also called a *mound*). The raised soil warms up more quickly than the surrounding soil and drains better. But be careful in midsummer not to let the mound dry out. You can easily construct a soil basin around the mound for watering (see Chapter 15).

## Thinning seedlings in your garden

Soon after seedlings grow their second set of true leaves, you need to thin them out. Don't neglect this important step; crowded seedlings turn into weak, spindly plants that don't produce well. Separate the plants by hand or with a narrow hoe according to the distances in Chapter 2.

When you thin plants, either discard the extra seedlings or move them to another part of your garden. Newly transplanted seedlings need extra attention until they get established. Shade them from the hot sun for a day or two and be sure to keep them well watered. Lettuce is one of the easiest vegetables to move when it's small. Root crops such as beets and carrots transplant poorly, as do beans and peas.

You can thin some crops in stages, with delicious results. Carrots, lettuce, and beets are all good candidates for gradual thinning. If you've ever tasted beet greens cooked up with tender, marble-sized beets still attached, you know what a real treat they are. Start thinning carrot, lettuce, and beet seedlings when they're 1 to 2 inches apart. After the plants grow to 6 to 8 inches tall, pull up every other one and enjoy them. Leave a final 4-to 6-inch spacing for larger plants to develop.

Your vegetable garden is now off and running, but you can't leave it now. Plants need water, fertilizer, and protection from pests; check out Chapter 15 for details. You may also want to page ahead to Chapter 22 to find how to get your plants off to a really fast start and protect them from unexpected frosts.

# Chapter 14

# Workin' the Dirt

● ● ● ● ● ● ● ● ● ● ● ● ● ● ● ● ● ● ● ● ● ● ● ● ● ● ● ● ● ● ● ● ● ● ● ● ● ● ● ● ● ● ● ● ● ● ● ● ● ● ● ● ●

## In This Chapter

▶ Clearing your garden plot

▶ Taking a closer look at your soil

▶ Adding the right nutrients and other stuff to your soil

▶ Turning your soil

▶ Making your own compost

● ● ● ● ● ● ● ● ● ● ● ● ● ● ● ● ● ● ● ● ● ● ● ● ● ● ● ● ● ● ● ● ● ● ● ● ● ● ● ● ● ● ● ● ● ● ● ● ● ● ● ● ●

*P*roperly preparing the soil before planting is an all-important first step toward a bountiful harvest. Don't take short cuts with your soil. You'll be cheating your plants at their roots, and they won't like it.

In this chapter, I tell you how to take care of your soil — clean it up, straighten it out, and make it an all-around better place for roots. Remember, good soil makes happy roots, and happy roots mean a healthy garden.

## Razing Your Garden Spot

After you choose a good sunny spot for your vegetable garden and draw a plan on paper (see Chapter 2 if you haven't done this preparatory work), you need to clean up the area where your garden will be so that the soil will be easier to work. You can clear your garden area any time during the year, but the season before planting works best — clear in the fall for spring planting, clear in the spring for summer or fall planting. Although you can clear the area the day before you plant, you may have more weed problems later.

If you already have an established garden, clean up any debris in fall or winter, depending on where you live, and till the ground before planting. Following are the basics of initially clearing your garden spot, which I explain in more detail in the sections that follow:

1. **Outline the areas of your garden plot that you want to clear.**

   - To get your edges straight for a square or rectangular vegetable plot, stretch a string between sticks and mark the line with a trickle of ground white limestone, which is available at garden centers.

   - For a round garden, use a hose or rope to lay out the area, adjusting the position to create a smooth curve.

   - If you want several individual beds separated by permanent paths, outline each bed independently so that you don't waste time improving soil that you'll never use. But if you think that you may change your garden layout from season to season or year to year, work the entire area within the outline.

2. **Clear the surface by first removing plants, weeds, sod, brush, and rock. If necessary, mow the site to cut back the grass and weeds close to the surface of the soil.**

   See the following section, "Killing weeds and aggressive grasses," for details on removing weeds.

3. **Dig out the roots of small trees and tough weeds with a hoe, shovel, or pick ax.**

4. **After the vegetation is manageable, remove the sod.**

   See the section "Stripping sod" for details on how to do this.

## Killing weeds and aggressive grasses

If your garden area contains a lot of perennial weeds (like quackgrass) — which are weeds that come back year after year — or if you need to clear an area of a warm-season lawn composed of vigorous grasses (like Bermuda grass), make sure that you first kill these weeds or grasses. If you simply dig out aggressive weeds or turf, they'll probably be back with a vengeance before you even get close to harvesting your first tomato. Although you can pull out or mulch out seedlings (see Chapter 15 for more on mulches and weeding), many aggressive weeds and turf spread by underground roots as well as seeds; these underground roots can haunt you for eons.

If you have an existing garden, you have to be diligent about weeding or start all over again with tilling and removing as much of the weed's root system as you can.

Basically, you can eliminate weeds and aggressive grasses two ways:

- **Use an herbicide.** Applying an herbicide is the most effective way to get rid of tough weeds. The herbicide glyphosphate, which kills roots and all, is the product of choice because it leaves little, if any, residue in your soil. But make sure that you read the directions carefully before spraying it on the weeds; killing the toughest weeds may take more than one application.

**Lovely trellised garden with a basket of veggie delights**

**A raised-bed lettuce garden with marigolds, harvest, and cat**

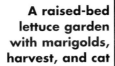

**Using bark mulch to suppress weeds and give a neat appearance**

A street-side kitchen garden served by plastic-covered cold frame and surrounded by lawn in Salem, Oregon

Squash vines trellised in a backyard vegetable garden

A sidewalk vegetable and flower garden in 5x5' boxes to grow hot-weather summer crops on a shady lot

Coleus and cucumber in window box

A basic mixed vegetable garden

Tomatoes, basil, and flowers growing in containers

**Vegetable garden in Anchorage, Alaska, with lush crops growing during long summer days despite short gardening season**

**Well-rooted seedling in peat pellet**

**Adding lime before planting to neutralize acidic soil**

**A compost pile with a green nitrogen layer like grass clippings alternating with brown carbon layers like straw**

**Using a pantyhose sling to protect Melon 'Salia' cantaloupe from falling as it ripens**

**Garden maintenance**

Garden row coverings — floating row covering fabric and poly plastic

Organic gardening technique showing young eggplants protected from flea beetles with nylon curtains

Romano Italian pole beans on tipi

Attractive garden with raised beds and straw mulch

Cucumbers growing in netting with mulch and marigolds

Using a plastic milk jug with top cut off and pin-holes in bottom as a reservoir to keep tomato plant moist between waterings

A colorful mix that includes chard, tomatoes, and parsley along with marigolds, nasturtiums, and lobelia

Italian heirloom vegetables

Heirloom tomato harvest

'Jingle Bells' sweet pepper

Heirloom winter squash collection

The 'Norland' potato

Asparagus spears emerging from spring soil ready for harvest

A collection of shell bean varieties

'Thumbellina' carrots

'Bright lights' Swiss chard

'Livette' Chicory

'Big Autumn' pumpkin

'Burpless Hybrid' Cucumber

'Neon' Eggplant

Lima bean seedlings ready for planting

'Grazer', 'Red Oak Leaf', 'Black Seeded Simpson, and 'New Red' lettuces

'Early Cascade' tomato

'North Star,' 'Yankee,' 'Bell,' 'Corona,' and 'Secret' bell peppers

North American
heirloom vegetables

✔ **Apply a covering.** An easy, chemical-free way to clear your garden is to cover it with clear or black plastic, cardboard, or even old rugs. After a month under these impermeable coverings, existing plants die from the lack of sunlight. You must plan ahead to use this method, and it may not look pretty, but it works like a charm especially on annual weeds. For perennial weeds, you may need to dig out their roots, too, after applying the plastic.

You can buy plastic in rolls at hardware stores or home improvement centers; check department stores for old pieces of cardboard and check carpet stores for old rugs. Use the thickest plastic or cardboard that you can find — at least 2 mil, but 4 mil is even better.

Controlling weeds and grasses by applying a covering to your garden area is easy; just follow these steps:

1. **Spread the covering over your entire garden area; secure the edges with spare rocks, bricks, or boards. (Place old rugs nap side down.)**

   Let neighboring pieces overlap by several inches so that no light can penetrate.

2. **Come back in a month to strip off any grass or weeds.**

   Use a shovel to cut off any grass or weeds at the root level (just below the soil surface). If they're not too thick, rototill them into the ground.

3. **Wet the area and wait about ten days for weeds to sprout.**

   Leave the covering off because you want weeds to sprout. You should get some growth because you haven't removed weed seeds.

4. **Use a hoe to kill the weeds.**

   Hoeing the weeds down is sufficient to kill annual weeds, but if you have perennial weeds, you need to dig out the roots.

## Stripping sod

When clearing your garden plot, you can strip the *sod* (grass and roots) without first killing the grass if your lawn consists of bluegrass and other less-spreading grasses; most lawns in the northern United States consist of these types of grasses. But you should kill weedier grasses, like Bermuda grass, before you strip the sod (see the preceding section for details on killing weedier grass). Stripping sod takes a lot of effort, but it works. Just follow these steps, and have your wheelbarrow handy, if you have one:

1. **Water the area that you want to clear for 15 minutes for each of the two days prior to digging up your sod.**

   Stripping sod is easier when the ground is slightly moist.

2. **Starting at one end of your plot, slip a spade under the grass and slide it under the sod.**

   An easier method is to precut the sod into square or rectangular sections and then loosen each section with a spade. Either way, don't dig too deep; you just want to remove the sod and 1 to 2 inches of roots.

3. **Pivot your spade up and let the sod flip off the spade and back onto the ground. Use your spade to slice off the sod section and then toss the sod into a wheelbarrow to discard it or to take it to a compost pile.**

4. **Repeat Steps 2 and 3 until your garden is cleared of sod.**

These steps should clear all the grass in your garden. You'll get new growth only if you have an aggressive grass like Bermuda and you don't get all the roots.

# Analyzing and Improving Your Soil

After clearing your garden area, you need to take a close look at your soil, maybe give it a good squeeze, have it tested, amend it, and then work it out to make sure that it's in shipshape. Good soil gives vegetable roots a balance of all the things they need — moisture, nutrients, and air. And knowing your soil type enables you to counteract problems that you may face gardening on that piece of land.

Three main types of soil exist, with a lot of variations in between. Hard clay is at one end of the spectrum; soft, sandy soil is at the other end; and loam is in the middle. Knowing your soil helps you know what to expect when gardening. Clay soil tends to have a lot of natural fertility but is heavy to work with and doesn't drain water well. Sandy soil drains water well (maybe too well) but doesn't have a lot of natural fertility. Loam soil is somewhere in between the two.

Here are general characteristics of the three basic types of soil:

- **Sandy soil** is composed of mostly large mineral particles. Water moves through this soil quickly, taking nutrients with it. Sandy soil is well aerated, quick to dry out and warm up, and often lacks the nutrients that vegetables need.

- **Clay soil** consists of mainly small particles that cling tightly together and hang onto water. It's slow to dry out and warm up, and has poor aeration.

- **Loam soil** is a happy mixture of large and small particles. It's well aerated and drains properly, but it can still hold water and nutrients. This is THE soil to have for a great vegetable garden.

To find out what type of soil you have, grab a handful of moist soil and squeeze it, as shown in Figure 14-1:

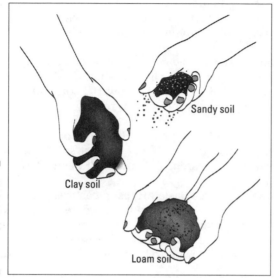

**Figure 14-1:**
Squeeze
your soil to
find out
what type
you have.

- Sandy soil falls apart and doesn't hold together in a ball when you let go. It feels gritty when you rub it between your fingers.

- Clay soil oozes through your fingers as you squeeze it and stays in a slippery wad when you let go. Rubbing clay soil between your fingers feel slippery.

- Loam soil usually stays together after you squeeze it, but it falls apart easily when you poke it with your finger.

If you have sandy or clay soil, don't despair; you can improve your soil and make it more like loam. Check out the section, "Adding dead stuff to your soil," later in this chapter, for details.

## *Putting your soil to the test*

Vegetables are kind of picky about soil chemistry. Too much of this nutrient or too little of that nutrient, and you have problems. If you don't believe me, check out Chapter 4 to see what happens when tomatoes grow in soil that's deficient in the nutrient calcium; they develop blossom-end rot. Yuck. Sometimes too much of a nutrient, such as nitrogen, will cause lots of leaf growth on plants (such as peppers) but few fruits. Getting the levels just right is important for the best harvest.

In addition to nutrient levels, soil pH is also an important factor in plant growth. The right pH enables vegetables to use nutrients from the soil. Soil is rated on a pH scale, with a pH of 1 being most acidic and a pH of 14 being most alkaline. Most vegetables grow well in a slightly acidic soil with a pH between 6 and 7. Potatoes, including sweet potatoes, prefer a slightly more acidic soil, in the 5 to 6 range. But in general, if you aim for a soil pH between 6 and 7, your vegetables should grow well.

If your soil's pH isn't within a suitable range, plants can't take up nutrients — like phosphorus and potassium — even if they're present in the soil in high amounts. On the other hand, if the pH is too low, the solubility of certain minerals, such as manganese, may increase to toxic levels.

The only way to find out whether your soil will be to your vegetables' liking is to test it. Here are two ways that you can test your soil (don't worry; analyzing your soil isn't complicated, and you don't need a lab coat):

✔ **Use a do-it-yourself kit.** This basic pH test measures your soil's acidity and alkalinity and sometimes major nutrient content. Buy a kit at a nursery, follow the instructions, and voilà — you know your soil's pH. However, the test gives you only a rough picture of the pH and nutrient levels in your soil. You may want to know more about your soil.

✔ **Have a soil lab do a test for you.** A complete soil test is a good investment because a soil lab can thoroughly analyze your soil. Here's what you can find out from a soil lab's test in addition to your soil's pH level:

   • **Your soil's nutrient content.** If you know your soil's nutrient content, you can determine how much and what kind of fertilizer to use. In fact, many soil tests tell you exactly how much fertilizer to add; see Chapter 15 for more on fertilizer.

   • **Soil problems that are specific to your geographic region.** A soil test may help you identify local problems. The soil lab should then give you a recommendation for a type and amount of fertilizer to add to your soil. For example, in dry-summer areas, you may have salty soil; the remedy is to add *gypsum,* a readily available mineral soil additive.

Of course, soil labs charge around $20 for this service. Your local Cooperative Extension office or a private soil lab can conduct a complete and reliable soil test. To locate a private lab, look in the Yellow Pages under *soil testing* or ask your Cooperative Extension office.

Fall is a good time to have a soil test done because labs aren't as busy. It's also a good time to add many amendments (materials that improve your soil's fertility and workability) to your soil because they work slowly.

To prepare a soil sample to use with a do-it-yourself kit or to send a sample to a soil lab, follow these steps:

1. **Fill a cup with soil from the top 4 to 6 inches of soil from your vegetable garden. Place the soil in a plastic bag.**

2. **Dig six to eight similar samples from different parts of your plot.**

3. **Mix all the cups of soil together; place two cups of the combined soil in a plastic bag — that's your soil sample.**

   From here, consult the instructions from your soil test kit or the testing lab.

If you're testing a soil imbalance — a known problem that you've identified in either pH or nutrients — you may want to test your soil every year because changes in pH and most nutrients are gradual. A home testing kit is a good way to test a pH imbalance. For nutrients, you may want to do a yearly test at a lab until the imbalance (high or low levels of a nutrient) is fixed. To maintain soil in good balance, test the soil every three to five years.

## Adjusting soil pH

Most garden soils have a pH between 5.5 and 8.0. This number helps you determine when and how to adjust your soil's pH level. The following guidelines help you interpret this number:

- If the number is below 6, the soil is too acidic, and you need to add ground limestone.

- If the measurement is above 7.5, the soil is too alkaline for most vegetables, and you need to add soil sulfur.

All Cooperative Extension offices, any soil lab, and many lawn and garden centers have charts showing how much lime or sulfur to add to correct a pH imbalance. The charts tell you how many pounds of material to add per 1,000 square feet, so you need to measure the size of your vegetable garden. Then use Tables 14-1 and 14-2 to figure out how much lime or sulfur you need to add to your soil.

| Table 14-1 | Pounds of Limestone Needed to Raise pH (Per 1,000 Square Feet) | | |
|---|---|---|---|
| **pH** | **Number of Pounds for:** | | |
| | **Sandy Soil** | **Loam Soil** | **Clay Soil** |
| 4.0 to 6.5 | 60 | 161 | 230 |
| 4.5 to 6.5 | 50 | 130 | 190 |
| 5.0 to 6.5 | 40 | 100 | 150 |
| 5.5 to 6.5 | 30 | 80 | 100 |
| 6.0 to 6.5 | 15 | 40 | 60 |

| Table 14-2 | Pounds of Limestone Needed to Lower pH (Per 1,000 Square Feet) | | |
| --- | --- | --- | --- |
| *pH* | *Number of Pounds for:* | | |
| | *Sandy Soil* | *Loam Soil* | *Clay Soil* |
| 8.5 to 6.5 | 45 | 60 | 70 |
| 8.0 to 6.5 | 30 | 35 | 45 |
| 7.5 to 6.5 | 10 | 20 | 25 |
| 7.0 to 6.5 | 2 | 4 | 7 |

In general, soils in climates with high rainfall — such as east of the Mississippi River (particularly east of the Appalachian Mountains) or in the Pacific Northwest — tend to be acidic. West of the Mississippi, where less rainfall occurs, soils are more alkaline. But regardless of where you live in the United States, you should easily be able to find the lime or sulfur that you need.

The best way to apply sulfur and limestone to your soil is to use a *drop spreader* (the same machine that you use to apply lawn fertilizer). This simple machine doesn't cost very much, and it helps you spread the material more evenly. Some nurseries may even loan you a spreader, or rent one to you inexpensively. You can also spread these materials by hand if you're careful and wear gloves; just make sure that you work the soil well after spreading them.

GARDEN JARGON

# What is organic gardening?

Many grocery stores and produce stands now feature organic produce. *Organic gardening* is the latest rage in vegetable gardening, but in many ways, organic gardeners use good, simple gardening practices and common sense. Some of the basic facets of organic gardening include feeding the soil — not just the plants — with organic fertilizers, manure, and organic matter; rotating crops (more on this in Chapter 16); planting a diverse group of crops; solving pest problems by planting disease-resistant varieties; using barriers (covers that keep bugs away from plants); releasing beneficial insects; and using the least harmful biological and plant-based sprays (more on these in Chapter 18).

The fertilizers and pesticides that commercial organic gardeners can use vary from state to state. A movement is in process to create national standards to define organic gardening, but the process is still moving — no standards are yet in place. As a home gardener, how you define organic gardening is a matter of personal preference.

Your soil uses limestone and soil sulfur most efficiently when it's tilled into the soil to a depth of 4 to 6 inches.

You can purchase and apply different types of limestone to your soil. Which type you use may depend on the type of nutrients your soil needs:

- **Dolomitic limestone** contains magnesium as well as calcium. Magnesium is one of the nutrients that a soil lab may test for, and although it's not in the top three (nitrogen, phosphorus, and potassium), it is as important as calcium for plant growth. Use dolomitic limestone to adjust the pH if your soil test shows that your soil is low in magnesium.

- **Pulverized limestone** is the most common and inexpensive acid neutralizer. Use this limestone if you don't need to add magnesium to your soil.

- **Pelletized pulverized limestone** is a little more expensive than ordinary powdered limestone, but it's cleaner and easier to use.

Sulfur usually comes only in powdered form, or mixed with other nutrients such as ammonium sulfate.

## Adding dead stuff to your soil

If you're like most people, your garden doesn't have the perfect loam soil. So to fix that mucky clay or loose sand, you need to add *organic matter* — once-living stuff like compost, sawdust, animal manure, ground bark, grass clippings, and leaf mold (composted tree leaves). You can't change the type of soil (clay, sand, or loam) you have, but adding organic matter makes your soil more like loam, which is perfect for vegetable roots. And even if you have loam soil, you should add organic matter to your soil every year.

Organic matter improves garden soil in the following ways:

- It helps loosen and aerate clay soil.

- It improves the water- and nutrient-holding capacity of sandy soil.

- It provides the once-living material that attracts microorganisms, beneficial fungi, worms, and other soilborne critters that improve the health of your vegetables.

Because organic matter is a good thing to add to your soil, work some into your soil before you plant each season. If you're using unfinished (raw) organic matter like leaves or undecomposed manure, add it to your soil at least one month before planting. Add finished compost and manures just before planting.

Follow these steps to add organic matter to your garden soil (for information on the best kinds of organic matter, see the following two sections):

1. **Add a 1- to 2-inch layer of organic matter to the area where you intend to plant your vegetables.**

   Go for the higher end (2 inches) if your garden is new or if your soil is heavy clay or very sandy. Use less if you've grown there for years or if your soil is pretty good.

   You need 3 cubic yards of compost to spread a 1-inch-thick layer over 1,000 square feet.

2. **Work in the organic matter to a depth of at least 6 inches.**

   There's nothing glamorous about spreading manure. The best way to spread manure or compost is with a wheelbarrow and a shovel.

Another way to add organic matter to your soil is to grow your own. You can find out more about growing green manure and cover crops in Chapter 16.

### The best choice: Compost

The best organic material to add to your soil is compost. Composting breaks down yard waste, agricultural waste, wood scraps, and even sludge into a crumbly soil-like material called *humus*.

Compost is usually clean, easy to use, and available. You can buy it in bags or have it delivered by the truckload. Most waste disposal sites make compost and sell it relatively cheap. You can also make your own compost; see "Making Your Own Compost" for details.

Before you buy compost, ask whether the compost contains any heavy metals, such as lead, and whether the compost is safe to use in a vegetable garden. Your local health department should be able to tell you what levels of lead and heavy materials are unsafe. The folks at the waste disposal site also may even be able to give you a precise nutrient content if they've performed any tests on the compost.

### Other organic materials, such as sawdust and manure

Using organic materials other than compost — such as sawdust and manure — is fine, but these materials present a few problems that compost does not. Here are some advantages and disadvantages:

✔ Adding sawdust adds organic matter to your soil, which eventually breaks down and forms humus. However, the sawdust also robs the soil of nitrogen when it decomposes, so you have to add more fertilizer to compensate (see Chapter 15).

## Charlie and the compost factory

Being an organic vegetable gardener, I'm pretty picky about the compost that I use in my vegetable garden (my head is hard enough without adding some lead to it). I prefer to make my own compost (see "Making Your Own Compost"), but I often need more than I can produce. So I purchase additional compost that I know has been made from plant refuse — no sludge and no ground-up boards with paint on them. I also make yearly trips to a local horse farm to load up on manure from the horses' old piles; the horse farm is more than happy to let me take as much as I want!

Because old manure is already composted, I can add it directly to my garden.

With fresh manure, I let it sit around (and get old) to complete the composting process so that I can apply it directly to my garden. Unfortunately, fresh mature smells like . . . manure! But after it's spread and incorporated into the soil, it doesn't smell anymore. I add partly decomposed manure the fall before planting and let it slowly break down until next spring planting.

 ✔ Livestock manure improves your soil's nitrogen level (see Chapter 15 for more information on manure). However, livestock diets often include lots of hay that's full of weed seeds, which may germinate in your vegetable garden.

Some manures (such as horse manure) add organic matter and some nutrients to your soil, but they're also loaded with bedding materials (like dried hay) that cause the same problem that adding sawdust causes.

If you use manure, make sure that it's *fully composted* — that is, it's been sitting around for a year or two, very little of the original material is visible, and the salts have been leached out (the nutrients have left the manure). Too much salt in the soil can be harmful to plants.

# Turning Your Soil

After adding nutrients and amendments to your soil, you need to mix them up. Turning your soil to mix the amendments enables them to break down faster and be available where the roots can use them.

If your soil is dry, water well, and let it sit for a few days before digging. Then, to determine whether your soil is ready to turn, take a handful of soil and squeeze it. The soil should crumble easily in your hand with a flick of your finger; if water drips out, it's too wet.

Don't work soil that's too wet. Working soil that's too wet ruins the soil structure — after it dries, the soil is hard to work and even harder to grow roots in.

The easiest way to turn your soil, especially in large plots, is with a *rototiller* (or *tiller,* for short). You can rent or borrow a tiller, or if you're serious about this vegetable-garden business, buy one. I prefer tillers with rear tines and power-driven wheels because you can really lean into the machines and use your weight to till deeper. If you have a small (less than 100 square feet) vegetable plot, consider using a minitiller. (See Chapter 21 for more on tools.)

If you use a rototiller, adjust the tines so that the initial pass over your soil is fairly shallow (a few inches deep). As the soil loosens, set the tines deeper with successive passes (crisscrossing at 90-degree angles) until the top 8 to 12 inches of soil are loosened.

To turn your soil by hand, use a straight spade and a digging fork. You can either dig your garden to one spade's depth, about 1 foot, or *double dig* (that is, work your soil to a greater depth), going down 20 to 24 inches. After turning the soil, level the area with a steel rake, breaking up clods and discarding any rocks. Although double digging takes more effort, it enables roots to penetrate deeper to find water and nutrients. If you're double digging, dig the upper part of the soil with a straight spade to remove the seal and loosen the subsoil (usually any soil below 8 to 12 inches) with a spade. Replace the original topsoil often when you loosen the subsoil.

# Making Your Own Compost

Making your own compost is a way to turn a wide array of readily available organic materials — such as grass clippings, household garbage, and plant residue — into a uniform, easy-to-handle source of organic matter for your garden. Although the finished compost is usually low in plant nutrients, composting enables you to enrich your soil in an efficient, inexpensive way. You can add organic matter that's not decomposed to your soil and get a similar result, but most people find that dark, crumbly compost is easier to handle than half-rotten household garbage — yuck.

A *compost pile* (a pile of organic matter constructed to decompose) can be free standing or enclosed and can be made any time of year. However, you'll have the most organic matter in summer and fall when the compost will happen faster due to the warm weather. Wire fencing, as shown Figure 14-2, makes a good container because it lets in plenty of air. You can also purchase easy-to-use composters at garden centers or through mail-order catalogs. Some composters simplify the turning process (see " Moisten and turn your compost pile" later in this chapter) because they rotate on swivels or come apart in sections or pieces. You can also build your own composter. For sample composter plans, check out *Decks & Patios For Dummies,* written by Robert J. Beckstrom and the Editors of the National Gardening Association (IDG Books Worldwide, Inc.).

**Figure 14-2:**
Layering brown and green organic matter in a 3- to 4-inch diameter cylinder creates the perfect mix in your compost pile.

## *How to build a compost pile*

Building a good compost pile involves much more than just tossing organic materials in a pile in the corner of your yard, though many people (including me at times) use this technique with varied success. You need to have a good size for your pile, add the right types and amount of materials, and provide the correct amount of moisture. Here are the characteristics of a well-made pile:

- ✔ It heats up quickly — a sign that the decay organisms are at work.
- ✔ Decomposition proceeds at a rapid rate.
- ✔ The pile doesn't give off any bad odors.
- ✔ The organisms that do all the decay work take up carbon and nitrogen (the stuff that they feed on and break down) in proportion to their needs.

You can easily come up with the correct amounts of materials for a compost pile by building the pile in layers, as shown in Figure 14-2. Just follow these steps:

1. **Choose a well-drained spot in your yard.**

2. **Create a 4- to 6-inch layer of "brown" materials that are rich in carbon.**

   These brown materials include plant residue, old grass clippings, dried hay, leaves, and so on. The more finely chopped these materials are, the more surface area that decay organisms can attack, and the faster the materials decompose.

3. **Add a thin layer of "green" materials that are high in nitrogen.**

   Green materials include green grass clippings, kitchen vegetable scraps, a 2- to 4-inch layer of manure, or a light, even coating of blood meal, cottonseed meal, or a chemical fertilizer high in nitrogen (see Chapter 15 for more on fertilizers).

4. **Repeat these green and brown layers (Steps 2 through 3) until the pile is no more than 5 feet high.**

   If a pile is higher than 5 feet, too little oxygen reaches the center of the pile, enabling some nasty anaerobic decay organisms to take over and produce bad odors; I hate that. Five feet is a good maximum width for the pile as well.

Here are a few additional ways to ensure success in your compost pile:

- ✓ **Moisten each layer of your compost pile lightly with a watering can as you build it, but don't let the pile get soggy.**

- ✓ **Cover the second layer with a few inches of garden soil.** The soil covers any material in the carbon layer that may attract flies, such as household garbage.

- ✓ **Add a dusting of ground limestone or wood ashes.** This keeps the compost's pH around the 6 to 7 mark that your plants like.

## *Materials that don't belong in compost*

A well-made pile heats up enough to kill off many insects and disease organisms, but the heating isn't uniform enough to be relied on to kill everything that you want it to. Don't add the following materials to your pile:

- ✓ **Diseased or infected plant material.**

- ✓ **Weeds that have gone to seed.** The heat may not be kill them.

- ✓ **Pieces of aggressive weeds like quackgrass or Bermuda grass.** Even a small piece of a root can produce a new plant.

- ✓ **Grass clippings from lawns treated with herbicides.** Some herbicides may not break down during the composting process.

🖊 **Meat scraps and fats.** They break down slowly and may attract animals to the pile.

🖊 **Dog or cat feces.** They may carry diseases that can be transmitted to humans.

## Moisten and turn your compost pile

After you build your compost pile, the decay process begins, causing the center of the pile to heat up. You must turn the pile periodically to aerate it, prevent it from overheating, and ensure that all the material decomposes uniformly. Proper moisture is also important so that decay organisms can work properly.

Following are some ways to keep your compost pile moist:

🖊 Water the pile as needed. To determine whether you need to water, dig about 1 foot into the pile and see if it's moist.

Be careful not to overwater your pile. It's easy to do. The water seeps in and tends not to evaporate readily, so people think the pile is dry when it's not.

🖊 If there's a long dry spell or if you live in a dry-summer area, water the entire pile to keep it lightly moist.

🖊 Make a depression in the top of the pile to collect rainfall.

You can turn your compost pile by forking the material from the outside of the pile to the center or by moving the pile from one area to another. If you made a pile out of wire fencing, simply unhook the ends, pull the fencing apart, and move the cylinder a few feet away from the pile. Then fork the materials from the pile into the empty wire cylinder.

How often you turn the pile and how quickly the compost is done depends on how quickly decay takes place. For example, green, succulent organic material — like fresh grass clippings — decays faster than dried plant material; cool fall temperatures or a spell of rainy days that turn the pile soggy slow things down. Follow these guidelines for deciding when to turn your pile:

🖊 If you added only shredded material, the pile may be ready for turning in a week.

🖊 If the pile contains a lot of big pieces of organic material, wait several weeks before turning.

🖊 If the pile heats up and then cools, turn it.

🖊 Turning the pile two to three times is plenty.

You can tell that decay has set in if your pile starts to smell bad. If this happens, hold your nose and fix things by spreading out the pile and reconstructing it.

Your compost is ready when the interior of the pile is no longer hot and all the material in the pile has broken down into a uniform, dark crumbly substance; this process takes about one to two months. To determine whether the pile is no longer hot, feel the interior of the pile with your hand. If you're squeamish, use a compost thermometer (available at garden centers).

Keep in mind that some rocks and big pieces of debris that didn't break down may still be present even though the pile has quit composting. If that's the case, you can still use the compost as is, or you may want to sift your finished compost through a sturdy mesh screen.

To make a mesh screen, build a 3-by-3-foot square frame out of two-by-fours, nail a screen to it, and then use it to sift the compost. You can either prop the screen up on an angle or support it with two sawhorses. Throw the compost on the screen and push it around with a shovel until it sifts through the screen.

# Chapter 15

# Maintaining Your Vegetable Garden

After planting your garden, you need to keep your vegetables growing vigorously until harvest. Maintaining your vegetable garden is similar to playing a football game. Your team is ready, the ball has been kicked off, and you need to stay injury-free and play hard until the game is over. If you let up anywhere in the game, the outcome will be disappointing. The same is true when you grow vegetables; after you plant your vegetables, you need to keep them healthy and well nourished throughout the growing season. If you let up just a bit on water or fertilizer, your harvest will be small or of poor quality. If you've ever tasted a cucumber harvested from a plant that has dried out, you know how bitter a poor harvest can be.

But don't worry. In this chapter, I tell you everything that you need to know to keep your vegetables happy — including keeping your soil moist and fertile, adding mulch, supporting your plants, and keeping those dreaded weeds at bay.

## Watering Basics

Although Mother Nature is often very generous with rain, there are times when she leaves gardens with a dry spell. Flooding isn't good for your garden, but neither is drought. If your plants don't have adequate water at the right time, they can easily die.

Different crops have different water needs. Some vegetables, like celery, are real water lovers and prefer to have moist soil around their roots at all times. Shallow-rooted crops (like onions and cabbage) need more careful watering during dry spells than deeper-rooted crops (like tomatoes) that can pull water from greater depths. The descriptions in Part II of this book provide specific watering information for different vegetables.

You also need to keep in mind a plant's growth stage when watering. Here are some general watering guidelines for different growth stages:

- **Watering seedlings and germinating seeds:** Seedlings with small root systems near the soil surface and germinating seeds benefit from frequent, gentle watering, which enables them to sprout and emerge quickly. Water once a day to a few inches deep if it doesn't rain.

- **Watering transplants:** Two weeks after you plant transplants in your garden, water frequently to help the roots recover from transplant shock. Water transplants every few days to 6 inches or so.

- **Watering established plants:** Plants that have been in your garden for a few weeks and that are beyond transplant shock need to be watered deeply. Try to wet the soil at least 6 inches deep; you can dig into the soil with a trowel to see how far the water has penetrated. Watering to this depth encourages roots to penetrate deeply, where they're less susceptible to drought. Give the soil a chance to dry out slightly before watering thoroughly again.

## How to tell when your veggies are thirsty

In general, most vegetables use about 1 inch of water per week (1 to 2 inches in hot, dry climates). If you don't get water from rainfall, you have to supply it. Here are some general guidelines for determining when your plants need water:

- **Your finger is the best indicator of when the soil has dried sufficiently to rewater.** Dig down several inches into the soil; if the soil is dry to your touch 3 to 4 inches down, it's time to water.

- **Wilting plants can be a sign that your soil needs water.** Wilting is when the leaves or stems of a plant droop, bend over, and look limp. These symptoms, however, can also be misleading at times. Some plants, like tomatoes, peppers, and eggplants, tend to droop slightly during the heat of the day, even if the soil has enough moisture. If your plants don't stand tall and proud and the soil feels dry, add water and watch them perk up fast.

Overwatering can also cause plants to wilt, so check the soil before watering to make sure that you don't overwater. If the soil is waterlogged, roots die from lack of air. With fewer roots, plants can no longer take up the water that they need from the soil, and they wilt. Root damage from insects and disease can also cause wilting.

✔ **Each vegetable has a critical period when you need to be especially careful about watering or your crop may be ruined.** Table 15-1 shows the important watering periods for different types of vegetables.

| Table 15-1 | Critical Watering Periods for Vegetables |
|---|---|
| *Vegetable* | *Important Watering Stage* |
| Bean, lima | When flowering and forming pods |
| Bean, snap | When flowering and forming pods |
| Broccoli | When forming a head |
| Cabbage | When forming a head |
| Carrots | When forming roots |
| Cauliflower | When forming a head |
| Corn, sweet | When silking, tasseling, and forming ears |
| Cucumber | When flowering and developing fruit |
| Eggplant | Give uniform supply of water from flowering through harvest |
| Melon | During fruit set and early development |
| Onion, dry | During bulb enlargement |
| Pea | When flowering and during seed enlargement |
| Pepper | Give uniform supply of water from flowering through harvest |
| Potato | When tubers set and enlarge |
| Radish | When forming roots |
| Squash, summer | When forming buds and flowering |
| Tomato | Give uniform supply of water from flowering through harvest |
| Turnip | When forming roots |

# Using a flowmeter to measure water flow

You can measure water flow by attaching an inexpensive flowmeter (available at hardware and garden supply stores) to your outdoor spigot. To figure out the flow rate at the spigot, turn off all the spigots and read your water meter. Then turn on the spigot serving the hose line for one minute. Reread the meter to find out how much water flows through the hose in one minute. You need about 60 gallons per 100 square feet of garden to get 1 inch of water.

## Some general watering tips

Here are some other watering pointers to keep in mind when tending to your crops:

- ✔ **Considering the time of day that you water is important, especially if you use a sprinkler.** You lose less water to evaporation (an important consideration in hot, dry climates) if sprinklers operate in the cool of the morning rather than during the afternoon heat. Watering in the morning also gives leaves a chance to dry off before evening; wet foliage is an ideal fungus-growing medium.

- ✔ **Frequent, shallow waterings do more harm than good.** They cause roots to develop mainly in the upper few inches of the soil, where they're susceptible to drying out.

- ✔ **If your garden has heavy clay soil or is on a slope, and you find that water begins to run off before it penetrates 6 inches deep in the soil, try watering at intervals to avoid this problem.** Water for 10 to 15 minutes, let the water soak in for 15 to 20 minutes, and then water again.

# Ways to Water Your Vegetable Garden

You can water your vegetable garden several different ways. The following sections discuss some of the basic techniques, from the simplest — furrows — to the most complicated — drip irrigation systems.

## Furrows

Furrows are shallow trenches between raised beds that channel water to plant roots. This watering method is based on an old farmer technique of planting on narrow raised mounds or beds and then using furrows to water. The beds can be 1 to 3 feet apart — the wider apart they are, the more water you need to add. You can use a hoe to dig a furrow at planting time and then plant the seeds or transplants on top of the raised beds, in between furrows. When you're ready to water, fill the furrows completely with water and then wait a while, or fill them more than once so that the water penetrates down as well as sideways into the raised soil. Poke around with your finger to make sure that the water has penetrated the bed.

Furrows work best on level or slightly sloping ground; otherwise, the water moves too fast down the furrows without sinking in. Furrows have traditionally been used in arid areas with clay soil, such as the Southwest, where streams or ground water can be used in the garden, but little natural rain falls during the growing season. Furrows don't work well in sandy soil because the water soaks in before it can reach the end of the furrow.

Furrows aren't the most efficient way to water. Here are a few reasons why:

- ✔ It takes time for the water to run from one end of a mound or bed to the other end.
- ✔ The beginning of a row always gets more water than the end.
- ✔ You have to move your hose around a lot to fill each furrow.

## Basins

A basin is a donutlike depression around a vegetable plant that you fill with water — almost like a "circular" furrow. You make a basin in a 2-foot diameter circle around the plant. Basins work particularly well for watering sprawling plants like melons and squash early in the season. After the plants mature, however, their roots will grow out of the diameter of the basin, and this method won't be effective any longer.

## Hoses

Watering with a hose is probably the most common way that gardeners water. It's simple, and some might say therapeutic. Who hasn't seen a gardener after a long day at work come home and take some time to hose down the garden with a cup of coffee or drink in hand?

However, watering with a hose is not the ideal watering system and probably is best for watering containers; for watering individual, large plants such as tomatoes; and when used in conjunction with the basin method. In these situations, you can be sure that you're applying the right amount of water to your plants.

Unless you check the amount of water you're applying by digging the soil after watering, you may not water your garden evenly. Some areas may have lots of water, whereas other areas may just have water on the surface. Also, like overhead sprinklers (described in the following section), using a hose is a more wasteful way of watering because much of the water falls in pathways or on the lawn around your garden. The best way to water your vegetable garden with a hose is to attach a bubbler (available at garden centers) to the end of the hose and leave the hose running in a basin near each plant until the water has soaked down at least 6 inches deep (see Figure 15-1).

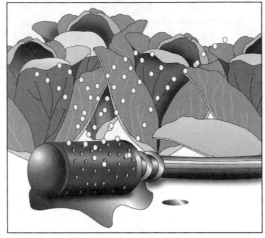

**Figure 15-1:**
Watering
with a hose
with a
bubbler
attached.

# Sprinklers

A sprinkler, shown in Figure 15-2, is very effective for watering vegetables planted in sandy soil that absorbs water quickly. It's also an effective way to water a large garden when you're pressed for time. Just set up the sprinkler, and based on the amount of time it takes to water to 6 inches deep (see the "How to tell when your veggies are thirsty," earlier in this chapter), you can set a timer and go about other business. However, if you have heavy clay soil that absorbs water slowly or if your garden is on a slope, the water may run off and not sink into the soil to where the plants need it.

For vegetable gardens, portable-type sprinklers (versus in-ground perma-nent sprinklers used in lawns) are best. You can move them around in your garden to cover a certain area or the whole garden. Some sprinklers throw water back and forth, whereas others send it in a circular direction. Choose the type that best suits your garden design.

Unfortunately, constantly wetting the foliage of vegetable plants can encour-age disease problems. So when you use a sprinkler, water in the morning so that the foliage can dry before nightfall and so that you lose less water to evaporation.

As taller plants such as corn and tomatoes grow, sprinklers tend to be less effective because the water hits the foliage, damaging it and not thoroughly watering the rest of the garden. Some gardeners use watering towers that have an overhead sprinkler attached to the top. You position the sprinkler a few feet above the plants, hook it up to a hose, and sprinkle the garden. However, even these sprinklers prove to be less effective when plants reach above 4- to 5-feet tall. For these taller plants, it's best to choose one of the other watering methods described in this chapter.

**Figure 15-2:**
Watering
with an
overhead
sprinkler.

## Soaker-hose irrigation

A soaker-hose system consists of a rubber hose perforated with tiny pores
that leak water, as shown in Figure 15-3. You can lay the hose between rows
or curve it around plants, similar to how you use a drip irrigation system
(described in the following section). Water leaks out of the hose and onto
the soil, leaving your plants dry and reducing evaporation.

Using a soaker-hose system is easier than using a drip irrigation system
because it involves fewer parts and no nozzles. It's primary limitation is that
it works best on flat terrain, often delivering water unevenly on a sloped or
even bumpy garden.

## Drip irrigation and microsprinklers

*Drip irrigation* provides water slowly through holes, or *emitters,* in flexible
black plastic pipes. Many different drip irrigation systems are available; they
can consist of a single pipe with flexible lines running off it, or a series of
pipes. You weave these pipes — which are connected to a water supply, a
filter, and often a pressure regulator — along rows of plants so that the
water flows directly to the roots of your vegetables, as shown in Figure 15-4.

**Figure 15-3:**
A soaker
hose.

**Figure 15-4:**
Drip
irrigation.

This watering technique is an effective and efficient way to water vegetables because water drips right to the roots of the plants and little water is wasted on pathways, in between plants, and in between rows. Drip irrigation works well even if your garden is on a slope, which poses problems for most other systems.

The downside to drip irrigation is that it's more costly than all the other methods listed in this chapter and more involved to set up and take down at the end of the season. It's best for those gardeners who are into technology, who don't have lots of time to water, and who live in water-restricted areas.

You can wet an entire bed from one end to the other at each watering with drip emitters. You snap the emitters in the pipes wherever you want them, or you can buy a pipe with emitters already evenly spaced along the length of the pipe. The moisture radiates sideways underground and wets the soil between emitters.

As an alternative to emitters, you may want to use *microsprinklers,* which are tiny sprinklers that hook to black plastic pipes like drip emitters. They're usually supported by 12- to 24-inch stakes and cover various-sized areas of soil with a fine spray of water. They're particularly useful for watering closely spaced vegetables like lettuce and root crops, or for watering germinating seeds.

Most nurseries sell drip irrigation systems, but you can also purchase them through the mail (see the appendix). Emitters and microsprinklers are available with different application rates, varying by the number of gallons applied per hour. Pressure-compensating emitters apply water consistently from one end of the line to the other, regardless of pressure changes due to uneven ground.

Follow these steps to set up a drip irrigation system in your garden:

1. **Lay the pipe (or pipes — depending on the system) on top of the soil and cover the pipe with plastic mulch, or bury the pipe a few inches below the surface of the soil.**

   Most people like to keep the pipe close to the surface so they can check it for clogs and fix breaks.

2. **If your pipe doesn't already have emitters in it, snap emitters in the pipe wherever you want them.**

   Position the emitters so that they are close to the bases of your plants.

3. **Run the drip system for at least several hours a day.**

   Watch the system carefully the first few times that you water. Dig around in your garden to see how far the water travels over a given time period. Then adjust your watering schedule in the future.

If you live in an area where the soil freezes, don't leave your drip irrigation system outside in the winter because it may burst. Instead, drain the water out, roll up the tubing, and store it in your garage.

# Mulching Magic

*Mulch* is any material, organic or inorganic, that you place over the surface of soil, usually right over the root zone of growing plants. It has many benefits depending on the type used. Mulch suppresses weeds, holds in moisture, lessens the chances of certain diseases attacking your plants, and adds an attractive look to your garden. Although some people may use compost as a mulch, compost has a different purpose than mulch. Compost is added and mixed into the soil to add nutrients and increase the work-ability of soil (water-holding capacity, aeration, and so on). Mulch generally doesn't add nutrients, but it helps hold in the ones already in the soil and prevents undesirables from attacking your growing plants.

You can choose from two basic types of mulch: organic and inorganic. For vegetable growers, each type of mulch has a purpose, as described in the following sections.

## Organic mulch

Organic mulch includes grass clippings, compost, leaf mold, pine needles, shredded bark, nut shells, cotton gin waste, stray hay, grain and fruit by-products, composted manure, mushroom compost, peat moss, and sawdust. Some mulches are easier to find in different parts of the country. You can even use newspaper as an organic mulch; black-and-white newspaper print is perfectly safe to use in your garden, and most colored inks are soybean based and biodegradable.

Generally, a 2- to 4-inch layer of mulch, spread evenly on the ground beneath your plants, is sufficient. However, you may have to replenish the mulch during the growing season because many organic mulches break down quickly.

Using organic mulch in your vegetable garden has many benefits:

  - Organic mulch conserves water by reducing the soil temperature and evaporation. It keeps the soil cool by buffering direct sunlight.
  - Organic mulch prevents wild fluctuations in soil moisture levels that can really spell disaster in hot weather.
  - Organic mulch smothers weed seeds and prevents them from germinating.

✓ Any weeds that do come up in a loose mulch are easy to pull.

✓ As the mulch breaks down, it adds nutrients and improves the texture of the soil that it covers.

✓ Organic mulch looks good; it makes the ground tidy and clean.

The following list includes some of the downsides of organic mulches. As minor as they are, they may lead you to choose one type of organic mulch over another:

✓ **Bark mulches, such as pine, are quite acidic.** So if you use them, keep a close eye on the pH level of your soil and correct it accordingly. (See Chapter 14 to find out how to test soil pH.)

✓ **Grass clippings decay quickly and must be replenished often.** Fortunately, grass clippings are usually pretty abundant. But if the grass goes to seed before you cut it, you may end up with grass growing in your flower bed. Also, make sure that no herbicides (weed killers) have been used on your lawn because the residue can damage or kill vegetables; if you have your lawn treated regularly, use another type of mulch.

✓ **Some organic mulches — such as fresh sawdust — rob nitrogen from the soil as they break down.** You may have to add supplemental nitrogen to your vegetables if they grow mysteriously slow or start to turn yellow. (Fertilizers are discussed later in this chapter in the section, "Using Fertilizer in Your Vegetable Garden.")

✓ **Some organic mulches such as peat moss or leaves can pack down or get hard and crusty when exposed to weather.** Water may not penetrate these mulches, running off the soil instead of soaking into the roots. My suggestion is to avoid peat moss or mix it with another organic mulch such as sawdust. It's also darn expensive.

✓ **Some lightweight mulches, like straw or cocoa hulls, can blow around in the wind.** You may want to avoid them if you live in a windy area.

✓ **Organic mulch, which keeps the soil cool, may slow the growth and maturity of warm-season crops such as tomatoes and melons.** This can especially be a problem in areas with cool summers. However in very hot-summer areas of the country, organic mulches work to keep the roots of even warm-season crops cool and healthy.

✓ **Composted manures may burn young vegetables if used as mulch because the manures vary in the amount of nitrogen they contain.** If you want to use composted manure, mix it with three times the volume of another organic mulch before applying it.

You can purchase organic mulches like shredded bark, compost, and leaf mold in bags or sometimes in bulk from nurseries and garden centers. Grass clippings, compost, and wood chips come free from your yard or garden.

# Inorganic mulch

*Inorganic mulches* include things like plastic, landscape fabric, and believe it or not, old carpet.

Mulching with black plastic works best when you install drip irrigation or a soaker hose underneath the plastic before planting. Otherwise, watering is difficult. You can place the irrigation on top of the plastic, which enables you to more easily check for clogs, but you have to run individual emitters to each plant.

Black plastic doesn't work well with vegetables that are planted very close together, such as root crops.

To mulch with black plastic, which is the most-used inorganic mulch for vegetable gardens, follow these steps:

1. **Purchase rolls or sheets of 2- to 4-mil (the thicker the better) black plastic (the thickness is on the label).**

   You can purchase black plastic at garden centers or hardware stores.

2. **If you're using irrigation under the plastic, lay down your drip irrigation and turn it on for several hours (see "Drip irrigation and microsprinklers," earlier in this chapter, for details). Note where the wet spots are in the soil.**

3. **A week or two before planting, water the entire area with a hose or sprinkler so that it's wet to 6 inches deep. Roll out the plastic over the planting area and cover the edges of the plastic with soil.**

4. **Cut holes in the plastic where you want to plant your transplants, as shown in Figure 15-5. You can also sow seed this way; just make sure that the seed can get through the holes in the plastic after it germinates.**

5. **Plant your seeds or transplants in the holes. Make sure that you plant in wet spots; otherwise, the plants may not get enough water.**

   If you live in a climate that gets very hot in the summer (Texas, for example), after the weather starts to warm, you may want to cover the black plastic with an organic mulch to prevent the soil from getting too warm or use white plastic.

You usually don't have to remove the plastic until the end of the season unless you have a problem with the irrigation system.

**Figure 15-5:**
Planting
through
black
plastic
mulch.

Black plastic is good for general use, but you may want to consider different-colored plastics as well:

- **Red plastic,** for example, is great for tomatoes (see Chapter 4).

- **Dark green IRT plastic** (infrared transmitting) lets through the warming, infrared rays of the sun, but blocks out the ultraviolet rays responsible for weed germination. This dark green plastic keeps the soil warmer than black plastic does, but still keeps weeds from growing. It's great for heat-loving vegetables, such as melons and okra.

- **White plastic** is good for hot climates where you want to stop weeds from growing but not heat up the soil.

You can also use the following inorganic mulches in your vegetable garden:

- **Landscape fabric:** This inorganic mulch doesn't warm the soil as much as black plastic, but it's permeable, enabling you to water through it. It also does a good job of keeping down weeds. You can find landscape fabric at your local nursery. You apply landscape fabric the same way that you do plastic.

- **Rug strips:** Roll out 3-foot rug strips and place them upside down, leaving about 6 inches of open soil between strips for irrigation and planting. Although rug strips look pretty weird in a garden, they keep the weeds down and make a nice path.

## *Knowing when and which mulch to use*

Choosing a mulch and deciding when to use it in your vegetable garden depends on the type of vegetables that you grow and when you plant them. Here are some mulching tips for different types of vegetables:

✔ **Cool-season vegetables planted in early spring:** You want the sun to warm your soil in the spring because lots of sun helps young plants get off to a fast start. Here are a few mulching pointers for these vegetables:

  • Lay down organic mulch when the soil starts to warm and when the plants need regular water. If you mulch too early, the soil stays too cold and wet for proper root growth.

  • In areas with short growing seasons, you can plant broccoli, cauliflower, and cool-season plants through plastic. Cover the plastic with organic matter when the weather warms.

✔ **Cool-season vegetables planted in late summer or early fall:** With these vegetables, you want the cooling effect, so put down an organic mulch right after planting. Here are a few other things to keep in mind:

  • When the weather starts to cool, rake off or remove the organic mulch so that the soil warms.

  • You can plant through plastic late in the year, but you should cover it with an organic mulch immediately so that the soil doesn't get too hot. Then remove the organic mulch when the weather cools and let the plastic warm the soil through harvest.

  • Many root crops can be stored in the ground well into winter if you cover them with a thick organic mulch like straw. Applied before the ground freezes, the mulch keeps the soil loose and unfrozen so that you can dig the vegetables later into winter.

✔ **Warm-season vegetables planted in spring:** With these vegetables, keep the ground clear if you're planting really early — the more heat the better. Planting through plastic works in early spring. In hot climates, apply an organic mulch when the weather starts to get really warm in summer.

# *Determining What Notable Nutrients Your Soil Needs*

Sixteen elements are essential for healthy plant growth. Of these elements, plants especially need carbon, hydrogen, and oxygen in large quantities, along with energy from sunlight for *photosynthesis,* the process by which plants use carbon dioxide from the air and water from the soil to produce sugars that enable them to grow. Nature — and your conscientious watering — supply these elements.

Plants also need nitrogen, phosphorus, and potassium in relatively large quantities. Plants take up these three nutrients — often called *macronutrients* — from the soil. If you soil doesn't contain enough of these nutrients, you can supply them by fertilizing.

Here's a list of important nutrients that your plants need, along with information to help you determine when you need to add nutrients to your soil. To find out what quantities to add, refer to the chapters on individual vegetables in Part II of this book:

- **Nitrogen (N),** a key component of proteins and *chlorophyll* (the plant pigment that plays a vital role in photosynthesis), is responsible for the healthy, green color of your plants.

  Nitrogen is a volatile creature. It easily moves around in the soil and can leach away from plant roots as a result of rain or watering. Therefore, you need to be sure that your plants receive a steady supply of nitrogen all season long.

  - *How to detect too little:* Plants with a nitrogen deficiency show yellowing (in older leaves first) and slowed growth. With plants like tomatoes, a nitrogen deficiency may first appear as a reddening of the stems and the undersides of the leaves.

  - *How to detect too much:* A plant with too much nitrogen has soft-textured, dark green foliage and an underdeveloped root system, and flowering and fruiting are delayed. Because nitrogen leaches out of the soil quickly, if you have too much, stop fertilizing, wait, and eventually the problem will solve itself.

  - *How to add it to your soil:* You can supplement soil nitrogen by adding chemical fertilizers, decomposing organic matter, or organic fertilizers, such as blood meal and cottonseed meal.

- **Phosphorus (P)** helps promote good root growth, increased disease resistance, and fruit and seed formation. It's less available in cooler soils, so adding a fertilizer containing phosphorus in spring is a good idea.

  - *How to detect too little:* Plants lacking in phosphorus are stunted and sport dark green foliage and purplish stems and leaves (on the older leaves first). Soil pH affects the availability of phosphorus to plants; a pH of 6 to 7.5 keeps it available. (See Chapter 14 for more on soil pH.)

  - *How to add it to your soil:* Sources of phosphorus include minerals, organic matter, inorganic fertilizers (such as rock phosphate), and organic fertilizers (such as bonemeal). Unlike nitrogen, phosphorus doesn't move quickly through soil, so add a fertilizer containing phosphorus to the root zone before planting, instead of sprinkling it on the soil surface.

✔ **Potassium (K)** promotes vigorous growth and disease resistance.

- *How to detect too little:* The first sign of a deficiency is slowed growth; brown leaf edges indicate a severe deficiency.

- *How to add to your soil:* Soil minerals provide potassium, as do organic matter and inorganic fertilizers, such as potassium sulfate, green sand, and granite dust.

✔ **Calcium, magnesium, and sulfur** are known as secondary nutrients. Plants need them in substantial quantities, but not to the same extent that they need nitrogen, phosphorus, and potassium.

- *How to detect too little:* Most alkaline soils contain these elements naturally, and few soils are deficient in sulfur. Most home garden soils contain these nutrients, but you can do specific tests on the leaves to detect any deficiencies.

- *How to add them to your soil:* In regions where the soil is acidic, liming to keep your soil's pH in a good growth range provides adequate calcium and magnesium (the latter if you use dolomitic limestone). See Chapter 14 for more on liming.

✔ **Micronutrients (iron, manganese, copper, boron, molybdenum, chlorine, and zinc)** are elements that plants need in tiny amounts. Too much of one of these elements is often as harmful as too little.

- *How to detect too little or too much:* A micronutrient deficiency or excess may mean that your soil is too acidic or too alkaline, so you can correct the problem by changing the pH rather than by adding more nutrients.

- *How to add them to your soil:* Sometimes, changing the pH sufficiently to increase micronutrient levels isn't practical, or you may need to give a plant a micronutrient quickly while you try to change the soil pH. In such cases, micronutrients are applied as *chelates* (from the Latin word for claw). Chelates are added to other chemicals, in this case micronutrients, to keep them available to plants when soil conditions are unfavorable. Apply chelated micronutrients to your soil, or better yet, spray them on plant foliage.

# Using Fertilizer in Your Vegetable Garden

Even if you have the healthiest soil around, growing vegetables is an intensive process that takes many important nutrients from the soil. So you need to add some fertilizer to your soil to keep it in optimum shape to feed your plants.

How much fertilizer you add depends on the soil and the plants you're growing. That's why it's hard to generalize across the board on what and how much fertilizer to use. Soil tests are a great way to know what to add. See Chapter 14 for more about soil tests.

## Reading a fertilizer label

Commercial fertilizers are labeled with three numbers, which indicate the fertilizer's nutrient content. The first number indicates the percentage of nitrogen (N), the second number shows the percentage of phosphate (the type of phosphorus, $P_2O_5$), and the third number represents the percentage of potash (the form of potassium used, $K_2O$). For example, a 5-10-10 fertilizer contains 5 percent nitrogen, 10 percent phosphate, and 10 percent potash, and it's called a *complete fertilizer* because it contains some of each type of nutrient. In contrast, bonemeal has an analysis of 4-12-0. It's a good source of phosphate but doesn't provide any potash. The other materials in a commercial fertilizer that the analysis numbers don't account for are generally filler — unimportant materials that add bulk to the bag so that the fertilizer is easier to spread.

How much to use? Soil tests are the best way to correct deficiencies (see Chapter 14 for details), but fertilizer bags also give general dosage recommendations for gardens. Most fertilizer recommendations for maintenance fertilization (rather than to correct a deficiency) are made according to how much nitrogen a crop needs. If you have a recommendation for 3 pounds of 5-10-10 fertilizer per 100 square feet, but the fertilizer that you have on hand is 5-10-5 fertilizer, apply 3 pounds of 5-10-5. Even though the 5-10-5 fertilizer's percentage of potash is less than that of the 5-10-10, it offers the same recommended amount of nitrogen.

## Choosing a fertilizer: Chemical or organic

You have to weigh the advantages and disadvantages of chemical and organic fertilizers to decide which products are best suited to your needs and preferences.

### Chemical fertilizers

Chemical fertilizers are synthetically manufactured. They include elements such as sodium nitrate, potassium chloride, and superphosphate. Chemical fertilizers come in liquid, granular, powder, or pellet form, and choosing a form is a personal thing. If you want to fertilize when you water with a watering can, use a liquid fertilizer. If you want to sprinkle some fertilizer around each plant, use a granular fertilizer or pellets.

You can combine different chemical fertilizers to produce a complete fertilizer with a balanced supply of nitrogen, phosphate, and potash, such as 6-18-6, 5-10-5, or 10-10-10. Or you can buy a balanced fertilizer and make life simple.

Here are the advantages to chemical fertilizers:

✓ Chemical fertilizers are widely available, relatively inexpensive, and easy to store, and vary widely in formulations and forms, so you can tailor a fertilizer program to your soil and plants.

✓ Most chemical fertilizers are rapidly available to plants. The exception is fertilizer that has been manufactured in slow-release form, in which case the fertilizer pellets break down and release the fertilizer slowly.

✓ A liquid or a dry powder chemical fertilizer that you mix with water is completely soluble, and its nutrients are quickly available to plants — an advantage when plants need a quick boost, such as right after transplanting.

Here are the disadvantages to using chemical fertilizers:

✓ Chemical fertilizers add no organic matter to your soil and contribute nothing to improving soil structure.

✓ Because chemical fertilizers are more concentrated than natural fertilizers, they can have a greater effect on soil pH, which can damage soil microorganisms.

✓ Manufacturing chemical fertilizers requires large amounts of energy, usually supplied by nonrenewable resources. Though not directly impacting your garden, producing chemical fertilizers does place a strain on the overall environment.

### Organic fertilizers

Natural fertilizers — animal and green manure, blood meal, fish emulsion, cottonseed meal, granite dust, and rock phosphate — have several advantages:

✓ Many natural fertilizers contribute organic matter to your soil, improving its structure, and they can contribute micronutrients.

✓ Most natural fertilizers supply a slow but steady diet for plants.

✓ Some natural fertilizers, such as manure, may be inexpensive.

Here are some disadvantages to using organic fertilizers:

✓ Some organic fertilizers are bulky and hard to store and transport.

✓ Their slow release of nutrients, in some cases dependent on the action of soil microorganisms, may not provide plants with an adequate nutrient supply when it's needed.

✔ Few natural fertilizers have a balanced ratio of nutrients; you must combine them to ensure that plants receive a good diet. For example, cow manure is low in phosphate in relation to nitrogen and potassium (and you may have to have it delivered by the truckload). To supply the deficient phosphate, you have to add another high-phosphate fertilizer, such as bonemeal. Complete organic fertilizers are available; as with complete chemical fertilizers, the three major nutrients are present, but usually in a lower concentration, such as 1-2-1.

## Side-dressing

Depending on the type of fertilizer you use, the crops you grow, and the type of soil you have, you may need to add repeat doses of fertilizer throughout the growing season — a practice called *side-dressing*. For example, because sandy soils don't hold nutrients well, giving plants small, regular fertilizer applications ensures a steady supply of nutrients. If you use a slow-release fertilizer, you may not need to side-dress until late in the season (if at all); check the label on the fertilizer package for details.

Both chemical and natural fertilizers can be used for side-dressing. A 5-10-10 fertilizer is a good choice for many crops. Use 1 to 2 tablespoons per plant, or 1 to 2 pounds for every 25 feet in a row, depending on the size of your plants. Sprinkle fertilizer around the base of the plant, about 6 to 8 inches from the stem, or spread it down the length of the row, 6 to 8 inches from plant stems, as shown in Figure 15-6.

**Figure 15-6:**
Ways to
fertilize
vegetable
plants.

## Using wood ashes to provide nutrients

Wood ashes are a source of potash and phosphate, although the exact amounts of these nutrients depend on the type of wood burned (hardwoods generally contain more nutrients than softwoods), the degree of combustion, and where the wood was stored (for example, dry storage prevents nutrient leaching). A general analysis is usually in the range of 0 percent nitrogen, 1 to 2 percent phosphate, and 4 to 10 percent potash. But the major benefit of wood ashes is as a liming agent to raise the pH of the soil. Naturally, if you live in an area where soils are alkaline, don't use wood ashes as a soil amendment; they raise the pH even higher.

Apply wood ashes to your soil in moderation (no more than 10 to 20 pounds per 1,000 square feet of garden) because they may contain small amounts of heavy metals, such as cadmium and copper. These metals build up in plants if you add too much wood ash to the soil *and can kill the plants or harm you if you eat lots of those plants.*

Depending on plant spacing, side-dress either in a narrow furrow down a row or around each individual plant (refer to Figure 15-6). In either case, spread granular fertilizer at least several inches away from the plant stem. Rake the fertilizer lightly into the soil and then water.

Adding liquid fertilizers to your watering can is an easy way to side-dress plants. You can use either natural (fish emulsion) or chemical soluble fertilizers. Follow the directions on the label. Pour the fertilizer around the bases of the plants.

For information on fertilizing vegetables growing in containers, see Chapter 17.

Too much fertilizer can be more harmful than too little. Excess fertilizer accumulates in the soil in the form of salts and damages plant roots. Be sure that growing conditions enable plants to use the fertilizer that you apply. For example, don't add fertilizer during a dry spell if you can't irrigate your garden, because without adequate soil moisture, roots can't take up nutrients. And if cool weather causes your plants to grow slowly, go easy on the fertilizer until the temperature warms up.

The kind of plants that you grow makes a difference in how much you side-dress. Plants that take a long time to mature (such as tomatoes and eggplants) and heavy feeders (like corn) generally benefit more from side-dressing than quick-maturing crops — such as lettuce, or legumes like peas and beans — that fix their own nitrogen. See Table 15-2 for some general side-dressing guidelines.

| Table 15-2 | Deciding When to Side-Dress Your Vegetables |
|---|---|
| **Vegetable** | **When to Side-Dress** |
| Beans, green | Not necessary. |
| Beet greens | Two weeks after leaves appear. |
| Beets | When tops are 4 to 5 inches high. Go light on nitrogen, which encourages leaf growth. |
| Broccoli | Three weeks after transplant. Go light on nitrogen. |
| Brussels | Three weeks after transplant; again when sprouts begin to appear. |
| Cabbage | Four to six weeks after planting. |
| Carrots | Three weeks after plants are well established and no longer seedlings. |
| Cauliflower | Four to six weeks after planting. |
| Celery | Three weeks after setting out; again six weeks later. |
| Corn, sweet | Three weeks after planting; again when plants are 8- to10-inches high; again when tassels appear. |
| Cucumbers | When they first begin to *run* (form vines and sprawl); again when blossoms set. |
| Eggplant | Three weeks after planting. |
| Kale | When plants are 6- to 8-inches tall. |
| Lettuce, head | Three weeks after transplant; again when heads form. |
| Melons | When they begin to run; again a week after blossom set; again three weeks later. |
| Onions | Three weeks after planting; again when tops are 6- to 8-inches tall; again when bulbs start to swell. |
| Peas, English | No need to side-dress. |
| Peppers, sweet | Three weeks after transplant; again after first fruit set. |
| Potatoes | When plants bloom. |
| Pumpkin | When plants start to run; again at blossom set. |
| Radishes | No need to side-dress. |
| Spinach | When plants are about 3- to 4-inches tall |
| Squash, summer | When plants are about 6-inches tall; again when they bloom. |
| Squash, winter | When plants start to run; again at blossom set. |
| Tomatoes | Two to three weeks after transplant; again before first picking; again two weeks after first picking. Go light on nitrogen. |

# Supporting Your Vegetables

Some vegetables, like peas and beans, have climbing habits that require some type of support to grow on. Other vegetables — including tomatoes, cucumbers, and even melons — have sprawling habits that benefit from some type of staking or support. Staking plants, tying them to a trellis, or growing them inside wire cylinders keeps their fruits off the ground where they may be attacked by bugs or become sunburned (fruit skins get burned due to sudden exposure to strong sun, and these fruits eventually rot). Supported plants are also easier to harvest and require less space to grow (they go *up* instead of *out*).

Figure 15-7 shows some techniques for supporting vegetables, but you can find more in Chapter 16. Following are some suggestions for supporting different types of vegetables:

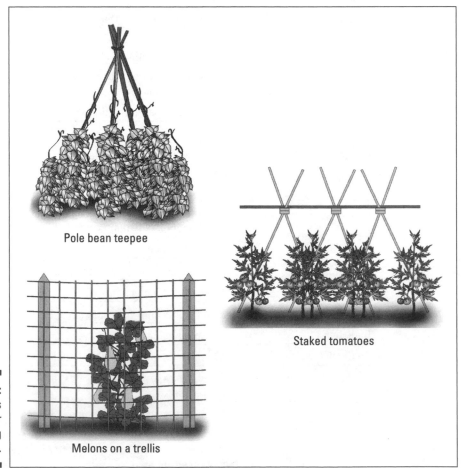

Pole bean teepee

Staked tomatoes

**Figure 15-7:**
Techniques
for
supporting
vegetables.

Melons on a trellis

✔ **Cucumbers and melons:** You can plant bush varieties inside small (2- to 3-foot high) wire cylinders similar to those used for tomatoes. But for more vigorous varieties, I like to use a more sturdy version of the A-frame trellis that's used for peas and beans. Instead of using string, I cut 6-foot-by-6-foot pieces of hog fencing (it has 6-inch squares) and nail them to each side of the trellis. The wire provides better support for heavy fruit (like melons) than string does, and the wide-open fencing doesn't constrict the growth of the fruit. You can purchase hog fencing at agricultural stores.

Yes, you can grow melons on a trellis. Choose small-fruited varieties of watermelon or any variety of cantaloupe, and plant your seeds at the base of the trellis. Tie the vines to the trellis as they grow. After a fruit forms, slip the leg of an old nylon stocking over the fruit, tying the bottom of the stocking in a knot. Then tie the other end of the stocking to the wire trellis so that the fruit is supported. As the melon grows, the stocking expands and supports the fruit, which may break off otherwise. See Figure 8-2 in Chapter 8 to see how this looks.

✔ **Peas and beans:** These twining or clinging plants grow best when they're supported by some type of string trellis. I like to use an A-frame trellis (see Chapter 7), which enables me to grow plants on both sides, but single poles are fine, too. Making an A-frame trellis is easy; just follow these steps:

1. **Using at least six 2-by-2-inch redwood or cedar stakes, build two 6-by-6-foot squares.**

2. **Secure the corners of the squares with metal corner braces and connect the two squares on one side with sturdy hinges.**

   The hinges enable you to easily move or store the trellis.

3. **Hammer small nails at 2- to 4-inch intervals along the top and bottom of the trellis.**

   Don't pound the nails in all the way; leave about 1 inch sticking out.

4. **Weave some sturdy twine or string up and down the trellis, between the nails.**

   Bingo; you have a string trellis.

✔ **Tomatoes:** You can support tomato plants several different ways:

   • Tie them to stakes, which you pound in the ground next to the plants.

   • Grow them inside wire cages, which you can buy at nurseries or easily build yourself out of hog fencing.

   • Construct string or wire trellises.

## Supporting your beans with a teepee

If you have kids, you may want to construct a teepee to support your beans. Here's how to make a teepee:

1. **Using four to six 2-by-2-inch redwood or cedar stakes 6- to 8-feet long, form a conelike teepee.**

2. **Tie the stakes together with twine at the top of the teepee.**

3. **Run some string or twine around the bottom of the teepee, securing the string or twine at each stake with a small nail.**

4. **Run more string back and forth around the stakes, from the top of the teepee to the bottom, leaving several inches between each run.**

Leave one side of the teepee open so that your kids can get inside, and plant beans around the base of the teepee. In time, the beans will cover the trellis, creating a great fort for your kids.

Which type of support you choose depends on the tomato varieties that you grow. Smaller determinate varieties grow well in small cylinders or cages. Larger indeterminate varieties need supports that are a little sturdier and more firmly anchored. (See Chapter 4 for more on determinate and indeterminate tomatoes.)

# Weed Wars

A *weed* is any plant that's growing where you don't want it to. Some weeds are worse than others, but in general, you don't want any weeds in your vegetable garden because they compete with vegetables for light, water, and nutrients. If you have a lot of weeds, you'll have weaker plants and a less substantial harvest. Besides, weeds look terrible.

The key to battling weeds is to get to them early before they're firmly established. When they're young, weeds are easier to pull, easier to till under, and less likely to produce seeds that cause problems down the road.

## Battling weeds before planting

You can reduce weeds in your vegetable beds many different ways. Here are some things that you can do *before* planting your garden:

✔ **Presprout weed seeds.** Presprouting — forcing weed seeds to germinate before you plant so that you can kill them early — really cuts down on the number of weeds. Follow these steps:

1. **Prepare your planting bed several weeks before you're ready to plant (see Chapter 2 for details).**

2. **Water the soil well and wait a few days.**

   Presto, young weeds.

3. **Kill the weeds one of two ways: pull them out by hand, or rake the bed lightly to uproot the seedlings and then let them dry out to die.**

   However you get rid of the young weeds, disturb the soil as little as possible when you do it; otherwise, you'll bring more seeds to the surface.

✔ **Plan for easy weeding.** Leave enough room between rows so that you can weed the soil easily.

✔ **Solarize the soil.** When you solarize the soil, you use the power of the sun to kill weeds. This technique works best in the middle of summer in hot climates like Arizona and Florida. The only downside to solarizing is that it takes a while. Follow these steps to solarize your soil:

1. **Prepare your bed for planting and water it well.**

2. **Dig a 6-to-12-inch-deep trench around the perimeter of the bed.**

3. **Cover the entire bed with thick clear plastic (4 mil) and place the edges of the plastic in the trenches and fill the trenches with soil. Then wait.**

   The temperature gets so hot underneath the plastic that it kills insects, disease organisms, and weeds. It usually takes a few months of solarizing to get a beneficial effect.

✔ **Plant your vegetables at the right time of year.** That way they get off to a fast start, and weeds have a harder time catching up with them. See Chapter 3 for details.

## Battling weeds after planting

After planting, you have several choices for reducing weeds:

✔ **Mulch.** Applying a good thick organic mulch is one of the best ways to battle weeds. Even if mulch doesn't smother the weeds and their seeds, the weeds that do come up are easy to pull. Planting through black plastic is also a very effective way to keep weeds from becoming a problem. See "Mulching Magic," earlier in this chapter, for more on mulch.

- ✔ **Pull the weeds by hand.** While they're young, weeds come out of the ground easily. Get 'em roots and all, whenever you see them.

- ✔ **Cultivate.** Simply hoeing or lightly turning the soil between vegetables exposes the weeds' roots and kills many of them. Cultivating is most effective when it's done often (a few times a week in the first month or so of gardening) and when the weeds are small. Some cultivating tools are designed especially for this purpose; see Chapter 21 for details.

- ✔ **Keep garden paths clean.** Try to keep your garden paths as weed free as possible; otherwise, weeds will creep into your planting beds. Try covering the paths with a thick mulch to keep weeds from becoming established.

# Chapter 16

# Some Cool Farmer Techniques

*P*eople have been growing vegetables for eons — probably since the days of Adam and Eve, though you usually associate them with fruits, not vegetables.

Over the years, farmers, and even gardeners for that matter, have tried almost anything to get a better or bigger harvest. Some of these techniques, such as planting according to the cycles of the moon, are rooted more in mysticism than in hard science. Others, such as using cover crops and succession planting, are commonsense approaches to farming that are now established practices in modern agriculture. They are also very useful techniques for vegetable gardeners.

Take a look at some cool farming techniques — some based on fact, some on fancy — and decide whether they'll work for you.

## Cover Crops and Green Manures

A *cover crop* is a general term for any plant grown to prevent erosion, to improve soil structure, and to maintain soil fertility. Sometimes, you'll hear cover crops referred to as *green manures*. Green manures are cover crops that are used primarily to add nutrients to the soil and are tilled into the soil when they are still green. Green manures are the most useful cover crop for vegetable gardeners.

The advantages of using cover crops are impressive:

- ✔ They add organic matter to the soil, improving water retention, aeration, and drainage.

- ✔ They prevent erosion by holding soil in place in windy or wet areas.

- ✔ They loosen compacted soils. Certain cover crops, such as oilseed radish, and bell beans, have aggressive taproots, sometimes reaching 3 feet deep, that help break up compacted soils.

- ✔ They add nutrients to the soil. Legume cover crops, such as hairy vetch and crimson clover, through a symbiotic (I scratch your back, you scratch mine) relationship with rhizobium bacteria on their roots, convert atmospheric nitrogen into a type that they can use to grow. The process is called *nitrogen fixing* (see Chapter 7 for more on this relationship). When the cover crop is tilled into the soil, the nitrogen is released for the next crop.

- ✔ They help control weeds by shading weed seeds so that they can't grow or by just being more aggressive than the weeds.

- ✔ They attract beneficial insects. Many cover crops attract good bugs that prey on garden pests, reducing insect problems on your vegetables.

If you want a healthier, more productive garden, and you have room, include cover crops each year in different parts of your veggie garden.

## Choosing cover crops

Cover crops can be annual (they die after flowering or over winter) or perennial (they regrow each year). For home gardeners, the best crops to sow are annual cover crops. These are easy to maintain and won't turn your vegetable garden into a cover crop garden. You have many choices of annual cover crops. If you want a wide selection plus a lot of helpful information, send for a catalog from Peaceful Valley Farm Supply (see the appendix for address information).

The most useful annual cover crops for home gardeners are listed here. All but the grasses and buckwheat are nitrogen fixing:

- ✔ **Annual ryegrass,** *Lolium multiflorum,* is a fast-growing, easy-to-establish grass that grows 2 to 3 feet high. It is hardy to –20°F but can become weedy. Sow $1/2$ to 2 pounds of seed per 1,000 square feet.

- ✔ **Berseem clover,** *Trifolium alexandrinum,* grows 1 to 2 feet high and is easy to mow and till under. It's hardy to 20°F. Sow 2 pounds of seed per 1,000 square feet. Crimson clover, *T. incarnatum,* is closely related, grows 18 inches high, and is hardy to 10°F. It has pretty red flowers that attract bees.

✔ **Buckwheat,** *Fagopyrum esculentum,* is fast growing, reaching 3 to 4 feet tall in about 40 days from seeding. It not only provides lots of organic matter, but also smothers weeds with its large leaves by shading them out, and it breaks down quickly in the soil after tilling. Sow 3 pounds of seed per 1,000 square feet. Buckwheat doesn't fix nitrogen and is frost sensitive, so grow it in summer when the temperatures are warm.

✔ **Fava beans,** *Vicia faba,* grow 3 to 8 feet high and are hardy to 15°F. Bell beans are a shorter (3 feet) relative. Edible varieties include 'Sweet Loraine' and 'Windsor.' Sow 2 to 5 pounds of seed per 1,000 square feet.

✔ **Field peas,** *Pisum arvense* or *P. sativus,* come in several varieties that range in height from 6 inches to 5 feet high. They are hardy to 10 to 20°F. Sow 2 to 4 pounds of seed per 1,000 square feet.

✔ **Hairy vetch,** *Vicia villosa,* is the hardiest annual legume (–15°F) and grows about 2 feet high. Sow 1 to 2 pounds of seed per 1,000 square feet.

✔ **Winter rye,** *Secale cereale,* is a very hardy grass (–30°F) that grows 4 to 5 feet high. It is the best grass for cold areas with poor, acidic soils and produces lots of organic matter. Sow 2 to 3 pounds of seed per 1,000 square feet.

## Planting cover crops

The best time to plant cover crops is late summer to early fall. In mild-winter areas, the plants will grow throughout winter and can be turned into the soil in spring. In cold-winter climates, plant hardy types that will grow for a while in fall, go dormant, and then grow again in spring before eventually dying. You can work them into the ground in late spring or early summer and plant soon after. Early spring planting also works in cold-winter climates, but you won't be able to work the plants in until later in the summer.

Because beds planted with cover crops won't be available for planting vegetables, you have to plan ahead to use your garden efficiently. If you are short on space, consider alternating vegetables and cover crops, so that each bed gets a cover crop every two or three years instead of each year.

If you plant cover crops in fall after your vegetables are done, you won't miss a beat and can plant vegetables in spring. If you plant cover crops during the spring or summer, you'll have to sacrifice some space in your veggie garden. I'd opt for this route only if your soil is very poor and you need to build it up, but want to grow vegetables at the same time. Just rotate where you plant the cover crops in your garden, and after a few years, your whole garden will get a cover cropping.

Plant cover crops by broadcasting seed. To make sure that the proper bacteria are present for nitrogen fixing in legume cover crops, most suppliers sell an inoculate that you mix with the seed. Till the soil, sow the seeds, and lightly cover the seeds with soil. If the weather is dry, water the seedbed to get the plants off to an early start and then keep the soil moist until it rains.

If you grow cover crops up to planting time (spring or fall) in your garden, the best time to work the cover crops into the ground is just before they start to bloom. With taller types, you may have to cut or mow the plants down before turning or tilling them in. After you work them in, wait about two weeks before planting vegetables.

# Companion Planting

A companion plant is one that provides some sort of benefit to other plants growing nearby. It's sort of like how a good friend makes life easier for you. Well, plants have good friends, too. I've already talked about some good companion plants. The cover crops that I talk about earlier in the chapter could be considered companion plants. They do all sorts of good things. And I list some plants that attract beneficial insects in Chapter 18.

But what I want to talk about here are companion plants that actually repel pests. In other words, I tell you about species that you can plant with your vegetables to drive bugs away. Is that really possible? Well, I'm not so sure. No hard evidence says that it does. In fact, I know of hard evidence that says it doesn't work. But some people swear by companion planting (Louise Riotte's *Carrots Love Tomatoes* published by Garden Way is devoted to the subject), so I'm going to tell you about it. It is true that a variety of plants, herbs, and flowers will provide a diverse ecosystem so that predatory insects are more likely to hang around and take care of the bad guys. Trying some of these combinations certainly won't hurt your garden.

These plants are thought to repel pests:

- **Anise** planted among members of the cabbage family (cabbage, broccoli, cauliflower, kale, and so on) is said to repel imported cabbage worms.
- **Catnip** is said to repel some types of aphids, flea beetles, squash bugs, and cucumber beetles.
- **Corn spurry,** *Spergula arvensis,* is supposed to repel Colorado potato beetles.
- **Garlic** may repel nematodes and other soil insects.
- **Gopher spurge,** *Euphorbia lathyris,* may repel gophers.
- **Marigolds** planted around vegetables are said to repel root nematodes, Mexican bean beetles, and Colorado potato beetles.

- ✔ **Mustard greens** are supposed to repel aphids.

- ✔ **Nasturtiums** are said to repel Colorado potato beetles.

- ✔ **Radishes** may repel striped cucumber beetles.

- ✔ **Ryegrass** may repel root-knot nematodes.

- ✔ **Southernwood** may repel moths and flea beetles.

- ✔ **Tansy** is supposed to repel some aphids, squash bugs, and Colorado potato beetles.

- ✔ **White clover** may repel cabbage root flies.

- ✔ **Wormwood** may repel flea beetles.

Many herbs, such as rosemary, oregano, and coriander, are also supposed to repel pests. Smaller companion plants, such as marigolds, can be interplanted with vegetables. Taller or more vigorous plants, such as ryegrass or wormwood, should be planted nearby — but not among — vegetables.

Hey, whatever works.

# Succession Planting

Succession planting is a method of extending the harvest of vegetables, such as radishes and corn, that ripen all at once and lose quality if left in the garden instead of being harvested. Farmers use the technique to ensure a constant supply of vegetables to take to market; you can use it to ensure a constant supply of vegetables to take to your table. Basically, you just make smaller plantings separated by two to three weeks instead of planting everything at once.

Here's how succession planting works:

1. **Figure out how much of a certain vegetable your family needs for a two- to three-week period and how much room it will take to grow it.**

   Check out Chapter 2 for information on how to plan your garden.

2. **Break your planting beds into three or four appropriate-sized sections to grow that much of the vegetable.**

3. **At the start of the planting season, plant the first bed; wait about two weeks and plant the second bed, and then plant the third bed about two weeks later.**

4. **Just about the time you finish harvesting the first bed, the second bed will be ready to harvest.**

The length of your planting season will determine how many successive plantings you can make and how successful the later plantings are. Depending on the weather, some of your later plantings may not yield well, but again, that's another reason to plant a number of plantings through the season so that you get some of every type of veggie. These vegetables work best:

- ✔ Bush beans
- ✔ Broccoli
- ✔ Carrots
- ✔ Corn
- ✔ Onions

- ✔ Beets
- ✔ Cabbage
- ✔ Radish
- ✔ Lettuce and other greens
- ✔ Spinach

Another way to ensure a constant harvest of vegetables is to plant using the square foot method. This method is for the mathematically inclined (even though you don't need an *A* in calculus to use it). You select a 4-foot-by-4-foot section of your garden and divide it into 16 squares (each section is 1 square foot). Each square will have a different number of plants, depending on what you're growing:

- ✔ **1 plant per square:** Tomatoes, peppers, broccoli, cabbage, cauliflower, eggplant, corn, melon, squash
- ✔ **4 plants per square:** Lettuce, garlic, Swiss chard
- ✔ **8 plants per square:** Pole beans, leeks, peas, spinach
- ✔ **16 plants per square:** Beets, carrots, radishes, onions

By planting so few plants, you will have many small harvests, and you can easily make more succession plantings and rotate plantings each year. We talk about crop rotation later in this chapter.

For more information about square foot gardening techniques, look for the book *Square Foot Gardening: A New Way to Garden,* by Mel Bartholomew, or visit this Web site: www.midnet.com/midnet/organic/squarefoot.htm.

# Intercropping

Intercropping is a space-saving technique in which you grow fast-maturing crops among slower-growing, larger vegetables. By the time the bigger plants start to take over, you have already harvested the crops in between. Intercropping makes one bed as productive as two. The best crops for intercropping include beets, carrots, lettuce, onions, radishes, spinach, and turnips. Use these examples to help you decide how to do it:

- ✔ Plant lettuce, carrots, or radishes among young tomatoes. For that matter, plant carrots and radishes wherever you have open space.
- ✔ Plant turnips and other root crops among your cabbage.

✔ Plant spinach or lettuce under your bean trellis. As the weather warms, the beans will shade the spinach and keep it cool.

✔ Plant green onions between rows of corn.

You get the picture.

# Crop Rotation

If you plant the same vegetables in the same spot year after year, you're going to cause a number of problems, including these:

✔ Insects and diseases that spend part of their life cycle in the soil will build up there and be harder to control.

✔ Specific nutrients that the vegetables need will consistently be depleted and will be harder to replace.

The way around these problems is to rotate your crops from season to season. In other words, plant them in different beds, as far away as possible from where they were planted before. Crop rotation is easy if you keep a journal and make note of what was planted where. And if you keep things out of the same beds for three years, you'll probably be in good shape.

It's important to do more than rotate individual crops. You should rotate families of crops. In Part II, I talk about vegetables such as tomatoes, peppers, eggplant, and potatoes being in the same family. A disease or insect that attacks one plant in a family is likely to attack others. Blight on tomatoes and potatoes is an example. When rotating crops, make sure that you don't plant a family member in the same spot three years in a row. For example, in one bed, plant beans (legume family), the next year plant potatoes (tomato family), and the third year plant cucumbers (squash family). After that, you can start over with another legume-family vegetable or start another rotation series. Keep the families apart for three years, and you'll have fewer problems in the veggie patch.

# Planting by Phases of the Moon

This isn't just a New Age technique. It's actually has been used for eons by many ancient farmers and gardeners. They noticed that certain vegetables perform better when planted during different moon phases. The planting seasons don't really change, but planting dates during those seasons become very important.

Basically, here's how moon gardening works: If you divide the 28-day moon cycle (from the new moon to the full moon and back to the new moon) into quarters, as any calendar does, certain quarters are thought to be better than others for planting specific vegetables. The following list gives you an idea of what to plant when, according to the moon cycle:

- **The first quarter,** when the moon goes from new moon (invisible) to a quarter visible, is thought to be best for planting asparagus, lettuce, broccoli, cabbage, cauliflower, and other vegetables that produce their seeds on parts of the plant that are not eaten.

- **The second quarter,** when the moon goes from half to full, is best for planting vegetables in which the seeds are eaten, such as beans, tomatoes, peppers, and squash.

- **The third quarter,** as the moon moves from full back to half again, is best for planting root crops such as beets, carrots, potatoes, radishes, and turnips.

- **The last quarter,** when the moon goes from half to invisible, is not thought of as a good planting time. Instead, it's a time to prepare the soil and rid the garden of pests and weeds.

You can get even more complicated than this by factoring in astrological signs and how they influence plant growth, but I'll leave that up to you and your further research. I haven't tried this, but I have a friend in India who swears by it, as do many others. For more on moon gardening, check out the book *Astrological Gardening: The Ancient Wisdom of Successful Planting & Harvesting by the Stars,* by Louise Riotte (Storey Books).

# French Intensive Method

The French intensive method is a labor-intensive (more soil preparation and watering) method of vegetable gardening that results in high yields per unit of space. It involves three basic steps:

- **Extensive soil preparation:** You should double dig the soil, as described in Chapter 14, with ample amounts of organic matter and nutrients worked in each season.

- **Formation of raised berms:** Form raised beds, arching mounds of soil that gently slope from the top to the sides, as described in Chapter 2. Large or sprawling vegetables can be planted in double-dug mounds.

- **Close planting:** Plant vegetables close together over the entire bed. As the plants grow, they shade the soil, keeping it cool and reducing weeds. Begin harvesting as soon as the plants reach edible size.

French-intensive gardening works for all vegetables, but it's best with lettuce, carrots, and radishes that can be harvested young and are normally planted fairly close.

# Chapter 17

# Growing Vegetables in Containers

. . . . . . . . . . . . . . . . . . . . . . . . . . . . . . . . . . . . . . . . . . . .

## In This Chapter

▶ Choosing the right size and type of container

▶ Taking a look at potting soil

▶ Finding out the best vegetables to grow in pots

▶ Caring for container-grown vegetables

▶ Combining vegetables to create beautiful pots

. . . . . . . . . . . . . . . . . . . . . . . . . . . . . . . . . . . . . . . . . . . .

**Y**ou can grow almost any vegetable in a container; just fill a big pot with good soil, and water and fertilize your plants regularly. But why not just grow vegetables in your garden? Well, maybe you aren't a farmer with a big backyard and a 10-horsepower rototiller. Maybe your soil is more appropriate for raising birds than raising plants. Maybe your garden is the balcony of your apartment or a tiny patio behind your condominium. You still have the right to fresh, home-grown tomatoes, don't you? You bet, and containers enable you to grow them.

Worried about insects and diseases harming your container plants? Don't be too concerned. In general, vegatables in containers have fewer pest problems because they're isolated from other plants. Insects aren't waiting on nearby weeds to jump on your plants, and sterilized potting soil (which I recommend for container gardening) doesn't have any disease spores. Plus, fertilizing is a snap because all the nutrients go right to the plant and not to any pathways.

Containers also enable you to grow vegetables that may not be able to grow in your garden. If you've tried to grow eggplant in a climate with cool summers, but it never matured before the first frost, try growing it in a container. Because containers heat up fast in spring, vegetables get a head start on the season.

Some people grow vegetables in containers simply because they like having their crops nearby — I certainly do. With containers, you can bring your crops close to your house where you can see and enjoy them (and eat them at the peak of freshness!). Because containers are so easy to move (or because you made them that way by putting them on wheels), containers are the great equalizer; if you need a little more or less sun, move the containers. (It's a heck of a lot easier than moving the sun!) Vegetables can be beautiful; I've seen pots of vegetables that are every bit as colorful as my favorite flowers.

Whew, I'm getting excited about growing vegetables in containers. And that's what this chapter is all about: how to get a bountiful and beautiful vegetable harvest from containers.

If you want more information about container gardening pick up a copy of *Container Gardening For Dummies,* by Bill Marken and the Editors of the National Gardening Association (IDG Books Worldwide, Inc.).

# What Type of Container Should You Use?

One trip to a nursery gives you an idea of just how many different styles and types of containers you can choose from. You can buy clay pots, glazed or not; plastic pots, pretty or ugly; or wood pots, big or small. And that's just the tip of the iceberg. Here are some things to keep in mind when choosing a pot for vegetables:

✔ **Size.** In most cases, pots that are bigger (in terms of width and volume) are better, especially for growing large plants like tomatoes. Lots of root space means that your vegetables are less likely to get cramped, and that they'll be easier to water and fertilize. If you want to grow one head of lettuce in a small pot, for example, you can do it, but you'll have to water it and fertilize it more frequently than if you had grown it in a larger pot. Although I've grown tomatoes in 5-gallon containers, I prefer at least the 15-gallon size.

With some vegetables, the depth of a container is as important — if not more important — as its width. You can grow quite a few carrots or radishes in a narrow container, but the container must be deep enough to accommodate the length of the plant's mature roots. See "Which Vegetables Grow in Pots," later in this chapter, for more on size issues for specific vegetables.

A half whiskey or wine barrel is a large, inexpensive container that can hold quite a few vegetables — ten heads of lettuce, ten bush bean plants, one or two small tomato plants, or four or five small cucumber varieties. You can purchase these containers at garden centers and nurseries.

✔ **Material.** What a pot is made of can affect how often you have to water and how long the container lasts. Pots made of porous materials like clay dry out faster than those made of plastic or wood, so you must water the plants in them more frequently, especially in hot or windy climates. If you want to use wood containers, they should be made of root-resistant materials like cedar or redwood; otherwise, they won't last very long. You can buy lumber that has been pressure-treated with preservatives and use that to build your own containers. But, even though there isn't strong proof that vegetable roots absorb these materials or any wood preservatives for that matter, I prefer not to use preservative-treated wood containers for growing vegetables or other edibles. If my redwood or cedar pots eventually rot after ten years, I just replace them — the same goes for my half whiskey barrels (my favorite containers).

✔ **Drainage.** Drainage holes should be in the bottoms of your pots; fortunately, almost all pots have these holes. But because a half barrel often doesn't, you can drill your own holes in the bottom of the container (eight to ten evenly spaced, 1-inch holes should be fine). If pots don't have drainage holes, the soil becomes a swampy mess, the roots drown, and the plants die. Bummer.

You need to consider two other accessories when you shop for pots:

✔ **A saucer to place underneath your pot.** A saucer collects water that runs out of the holes in the bottom of a pot and prevents the pot from staining whatever it's sitting on. You can find saucers made of the same or similar material as your pot or ones made of clear plastic. Plastic saucers are least likely to stain.

Saucers can also help you water your pots (see "Caring for Container Veggies," later in this chapter). Just make sure that you don't let water stand too long in the saucer; water rots roots and wooden pots. Better yet, raise the bottom of your pot out of the saucer by placing it on bricks or pieces of wood.

✔ **Wheels for mobility.** Most nurseries sell wheeled platforms that you place under pots to move them easily. Otherwise, you have to lift heavy pots or cart them around on a hand-truck.

# Potting Soil Made Simple

Remember this one rule: Don't fill your pot with soil from your garden even if your garden has the very best soil on the planet. It's too heavy and too dirty (you know, weed seeds, bugs, bacteria — stuff that you don't want in your pots), and it may not drain properly in a pot.

Instead, use potting soil. I can tell you a lot about potting soil: how it's well aerated, sterile, lightweight, and made of a good balance of organic material and mineral particles like sand or perlite. I can even give you a recipe to make your own, but you'd nod off in a second. Either that or you'd hurt your back mixing a batch. Besides, I cover potting soil in a little more detail in Chapter 13.

At your local nursery or garden center, buy whatever packaged potting soil is cheapest and comes in the prettiest bag. If you need a large quantity, many nurseries sell soil in bulk.

You may want to try different brands of potting soil over time to see which ones are easiest to wet and which ones have the best moisture-holding capacity and drainage. But don't have a personal crisis over which brand of potting soil you buy; caring for your vegetables properly after you plant is more important than choosing the perfect potting soil.

# Which Vegetables Grow in Pots

If you're persistent, you can grow any vegetable in a pot. However, some of the bigger plants, like squash and watermelon, are pretty tricky to grow in containers and tend to get unruly. But don't worry, many other vegetables fit perfectly in pots.

Vegetable breeders have long had container gardeners in mind. They breed many small-space varieties (of even the most sprawling plants) that are ideal for growing in pots. So in the following list, I take a look at the most common vegetables to grow in containers (for more information on varieties, see Part II). If you can't find the dwarf varieties that I mention, try anything with *compact, bush, baby, midget, dwarf, tiny,* or *teeny* in the name.

- ❀ **Beans:** Bush varieties like 'Provider' and Derby' are best; you can grow three to four plants in a 12-inch pot. You can grow pole types in a long narrow box, but you have to attach some type of trellis (see Chapter 15 for more on trellises). If you don't want to bother with a trellis, just grow bush types.

- ❀ **Beets:** Any variety grows well in a pot, and smaller varieties like 'Action' and 'Kestrel' will grow in smaller pots. Make sure that your pot is big and deep enough (at least 12 inches); beets don't like to be crowded. You should end up having about six plants in a 12-inch pot — more if you're growing them for greens or will pick them as baby beets.

- ❀ **Carrots:** Carrots are a perfect vegetable to grow in a pot. Start with baby varieties like 'Baby Spike,' 'Short 'n Sweet,' or 'Thumbelina.' If you water diligently, you can get a bumper harvest in pots as shallow as 6 to 8 inches deep. Longer varieties need deeper pots. After thinning, you should end up with 20 or so carrots per 12-inch pot.

- ❀ **Cole crops — broccoli, cabbage, cauliflower, and so on:** All the cole crops grow well in containers as long as your pots are big enough; try planting three or four plants in a half barrel. Plant early varieties whenever possible because the quicker you can harvest, the less likely the plants will get root bound.

❀ **Corn:** You've got to be kidding — corn in a pot? Sure. For most varieties, you need a large pot, like a half barrel, but if you plant shorter, early varieties, like 'Sugar Buns' and 'Quickie,' you can get away with a smaller container. Even a short popcorn variety called 'Tom Thumb' will grow in a container. Plant 10 to 15 seeds per half barrel, and then fertilize and water like crazy. You may get only one ear per plant, but hey, it's fresh corn.

❀ **Cucumbers:** You can't go wrong growing small cucumber types like 'Bush Pickle' and 'Salad Bush.' I've harvested cucumbers out of 12-inch-diameter, hanging pots — planted with three seeds to a pot. And plants dangling over the edges of a hanging pot are something to behold. Plant large-growing varieties in bigger pots and slip a sturdy wire cylinder into the outside edge of the pot for the plants to climb on.

❀ **Eggplant:** An eggplant's purple foliage and compact habit are perfect for pots; any variety works as long the container is at least 5 gallons. Plant one eggplant per 5-gallon pot. If a plant gets floppy, push a small stake in the pot to support the plant.

❀ **Lettuce and other greens:** Lettuce and greens may be the perfect container vegetables. The size of your pot doesn't really matter — just sprinkle some seeds in it, keep the soil moist, and then get out your salad bowl for a great harvest. You can harvest the whole plant or snip off just what you need. In the smallest pots (would you believe 4 inches wide?), try butterhead lettuce types like 'Tom Thumb.' If you want something really pretty, plant some red-leaf Swiss chard.

❀ **Melons:** Melons aren't ideal container subjects; they're wild and unruly. But through the magic of modern science, some dwarf varieties, like 'Bush Sugar Baby' watermelon, grow well in containers. Plant one to two plants in a big pot (at least 5 gallons) and let the vines sprawl over the edges, supporting the fruit if necessary. And don't let up on water and fertilizer.

❀ **Onions:** Green onions — scallions or bunching onions if you prefer to call them that — grow well in containers. Just buy a bag of sets, plant them 2- to 3-inches deep, and you're in business. You can grow onions to full bulb size; just make sure that you use a big pot (preferably 5 gallons) and give them plenty of room to grow.

❀ **Peas:** Go with dwarf pea varieties like 'Green Arrow' and 'Maestro' English peas, 'Sugar Bon' snap peas, or 'Dwarf Grey Sugar.' Any variety larger than that needs a trellis. Planting six plants in a 12-inch pot should be fine.

❀ **Peppers:** You can grow any pepper variety in a pot, but the bigger the pot the better. I like to grow small-fruited varieties like 'Serrano' and purple Thai peppers; they produce so much colorful fruit that their containers become showpieces. A 5-gallon pot should hold one to two plants. You may need to stake the plants if they get floppy.

❀ **Potatoes:** Potatoes are fun vegetables to grow in a container. Just place 8 to 10 inches of potting soil in a big pot (at least a 5-gallon size). Plant two to three potato eyes, 2 to 3 inches from the bottom of the pot, and water them in. After the plants start to grow, cover the stems with more soil (leaving the very top exposed) until the pot is full. In a couple of months, you can harvest a pot full of spuds. Start harvesting earlier for new potatoes, later for larger ones. For more on growing potatoes in small spaces, see Chapter 6.

❀ **Radishes:** Growing radishes is quick and easy even in the smallest container. Scatter some seeds in the top of a pot, keep the soil moist, and you'll have radishes in less than a month.

❀ **Squash:** I have to be honest, bush zucchini plants are too productive even in pots. But plant space-saving winter squash varieties — like 'Cream of the Crop,' 'Green Magic II,' or 'Table King' — and you're in business.

❀ **Tomatoes:** Everyone deserves fresh tomatoes, and anyone can grow them in pots. Try your favorite determinate variety in a container that's at least 5 gallons (bigger is better), but be ready to stake tall plants to a wall or a post. Or you can grow dwarf varieties like 'Patio,' 'Tiny Tim,' or 'Micro-Tom,' which fit perfectly in pots, even smaller sizes.

Most herbs grow well in containers; see Chapter 12 for details.

# Planting in Pots

Planting in containers is very much like planting in open ground (see Chapter 13). But with containers, you can plant seedlings or seeds a little closer together because you're concentrating water and nutrients in a small space, so the seedlings and seeds, not the general soil, get more of what they need to grow. You also don't have to form *berms* or basins in the soil with container gardening. Here's how to plant vegetables in a container:

1. **Fill your container with soil mix so that the soil reaches almost to the top of the container.**

2. **Wet the soil thoroughly.**

   Wetting the soil will probably take several passes with a hose. After the soil drains, it will have settled several inches.

3. **After the water settles, add more soil until the soil level is within 2 to 3 inches of the rim.**

   Level the top of the soil with your hands.

4. **If you're planting seedlings, make a small hole in the soil for each transplant. Place one seedling in each hole.**

The top of the *root ball* (the soil held together by the roots) should be level with or slightly below the surrounding soil. Use your finger to gently press down the soil around each seedling.

5. **If you're sowing seeds, plant them at the appropriate depth according to the information in Chapter 13.**

6. **Water the container gently with a watering can or hose until the soil is thoroughly moist.**

   A watering can or a hose with a bubbler extension works best because it's less likely to wash soil out of the pot or dislodge seeds.

Care for your new plantings as described in Chapter 13, making sure to keep the soil moist until the seedlings are established or until the seeds germinate.

# Caring for Container Veggies

Here are some pointers for taking care of your container vegetables as compared to vegetables in your garden:

- **Water more frequently.** Because potting soil dries out faster than regular garden soil, container vegetables need more frequent watering. In really hot weather, you may have to water more than once a day, especially if the plants are large and roots fill the pots. If you let your vegetables go dry just once, you may spoil your harvest, causing conditions such as blossom-end rot, which can affect tomatoes.

  Here are a couple of ways to check whether your container is dry:

  - **Stick your finger in the soil.** If the top few inches are bone dry, you should water.

  - **Lift or tip the container on its side.** If the soil is dry, the container will be very light.

- **Water more thoroughly.** Wetting dry potting soil can be tricky. Sometimes, the root ball of the plant (or plants) shrinks a bit and pulls away from the side of the pot as the soil dries so that when you water, all the water rushes down the space on the side of the pot without wetting the soil. To overcome this problem, make sure that you fill the top of the pot with water more than once so that the root ball can absorb the water and expand. In fact, you should always water this way to make sure that the root ball is thoroughly wet. It's also important to avoid overwatering the soil; do the finger check before watering (see Chapter 15 for details).

If you still have problems wetting the root ball, place your pot in a saucer and fill the saucer repeatedly with water. The water soaks up into the root ball and slowly wets all the soil.

If you have a lot of pots, you may want to hook up a drip irrigation system to an automatic timer to water them; nurseries and garden centers sell special drip emitters designed for pots (see Figure 17-1). You can find out more about drip irrigation and emitters in Chapter 15.

✔ **Fertilize more frequently.** Because nutrients are leached from the soil when you frequently water container vegetables, you need to fertilize your plants more often — at least every two weeks. Here are a few tips for fertilizing your container vegetables (see Chapter 15 for more detailed fertilizer info):

- Liquid or water-soluble fertilizers (you just add them to water) are easiest to use and get nutrients down to the roots of your pants. A complete fertilizer that includes micronutrients (like iron) is best.

- Add a slow-release fertilizer, such as Osmocote, to the soil before you plant. These small pellets release nutrients over time, but they may not provide enough food for your vegetables during their most critical periods. In such cases, you may have to add a liquid fertilizer, perhaps at half strength, to supplement the slow-release fertilizer.

**Figure 17-1:**
You may need to set up a drip irrigation system for your containers.

✔ **Watch for pests.** Even though container vegetables tend to have fewer pest problems — because only a few plants are in a concentrated area — you should quickly deal with any problems that arise so that your whole crop isn't wiped out. Solve your pest problems by using the same techniques that you use in your garden. Check out Chapter 18 for controls for specific diseases and insects.

One last point: Because container vegetables are often located on patios or decks that are close to the house, special care should be used in spraying them for pests. I know that I said container vegetables don't get as many pests as in the garden, but you may have to spray occasionally, so if possible move the containers away from the doors and windows to spray.

# Some Bee-U-tee-ful Vegetable Combos

I'm a firm believer that anything growing in a pot, including vegetables, should look good enough to place on a patio or deck. So I like to combine different vegetables that look good together, and sometimes I even throw in some flowers. Here are some of my favorite container vegetable combinations:

✔ **Mixed leaf-lettuce varieties:** All the different reds, greens, and purples form a soft, textured kaleidoscope of colors. You can sow premixed seeds, but I prefer to use transplants so that I can evenly space them for a more structured look.

✔ **Cool season masterpiece:** In a half barrel, place one or two red chard plants in the middle, and then surround them with red and green leaf lettuce, a few parsley plants, and some white pansies. Whew!

✔ **A salad bowl:** Are you starting to see how much I like to use lettuce as an ornamental? Plant some different lettuces or other greens with parsley, chives, green onions, and other herbs. If you really want to get fancy, add some edible flowers like pansies and violas. (For more on growing herbs, check out Chapter 12.)

✔ **Tomatoes and herbs:** Plant one of the smaller tomato varieties, like 'Patio,' in the middle of a large pot. Surround it with basil or thyme, and mix in several dwarf yellow marigolds.

✔ **Cabbage and kale:** A large pot works best with these vegetables. Just mix red and green cabbage with some crinkly kale. Keep the older leaves trimmed so that the arrangement looks nice and clean. If you really want a knock-out display, plant some red tulip bulbs about 4 inches deep in the soil.

Well, I've given you five good combinations. Using your imagination, you should be able to come up with plenty more possibilities. But do you want one more for the road? Try planting rhubarb in a pot; the big leaves and colorful stems are stunning.

# Greenhouses and Hydroponics

You can grow cucumbers and tomatoes and other vegetables in the dead of winter in a *greenhouse* (an enclosed, heated, controlled-atmosphere room). In fact, farmers throughout the world do it all the time. But greenhouse growing isn't easy — it's container gardening and vegetable growing at it's highest level; everything has to be just right to get a good crop. But maybe I've helped turn you into a really good gardener, so everything will be just right. That was the point of this book, right?

You need to pay attention to many more conditions in a greenhouse, such as too hot and too cool temperatures, fertility, pests (once they get started, they're tough to stop in a greenhouse), pollination for crops like cucumbers and melons, and so on. You generally have to be more into vegetable gardening to grow good crops in greenhouse. The easiest time to grow them is in the spring and fall to extend the season. Winter and summer are the toughest times to grow plants in a greenhouse because of the hot/cold, dark/bright weather.

Another term that's associated with container vegetables is *hydroponics*. You may have seen hydroponic tomatoes in grocery stores or seen the amazing hydroponic lettuce at Disney World. Hydroponics means growing plants in a soilless, liquid solution that provides all the plant's nutrient needs. You need special equipment and growing techniques, but you can grow any plant this way.

If you're interested in finding more information about successfully growing vegetables hydroponically or in a greenhouse, here are two books that I suggest: *Beginning Hydroponics: Soilless Gardening: A Beginner's Guide to Growing Vegetables, House Plants, Flowers, and Herbs Without Soil* by Richard E. Nicholls, (Running Press) and *Gardening in Your Greenhouse (Greenhouse Basics, No 2)* by Mark Freeman (Stackpole Books).

Now your pot runneth over with the scoop on growing vegetables in containers.

# Chapter 18

# Off with the Bugs: Keeping Plants Pest-Free and Healthy

Considering how tasty home-grown vegetables are, you shouldn't be too surprised to find that other creatures want to share in your harvest. And, no, I'm not talking about your neighbors. I'm talking about garden pests, insects that want to munch on your tomatoes, and animals, like deer, raccoons, and rabbits, that are just plain hungry. In addition, your plants face the threat of diseases, such as blight, which turns your potatoes to mush. With diseases, prevention is the key; once they take hold, they're almost impossible to eliminate.

Does the thought of all these potential problems make you want to run for cover? Well, you don't need to. It's true that insects, diseases, weeds, and animal pests can be very frustrating, but only if the damage gets out of hand. The secret is to nurture a healthy, naturally balanced garden. Every garden can withstand some damage, and there are many ways to prevent pest problems from getting out of control.

You can find help in this chapter. I tell you how to garden to prevent severe pest problems and how to identify the enemies, as well as discuss safe ways to deal with them.

Don't believe me? Then read on.

# For Pest Control: Empower the Good Guys

Most gardens are populated by a huge number of insects, most of which are neither good nor bad. They're just hanging out in your garden at no expense to your plants. But some insects are beneficial, waged in a constant battle with the bugs that are harming your plants.

To get the good insects to stick around, follow these tips:

- ✔ Avoid indiscriminately using broad-spectrum chemical or organic pesticides, which kill everything, the good bugs and the bad bugs. If you do spray, use a spray that specifically targets the pest that you want to eliminate and that has minimal effect on beneficial insects; the label on the spray usually gives you this information.

- ✔ Plant a diverse garden with many kinds and sizes of plants, including flowers and herbs. Doing so gives the beneficials places to hide and reproduce. A garden with a variety of plants can also provide an alternative food source, because many beneficials like to eat pollen and flower nectar, too. Some plants that attract beneficials include Queen Anne's lace, parsley (especially if you let the flower develop), sweet alyssum, dill, fennel, and yarrow.

- ✔ If beneficials are not as numerous in your garden as you would like, you can buy them from mail-order garden suppliers (I list several in the appendix). If you know that a particular pest is likely to appear, order beneficials in advance. That way you can release the beneficials in time to prevent problems.

Following are some beneficial insects that you can buy inexpensively to help control pests that harm vegetables:

- ✔ **Green lacewings:** These beneficial insects are some of the most effective insects for garden use. Their voracious larvae feed on aphids, mites, thrips, and various insect eggs. Release them in your garden in late spring, after the danger of frost has passed.

- ✔ **Lady beetles:** These insects are your basic ladybugs. Both the adults and the lizardlike larvae are especially good at feeding on small insects like aphids and mites. But releasing adults sometimes isn't very effective because Mother Nature has preprogrammed them to migrate down the road, so they leave your garden quickly. So try preconditioned lady beetles, which have been deprogrammed (don't worry — the procedure is safe), so they're more likely to stick around. Release lady beetles just before sundown; that way, they'll at least spend the night. Release a few thousand of them in spring as soon as you notice the first aphid.

- ✔ **Parasitic nematodes:** These microscopic worms parasitize many types of soil-dwelling and burrowing insects, including cutworms and grubs of Japanese beetles. Because grubs usually inhabit lawns, you have to apply these worms there, too, as well as around the bases of your plants. Mix the nematodes with water, and spray them on the soil around the bases of your plants once in spring.

- ✔ **Predatory mites:** These types of mites feed on spider mites and other small pests. Add predatory mites to your garden in the spring as soon as the danger of frost has passed.

- ✔ **Trichogramma wasps:** These tiny wasps (which are harmless to humans) attack moth eggs and butterfly larvae (that is, caterpillars). Release these garden good guys when air temperatures are above 72°F.

Good bugs are smart; they hang out in gardens that offer the most diverse and reliable menu. That's why eliminating every last insect pest from your garden is not a good idea.

My approach to pest control is to have a maximum diversity of bugs in my garden. And having some bad bugs around is important. Aphids are like hors d'oeuvres for some helpful insects, so it's okay to have a few in your garden. Otherwise, what will the good bugs eat? But accepting the bad bugs also means that you have to accept a little damage once in a while. So just try to manage the pests, not nuke them off the face of the earth. You want to keep them at acceptable levels, without letting them get out of control.

## Know your enemy: A bad-bug roundup

It helps to know your enemy, and insect pests command the largest army of invaders. The following list includes the most common insect pests that are likely to infest your vegetables as well as the best ways to control them. You can find control measures for pests that prey primarily on specific vegetables in the individual descriptions of those vegetables in Part II of this book.

- ✔ **Aphids** are tiny, pear-shaped pests that come in many colors including black, green, and red (see Figure 18-1). They congregate on new growth and flower buds, sucking plant sap through their needlelike noses. Heavy infestations can cause distorted growth and weaken your plants. Many vegetables can be infested, including cabbage, cucumbers, and broccoli. Aphids leave behind a sticky sap that may turn black with sooty mold and may carry diseases, such as viruses, that infect your plants.

  Aphids are easy to control. A strong jet of water from a hose can knock them off sturdy plants, or you can use insecticidal soap or pyrethrins. Insecticidal soap also helps wash off the sooty mold (the harmless black gunk that comes with aphids). But if you have only a few aphids, wait a week for beneficial insects, especially lady beetles, to move into your garden; they usually take matters into their own hands before serious damage occurs.

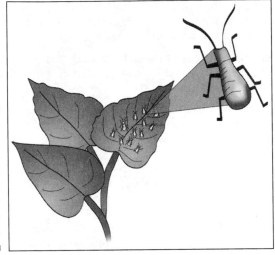

**Figure 18-1:**
Control
aphids with
insecticidal
soap, neem
oil, or
pyrethrin
spray.

✔ **Caterpillars and worms,** moth and butterfly larvae, are avid eaters and
   can cause a lot of damage to a variety of plants. Some are hairy caterpillars; others are smooth skinned and more wormlike. Caterpillars
   include tomato hornworms and cabbage loopers, which are described
   in Chapters 5 and 9 respectively. You can handpick caterpillars and
   worms to reduce numbers, release trichogramma wasps, or use pyrethrins. But the most effective way to get rid of them is to spray with Bt.

✔ **Corn earworms** are found throughout the United States. These $1^1/_2$-
   inch-long caterpillars with alternating light and dark stripes may be
   green, pink, or brown. In spring, night-flying moths lay yellow eggs on
   the undersides of leaves. The resulting first-generation caterpillars feed
   on the leaves. The eggs of later generations can be found on corn silks;
   the emerging caterpillars feed on the silks and the kernels at the tips of
   the corn ears, just inside the husks, as shown in Figure 18-2. The
   earworms, also called fruitworms, attack a variety of plants including
   tomatoes, beans, peas, peppers, potatoes, and squash.

   The easiest way to deal with corn earworms on your corn plants is to
   just cut off the tip of the ear before you cook it. Or to prevent worms,
   you can spray Bt before the caterpillars enter the ears or fruit, but that
   doesn't always work. You can also place a few drops of mineral oil on the
   silks of each ear just as the silks wilt and start to turn from white or
   yellow to brown (don't do it too early or you'll interfere with pollination,
   but dont wait until the silks are all brown and shriveled either; you have
   about a week in which to work) — that should prevent worms from
   entering ears.

✔ **Cutworms** are $^1/_2$-inch-long, grayish caterpillars. They emerge on spring
   and early summer nights to eat the stems of young seedlings, causing
   the seedlings to fall over like small timbers. Cutworms also climb up to
   older plants and feed on leaves and flowers.

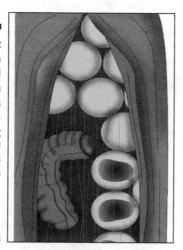

**Figure 18-2:**
Corn infested with earworms is still fine to eat. Just break off the tip of the ear of corn and munch away.

To protect seedlings, surround their stems with barriers that prevent the cutworms from crawling close and feeding. These devices can be as simple as empty cardboard toilet paper rolls, Styrofoam cups with the bottoms cut out, or collars made from aluminum foil — just make sure that they encircle the stem completely and are set 1 inch deep in the soil. You can also trap cutworms by leaving boards around your garden; the worms hide under the boards during the day, enabling you to collect them. Parasitic nematodes are also effective against cutworms.

✔ **Flea beetles** are tiny $\frac{1}{16}$-inch beetles that feed on vegetable leaves, riddling them with small shot holes. These beetles jump rapidly when disturbed, like fleas — hence their name. Various species feed on just about any plant in a garden including eggplant, tomatoes, broccoli, cabbage, corn, potatoes, spinach, peppers, and sweet potatoes. Adult beetles can spread diseases — wilt in sweet corn, for example — and larvae feed on roots. Adults overwinter in the soil and on garden debris, emerging in early spring, and can destroy young plants quickly.

To control flea beetles, make sure that you clean up garden debris in the winter and till the soil. Use a floating row cover to exclude adults, and release parasitic nematodes to attack the larvae. Rotenone, pyrethrins, and insecticidal soap also provide some control.

✔ **Japanese beetles** can really be troublesome east of the Mississippi River. These $\frac{1}{2}$-inch-long beetles have coppery bodies and metallic green heads. They feed on the foliage of many vegetables including corn, beans, and tomatoes.

Controlling Japanese beetles can be tough. Treating your lawn and garden soil with parasitic nematodes or with milky spore (another biological spray) may reduce the white C-shaped larvae, but more adults will probably fly in from your neighbor's yard. Floral-scented traps that attract adult beetles are available, but the traps may attract more beetles than you had before. If you try the traps, keep them at least 100 feet from your vegetables and encourage your neighbors to use them, too, to control the beetles community-wide.

Insecticidal soap, rotonone, and pyrethrins are effective against adult beetles. You can also just handpick the beetles off your vegetables and stomp on them. Picking in early morning or evening is easiest because the beetles are sleepy then and tend not to fly away.

✔ **Nematodes** are microscopic wormlike pests that can infect soil, especially in warm climates. They feed on the roots of plants and attack many vegetables including carrots, tomatoes, and potatoes. Nematodes thrive in sandy, moist soil and can quickly stunt plants and cause roots to look hairy and knotted. Your best defense is to plant nematode-resistant varieties and rotate your crops (see Chapter 16) to prevent a population from building. These nematodes are different from the parasitic nematodes that I mention later in the chapter, which are actually good for your garden.

✔ **Snails and slugs** are soft-bodied mollusks that feed on tender leaves and flowers during the cool of the night or during rainy weather. Snails have shells; slugs don't. Snails and slugs proliferate in damp areas, hiding under raised containers, boards, or garden debris. To control them, roam through your garden at night with a flashlight and play pick-and-stomp, or trap them with saucers of beer, setting the rims at ground level. They'll jump in to drink the beer, not be able to climb out, and drown. What a way to go! Refill the saucers regularly (these pests seem to like imported beers best, but why waste good beer on a slug?). Snails and slugs will not cross copper (because they'll get an electrical shock), so you can also surround raised beds or individual containers with a thin copper stripping, which is sold at most nurseries. In California, you can release decollate snails, which prey on pest snails; ask you Cooperative Extension office for information. If all else fails, you can use poison snail bait.

✔ **Spider mites** are tiny, spiderlike arachnids that you can barely see without a magnifying glass. If the population gets big enough, you can see their fine webbing beneath the leaves of your plants. As they suck a plant's juices, the leaves become yellowish with silvery stippling (small yellow dots on the leaves) or sheen. If things get really bad, the plant may start dropping leaves. Mites are most common in hot, dry summer climates and on plants with dusty (sooty) leaves. Tomatoes and beans are commonly infested. A daily bath with a strong jet of water from a hose helps keep infestations down. You can control spider mites with insecticidal soap, which also helps clean off the plants' leaves. Applying summer oil or neem oil and releasing predatory mites are also effective.

✔ **Thrips** are almost-invisible troublemakers. They feed on leaves giving them a stippled look and making them deformed. You can distinguish thrips from spider mites by looking for the small fecal pellets that thrips leave behind. Thrips often pass on diseases as they feed. Beans, cabbage, onions, and eggplants are commonly infested. Many beneficials (beneficial insects) feed on thrips, especially lace-wings. Insecticidal soaps and pyrethrins are also effective.

✔ **Whiteflies** look like small white gnats, but they suck plant juices and can proliferate in warm climates and greenhouses. They tend to congregate on the undersides of leaves, especially on tomatoes and beans. You can trap whiteflies with yellow sticky traps, which are sold in nurseries. In greenhouses, release Encarsia wasps, which prey on greenhouse whiteflies. Insecticidal soaps, summer oil, neem oil, and pyrethrins are effective sprays.

If you need more help identifying garden pests and other plant problems, contact a full-service garden center with a variety of reference books that you can look through as well as employees who have personal experience with local problems. Also check with a botanical garden, library, or local Cooperative Extension Service office. You should be able to find your county Extension office listed under county offices (these services are usually managed by area land-grant universities) or under *Cooperative Extension* or *Farm Advisor.* Often a well-trained home gardener called a Master Gardener will be on duty to answer gardening questions just like yours.

## Attack when necessary

If you need to take further action, start with what I consider the first line of defense against pest outbreaks: physical barriers that keep the bugs away from your plants. The next step is using pesticides that are effective against a certain pest, that are pretty safe to use, and that have a mild impact on the rest of your garden's life forms. In general, these products are short-lived after you use them in your garden — that's what makes them so good. However, in order to get effective control, you often have to use them more frequently than stronger chemicals.

You can physically prevent pests from damaging your vegetables a number of ways. One of the best ways is to grab bugs by their tails, body slam them to the ground, and stomp on them. *Handpicking,* as it's usually called, works best with large bugs like tomato hornworms, snails, and slugs, and the best time to handpick slugs is at night, using the light of a flashlight. If you're wimpy and have problems squashing bugs, drop them in a jar of soapy water instead. Here are some other physical controls to try:

✔ **A strong jet of water** often dislodges insects like aphids and spider mites from the leaves of vegetables. It also keeps the foliage clean.

✔ **Barriers** keep pests from reaching your vegetables. For example, place a small copper strip around the outside of raised beds or containers to keep snails from reaching your plants; snails won't cross the copper stripping. *Floating row covers,* (see Figure 18-3) those lightweight, blanketlike materials described in Chapter 22, also keep pests away from plants. And if you have problems with cutworms, push a small cardboard collar (a paper cup with the bottom pushed out works well) into the ground around seedlings to keep bugs from reaching the stems.

✔ **Trapping** pests before they reach your vegetables is another way to reduce problems. Trapping works best with night feeders — such as slugs and earwigs — that seek shelter during the day and that are attracted to dark, moist environments. You can trap snails and slugs under a slightly raised board at night, and then dispose of the board in the morning. Earwigs will collect in rolled-up newspapers.

**Figure 18-3:**
Remember to remove floating row covers for crops that need bees to pollinate them.

Here are my favorite safe spray methods of controlling harmful bugs:

✔ **Biological controls:** Using biological controls involves pitting one living thing against another. Releasing beneficial insects is one example of biological control, but you can also use bacteria that, while harmless to humans, makes insect pests very sick and eventually very dead. The most common and useful biological controls are forms of *Bacillus thuringiensis,* or Bt, which kill the larvae of moths and butterflies (that is, caterpillars). Another variety of Bt, *B.t. tenebrionis* or *B.t. San Diego,* kills the larvae of Colorado potato beetles. Bacillus popilliae (milky spore disease) is an effective control of Japanese beetle grubs.

Recently, plant breeders have used genetic engineering techniques (see Chapter 1 for more on genetically modified plants) to insert the Bt toxin into plants, such as corn and potatoes, so that when an insect eats any part of the plant, it automatically ingests the toxin and dies. Initial results show that this technology does reduce the need to spray to control pests such as corn borers on corn and potato beetles on potatoes, but many questions remain about the long-term effectiveness and consequences of using this technology.

✔ **Botanical insecticides:** These insecticides are derived from plants. The following are the most useful insecticides against vegetable pests:

- **Pyrethrins** are derived from the painted daisy, *Chrysanthemum cinerariifolium*. They're broad-spectrum insecticides, which means that they kill a wide range of insects. Unfortunately, that means some of the good guys are killed, too. So to avoid killing bees, for example, spray pyrethrins late in the evening. The advantage to using this insecticide is that it kills pests like aphids and beetles quickly, and has low toxicity to mammals, which means that it's essentially harmless to humans and the environment. However, always follow the label and never apply more than is recommended.

- **Rotenone** is derived from the roots of tropical legumes. It breaks down quickly but is more toxic than some commonly used chemical insecticides. It's a broad-spectrum insecticide, killing beneficials (including bees) and pests. Use rotenone as a last resort to control various caterpillars, beetles, and thrips. It is also deadly to fish, so never use it around water.

✔ **Summer or horticultural oil:** When sprayed on a plant, this highly refined oil smothers insect pests and their eggs. The words *highly refined* mean that the sulfur and other components of the oil that damage the plant are removed. This oil is relatively nontoxic and short lived. Use it to control aphids, mites, thrips, and certain caterpillars.

Make sure that you don't confuse summer oil with dormant oil. Dormant oil should be applied to leafless trees and shrubs during the winter. It isn't meant to be used on vegetables.

Double-check the oil's product label to make sure that you can use the oil on plants during the growing season. Then follow the mixing instructions carefully. Water your plants before and after applying the oil. But don't apply the oil if temperatures are likely to rise above 85°F. When it's that hot, the oil can damage plant leaves.

✔ **Insecticidal soaps:** Derived from the salts of fatty acids, insecticidal soaps kill mostly soft-bodied pests like aphids, spider mites, and whiteflies. They can also be effective against Japanese beetles. They work fast, break down quickly, and are nontoxic to humans. Insecticidal soaps are most effective when mixed with soft water because soaps can sometimes burn tender foliage.

✔ **Neem oil:** This relatively new insecticide is extracted from the seed of the tropical neem tree. Neem oil has been used for centuries in India as an insecticide, to kill parasites in cattle, and even as a toothpaste for humans. Needless to say, it's very safe. Now, home gardeners can purchase neem oil to repel and kill a wide variety of insects including aphids, whiteflies, leaf miners, caterpillars, and many others. Check garden centers for trade names such as Bioneem and Fruit, Nut & Vegetable Spray.

✔ **Home remedies:** Not all pesticides are exotic. Many gardeners (myself included) have had great success using common household products to control insects in their gardens. One of my favorite home remedies is adding a clove or two of garlic and a few teaspoons of cayenne to a quart of water and then blending it all in a mixer. You then strain the solution to remove the chunks, and using a hand-held sprayer, spray your plants to control insects, such as aphids and whiteflies, and repel animals, such as rabbits and deer. Of course, after it rains, you have to reapply the mix. Commercial insecticide products, such as Hot Pepper Wax and Garlic Barrier, which are based on the common foods, are also available. Either type of product is effective, simple, safe, and fun to try.

You should be able to successfully control most insect problems using the techniques and products that I covered previously. However, if a pest really gets out of hand on a prized planting, you may want to use something more serious. Several synthetic chemicals, such as malathion, diazinon, and sevin can be used on vegetable plants. Personally, I don't use them on any plants that I intend to eat.

## Watch out when using pesticides

Even pesticides that have relatively low impact on your garden environment can be dangerous to use as well as toxic to humans; this is true of several commonly used botanical insecticides such as rotenone and pyrethrin.

Always follow the instructions on the product label exactly. In fact, not following these instructions is against the law. Both the pest that you're trying to control and the plant that you're spraying must be listed on the label (sometimes plants are listed as groups, such as flowers). Each label also provides the number of days between the time that you spray the vegetable and the time that the vegetable is safe to eat. This number can range from one day up to two weeks. Obviously, paying attention to this number is important.

Wear gloves when mixing and spraying pesticides. Spray when the wind is calm. Store the chemicals in properly labeled containers that are well out of the reach of children (a locked cabinet is best). Dispose of empty containers as described on the label, or contact your local waste disposal company for appropriate disposal sites.

Remember, no matter which pesticides you decide to use, you must use them correctly and take precautions against accidentally doing harm. There's no such thing as a truly safe pesticide — after all, it's meant to kill bugs, right?

GARDEN JARGON

## Use INs, not OIDs

The terminology can be confusing. *Pyrethrum* is the ground-up flower of the daisy. *Pyrethrins* are the insecticide components of the flower. You may also see insecticides called *pyrethroids,* however. Pyrethroids, such as permethrin and resmethrin, are synthetic compounds that resemble pyrethrins but are more toxic and persistent. Consequently, I prefer to avoid pyrethroids for home garden use.

# Gardening to Eliminate Diseases

Diseases differ from insects in that, with bugs, you can take action after you see them. With diseases, once you see symptoms, it's often difficult to stop the diseases from spreading. However, you can prevent or at least reduce most vegetable diseases by using good growing practices or by planting resistant varieties. Most vegetables have some varieties with disease resistance; see the chapters on individual vegetables in Part II of this book for details. The following list includes some cultural practices that can help you avoid plant diseases:

- ✓ **Remove infected plants.** Once you notice a plant with a problem, yank out the entire plant. Even picking off infected leaves helps prevent a disease from spreading.

- ✓ **Avoid overhead watering** (or at least water early in the morning so that plants have a chance to dry out before nightfall). Using drip irrigation or watering in furrows also helps keep foliage dry (see Chapter 15). Overhead watering can encourage foliage disease organisms to prosper.

- ✓ **Space plants properly.** Planting vegetables too close together reduces air circulation between them, a condition that favors disease and allows diseases to spread from plant to plant more readily. Keep your eyes open for developing problems.

- ✓ **Keep your garden clean and tidy.** Many diseases spread on plant debris, so rake up fallen leaves and remove dead plants. Also, keep the spaces under any containers clean. Removing diseased leaves can slow the spread of some organisms.

- ✓ **Rotate plants.** Don't plant the same vegetables in the same place year after year. Otherwise, you create a nursery for disease. Move things around as described in Chapter 16.

- ✓ **Mulch.** A layer of mulch on the soil can act like a physical barrier, keeping disease spores in the soil and off the plants. See Chapter 15 for more on mulches.

The following list includes tips on how to prevent, identify, and treat (if possible) some common diseases that affect vegetables. Controls for diseases that are most troublesome for a specific vegetable are included with the description of that vegetable in Part II of this book:

- **Damping off:** This fungus attacks the bases of seedling stems, causing them to wilt and fall over. I discuss ways to prevent damping off in Chapter 13, which covers all aspects of growing vegetables from seed.

- **Powdery mildew:** This fungus coats leaves and flowers with a white powder. It's most common when days are warm but nights are cool. This disease is particularly troublesome to squash, cucumbers, melons, and peas. Controlling powdery mildew is difficult, but resistant varieties are available. The disease becomes less of a problem as the weather changes.

  Some gardeners have had some success mixing 1 tablespoon of summer oil and 1 to 2 teaspoons of baking soda in 1 gallon of water. You have to use the mixture often to protect new foliage. You also may have some success spraying your plants with antitranspirants, which you need to apply only once. These materials, sold under names like Cloud Cover or Wiltpruf, coat the leaves with a thin waxy film that seems to prevent the mildew from getting established. They're worth a try. Some forms of neem oil are also registered for use on vegetables.

- **Root rots:** A number of soilborne fungi cause plants to have, basically, the same damage — regardless of whether the soil is moist. Lettuce is notorious for dying like this. The best way to prevent root rot is to make sure that soil drainage is good and to avoid overwatering — let the soil dry partially between waterings. Otherwise, all that you do to control root rot is remove the dead plants. Few other control measures are effective.

- **Southern blight:** This rather nasty disease that affects corn is common in the southeastern United States. Southern blight causes plants to rot at the base of their stems, wilt, turn yellow, and die. Unfortunately, this disease is hard to control. Your best bet is to rotate your crops each year, get rid of all infected plant material, and turn your soil in the fall. You can also try soil solarization, as described in Chapter 15.

- **Viruses:** These diseases affect many vegetables including tomatoes, peppers, peas, beans, cucumbers, beets, potatoes, and squash. When infected with a virus, leaves and fruits often have mottled yellow spottings and are deformed. Plants are stunted and die young, often not producing usable fruit. Virus diseases are sometimes specific to certain vegetables and spread by insects such as cucumber beetles (see Chapter 8 for more on controlling this pest), aphids, and whiteflies, so stopping these pests many times stops the disease. You should also destroy infected plants and try to plant disease-resistant varieties.

## My outlook on fungicides: Avoid 'em

Chemical fungicides (substances that kill fungus) are a nastier bunch of pesticides. I prefer not to use them on my vegetables. If you get a really stubborn disease in a prized planting, however, you may have no other choice than to use fungicides. The following lists some of the "safer" ones:

✔ Some mineral-based fungicides — such as copper for blight on tomatoes and sulfur for mildew on peas — are less toxic, but you should still use them only sparingly. They are most effective preventing the disease, so they need to be applied early.

✔ Neem oil has also been proven effective as a fungicide, making it another option. But before you spray, make sure that you've properly identified the disease.

When considering a fungicide, enlist help from the folks at a local nursery or from a specialist at the Cooperative Extension office to be sure that you need one. Then use a product that's specifically designed to treat the disease that's infecting your plants. Follow the instructions on the label carefully and exactly.

# Keeping Animals Out of Your Garden

Besides insects and diseases, you should keep an eye out for 2- and 4-footed pests. Whether or not one of the critters described in this section will cause problems in your garden depends a lot on where your garden is located. If woods adjoin your property, squirrels and raccoons may become pests; if you're surrounded by fields, mice and woodchucks may invite themselves in to dine on your tender young plants. Be sure to properly identify the pest; this may take some late night work with a flashlight.

As you read the control suggestions in this section, you'll notice that fencing is one of my most common recommendations. Although fencing can be expensive, it's the most reliable means of keeping animals out of your garden. But even a sturdy fence isn't a 100-percent guarantee, so sometimes live trapping and relocating may be the only solution to an especially persistent woodchuck or raccoon. (Make sure that you check first with your state Fish and Game Department to find out if there are any regulations governing trapping the animal that you have in mind. If you're a little more brutal, ask the folks there how to poison small pests like mice or gophers.) You can purchase live traps at most hardware stores; get the appropriate size for the animal that you want to catch. Once you have the animal in the trap, be sure to release it in areas recommended by your local state Fish and Game Department officials.

Although letting your family dog or cat prowl your grounds to ward off wild animals may sound like a good idea, in reality keeping your pets indoors or restrained is the best idea, especially when large animals are around. Rabies is a problem with many wild animals, such as raccoons, and some wildlife, such as woodchucks, which are ferocious fighters.

The following list identifies animal pests that are common to vegetable gardens, and methods to control these critters so that you have some veggies left for you to enjoy:

- **Birds:** Starlings and crows have an uncanny sense of where you planted your corn seeds. To keep birds from eating seeds or pulling up newly sprouted plants, protect your seedbed with a bird tunnel (see Figure 18-4) or use a floating row cover. By the time that the plants outgrow the cover, they're no longer at the stage that's appetizing to birds.

**Figure 18-4:** Covering young seedlings with a portable bird tunnel is a sure way to keep the birds away.

- **Cats and dogs:** Fences work best to keep these pests — and your neighbors — out of your garden. Cats are a problem early in the season when they like to dig in newly tilled ground; laying chicken wire or hardware cloth over your seedbed until plants sprout encourages cats to dig elsewhere. Try spraying a pepper and garlic spray (see "For Pest Control: Empower the Good Guys" for details) to deter these critters.

- **Deer:** A slanted fence is a good way to keep deer out of your garden because their instinct is to try to crawl under a fence before jumping it and they're less likely to jump a wide fence. A slanted fence can be 4 to 5 feet high, as shown in Figure 18-5, whereas a vertical fence must be at least 8 feet high to keep deer from jumping over it.

- **Gophers:** In the western United States, gophers can wreak havoc on gardens, eating roots and underground parts of the plants. Trapping is the most practical solution in most cases. Find an active runway by probing the soil near a fresh mound of dirt with a crowbar. Set two traps in the runway, one facing each direction. Tie the traps together and cover them lightly with soil to keep out all light.

If your garden is small or organized into small beds, you may want to construct a gopher barrier, as shown in Figure 18-6. It's a lot of work, but it does the trick. Basically, you dig the soil out of the bed to a depth of at least 12 inches and line the bottom and sides with 1-inch chicken wire, carefully attaching the edges with wire. Then replace the soil. The wire should last about five years. You can also line the bottom of raised beds to keep gophers out.

✔ **Mice and small rodents:** A 12-inch-high fence made of ¹/₄-inch mesh hardware cloth, with another 12 inches buried underground, keeps mice, chipmunks, and other small rodents out of your garden. Also, keeps your garden free of weeds and keeps your yard mowed because mice don't like to cross an open area and expose themselves to predators. You can also set traps in your garden, but make careful note of where they are so that you don't catch an unsuspecting human harvester.

**Figure 18-5:**
A slanted fence is the best design to keep deer out of your garden.

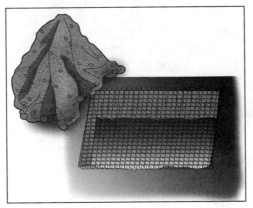

**Figure 18-6:**
Fencing is the safest and most effective way to deter digging animals like gophers.

✔ **Moles:** Moles do not feed on plants; they eat insects, such as grubs and earthworms. However, their tunneling may damage the roots of plants. The most effective way to control moles in your garden is repel them. Moles also don't like the smell of castor oil, so spray a mole repellent, such as Mole Med, that contains castor oil to ward off these pests. If the problem is severe, try to set traps in the tunnels. To find active tunnels, tamp down raised soil, which indicates tunneling. The tunnels that are raised the day after you tamp the soil are active.

✔ **Rabbits:** A 2-foot-high fence made of $1^1/_2$-inch mesh should keep rabbits out of your garden. Make sure that the bottom is tight to the ground or bury the bottom edge as recommended for woodchucks. Try a pepper and garlic spray that's designed to repel cats and dogs.

✔ **Raccoons:** A 4-foot-high fence that's similar to the one recommended for woodchucks usually keeps raccoons out of your garden. A strand of electric fence on top serves as an added deterrent.

✔ **Woodchucks:** Also known as groundhogs, woodchucks feed happily on just about anything in your garden. A fence that's at least 3 feet high with another 12 inches underground is the best way to keep them out (see Figure 18-7). Leave the top 18 inches of the fence unattached to support posts. This way, as the woodchuck attempts to climb over the fence, the fence will bend back down under the animal's weight. A strand of electric wire at the top of a woven wire fence will also discourage them.

**Figure 18-7:**
Build a fence to keep out woodchucks and raccoons, making sure to keep the top 18 inches unattached to the stakes.

Now you can't say you don't know how to deal with what's bugging you about your garden.

# Chapter 19

# Harvesting and Storage

. . . . . . . . . . . . . . . . . . . . . . . . . . . . . . . . . . . . . . .

## In This Chapter

▶ Knowing when and how to harvest your vegetables

▶ Storing your crops

▶ Preserving your crops by freezing, drying, or canning

. . . . . . . . . . . . . . . . . . . . . . . . . . . . . . . . . . . . . . .

**S**uppose that you've done everything you need to do: You planted at the right time, watered and fertilized as needed, and kept an eye out for pests. Way to go. What might you be forgetting as you watch your garden grow? Oh yes, don't forget when it's time to eat!

To get all the best flavor and highest nutritional value from your vegetables, you need to pick them at just the right time. Some vegetables taste terrible if you pick them too early; others are tough and stringy if you pick them too late.

And after you pick your vegetables, what if you can't eat them right away? Properly stored, most vegetables will last a while without rotting or losing too much flavor (of course, eating them fresh picked is always best). In fact, you can store some vegetables, like potatoes and winter squash, for months.

So in this chapter, I discuss harvesting and storing fresh vegetables. You put in too much work not to do the final steps just right.

## When and How to Harvest

You should harvest most vegetables when they're young and tender, which often means harvesting plants, roots, or fruits before they reach full size. A 15-inch zucchini is impressive, but it tastes better at 6 to 8 inches. Carrots and beets get woody (tough textured) and bland the longer that they stay in the ground. Other plants are harvested to keep them productive. If you keep harvesting vegetables like snap beans, summer squash, lima beans, snow and snap peas, broccoli, okra, spinach, and lettuce, they'll continue to produce pods, shoots, or leaves.

A good rule for many of your early crops is to start harvesting when you have enough of a vegetable for a one-meal serving. Spinach, Swiss chard, scallions, radishes, lettuce, and members of the cabbage family certainly fit the bill here. They don't grow as well in warm weather, so pick some of these crops in the spring when temperatures are cooler.

Once you start harvesting, visit your garden and pick something daily. Take along a good sharp knife and paper bags, buckets, or baskets. A wire or wood bucket works well because you can easily wash vegetables in it. Table 19-1 provides information on when to harvest.

| Table 19-1 | Harvesting Fresh Vegetables |
|---|---|
| *Vegetable* | *When to Harvest* |
| Asparagus | When spears are 6 to 9 inches long |
| Beans, snap | Start about two to three weeks after bloom, before seeds mature |
| Beets | When 1 to 3 inches wide |
| Broccoli | When flower heads are tight and green |
| Brussels sprouts | When sprouts reach 1 inch wide |
| Cabbage | When heads are compact and firm |
| Carrots | When tops are 1 inch wide |
| Cauliflower | While heads are still white but not ricey (the florets split apart) |
| Corn | When silks are dry and brown; kernels should be milky when cut with a thumbnail |
| Cucumbers | For slicing when 6 inches long; picklers at least 2 inches long |
| Eggplant | Before color dulls |
| Kohlrabi | When 2 to 3 inches wide |
| Lettuce and other greens | While leaves are tender |
| Muskmelons | When fruit slips off vine easily, while netting (raised area on skin) is even, fruit firm |
| Onions | When necks are tight, scales dry |
| Parsnips | When roots reach desired size, possibly after light frost |
| Peanuts | When leaves turn yellow |
| Peas | While pods are still tender |
| Peppers | When fruits reach desired size and color |

| Vegetable | When to Harvest |
|---|---|
| Potatoes | When vines die back |
| Pumpkins | When shells harden, before frost |
| Radishes | When roots are up to 1¼-inches wide |
| Rutabagas | When roots reach desired size |
| Spinach | When leaves are still tender |
| Squash, summer | When 6 to 8 inches long |
| Squash, winter | When shells harden, before frost |
| Sweet potatoes | When they reach adequate size |
| Tomatoes | When uniformly colored |
| Turnips | When 2 to 3 inches wide |
| Watermelons | When undersides turn yellow and produce dull sound when thumped |

The harvesting information in Table 19-1 is based on picking mature vegetables. But many vegetables can be picked smaller and still have excellent flavor. Pick baby vegetables whenever they reach the size that you want. The following vegetables can be picked small: beets, broccoli, carrots, cauliflower, cucumbers, lettuce and other greens, onions, peas, potatoes, radishes, snap beans, summer squash, swiss chard, turnips. In addition, some small varieties of corn and tomatoes fit the baby-vegetable mold.

Try to avoid harvesting when plants, especially beans, are wet. Many fungal diseases spread in moist conditions, and if you brush your tools or pant legs against diseased plants, you can transfer disease organisms to other plants down the row.

Also avoid harvesting in the heat of the day if you can. For the freshest produce, harvest early in the day when vegetables' moisture levels are highest and the vegetables are at peak flavor. Then refrigerate the produce and prepare it later in the day.

In the fall, wait as long as you can to dig up root crops such as carrots, rutabagas, and beets if you intend to store them in a root cellar or cold storage room. Root crops can withstands frosts, but harvest them before the ground freezes. They'll come out of the ground easiest if the soil is slightly moist.

Don't wash crops that are going to the root cellar; instead, just gently brush away soil crumbs. Use any blemished or cut vegetables within a few days.

# Pick 'em, Eat 'em, or Put 'em Away

You have only two choices when you harvest your crops: eat the veggies right away, or store them to use later. Different vegetables need different storage conditions to maintain their freshness. These conditions can be summarized as follows:

- **Cool and dry.** Ideally, temperatures should be between 50 and 60°F, with 60-percent relative humidity — conditions that you usually find in a well-ventilated basement.

- **Cold and dry.** Temperatures should be between 32 and 40°F, with 65-percent humidity. You can achieve these conditions in most home refrigerators or in a cold basement or garage.

- **Cool and moist.** Temperatures should be between 50 and 60°F with 90-percent humidity. You can store vegetables in a cool kitchen or basement in perforated plastic bags.

- **Cold and moist.** Ideally, your storage area should be 32 to 40°F, with 95-percent humidity. You can create these conditions by placing your vegetables in perforated bags (bags without ventilation are likely to degrade faster) and then storing the bags in a refrigerator. You can also create these conditions in a root cellar, which I discuss later in this section.

In Table 19-2, I provide specifics on how to store the vegetables so that, after you pick them, you'll quickly know what to do with them (that is, if you don't eat them). Table 19-2 also includes information on whether you can dry, can, or freeze vegetables, topics that I cover later in this chapter in "Freezing, Canning, and Drying Veggies."

| Table 19-2 | Storing Fresh Vegetables | | |
|---|---|---|---|
| *Vegetable* | *How to Store* | *Expected Storage Life* | *Comments* |
| Asparagus | Cold and moist | Two weeks | Store upright. Freeze, dry, or can. |
| Beans, snap | Cool and moist | One week | Pods will scar below 40°F. Freeze. |
| Beets | Cold and moist | Five months | Store without tops. Can, freeze, or dry. |
| Broccoli | Cold and moist | Two weeks | Freeze or dry. |
| Brussels sprouts | Cold and moist | One month | Freeze or dry. |
| Cabbage | Cold and moist | Five months | Freeze or dry. |

| Vegetable | How to Store | Expected Storage Life | Comments |
|---|---|---|---|
| Carrots | Cold and moist | Three weeks | Store without tops. Can, freeze, or dry. |
| Cauliflower | Cold and moist | Three weeks | Freeze or dry. |
| Corn | Cold and moist | Five days | Can, freeze, or dry. |
| Cucumbers | Cool and moist | One to two weeks | Will scar if stored below 40°F. Can be stored in a cool kitchen in a perforated bag. Don't store with apples or tomatoes. Can. |
| Eggplant | Cool and moist | One week | Prolonged storage below 50°F causes scarring. Freeze or dry. |
| Kohlrabi | Cold and moist | Two months | Store without tops. Freeze. |
| Lettuce and other greens | Cold and moist | One week | |
| Muskmelons | Cold and moist | One week | Freeze. |
| Onions | Cold and dry | Four months | Cure (let dry) at room temperatures for two to four weeks before storing. Keep green onions cool and moist for one to four months. Can, freeze, or dry. |
| Parsnips | Cold and moist | Will sweeten after two weeks at 32°F. | Freeze. |
| Peanuts | Cool and dry | Four months | Pull pods after plant has dried for several weeks. Store dried in bags. |
| Peas | Cold and moist | One week | Can, freeze, or dry. |
| Peppers | Cool and moist | Two weeks | Will scar if stored below 45°F. Can, freeze, or dry. |

*(continued)*

**Table 19-2 (continued)**

| Vegetable | How to Store | Expected Storage Life | Comments |
|---|---|---|---|
| Potatoes | Cold and moist | Six months | Keep out of light. Cure at 50 to 60 °F for 14 days before storage. Can, freeze, or dry. |
| Pumpkins | Cool and dry | Two to five months | Very sensitive to temperatures below 45°. Can, freeze, or dry. |
| Radishes | Cold and moist | One month | Store without tops. |
| Rutabagas | Cold and moist | Four months | Freeze. |
| Spinach | Cold and moist | Ten days | Freeze. |
| Squash, summer | Cool and moist | One week | Do not store in refrigerator for more than four days. Can, freeze, or dry. |
| Squash, winter | Cool and dry | Two to six months | Can, freeze, or dry. |
| Sweet potatoes | Cool and moist | Four months | Cure in the sun. |
| Tomatoes | Cool and moist | Five days | Loses flavor if stored below 55°F. Do not refrigerate. Can, freeze, or dry. |
| Turnips | Cold and damp | Two to four months | |
| Watermelons | Cool and moist | Two weeks | Will decay if stored below 50°F. Can. |

If you want to store vegetables, make sure that you harvest them at their peak ripeness and avoid bruising the produce, which hastens rotting. Storage times are only estimates; they can vary widely depending on conditions.

If you live in an area where the ground freezes in the winter, you can actually store some root crops — including carrots, leeks, rutabagas, and turnips — in the ground and harvest all winter long. After a good, hard frost, but before the ground freezes, cover your vegetable bed with a foot or more of dry hay. Cover the hay with heavy plastic (4 to 6 mil) and secure the edges with rocks, bricks, or heavy boards. The plastic keeps rain and snow from trickling down through the hay and rotting your vegetables yet keeps the soil from freezing solid. You can harvest periodically through winter, being careful to re-cover the opening after each harvest.

In cold-winter climates, root cellars were once popular places to store vegetables that needed to be kept cold and moist. An unheated basement works well as a root cellar, but these days, most homes have heaters or furnaces in the basement, which make the conditions too warm for storing vegetables. However, if you don't have a heater or can section off a portion of your basement and keep temperatures just above freezing, you can store vegetables like root crops and even cabbage for long periods of time.

You should store only the highest quality vegetables for long periods of time. Any vegetables that are damaged or scarred are likely to rot and spoil everything nearby.

Make sure that your vegetables are well ventilated; you can store onions, potatoes, and other root crops in mesh bags. Shoot for a humidity level that is as high as you can get. To increase humidity, spread moist wood shavings or sawdust on the floor but keep the vegetables elevated on wooden boxes.

# *Freezing, Canning, and Drying Veggies*

You can preserve vegetables three different ways — by freezing, canning, or drying them — to make your harvest last longer than if you stored your vegetables fresh. Refer to Table 19-2 for information on whether a particular vegetable can be frozen, canned, or dried. Although I don't have room to cover all the details about these different methods, the following list gives you a thumbnail sketch of each technique as well as good sources for additional information. Your local Cooperative Extension office is also a very good source of information on preserving vegetables:

- **Freezing.** This is probably the easiest way to preserve vegetables. Heck, if you want, just puree up some tomatoes, put them in a container, and throw them in the freezer — they'll last for months. The mix is great to use in spaghetti sauce or soups. You can also freeze some vegetables, like beans or peas, whole. But usually you have to blanch them first to preserve their color and texture. *Blanching* is simply the process of dipping the vegetables in boiling water for one minute and then placing them in ice water to cool them off. Then you dry the vegetables with a towel and freeze them in labeled plastic freezer bags. Simple.

- **Drying.** This technique can be pretty easy, but it must be done properly to prevent spoilage. Basically, you dehydrate the vegetables by laying them out in the sun to dry, by slow baking them in the oven, or by using a commercial dehydrator, which you can buy in most mail-order catalogs (see the appendix). In hot, sunny climates like California, you can dry 'Roma' tomatoes by slicing them in half and laying them out in the sun on a screen. But spoilage is always a concern, so before drying your vegetables, you may need to get some additional information. You usually store dried vegetables in airtight containers like lidded jars. You can use dried vegetables to make to soups and sauces.

✔ **Canning.** Of all preserved vegetables, I like the taste of canned tomatoes the best. Nothing tastes better in the middle of winter. But canning is a delicate and labor-intensive procedure that can require peeling, sterilizing jars, cooking, boiling, and a lot of other work. I usually set aside a whole weekend to can tomatoes. I don't want to discourage you, but you need some good recipes, some special equipment, and probably some help if you want to can vegetables.

I like to refer to the Ball and Kerr Company for canning help. The company has a hotline (800-344-5377) and a good book: *Ball Blue Book: Guide to Home Canning, Freezing & Dehydration* (Alltrista Corp.). Want to know more about canning, freezing, and drying your vegetable bounty? Try these books: *Preserving Summer's Bounty: A Quick and Easy Guide to Freezing, Canning, and Preserving, and Drying What You Grow* by Susan McClure and *Putting Food* by Janet C. Greene, Ruth Hertzberg, and Beatrice Vaughan. For good Web sites, try the home canning guides at www.home-canning.com and the University of Florida's Selecting, Preparing, and Canning Vegetables and Vegetable Products site at hammock.ifas.ufl.edu/txt/fairs/39653.

# Saving Vegetable Seeds

If you have a favorite vegetable variety that is suited to your tastes or growing conditions, or if you have a particular plant that thrives in your garden, you can save those plants' seeds and possibly even improve their qualities to better fit your needs. If you collect seeds from only the best plants year after year, the qualities that you want will eventually be more present and predictable. Just remember that hybrid seeds won't come true to type (the exact same plant) if you collect the seeds and try to grow them a year later. Open-pollinated varieties are more likely to give you what you expect. See Chapter 2 for more on hybrids. Saving your own seeds also may be the only way to keep some heirloom varieties alive. Many heirlooms are difficult or impossible to obtain, but have something special to offer, such as adaptation to a specific climate, certain types of disease resistance, or especially good flavor. Heirloom varieties represent a reservoir of genes that plant breeders can use to improve present and future crops. The appendix lists sources for obtaining detailed information on saving seeds and on organizations dedicated to heirloom varieties.

# Part IV
# The Part of Tens

Whoever said having a rooftop vegetable garden was fun never lived in the Chrysler building.

# In this part . . .

One of the messages of this book is to keep your vegetable gardening simple. That's what I help you to do here in this part. I give you lists of which vegetables to grow in almost any situation, plus what to do with those pesky zucchinis that just keep coming up. Special tools make the weeding and planting a lot easier, and if you just can't get enough of that great produce, I've included way to extend your growing season beyond the limits of Jack Frost.

# Chapter 20

# Sets of Ten
# Special-Purpose Vegetables

· · · · · · · · · · · · · · · · · · · · · · · · · · · · · · · · · · · · · · · · · ·

## In This Chapter

▶ Vegetables for short seasons, hot weather, and shade

▶ Kid-friendly vegetables

▶ Vegetables that are easy to grow that look good

· · · · · · · · · · · · · · · · · · · · · · · · · · · · · · · · · · · · · · · · · ·

*I* cover quite a few vegetables throughout this book, so this chapter is a quick reference to help you determine which vegetables are good for your particular needs:

✔ **Ten short-season vegetables.** If your growing season is short and sweet, try growing these ten vegetables: bush beans, carrots, cress, lettuce, scallions, peas, radishes, spinach, mesclun greens, and summer squash.

✔ **Ten heat-loving vegetables.** These vegetables can take the heat — perhaps even better than you can: beans, corn, eggplant, melons, okra, peanuts, peppers, sweet potatoes, tomatoes, and watermelon.

✔ **Ten easy-to-grow vegetables.** If you plant at the right time of the year, these vegetables are almost foolproof: broccoli, bush beans, cucumber, eggplant, lettuce, peas, pepper, potatoes, squash, Swiss chard, and tomatoes.

✔ **Ten vegetables for shadier gardens.** If you have a garden plot that receives less than six hours of direct sunlight, try these vegetables: beets, carrots, kale, lettuce, potatoes, scallions, radishes, rhubarb, spinach, and Swiss chard.

✔ **Ten vegetables kids love to grow.** The following vegetables and flowers are fun, easy-to-grow plants, and kids love to harvest and eat them — sometimes right in the garden: pole beans on a teepee, carrots, Swiss chard, cherry tomatoes, blue potatoes, gourds, peanuts, pumpkins, sweet potatoes, sunflowers, and seedless watermelons.

✔ **Ten attractive vegetables.** Why hide your love of vegetables? Plant these vegetables right in your front yard where everyone can enjoy their beauty. Try these vegetables for an attractive-looking as well as productive garden: asparagus, eggplant, fennel, Jerusalem artichoke, kale, lettuce, pepper, rhubarb, sunflower, and Swiss chard.

✔ **Ten things to do with zucchini.** Now that you're a great gardener, you'll invariably make the common mistake that all great gardeners make: planting too much zucchini. Short of giving your crops away (and risking your zucchini's scorn) to every neighbor, friend, relative, and charitable organization in town, try these ten creative ideas to use all those leftover zucchini:

- **Zucchini bowling.** Cut the big zucchini in half, stand them up on the flat end, and bowl them over with a winter squash or the 'Roly Poly' variety of summer squash.

- **Teach yourself to juggle them.** Don't worry, you'll go through a lot of zucchini this way.

- **Carve them for Halloween.** The really big, mature zucchini carve up pretty nice with a looooonnnngggggg face.

- **Make vegetable animals.** Use carrots for legs, peppers for eyes, and watch your neighbors move out of town.

- **Make them into boats.** Hollow out the big zucchini and float them down a stream.

- **Make zucchini bread.** Zucchini bread is actually pretty good and freezes well.

- **Make zucchini parmesan.** Use thinly sliced zucchini instead of eggplant.

- **Stuff 'em.** No, I'm not being rude. Hollow out the mild zucchini, add vegetables and stuffing, and bake the whole thing. Yummy.

- **Use them to expand your shoes.** Really! Take cooked zucchini, place it in a sealed plastic bag and stuff it into a shoe that is one size too small. Now place the shoe in the freezer and as the zucchini freezes, it expands and pushes out the shoe. Pull the shoe out of the freezer, let the zucchini bag thaw, and remove it. Pretty weird, but if the shoe fits. . . .

- **Yank nine of your ten plants out.** You planted way too much.

# Chapter 21

# Ten Tools of the Trade

You've heard this saying a hundred times: "Use the right tool for the job." It's as true in vegetable gardening as for any other project. The right tool can enable you to finish a job faster, and even more importantly, make working in your garden easier on your body. After all, most people garden not to labor and sweat but to enjoy the vegetables and the relaxing environment.

As a new gardener, however, you may find that knowing which tools to pick is often confusing. You can spend hundreds of dollars buying tools for every imaginable use, but you may end up spending more time in your tool shed choosing and maintaining your tools than in your garden. So when you're selecting your tools, my solution is to keep it simple — that's why I chose only ten tools in this chapter, and even these tools may not be appropriate for all garden situations.

Many of the items that you need are probably already around your house — especially if you're working on other outdoor projects. Here is a short list of some useful gardening gear:

✔ Gloves help you grip tools better and help you avoid hand blisters. Cotton gloves are the cheapest, but the more expensive animal skin gloves — made of goat and sheep, for example — last longer.

✔ A good straw hat with ventilation keeps the sun off your skin and allows air to move through and cool your head.

✔ A good pocketknife or pruning shears are great for cutting strings and vines.

✔ Sturdy rubber boots, garden clogs, or work boots repel water and provide support for digging.

Now on to the specific garden tools that you need. Depending on the size and type of garden you have, the "right tool" can vary widely. In this chapter, I describe ten essential tools and talk about the garden situations for which they're best suited. Many gardening tools are ergonomically designed to work more efficiently and put less stress on your joints. I highlight these ergonomic tools as well as provide helpful tips on how to use the tools and put less strain on your back, arms, wrists, and legs. So get ready to start digging in your garden!

## Watering cans and hoses

Shall I start with the most obvious tools? I dare say, yes. Plants need water to grow, and if Mother Nature isn't cooperating, you need to water regularly (see Chapter 15 for watering techniques). For a large garden, you may need elaborate soaker hoses, sprinklers, and drip irrigation pipes. But for most small-scale home gardeners, a simple hose and watering can will do.

Rubber hoses are less likely to kink than vinyl or nylon hoses, but they tend to be much heavier to move around. Be sure to get a long enough hose so that you can reach plants in all areas of your garden without having to shoot water across the beds to reach distant plants. Choose a hose that has brass fittings and a washer integrated into the hose because it's less likely to fail after prolonged use.

Watering cans can be made of simple, inexpensive plastic or high-end, fancy galvanized metal. Plastic is lighter, but galvanized metal is rustproof and more attractive. Watering cans also come in different sizes, so try a few out for comfort before buying. Make sure that you can easily remove the sprinkler head, or *rose,* for cleaning.

For watering tender seedlings, buy a can with an oval rose (nozzle with holes) that points upward and applies water with less pressure. The traditional round rose is better for watering more mature plants.

## Hand trowel

Hand trowels are essential for digging in containers, window boxes, and small raised beds. The wider-bladed hand trowels, which are scoop shaped and rounded on the end, are easier to use to loosen soil than the narrower-bladed, V-pointed ones. The narrower blades are better for digging tough weeds, such as dandelions.

Hand trowel blades are usually made of steel or plastic. Steel blades are more durable, but plastic blades are lighter. Although stainless steel versions are more expensive, they're easier to clean and easier to find if you lose them. The handles may be steel, wooden, or plastic. Choose a trowel that's forged as one piece of metal or that has secure attachments between the blade and handle.

Try out different hand trowels before buying, choosing one that feels comfortable and fits your hand well. Ergonomic versions of hand trowels have forearm supports and cushioned grips.

## Hand cultivator

After you plant your small container or raised bed, the weeds will come. A three-pronged hand cultivator (see Figure 21-1) is a handy tool to break up soil clods, smooth seed beds, work in granular fertilizer, and remove young weeds as they germinate. When you're digging a planting hole, a hand cultivator breaks up the soil more easily than a hand trowel.

**Figure 21-1:** A handheld, three-pronged cultivator is great for creating seed beds, digging out furrows for planting, and weeding.

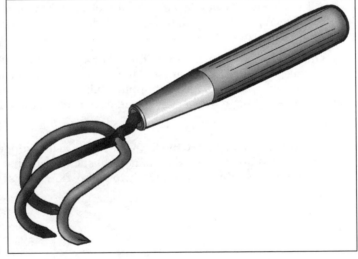

As with a hand trowel, choose a hand cultivator that feels comfortable in your hand and that has a handle securely fastened to the blade. The steel-bladed types are the most durable.

## Hoe, hoe, hoe

If you want to become a connoisseur of gardening equipment, then hoes are a good place to start. I could wax poetically about garden hoes for a whole chapter, but I'll cut to the chase and get down to the basics.

Hoes are available for all occasions — hoes for digging furrows, hoes for weeding, hoes for wide rows, hoes for tight rows, hoes that scuffle, hoes that oscillate, and even hoes for specific vegetables such as the onion hoe. What you need largely depends on the design of your garden. The best hoes have long hardwood handles and single-forged steel blades strongly attached to their handles. Here are three favorites:

- **Common garden hoe:** This classic hoe has a broad, straight, 6-inch steel blade that's good for all types of gardening, including digging, weeding, chopping, hilling, and cultivating. Longer- and narrower-bladed versions, such as the Collinear hoe, are good for weeding in tight spots.

- **Oscillating hoe (also known as stirrup hoe):** This hoe, shown in Figure 21-2, is primarily used for weeding. Unlike the other hoes mentioned in this section, which cut weeds on the pull stroke, this hoe cuts weeds on the pull stroke *and* the push stroke, enabling you to weed faster. The 4- to 7-inch-wide steel stirrup is hinged so that it moves back and forth, digging about $1/4$ inch deep into the soil. It's good for pulling young weeds. This hoe works well in gardens with clearly defined rows and spaces between plants. Like all hoes, the blade works best when it's sharpened regularly.

- **Tined hoe:** This hoe is my favorite. It has 3 or 4 steel tines attached to the bottom of a 5- to 6-inch-diameter steel head. Tined hoes are good for weeding, cultivating, digging, chopping, hilling, and breaking up soil clods. They're lighter, more versatile, and easier to use than common hoes.

If hoeing gives you a sore back, try the Swan-Neck hoe. This wooden-handled, metal-bladed hoe is curved at its neck in such a way that you can stand straight up (not bending) as you work your way down those rows of beans.

**Figure 21-2:**
An oscillating hoe.

## Spades and shovels

Spades and shovels are two of the most commonly used gardening tools. The difference between the two is simple: A spade is designed for digging, and a shovel is designed for scooping and throwing. Shovels traditionally have rounded and pointed blades, whereas spades have flat, straight, almost rectangular blades. A good shovel is essential in any garden for spreading compost, manure, or fertilizer. A spade is essential for edging or breaking new ground. However, many gardeners use spades for anything from cutting open fertilizer bags to hammering in stakes. Good spades are that rugged.

Both spades and shovels come in short- and long-handled versions. A long handle gives you more leverage when digging holes, so keep that in mind if you're purchasing a spade. I find that I use a short-handled shovel with a D-shaped grip more often in my garden than a spade. Choose a spade or a shovel that has a single piece of metal attached to a wooden handle with either a single socket or a single socket that runs 1 foot up the handle (solid strap). These models are heavier, but they're much more durable.

To get a more comfortable grip on long-handled tools, try low-cost foam grippers that fit on handles (see Figure 21-3). These grippers make the diameter of a handle larger and more cushioned, reducing the amount of blistering and cramping in your hands.

**Figure 21-3:**
Comfort grips on a long-handled tool.

## Garden rakes

After you dig soil, you need to level it, break up soil clods, and smooth the seedbeds (especially if you're growing raised beds, which are described in Chapter 2). An iron rake is the right tool for the job even though you may use it for this purpose only a few times a year. A 14-inch-diameter, iron-toothed rake should have a long, wooden handle that's securely attached to a metal head. You can flip the metal head over to really smooth a seedbed flat. For a lightweight but less durable version of an iron rake, try an aluminum rake.

## Garden forks

As handy as a spade is for turning fresh garden soil, I find that an iron fork is a better tool for turning beds that have been worked before. The fork digs into the soil as deep as 12 inches, and at the same time breaks up clods, and loosens and aerates the soil better than a spade. Iron forks look similar to short-handled spades except that they have three to four iron tines on their heads. The best ones are those forged from one piece of steel with hard-wood handles firmly attached. They're great not only for turning soil but for turning compost piles and digging root crops, such as potatoes and carrots.

To keep your metal hand tools functioning for years, clean and store them properly. After you're finished using a tool, wash all soil off of it. Yearly, sharpen the blades of weeders, spades, and shovels; oil wooden handles with linseed oil; and tighten any nuts and screws on the handles.

## Buckets, wagons, and baskets

Okay, you don't have a 1,000-square-foot garden. But you still need to carry seeds, tools, fertilizer, and other items around. I love talking about storage containers because this is where the tools of the trade get really simple. For fertilizers, potting soil, and hand tools, a 5-gallon plastic bucket is the perfect container. You can probably get one free from a construction site; just make sure that you clean it out well. For a more durable but smaller bucket, buy one made from galvanized steel.

For bulkier items, such as flats of seedlings, use your child's old red wagon. Wagons are great for moving plants and small bags of fertilizer in your garden, and the lip on the wagon bed helps hold these items in place when you cover bumpy ground.

Finally, to gather all that great produce, invest in a wire or wicker basket. Wire baskets are easier to use because you can wash the produce while it's still in the basket. Wicker and wooden baskets, though less durable than metal, are more aesthetically pleasing and stylish in your garden. Piling your produce in either basket is a lot more functional than trying to balance zucchinis in your arms while carrying them from your garden to your kitchen.

## Wheelbarrows and garden carts

Invariably you need to move heavy items such as soil and fertilizer from one spot to another in your garden. The two main options for moving "larger than a bread box" stuff are wheelbarrows and garden carts. The basic difference between the two vehicles is the wheels. Wheelbarrows have one wheel and an oval, metal tray; garden carts have two wheels and a rectangular wooden tray.

Wheelbarrows are very maneuverable in tight places, can turn on a dime, and are easy to dump. A contractors-type wheelbarrow has a deeper box and is worth the extra investment because of its superior quality. For a lighter weight wheelbarrow, try one with a box made out of plastic.

Garden carts are better balanced, can carry larger loads, and are easier to push than wheelbarrows. A larger-sized garden cart can handle loads of compost, soil, rocks, and bales of hay very easily. Some garden carts have removable back panels that make dumping easier.

## Power tillers

The old fashioned rear- or front-tined tiller was designed to help large-scale gardeners save time turning their gardens in spring and fall. The large (more than 5-horsepower engine) power tillers are best if you have 1,000 square feet or more to till. They also can be indispensable tools for forming raised beds and breaking sod.

If you only need to use a large tiller once a year, consider renting one from a local rental store, hiring someone to till for you, or chipping in with a neighbor to buy one.

Because home gardens have gotten smaller, tiller manufacturers have responded by designing a new group of tillers called minitillers (see Figure 21-4). These two-cycle, 1- to 2-horsepower tillers weigh only 20 to 30 pounds, are easy to handle, and can till in tight places. Not only do they have tilling tines, but they come with other attachments such as lawn aerators, edgers, and lawn dethatchers.

**Figure 21-4:**
A minitiller.

Minitillers work best in previously worked, loamy soil without large stones. Unlike their larger cousins, minitillers are easy to handle when you're weeding between rows of vegetables and close to plants. However, they're not good for breaking new ground or tilling stony or heavily weeded areas in your garden. Because they're lightweight, they till raised beds and small gardens very well. Electric models are available if you don't *like* the noise and smell of a two-cycle engine. Though not essential for your garden, if you like power equipment and need a little help keeping your garden looking good, check out minitillers. (See the appendix to find out how you can get minitillers.)

# Chapter 22

# Ten Ways to Extend Your Growing Season

. . . . . . . . . . . . . . . . . . . . . . . . . . . . . . . . . . . . . . . . . . . .

### In This Chapter

▶ Starting your veggies earlier in the season

▶ Extending your harvest into the cold-weather season

. . . . . . . . . . . . . . . . . . . . . . . . . . . . . . . . . . . . . . . . . . . .

*O*nce you start vegetable gardening, you may get hooked on having fresh vegetables from your garden year-round. Unless you live in a mild climate, such as zones 9 and 10, the best way to get the most vegetables from your garden is to use season-extending devices. These devices protect your vegetables from killing frosts in fall and enable you to get an earlier start in spring. Of course, selecting the right vegetables to grow is vital to your success. In general, greens, root crops, and cool-season cole crops are the best vegetables to grow in cold weather. (See the specific chapters on these vegetables for growing information.) However, you also can extend the length of time that you harvest warm-season crops — such as melons, tomatoes, and peppers — by using these methods. Whatever plants you grow, these season-extending techniques enable you to harvest fresh vegetables for most of the year.

## Location, location, location

*Where* you plant your vegetables has much to do with avoiding frosts and cold weather as *when* you plant. Every yard has pockets or areas that warm up earlier in spring and stay warmer later into the fall. For example, the nook near my chimney on the south side of my house is such a location. That area is the first place that snow melts, and plants grow well past the time frost has killed vegetables in my main garden. Find these nooks in your yard, plant cold-hardy vegetables like spinach and broccoli, and enjoy harvesting earlier and later than anyone else. Some good nook areas to check out are the south side of any building, especially if you can find a spot that's protected from wind. Courtyards are notoriously good microclimates. (See Chapter 2 for more on microclimates.) Other good spots include areas around evergreen shrubs (as long as enough sun pokes through to grow the plants) and near paved surfaces such as driveways, or walkways — especially if the pavement is dark colored.

## Timing of planting

Timing is important when you grow vegetables. If you want early vegetables, start your seeds indoors and then transplant young seedlings into a season extender, such as a cold frame, cloche, or hot cap. If you want your vegetables to last longer into winter, start them early enough so that by the dark months (December and January), they'll be full-sized and edible. During these months, don't expect much growth, even in warm areas, because the light is less intense and the day is much shorter. Make sure that the vegetables are at or close to maturity heading into this period (unless you're in a warm location and trying to overwinter these vegetables for a spring harvest; see Chapter 19).

## Hot caps

For individual prized plants, hot caps are a great way to protect them from the cold. A *hot cap* is usually a clear plastic, pyramid-shaped cone with an opening in its top to let hot air out. You can buy these cones at garden centers or create your own by cutting the bottoms out of clear plastic milk jugs. Be sure to create a vent at the top of the milk jugs to let hot air out on sunny days, or use them only at night. You can cover the hole with a blanket at night if you expect chilly temperatures.

## Glass cloches

If you really want something elegant in your garden, you can spend up to $50 on tinted glass hot caps, affectionately called *cloches,* as shown in Figure 22-1. They're sturdy and beautiful, and yes, they protect tender plants from the cold, a little better than plastic hot caps do. However, cloches don't have vents, so remove them during sunny days or prop them up to let cool air in. If you want a classy-looking vegetable garden, glass cloches are the way to go.

## Hay bales

If you don't like building things or buying expensive prefabricated cold frames, the easiest season-extending devices that I've seen are hay bales. Hay bales are a great way to grow greens early and late into the season without any extra work.

**Figure 22-1:**
A glass
cloche.

Find a 6-foot-long garden spot along a south-facing wall of your house, garage, or shed. Till up the soil and create a 3-foot-by-6-foot box by placing six, 3-foot-wide hay bales flat around the area (one on each side, two in the front and back). Then find an old window sash and drop it over the bales, covering the garden spot. Voilà! You've created a season-extending cold frame. This type of cold frame isn't as air tight or as well-insulated as a wooden or plastic cold frame, and it doesn't let in as much light, but it's simple, and it works.

## Cold frames

Cold frames essentially are mini-greenhouses. They're usually wooden boxes covered with windowpanes or clear plastic (see Figure 22-2). The French perfected cold frames in the early 1900s, using elaborate systems of them to grow produce year-round for major cities such as Paris. Some professional gardeners as far north as zone 5, where winter temperatures can dip down to –20°F, can harvest vegetables every month of the year by planting cold-weather-tolerant crops and by using cold frames.

You can purchase a premade cold frame for $100 to $200, or create your own simple cold frame by following these steps:

1. **Build a 3-foot-by-6-foot box from untreated lumber. Cut the box so that the back is 18 inches high, sloping to a front height of 14 inches.**

   This sloping angle enables more sun to reach the plants, and it sheds rain and snow as well.

2. **Hinge an old window sash over the top of the cold frame or make a frame by using tightly stretched clear plastic, which creates a sealed growing environment.**

   You can insulate the cold frame by adding rigid foam insulation around the insides of the cold frame and by weather stripping along the top edge.

3. **Position the cold frame so that it faces south.**

   It's best to put a cold frame next to a structure, such as a house, pointing south.

Even though the purpose of a cold frame is to trap heat, on sunny days, even in winter, a cold frame can get so hot that it burns the plants. Check your cold frame once a day on sunny days, opening or venting the top slightly to allow hot air to escape.

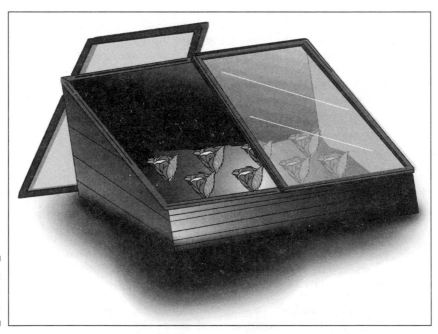

**Figure 22-2:**
A simple
cold frame.

## Row covers

A row cover can be a clear plastic cover draped over half-circle wire hoops to create a tunnel effect (see Figure 22-3), or it can be a new lightweight cheesecloth-like fabric that's so light that it floats on top of vegetables. Both plastic and floating row covers protect plants from light freezes; however, if you expect really chilly temperatures (around 20°F), use another protection device. Clear plastic heats up your crops faster and warmer than floating row cover material, but it needs venting to keep the plants from overheating. Floating row covers let in air, light, and water and don't overheat as easily as clear plastic row covers. You also can use both materials to protect your plants from insects.

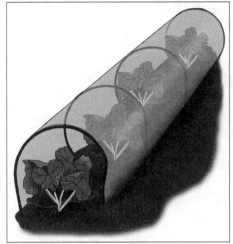

**Figure 22-3:**
A clear plastic grow tunnel.

# Wall O' Waters

*National Gardening* magazine was the first publication to introduce Wall O' Waters (shown in Figure 22-4) to the world. These double-walled, clear-plastic cylinders hold narrow columns of water around your favorite vegetables.

By placing Wall O' Waters around heat-loving plants, such as tomatoes, you can get a jump on spring. The water in the cylinders absorbs the warmth of the sun during the day and slowly releases the stored heat at night to protect your plants in cold temperatures. Even if the water freezes, it releases enough heat to protect your plants. Wall O' Waters have been reported to protect tomatoes in temperatures as low as 16°F. To prevent overheating during the day, leave the tops open. For added protection at night, collapse the tops of these devices into a pyramid shape. Of course, after a plant has grown for a few weeks, it will outgrow the plastic cylinder, so you'll have to remove the Wall O' Water. But what a jump on the growing season you'll have by then!

## Growing in containers or indoors

If you want to protect your plants without covering them, grow them to maturity indoors under lights (see Chapter 13) or grow them in movable containers (see Chapter 17). You can grow your plants in small containers, such as a 5-gallon bucket, or larger containers, such as a container with casters that's half the size of a whiskey barrel. When cold weather threatens, just roll or carry the container into your garage or house. Containers may require a lot of lifting and carrying, but great-tasting tomatoes later in the season will be your reward for all that hard work.

## Portable greenhouses

If you really want to extend the growing season, stop fooling around with hot caps and blankets and buy a greenhouse. You can find many different free-standing portable greenhouses on the market that are great for getting an early jump on the growing season and extending it into the fall. Portable greenhouses usually aren't designed for heavy snow or extreme cold, so don't expect to be growing year-round in the North with these. Greenhouses can range in price from $200 to $2,000, depending on the materials and size. In the appendix, I list a number of greenhouse manufacturers and suppliers that can help you choose the right greenhouse for your location.

# Appendix

# Planning Guide and Other Resources

• • • • • • • • • • • • • • • • • • • • • • • • • • • • • • • • • • • • • • • •

*T*his section is vegetables by the numbers. All the distances, depths, and yields for more than 40 vegetables are listed in "Guidelines for Planting," which includes a chart that provides a great way for you to start out and sketch your garden before you plant. "Frost Dates and Length of Growing Season" tells you what you need to know to avoid freezing out your veggies and stunting your crop. And I provide a guide to the hardiness zones in the final section. I also include a list of suppliers of vegetable seeds and other materials to get you started.

## *Guidelines for Planting*

The best way to plan your garden is to start with how much produce you want. For example, if you like lettuce, 25 heads will take approximately 25 feet of row. The recommended distances between rows will tell you how much space to leave between crops.

Use the information in Table A-1 as a general guideline. You may choose to vary the distance between rows, for example, depending on the method of planting or cultivating. You can usually hand-hoe weeds between rows adequately in 18- or 24-inch-wide pathways; rototilling is faster, but pathways should be 30 or 36 inches wide. If you garden intensively, such as in raised beds, you can space plants closer than indicated in the chart.

The days to maturity and the yield figures are averages. Depending on weather, soil fertility, pests, and weed pressure, yield and maturities in your garden can vary greatly. Just remember, there are always friends, relatives, and bunnies who'd love some fresh, home-grown produce.

## Table A-1 Planting Guide

| Crop | Seed/Plants per 100 ft. of Row | Frost Tolerance | Planting Depth (Inches) | Spacing between Rows (Inches) | Spacing Between Plants (Inches) | Soil Temp. for Germ.* | Ave. Days to Germ. | Ave. Days to Maturity | Ave. Yield per 10 ft. of Row |
|---|---|---|---|---|---|---|---|---|---|
| Asparagus | 65pl./1 oz. | Very hardy (R) | 1/2 | 36–48 | 18 | 50–95 (75) | 7–21 | 2 years | 3 lbs. |
| Beans, snap (bush) | 1/2 lb. | Tender | 1–1 1/2 | 24–36 | 3–4 | 60–95 (85) | 6–14 | 45–60 | 12 lbs. |
| Beans, snap (pole) | 1/2 lb. | Tender | 1–1 1/2 | 36–48 | 4–6 | 60–95 (85) | 6–14 | 60–70 | 15 lbs. |
| Beans, lima (bush) | 1/2 lb. | Very tender | 1–1 1/2 | 30–36 | 3–4 | 60–85 (80) | 7–12 | 65–80 | 2.5 lbs., shelled |
| Beans, lima (pole) | 1/4 lb. | Very tender | 1–1 1/2 | 36–48 | 12–18 | 60–85 (80) | 7–12 | 85–90 | 5 lbs., shelled |
| Beets | 1 oz. | Hardy | 1/2 | 15–24 | 2 | 40–95 (85) | 7–10 | 50–60 | 15 lbs. |
| Broccoli | 45 pl./1/4 oz. | Very hardy (P) | 1/4 | 24–36 | 14–24 | 40–95 (85) | 3–10 | 60–80 | 10 lbs. |
| Brussels sprouts | 55 pl./1/4 oz. | Very hardy (P) | 1/4 | 24–36 | 14–24 | 40–95 (85) | 3–10 | 90–100 | 7.5 lbs. |
| Cabbage | 55 pl./1/4 oz. | Very hardy (P) | 1/4 | 24–36 | 14–24 | 40–95 (85) | 4–10 | 60–90 | 15 lbs. |
| Carrots | 1/2 oz. | Hardy | 1/4 | 15–24 | 2 | 40–95 (80) | 10–17 | 70–80 | 10 lbs. |
| Cauliflower | 55 pl./1/4 oz. | Hardy (P) | 1/4 | 24–36 | 14–24 | 40–95 (80) | 4–10 | 70–90 | 10 lbs. |
| Celery | 200 pl. | Hardy | 1/8 | 30–36 | 6 | 40–75 (70) | 9–21 | 125 | 18 stalks |
| Chinese cabbage | 65 pl./1/4 oz. | Hardy (P) | 1/4 | 18–30 | 8–12 | 40–105 (80) | 4–10 | 65–70 | 8 heads |
| Corn | 3–4 oz. | Tender | 2 | 24–36 | 12–18 | 50–105 (85) | 6–10 | 70–90 | 1 dozen |

| Crop | Seed/Plants per 100 ft. of Row | Frost Tolerance | Planting Depth (Inches) | Spacing between Rows (Inches) | Spacing Between Plants (Inches) | Soil Temp.* for Germ. | Ave. Days to Germ. | Ave. Days to Maturity | Ave. Yield per 10 ft. of Row |
|---|---|---|---|---|---|---|---|---|---|
| Cucumbers | 1/2 oz. | Very tender | 1 | 48–72 | 24–48 | 60–105 (95) | 6–10 | 50–70 | 12 lbs. |
| Eggplant | 1/8 oz. | Very tender (P) | 1/4–1/2 | 24–36 | 18–24 | 65–95 (85) | 7–14 | 80–90 | 10 lbs. |
| Leeks | 1/2 oz. | Very hardy | 1/2–1 | 12–18 | 2–4 | 45–70 (75) | 7–12 | 130–150 | 12 lbs. |
| Lettuce, heading | 1/4 oz. | Very hardy | 1/4–1/2 | 18–24 | 6–10 | 32–75 (75) | 4–10 | 70–75 | 10 heads |
| Lettuce, leaf | 1/4 oz. | Very hardy | 1/4–1/2 | 15–18 | 2–3 | 32–75 (75) | 4–10 | 40–50 | 5 lbs. |
| Muskmelon | 50 pl./1/2 oz. | Very tender | 1 | 60–96 | 24–36 | 65–105 (95) | 4–8 | 85–100 | 5 fruits |
| Okra | 2 oz. | Very tender | 1 | 36–42 | 12–24 | 65–80 | 7–14 | 55–65 | 10 lbs. |
| Onion, seed | 1 oz. | Very hardy | 1/2 | 15–24 | 3–4 | 32–95 (80) | 7–12 | 90–120 | 10 lbs. |
| Onion, sets | 400–600 pl. | Very hardy | 1–3 | 15–24 | 3–4 | NA | NA | 80–120 | 10 lbs. |
| Parsley | 1/4 oz. | Hardy | 1/4–1/2 | 15–24 | 6–8 | 50–85 (70) | 14–28 | 70–90 | 4 lbs. |
| Parsnips | 1/2 oz. | Hardy | 1/2 | 18–30 | 3–4 | 32–85 (70) | 15–25 | 120–170 | 10 lbs. |
| Peas | 1 lb. | Very hardy | 2 | 18–36 | 1 | 40–85 (75) | 6–15 | 55–90 | 2 lbs. |
| Peppers | 1/8 oz. | Very tender | 1/4 | 24–36 | 18–24 | 60–95 (85) | 10–20 | 60–90 | 6 lbs. |
| Potatoes, Irish | 6–10 lbs. seed potatoes | Very hardy (R) | 4 | 30–36 | 8–10 | NA | NA | 75–100 | 10 lbs. |
| Pumpkins | 1/2 oz. | Very tender | 1–2 | 60–96 | 36–48 | 65–105 (95) | 6–10 | 75–100 | 10 lbs. |

*(continued)*

**Table A-1 (continued)**

| Crop | Seed/Plants per 100 ft. of Row | Frost Tolerance | Planting Depth (Inches) | Spacing between Rows (Inches) | Spacing Between Plants (Inches) | Soil Temp.* for Germ.* | Ave. Days to Germ. | Ave. Days to Maturity | Ave. Yield per 10 ft. of Row |
|---|---|---|---|---|---|---|---|---|---|
| Radishes | 1 oz. | Hardy | ½ | 14–24 | 1 | 40–95 (80) | 3–10 | 25–40 | 10 bunches |
| Rhubarb | 20 pl. | Very hardy (R) | 4 | 36–48 | 48 | NA | NA | Two years | 7 lbs. |
| Southern peas | ½ lb. | Very tender | ½–1 | 24–36 | 4–6 | 60–95 (85) | 7–10 | 60–70 | 4 lbs. |
| Spinach | 1 oz. | Very hardy | ¾ | 14–24 | 3–4 | 32–75 (70) | 6–14 | 40–60 | 4–5 lbs. |
| Squash, summer | 1 oz. | Tender | 1 | 36–60 | 18–36 | 65–105 (95) | 3–12 | 50–60 | 15 lbs. |
| Squash, winter | ½ oz. | Very tender | 1 | 60–96 | 24–48 | 65–105 (95) | 6–10 | 85–100 | 10 lbs. |
| Sweet potatoes | 75–100 pl. | Very tender (P) | NA | 36–48 | 12–16 | NA | NA | 100–130 | 10 lbs. |
| Tomatoes | 50 pl./⅛ oz. | Tender | ½ | 24–48 | 18–36 | 50–95 (80) | 6–14 | 70–90 | 10 lbs. |
| Turnips | ½ oz. | Very hardy | ½ | 14–24 | 2–3 | 50–105 (80) | 3–10 | 30–60 | 5–10 lbs. |
| Watermelon | 1 oz. | Very tender | 1 | 72–96 | 36–72 | 65–105 (95) | 3–12 | 80–100 | 4 fruits |

P — plants
R — roots
NA — not applicable
Very hardy — plant outside four to six weeks before last spring frost date
Hardy — plant outside two to three weeks before last spring frost date
Tender — plant outside on date of last spring frost
Very tender — plant outside one to two weeks after last spring frost date
*Range of germination temperature; optimum germination in parentheses

# Frost Dates and Length of Growing Season

You can grow vegetables anywhere! Some of the largest, most beautiful vegetables I've ever seen are grown by avid gardeners in Alaska. If you can grow vegetables where the sun doesn't shine for six months of the year, you know that they must be easy to grow.

Table A-2 is a chart of the average annual first and last frost dates as well as the length of the frost-free growing season in 100 cities across the United States. Of course, this chart is only a guide, and your local climate will vary depending on many factors, including the variation in weather from year to year. To get more accurate dates, contact your local weather service or the Cooperative Extension Service in your area.

| Table A-2 | First and Last Frost Dates | | |
|---|---|---|---|
| *City* | *Last Frost Date* | *First Frost Date* | *Length of Season* |
| Birmingham, Alabama | March 29 | November 6 | 221 days |
| Mobile, Alabama | February 27 | November 26 | 272 days |
| Juneau, Alaska | May 16 | September 26 | 133 days |
| Flagstaff, Arizona | June 13 | September 21 | 99 days |
| Phoenix, Arizona | February 5 | December 15 | 308 days |
| Tucson, Arizona | February 28 | November 29 | 273 days |
| Fayetteville, Arkansas | April 21 | October 17 | 179 days |
| Little Rock, Arkansas | March 23 | November 9 | 230 days |
| Fresno, California | February 22 | November 25 | 273 days |
| Los Angeles, California | None likely | None likely | 365 days |
| San Bernardino, California | February 23 | December 8 | 294 days |
| San Francisco, California | January 8 | January 5 | 362 days |
| Sacramento, California | February 14 | December 1 | 287 days |
| San Jose, California | January 22 | December 25 | 338 days |
| San Diego, California | None | None | 365 days |
| Santa Rosa, California | March 26 | November 19 | 236 days |
| Denver, Colorado | May 3 | October 8 | 157 days |
| Durango, Colorado | June 4 | September 18 | 105 days |

*(continued)*

## Table A-2 *(continued)*

| City | Last Frost Date | First Frost Date | Length of Season |
|------|-----------------|------------------|------------------|
| Hartford, Connecticut | April 25 | October 10 | 167 days |
| New Haven, Connecticut | April 15 | October 27 | 195 days |
| Dover, Delaware | April 9 | October 28 | 202 days |
| Wilmington, Delaware | April 13 | October 29 | 198 days |
| Washington, DC | April 10 | October 31 | 203 days |
| Jacksonville, Florida | February 14 | December 14 | 303 days |
| Miami, Florida | None | None | 365 days |
| Orlando, Florida | January 31 | December 17 | 320 days |
| Tallahassee, Florida | March 12 | November 14 | 246 days |
| Atlanta, Georgia | March 13 | November 12 | 243 days |
| Savannah, Georgia | March 10 | November 15 | 250 days |
| Boise, Idaho | May 8 | October 9 | 153 days |
| Pocatello, Idaho | May 20 | September 20 | 122 days |
| Chicago, Illinois | April 14 | November 2 | 201 days |
| Indianapolis, Indiana | April 18 | October 22 | 186 days |
| Cedar Rapids, Iowa | April 29 | October 7 | 161 days |
| Des Moines, Iowa | April 19 | October 17 | 180 days |
| Manhattan, Kansas | April 23 | October 16 | 176 days |
| Wichita, Kansas | April 13 | October 23 | 193 days |
| Lexington, Kentucky | April 17 | October 25 | 190 days |
| Louisville, Kentucky | April 1 | November 7 | 220 days |
| New Orleans, Louisiana | February 20 | December 5 | 288 days |
| Portland, Maine | May 10 | September 30 | 143 days |
| Baltimore, Maryland | March 26 | November 13 | 231 days |
| Amherst, Massachusetts | May 9 | September 29 | 142 days |
| Boston, Massachusetts | April 6 | November 10 | 217 days |
| Detroit, Michigan | April 24 | October 22 | 181 days |
| Marquette, Michigan | May 12 | October 19 | 159 days |
| Minneapolis—St. Paul, Minnesota | April 30 | October 13 | 166 days |
| Duluth, Minnesota | May 21 | September 21 | 122 days |

| City | Last Frost Date | First Frost Date | Length of Season |
|------|-----------------|------------------|------------------|
| Columbus, Mississippi | March 27 | October 29 | 215 days |
| Jackson, Mississippi | March 17 | November 9 | 236 days |
| Jefferson City, Missouri | April 26 | October 16 | 173 days |
| St. Louis, Missouri | April 3 | November 6 | 217 days |
| Billings, Montana | May 12 | September 23 | 133 days |
| Helena, Montana | May 18 | September 18 | 122 days |
| Lincoln, Nebraska | March 13 | November 13 | 180 days |
| North Platte, Nebraska | May 11 | September 24 | 136 days |
| Las Vegas, Nevada | March 7 | November 21 | 259 days |
| Concord, New Hampshire | May 23 | September 22 | 121 days |
| Newark, New Jersey | April 4 | November 10 | 219 days |
| Trenton, New Jersey | April 6 | November 7 | 214 days |
| Albuquerque, New Mexico | April 16 | October 29 | 196 days |
| Los Alamos, New Mexico | May 8 | October 13 | 157 days |
| Albany, New York | May 7 | September 29 | 144 days |
| New York, New York | April 1 | November 11 | 223 days |
| Rochester, New York | May 3 | October 15 | 164 days |
| Syracuse, New York | April 28 | October 16 | 170 days |
| Asheville, North Carolina | April 10 | October 24 | 195 days |
| Charlotte, North Carolina | March 21 | November 15 | 239 days |
| Raleigh, North Carolina | April 11 | October 27 | 198 days |
| Fargo, North Dakota | May 13 | September 27 | 137 days |
| Akron, Ohio | May 3 | October 18 | 168 days |
| Cincinnati, Ohio | April 14 | October 27 | 195 days |
| Columbus, Ohio | April 26 | October 17 | 173 days |
| Oklahoma City, Oklahoma | March 28 | November 7 | 224 days |
| Tulsa, Oklahoma | March 30 | November 4 | 218 days |
| Ashland, Oregon | May 13 | October 12 | 152 days |
| Pendleton, Oregon | April 15 | October 21 | 188 days |
| Portland, Oregon | April 3 | November 7 | 217 days |
| Allentown, Pennsylvania | April 21 | October 18 | 179 days |

*(continued)*

## Table A-2 *(continued)*

| City | Last Frost Date | First Frost Date | Length of Season |
|------|-----------------|------------------|------------------|
| Pittsburgh, Pennsylvania | April 16 | November 3 | 201 days |
| State College, Pennsylvania | April 27 | October 15 | 170 days |
| Kingston, Rhode Island | May 8 | September 30 | 144 days |
| Charleston, South Carolina | February 17 | December 10 | 296 days |
| Columbia, South Carolina | April 4 | November 2 | 211 days |
| Memphis, Tennessee | March 23 | November 7 | 228 days |
| Nashville, Tennessee | April 5 | October 29 | 207 days |
| Amarillo, Texas | April 14 | October 29 | 197 days |
| Dallas, Texas | March 18 | November 12 | 239 days |
| Houston, Texas | February 4 | December 10 | 309 days |
| Cedar City, Utah | May 20 | October 2 | 134 days |
| Salt Lake City, Utah | April 12 | November 1 | 203 days |
| Burlington, Vermont | May 11 | October 1 | 142 days |
| Norfolk, Virginia | March 23 | November 17 | 239 days |
| Richmond, Virginia | April 10 | October 26 | 198 days |
| Seattle, Washington | March 24 | November 11 | 232 days |
| Spokane, Washington | May 4 | October 5 | 153 days |
| Parkersburg, West Virginia | April 25 | October 18 | 175 days |
| Green Bay, Wisconsin | May 12 | October 2 | 143 days |
| Milwaukee, Wisconsin | May 5 | October 9 | 156 days |
| Cheyenne, Wyoming | May 20 | September 27 | 130 days |

Keep in mind that, just because your frost-free growing season is only so many days, many vegetables that I list can tolerate a light frost. And you can extend your growing season by using special growing techniques, as described in Chapter 22. However, warm-season vegetables such as tomatoes don't like even a touch of frost, so this guide is much more accurate for estimating how many days you have to grow your favorite heat-loving vegetables.

# Check Out Your Hardiness Zone

The U.S. Department of Agriculture has helpfully divided North America into plant hardiness zones based on average annual minimum temperatures. Planting instructions regarding depth and timing may change depending on what zone you're in. I refer to these hardiness zones throughout this book. You can find a map of these zones in *Gardening For Dummies* by Michael MacCaskey and the Editors of the National Gardening Association (IDG Books Worldwide, Inc.).

Your hardiness zone isn't as critical for vegetable growing as it is for growing fruits, perennial flowers, trees, and shrubs. However, knowing your hardiness zone is a good idea because in some warm areas, such as zones 7 and 8, you can grow two or three crops of the same vegetable in one year or even grow vegetables throughout the winter. The table that follows helps you determine your hardiness zone.

| *Zone* | *Minimum Temperature* | |
|--------|-----------------------|---|
| | *Fahrenheit* | *Celsius* |
| Zone 1 | Below –50°F | Below –46°C |
| Zone 2 | –50°F to –40°F | –46°C to –40°C |
| Zone 3 | –40°F to –30°F | –40°C to –34°F |
| Zone 4 | –30°F to –20°F | –34°C to –29°C |
| Zone 5 | –20°F to –10°F | –29°C to –23°C |
| Zone 6 | –10°F to 0°F | –23°C to –18°C |
| Zone 7 | 0°F to 10°F | –18°C to –12°C |
| Zone 8 | 10°F to 20°F | –12°C to –7°C |
| Zone 9 | 20°F to 30°F | –7°C to –1°C |
| Zone 10 | 30°F to 40°F | –1°C to 4–C |
| Zone 11 | 40°F and above | 4°C and up |

# Where to Find Seeds and Other Resources

Vegetable seeds are available seemingly everywhere in the spring. From grocery stores to local garden centers, home centers, and hardware stores, everyone seems to sell seed packets. If you're interested in the standard vegetable varieties, these locations are great places to get them. However, if you're interested in some of the more unusual varieties mentioned in this book, try the catalog companies listed in this appendix.

You may also want to avoid seed starting altogether and buy transplants. Local garden and home centers offer a broad selection of vegetable and fruit plants for sale in spring. Also, some catalog companies now offer transplants through the mail. In this appendix, I indicate which companies currently offer transplants through their catalogs.

I also include a list of fruit and berry nurseries for a broader selection and cheaper prices than what you may find locally, and a list of tool and equipment suppliers for many of the products and devices mentioned in this book. Part of the fun of gardening is shopping for new stuff, so write away for as many catalogs as you're interested in. Some companies charge a small fee for their catalogs, but most are free. Many catalogs are now online, so you can browse and buy via the Internet.

# *Vegetables, herbs, and flowers*

**Abundant Life Seed Foundation,** P.O. Box 772, Port Townsend, WA 98368; phone 360-385-5660, fax 360-385-7455; e-mail abundant@olypen.com. Nonprofit seed organization dedicated to the preservation of unusual heirloom vegetable, herb, grain, and flower seeds. The organization offers organically grown and untreated seeds and sponsors the World Seed Fund, dedicated to helping Third World farmers obtain seeds.

**Bethlehem Seed Co.,** P.O. Box 1351, Bethlehem, PA 18018; phone 610-954-5443; Web site www.bethlehemseed .com. Broad selection of vegetables and flower seeds at inexpensive prices.

**Bountiful Gardens,** 18001 Shafer Ranch Rd., Willits, CA 95490; phone or fax 707-459-6410; e-mail: bountiful@zapcom .net. Specialize in untreated, unusual varieties of vegetables, cover crops, herbs, and grains.

**Burrell Seed Co.,** P.O. Box 150, Rocky Ford, CO 81067; phone 719-254-3318, fax 719-254-3319. A complete line of vegetables, specializing in cantaloupes and watermelons.

**The Cook's Garden,** P.O. Box 535, Londonderry, VT 05148; phone 800-457-9703, fax 800-457-9705; Web site www.cooksgarden.com. Wide selection of culinary vegetables, herbs, and flowers, including European and hard-to-find salad greens.

**DeGiorgi Seed Co.,** 6011 'N' St., Omaha, NE 68117-1634; phone 800-858-2580, fax 402-731-8475. A full line of vegetables and flowers. Catalog $2.

**Dill's Atlantic Giant Pumpkins,** Howard Dill, 400 College Rd., Windsor, N.S., Canada B0N 2T0; phone 902-798-2728. Seed for the world's largest pumpkins — 'Atlantic Giant' and other pumpkin varieties.

**Dixondale Farms,** P.O. Box 127, Carrizo Springs, TX 78834; phone 210-876-2430, fax 210-876-9640. Specialists in sweet onion plants.

**Evergreen Y.H. Enterprises,** P.O. Box 17538, Anaheim, CA 92817. Specialists in Oriental vegetables.

**Fedco Seeds,** P.O. Box 520, Waterville, ME 04903-0520; phone 207-873-7333. A full line of vegetables including a good selection of potatoes. Also offers books, tools, and products.

**Ferry-Morse Seed Co.,** P.O. Box 488, Fulton, KY 42041-0488; phone 800-283-6400, fax 800-273-2700; Web site Gardenet.com/Ferry-Morse. Full-line seed and nursery catalog.

**Filaree Farm,** 182 Conconully Hwy., Okanogan, WA 98840; phone 509-422-6940. Catalog $2. More than 350 varieties of garlic.

**Fox Hollow Seed Co.,** P.O. Box 148, McGrann, PA 16236-0148; phone 888-548-7333, fax 724-543-5751. Heirloom and unusual vegetable, herb, and flower seeds. Catalog $1.

**Garden City Seeds,** 778 Hwy. 93 N., Hamilton, MT 59840-9448; phone 406-961-4837, fax 406-961-4877; e-mail seeds@juno.com. Specialists in open-pollinated, short-season vegetable seeds.

**Gurney Seed Company,** 110 Capital St., Yankton, SD 57079; phone 605-665-1930, fax 605-665-9718. Full-line seed and nursery catalog.

**Harris Seeds,** 60 Saginaw Dr., P.O. Box 22960, Rochester, NY 14692-2960; phone 800-514-4441, fax 716-442-9386; Web site www.Harriseeds.com. Vegetable and flower seeds, gardening accessories, and vegetable transplants.

**Heirloom Seeds,** P.O. Box 245, W. Elizabeth, PA 15088-0245. A small company specializing in heirloom seeds. Catalog $1.

**Henry Field's Seed & Nursery Co.,** 415 North Burnett Rd., Shenandoah, IA 51602; phone 605-665-9391, fax 605-665-2601. Basic vegetable, flower, and fruit catalogs with some products.

**High Altitude Gardens,** P.O. Box 1048, Hailey, ID 83333-1048; phone 208-788-4363, fax 208-788-3452; Web site www.seedsave.org. More than 180 varieties of open-pollinated vegetables for high-altitude gardens. Also a good selection of Russian heirloom tomatoes, herbs, flowers, and tools.

**Jersey Asparagus Farms, Inc.,** 105 Porchtown Rd., Pittsgrove, NJ 08318; phone 800-499-0013, fax 609-358-6127; Web site www.jerseyasparagus.com. Specialists in asparagus and strawberries.

**Johnny's Selected Seeds,** Foss Hill Rd., Albion, ME 04910; phone 207-437-4301, fax 207-437-2165. Web site www.johnnyseeds.com. Vegetable, herb, cover crop, and flower seeds. Also vegetable seeds for sprouting.

**Jung Seeds,** 335 S. High St., Randolph, WI 53957; phone 800-247-5864, fax 800-692-5864. Wide selection of vegetable seeds and products.

**Kilgore Seed Co.,** 1400 W First St., Sanford, FL 32771; phone 407-323-6630. A complete line of vegetable and flower seeds for Florida.

**Liberty Seed Company,** P.O. Box 806, New Philadelphia, OH 44663; phone 800-541-6022, fax 330-364-6415; Web site www.libertyseed.com. A complete line of vegetable and flower seeds including the company's own sweet corn varieties.

**Lockhart Seeds Inc.,** P.O. Box 1361, Stockton, CA 95205; phone 209-466-4401. Full line of vegetable and cover crop seeds, especially varieties adapted for California.

**Native Seeds/SEARCH,** 526 North 4th Ave., Tucson, AZ 85705; phone 520-622-5561, fax 520-622-5591; Web site desert.net/seeds/home/htm. Specialize in Native American varieties of vegetables adapted to the desert Southwest.

**Nichols Garden Nursery,** 1190 N. Pacific Hwy., Albany, OR 97321-4598; phone 541-928-9280, fax 541-967-8406; Web site www.pacificharbor.com/nichols/. Asian and unusual vegetables and good selection of herb seeds and plants.

**Nourse Farms, Inc.,** 41 River Rd., South Deerfield, MA 01373; phone 413-665-2658; Web site www.noursefarms.com. Good selection of small fruits and asparagus.

**Park Seed Company,** Cokesbury Rd., Greenwood, SC 29647-0001; phone 800-845-3369, fax 800-275-9941; Web site www.parkseed.com. Wide variety of vegetable, herb, and flower seeds. Good selection for the South.

**The Pepper Gal,** P.O. Box 23006, Ft. Lauderdale, FL 33307-3006; phone 954-537-5540, fax 954-566-2208. More than 250 varieties of sweet and hot peppers listed. Catalog $2.

**Piedmont Plant Co.,** P.O. Box 424, Albany, GA 31702; phone 800-541-5185, fax 912-432-2888; e-mail piedmont@surfsouth.com. Wide selection of field-grown vegetable transplants shipped through the mail.

**Pinetree Garden Seeds,** P.O. Box 300, New Gloucester, ME 04260; phone 207-926-3400, fax 888-527-3337; Web site www.superseeds.com. Large selection of vegetables, herbs, and flowers. Small-sized packets at low prices. Also, tools and books.

**R. H. Shumway's,** P.O. Box 1, Graniteville, SC 29829; phone 803-663-7277, fax 888-437-2733. Wide selection of vegetable seeds.

**Richters Herbs,** Goodwood, Ontario, Canada L0C 1A0; phone 905-640-6677, fax 905-640-6641; Web site www.richters.com. An extensive selection of herb seeds, plants, and products.

**Ronniger's Seed and Plant Company,** P.O. Box 307, Ellensburg, WA 98926; phone 509-925-6052. More than 60 varieties of potatoes; also a good selection of onions and garlic. Catalog $2.

**Santa Barbara Heirloom Nursery,** P.O. Box 4235, Santa Barbara, CA 93140; phone 805-968-5444, fax 805-562-1248; Web site www.heirloom.com/heirloom/. Wide selection of heirloom vegetable varieties sold and shipped as transplants.

**Seed Dreams,** P.O. Box 1476, Santa Cruz, CA 95061-1476; phone 408-458-9252. A small company specializing in heirloom vegetables and grains.

**Seed Savers Heritage Farm,** 3076 North Winn Rd., Decorah, IA 52101; phone 319-382-5990, fax 319-382-5872. Offers a good selection of heirloom vegetable varieties from the United States and Europe. Associated with the largest nonprofit seed-saving organization in the United States: Seed Savers Exchange.

**Seeds Blum,** HC 33 Idaho City Stage, Boise, ID 83706; phone 800-528-3658, fax 208-338-5658; Web site www.seedsblum.com. Large selection of heirloom vegetables, herbs, and flowers. Catalog $3.

**Seeds of Change,** P.O. Box 15700, Santa Fe, NM 87506-5700; phone 888-762-7333, fax 888-329-4762; Web site www.seedsofchange.com. Organic, open-pollinated vegetable, flower, and herb seeds and seeds for sprouting.

**Shepherd's Garden Seeds,** 30 Irene St., Torrington, CT 06790; phone 860-482-3638, fax 860-482-0532. Web site www.shepherdseeds.com. Features European and Asian gourmet vegetable and herb varieties and recipes.

**Steele Plant Co.,** Gleason, TN 38229; phone 901-648-5476. Specialists in sweet potato plants.

**Southern Exposure Seed Exchange,** P.O. Box 170, Earlysville, VA 22936; phone 804-973-4703, fax 804-973-8717; Web site www.southernexposure.com. Over 500 varieties of heirloom and traditional vegetables, flowers, and herbs especially adapted in the South. Catalog $2.

**Southern Seeds,** P.O. Box 803, Lutz, FL 33548. Many varieties of vegetables adapted in the South and some tropical fruits such as bananas.

**Stokes Seeds, Inc.,** P.O. Box 548, Buffalo, NY 14240; phone 716-695-6980, fax 888-834-3334; Web site www.stokeseeds.com. Complete listing of flower and vegetable seeds, including cultural information.

**Sunrise Enterprises,** P.O. Box 1960, Chesterfield, VA 23832; phone 804-796-5796, fax 804-796-6735; Web site commercial.visi.net/sunrise/. Oriental vegetable seed specialists. Catalog $2.

**Territorial Seed Company,** 20 Palmer Ave., Cottage Grove, OR 97424; phone 541-942-9547, fax 888-657-3131; Web site www.territorial-seed.com/. Vegetable, herb, and flower seeds, especially varieties suited to the Pacific Northwest. Also sell and ship transplants.

**Thompson & Morgan Seed Co.,** P.O. Box 1308, Jackson, NJ 08527-2225; phone 800-274-7333, fax 908-363-9356; Web site www.thompson-morgan.com. Wide selection of English flowers and vegetables. The company also sells and ships transplants.

**Tomato Growers Supply Co.,** P.O. Box 2237, Fort Myers, FL 33902; phone 888-478-7333, fax 888-768-3476. More than 400 kinds of tomatoes and peppers.

**Totally Tomatoes,** P.O. Box 1626, Augusta, GA 30903; phone 803-663-0016, fax 888-477-7333. More than 350 varieties of tomatoes and peppers.

**Underwood Gardens,** 4N381 Maple Ave., Bensenville, IL 60106; fax 888-832-7041. Specialize in heirloom vegetables and flowers. Catalog $1.

**Vermont Bean Seed Company,** 32 Garden Ln., Fair Haven, VT 05743; phone 802-273-3400, fax 803-500-7333. Specialize in more than 100 varieties of beans, plus other vegetable seeds.

**Vesey's Seed Ltd.,** York, Prince Edward Island, Canada C0A 1P0; phone 800 363-7333, fax 800-686-0329; Web site www.veseys.com. Wide selection of vegetable and flower seeds adapted to short-growing-season conditions.

**W. Atlee Burpee & Co.,** 300 Park Ave., Warminster, PA 18974; phone 800-333-5808, fax 800-487-5530; Web site www.burpee.com. Wide selection of flower and vegetable seeds, plants, and supplies. Also has a separate heirloom vegetable catalog.

**Wild Garden Seeds,** Shoulder to Shoulder Farm, Box 1509, Philomath, OR 97370; phone 541-929-4068. A selection of vegetables and beneficial-insect-attracting plants bred on the farm. Catalog $4.

**Willhite Seed Inc,** P.O. Box 23, Poolville, TX 76487; phone 800-828-1840, fax 817-599-5843. Good selection of vegetable seeds for warm growing areas. Special section on Indian vegetable varieties.

**William Dam Seeds,** P.O. Box 8400, Dundas, Ontario, Canada L9H 6M1; phone 905-628-6641, fax 905-627-1729. A full line of vegetable, flower, and wildflower seeds and some products for Northern gardeners.

**Wood Prairie Farm,** RFD 1, Box 164, Bridgewater, ME 04735; phone or fax 800-829-9765. Specialize in potato varieties.

## Seed-Savers

Following are some seed-saving organizations and small, nonprofit organizations specializing in historic and unusual heirloom varieties. The seed-saving organizations often have seed swaps for members so that you can share and try unusual heirloom varieties from around the world, and they offer special programs promoting the reintroduction of heirloom plants. You may have to become a member to receive the seeds.

**Abundant Life Seed Foundation,** see description in the preceding section.

**Eastern Plant Conservancy,** 222 Main St., Box 451, Great Barrington, MA 01230; phone 413-229-8316; Web site www. berkshire.net/ensc seedmain.html. A seed-saving organization dedicated to the preservation of rare, Native American varieties of vegetables and medicinal plants of the eastern United States.

**Genesee County Museum,** P.O. Box 310, Mumford, NY 14511-0310; phone 716-538-6822. Dedicated to the preservation of nineteenth-century heirloom vegetable varieties grown in the Genesse, New York, area.

**Landis Valley Museum and Heirloom Seed Project,** Landis Valley Museum, 2451 Kissel Hill Rd., Lancaster, PA 17601-4899; phone 717-569-0401. Dedicated to the preservation of heirloom vegetable, flower, and herb varieties grown by the Pennsylvania Dutch farmers. Catalog $4.

**Native Seed /SEARCH,** see the description in the preceding section.

**Old Sturbridge Village Heirloom Seeds and Plants,** 1 Old Sturbridge Village Rd., Sturbridge, MA 01566; 508-347-3362, fax 508-347-5275. A listing of vegetable, flower, and herb varieties grown in Colonial New England.

**Seed Savers Exchange,** see description under Seed Savers Heritage Farm in the preceding section.

**Thomas Jefferson Center for Historic Plants,** Monticello, P.O. Box 316, Charlottesville, VA 22902; phone 804-984-9821, fax 804-977-6140; Web site www.monticello.org. A listing of flowers, trees, shrubs, vegetable, herbs, and fruits grown at Thomas Jefferson's home in Virginia.

## Fruits and berries

**Bay Laurel Nursery,** 2500 El Camino Real, Atascadero, CA 93422; phone 805-466-3406, fax 805-466-6455. Good selection of apples, apricots, cherries, nectarines, peaches, pears, and plums for the Southwest.

**Brittingham Plant Farms,** P.O. Box 2538, Salisbury, MD 21802; phone 410-749-5153, fax 800-749-5148. Strawberries, raspberries, blackberries, blueberries, asparagus, and grapes. Catalog $1.

**Edible Landscaping,** 316 Spirit Ridge Ln., P.O. Box 77, Afton, VA 22920; phone 800-524-4156, fax 804-361-1916; Web site www.eat-it.com. Good selection of unusual fruits such as kiwi, fig, and citrus.

**Indiana Berry & Plant Co.,** 5218 W. 500 South, Dept. NG-96, Huntingburg, IN 47542; phone 800-295-2226, fax 812-683-2004. Strawberries, blueberries, raspberries, blackberries, asparagus, and grapes.

**Ison's Nursery & Vineyards,** 6855 Newnan Hwy., Brooks, GA 30205; phone 800-733-0324, fax 770-599-6970. Mucho muscadines (grapes for the southern U.S.), plus dozens of other fruits, large and small.

**Johnson Nursery,** Rt. 5, Box 29J, Hwy. 52 E., Ellijay, GA 30540; phone 888-276-3187, fax 706-276-3187. Hardy and antique fruit trees. Also grapes, berries, persimmons, and supplies.

**Just Fruits,** 30 St. Francis St., Crawfordville, FL 32327; phone 904-926-5644. Good selection of tropical fruits, citrus, persimmon, and many other fruit varieties adapted to warm growing regions.

**Miller Nurseries,** 5060 West Lake Rd., Canandaigua, NY 14424; phone 800-836-9630 or 716-396-2647, fax 716-396-2154. Complete selection of fruiting plants, including many varieties of antique dwarf apples.

**Northwoods Retail Nursery,** 27634 S. Oglesby Rd., Canby, OR 97013; phone 503-266-5432, fax 800-924-9030; Web site www.northwoodsplants.com. Unusual hardy edibles and ornamentals.

**Pacific Tree Farms,** 4301 Lynwood Dr., Chula Vista, CA 91910; phone 619-422-2400, fax 619-426-6759. Extensive collection of citrus, other exotic fruit plants, and rare and unusual trees and shrubs. Catalog $2.

**Raintree Nursery,** 391 Butts Rd., Morton, WA 98356; phone 360-496-6400, fax 360-496-6465. Fruits, nuts, berries, and bamboo.

**Stark Bros.' Nursery,** P.O. Box 10, Hwy. 54 W., Louisiana, MO 63353; phone 800-325-4180, fax 573-754-5290; Web site www.starkbros.com. Fruit trees, berries, and landscape plants.

**Womacks Nursery,** Rt. 1, P.O. Box 80, DeLeon, TX 76444-9631; phone 254-893-6497, fax 254-893-3400. Fruit and pecan trees.

# Tools and supplies

**A. M. Leonard, Inc.,** 241 Fox Dr., Piqua, OH 45356; phone 800-543-8955, fax 800-433-0633; Web site www.amleo.com. Professional nursery and gardening supplies. Catalog $3.

**Arbico,** P.O. Box 4247 CRB, Tucson, AZ 85738-1247; phone 800-827-2847, fax 520-825-2038; Web site www.usit.net/hp/bionet/gardencat.html. Beneficial insects and other environmentally friendly products for pest control.

**Charley's Greenhouse Supply,** 1569 Memorial Highway, Mount Vernon, WA 98273; phone 800-322-4707, fax 360-428-0310; Web site www.charleysgreenhouse.com. Good listing of small greenhouses and greenhouse supplies. Catalog $2.

**Fungi Perfecti,** P.O. Box 7634, Olympia, WA 98507; phone 206-426-9292, fax 206-426-9377; Web site www.fungi.com. Full line of mushroom-growing kits and supplies.

**Gardener's Supply Company,** 128 Intervale Rd., Burlington, VT 05401; phone 800-863-1700, fax 800-551-6712; Web site www.gardeners.com. Hundreds of innovative tools and products for gardeners.

**Gardens Alive,** 5100 Schenley Pl., Dept. 5672, Lawrenceburg, IN 47025; phone 812-537-8650, fax 812-537-5108. One of the largest organic pest control suppliers.

**Gempler's,** 100 Countryside Dr., P.O. Box 270, Belleville, WI 53508; phone 800-382-8473, fax 800-551-1128; Web site www.gemplers.com. Extensive listing of tools and products for the professional and amateur gardener.

**Harmony Farm Supply,** P.O. Box 460, Graton, CA 95444; phone 707-823-9125, fax 707-823-1734; Web site www.harmonyfarm.com. Drip and sprinkler irrigation equipment, organic fertilizers, beneficial insects, power tools, and composting supplies. Catalog $7.

**Hoop House Greenhouse Kits,** Dept. N, 1358 Route 28, South Yarmouth, MA 02664; phone 800-760-5192. Hoop house greenhouse kits.

**Hydrofarm,** 3135 Kerner Blvd., San Rafael, CA 94901; phone 800-634-9999, fax 415-459-3710; Web site www. hydrofarm.com. One of the largest selections of indoor growing lights and hydroponic supplies available.

**IPM Labs,** P.O. Box 300, Locke, NY 13092-0300; phone 315-497-2063, fax 315-297-3129; Web site www.ipmlabs.com. Specialists in beneficial insects.

**Kinsman Company,** River Rd., Pt. Pleasant, PA 18950; phone 800-733-4146, fax 215-297-0450. Gardening supplies and quality tools.

**Langenbach,** 644 Enterprise Ave., Galesburg, IL 61401; phone 800-362-1991, fax 800-362-4490. Fine-quality tools and garden gifts.

**Lee Valley Tools Ltd.,** P.O. Box 1780, Ogdensburg, NY 13669-6780; phone 800-871-8158, fax 800-513-7885; Web site www.leevalley.com. Quality tools and products for home gardeners.

**Mellinger's, Inc.,** 2310 W. South Range Rd., N. Lima, OH 44452; phone 800-321-7444, fax 330-549-3716; Web site www.mellingers.com. Broad selection of gardening tools, supplies, fertilizers, and pest controls as well as seeds and plants.

**Natural Gardening,** 217 San Anselmo Ave., San Anselmo, CA 94960; phone 707-766-9303, fax 707-766-9747; Web site www.naturalgardening.com. Organic gardening supplies, seeds, and transplants.

**Peaceful Valley Farm Supply,** P.O. Box 2209, Grass Valley, CA 95945; phone 888-784-4769, fax 530-272-4794; Web site www.groworganic.com. Large selection of organic gardening supplies and quality tools.

**Planet Natural,** 1612 Gold Ave., Bozeman, MT 59772; phone 800-285-6656, fax 406-587-0223; Web site www. planetnatural.com. Environmentally friendly products for lawn, garden, and farm.

**Plow & Hearth,** P.O. Box 5000, Madison, VA 22727; phone 800-627-1712. A wide variety of home and garden products.

**Smith & Hawken,** 2 Arbor Ln., P.O. Box 6900, Florence, KY 41022-6900; phone 800-776-3336, fax 606-727-1166; Web site www.smith-hawken.com. Wide selection of high-end tools, furniture, plants, and outdoor clothing.

**Snowpond Farm Supply,** RR 2, Box 4075, Belgrade, ME 04917-9441; phone 800-768-9998, fax 207-872-0929; Web site www. snowpond.com. Good selection of tools, organic gardening supplies, pest controls, and potatoes.

**The Urban Farmer Store,** 2833 Vicente St., San Francisco, CA 94116; phone 800-753-3747 or 415-661-7827. Garden tools and drip irrigation supplies. Catalog $1.

**Walt Nicke Co.,** P.O. Box 433, Topsfield, MA 01983; phone 800-822-4114, fax 508-887-9853; Web site www.gardentalk.com. Good selection of gardening tools.

**Worm's Way Garden Center,** 7850 North Hwy. 37, Bloomington, IN 47404; phone 800-274-9676, fax 800-316-1264; Web site www.wormsway.com. Wide variety of gardening supplies including irrigation supplies, pest controls, mushroom kits, organic fertilizers, and of course, worms for composting.

# U.S. and Canadian Master Gardeners

The umbrella organization for all the regional master gardener programs is Master Gardeners International, 424 N. River Dr., Woodstock, VA 22664; phone 540-459-5656. If you write for information, include a self-addressed, stamped envelope. The e-mail address is mgic@capaccess.org. Following is a list of contact persons and telephone numbers for each state and participating province:

**Alabama:** Mary Beth Musgrove, 334-844-5481

**Alaska:** Wayne Vandre, 907-279-6575

**Arizona:** Lucy Bradley, 602-470-8086, ext. 323

**Arkansas:** Janet Carson, 501-671-2174

**British Columbia:** MG Coordinator, Van Dusen Botanical Gardens, 604-257-8672

**California:** Pam Elam, 209-456-7554, or Nancy Garrison, 408-299-2638

**Colorado:** Marlo Meakins, 970-491-7887

**Connecticut:** Norman Gauthler, 860-241-4940

**Delaware:** Susan Barton, 302-831-2532

**District of Columbia:** M. Khan, 202-274-6907

**Florida:** Kathleen C. Ruppert, 352-392-8836

**Georgia:** Bob Westerfield, 912-875-6269

**Hawaii:** H. Dale Sato, 808-453-6059

**Idaho:** Dr. Michael Colt, 208-722-6701

**Illinois:** Floyd A. Giles, 217-333-2125

**Indiana:** B. Rosie Lerner, 765-494-1311

**Iowa:** Linda Naeve, 515-294-2710

**Kansas:** Charles Marr, 785-532-6173

**Kentucky:** Sharon Bale, 606-257-8605

**Louisiana:** Dr. Tom Koske, 504-388-4141

**Maine:** Lois Berg Stack, 207-581-2949

**Maryland:** Jon Traunfeld, 800-342-2507 in state; 410-531-5572 out of state (Monday through Friday, 8 a.m. to 1 p.m.)

**Massachusetts:** Bruce Roberts, 617-536-0916, or Suzanne A. Siegel, 617-536-9280

**Michigan:** Mary McLellan, 517-353-3774

**Minnesota:** Dr. Mary H. Meyer, 612-443-2460, ext. 639

**Mississippi:** Dr. Freddie Rasberry, Mississippi State University, 601-325-2311

**Missouri:** Denny Shrock, 573-882-9633

**Montana:** Bob Gough, 406-994-6523

**Nebraska:** Susan Schoneweis, 402-472-1128

**Nevada:** Richard Post, 702-784-4848

**New Hampshire:** Virginia Hast, 603-796-2151

**New Jersey:** Rutgers Cooperative Extension, 908-526-6293

**New Mexico:** Dr. Curtis Smith, 505-275-2576

**New York:** Robert Kozlowski, 607-255-1791

**North Carolina:** Larry Bass, 919-515-1200

**North Dakota:** Dr. Ronald Smith, 701-231-8161

**Ohio:** Mary Riofrio, 614-292-8326

**Oklahoma:** Dale Hillock, 405-744-5158

**Ontario:** Ramona Cameletti, 519-826-3115

**Oregon:** Ann Marie VanDerZanden, 541-737-2503

**Pennsylvania:** Toni Bilik, 814-863-7716

**Rhode Island:** Roseanne Sherry, 401-792-2900

**Saskatchewan:** Sara Williams, 306-966-5593

**South Carolina:** Robert F. Polomski, 864-656-2604

**South Dakota:** David F. Graper, 605-688-6253

**Tennessee:** Dr. David Sams, 901-425-4721

**Utah:** Dr. Dan Drost, 801-797-2258

**Vermont:** Robyn Osiecki, 802-656-9262

**Virginia:** Sheri Dorn, 540-231-6524

**Washington:** Van Bobbitt, 206-840-4547

**West Virginia:** John Jett, 304-293-4801

**Wisconsin:** Helen Harrison, 608-262-1749

**Wyoming:** Rodney Davis, 307-235-9400

# Web Sites about Vegetables

The following sites offer a broad spectrum of general gardening information and links.

**California Garden Calendar** (www.geocities.com/RainForest/1079/calendar.html): A detailed monthly calendar of gardening chores for Californian gardeners. Links to other sites.

**Garden Escape** (www.garden.com): One of the largest online sources for all your gardening needs, from plants to tools to information.

**Garden Guides** (www.gardenguides.com): This site provides good information on vegetable and herb gardening, descriptions of and links to selected Internet gardening sites, Web pages, and discussion groups.

**Gardening.com** (www.gardening.com): This site features a searchable plant encyclopedia with over 1,500 plants; access to the *Ortho Problem Solver,* an illustrated pest and disease guide; a magazine rack, which includes gardening articles from your favorite publications; and information about obtaining gardening software.

**GardenMart** (www.gardenmart.com): This site has a searchable database, an "ask the experts" section, and an electronic bulletin board. The site has links to horticultural resources for areas of interest such as organic gardening and roses and links to take you to other seed and gardening supply companies.

**GardenNet** (www.GardenNet.com): This weekly online newsletter — The Ardent Gardener — features articles, tips, and a question-and-answer section.

**GardenWeb's The Spider's Web** (www.gardenweb.com/spdrsweb): This site provides links to many, many other gardening Web sites.

**National Gardening Association** (www.garden.org): My personal favorite! Look to this site for everything from the largest national association of home gardeners, including several years of *National Gardening* magazine, applications for garden grants, an online newsletter, and more.

**USDA Gardening Page**
(`www.usda.gov/news/garden.htm`):
This site has multiple sections including
a horticultural solutions section, lawn
and garden care, an eco-regions map,
and more.

**USDA Partners of the Cooperative State
Research, Education, and Extension
Service** (`www.reeusda.gov/new/
statepartners/usa.htm`): A directory
of land-grant universities, which are
state partners of the Cooperative
Extension Service, with links to all
partners. Here's a quick way to find your
state's Cooperative Extension Web site.

**Weekend Gardener** (`www.chestnut-
sw.com/seeds/vegseed.htm`): A site
dedicated to seed-starting vegetables
and herbs. A great place to get information on starting off on the right foot.

## State sites

Many state Cooperative Extension
Services have great information on
home vegetable gardening. Here are
some of my favorites.

**North Carolina State University:**
`www2.ncsu.edu/ncsu/cals/
sustainable/peet/`

**Ohio State University:** `www.ag.ohio-
state.edu/~ohioline/hyg-fact/
1000/1609.html`

**Oregon State University:**
`www.orst.edu/Dept/NWREC/
vegindex.html`

**Purdue University:**
`www.hort.purdue.edu/rhodcv/
hort410/`

**Texas A & M University:** `aggie-
horticulture.tamu.edu/
PLANTanswers/vegetables/`

**University of Arizona:**
`ag.arizona.edu/maricopa/garden/`

**University of California:**
`vric.ucdavis.edu/vrichome/html/
selectnewtopic.garden.htm`

**University of Florida:**
`hammock.ifas.ufl.edu/`

**University of Illinois:**
`www.ag.uiuc.edu/~robsond/
solutions/horticulture/
veggies.html`

## Cyber-veggies

The following Web sites have
information just on the specific
vegetables mentioned. Some are
company sponsored (such as
Sunspiced Produce), some are
organizations (such as the Leafy
Greens Council), and others are just
personal sites (such as B's Cucumber Page). Many have great links to
other sites. The following list is only
the beginning, but if you have a
favorite vegetable and need to know
more. . . .

**Beans:** Bean Ref, at `scaffold.
biologie.uni-kl.de/Beanref/
prodcon.htm`

**Cabbage:** The Cabbage Page, at
`discworld.imaginary.com:5678/
cabbage/`

**Carrots:** The Carrot, at
`www.carbon.org/hydro/book/food/
carrot.htm`

**Cucumbers**: B's Cucumber Page, at
`www.lpl.arizona.edu/~bcohen/
cucumbers/info.html`

**Greens**: Leafy Greens Council, at www.leafy-greens.org/

**Onions:** Sunspiced World of the Onion, at www.sunspiced.com/olinks.html

**Peas:** Snow and Sugar Snap Peas (Australian), at www.agric.nsw. gov.au/Hort/Veg_pub 011999.00186.html

**Peppers:** The World of Hot Peppers, at www.wfu.edu/users/patelpp/ Peppers.html

**Potatoes:** Sunspiced World of the Potato, at www.sunspiced.com/ plinks.html

**Pumpkins:** World Class Giant Pumpkins, at www.athenet.net/~dang/ pumpkins.html

**Tomatoes:** Growing Big Tomatoes, at www.njtomato.com/indice.html, Power Tomato Growing, at www.ars. usda.gov/is/tom/, and On-Line Tomato Vine, tomato.vbutler.com/

**Squash and Cucurbits:** Cucurbit-Related World Wide Web sites, at probe. nalusda.gov:8000/otherdocs/cgc/ tcn/links.html

# Magazines

*Herb Companion,* published bimonthly. Interweave Press, 201 East Fourth Street, Loveland, CO 80587-5655; phone 800-272-2193. $24. Subscriptions: Herb Companion, phone 800-645-3675; Web site www.interweave.com.

*Kitchen Garden,* published bimonthly. Taunton Press, 63 S. Main St., Newtown, CT 06470-5506; phone; 800- 283-7252 or 203-426-8171; Web site www. taunton.com/kg. $24. To order by phone, call 800-888-8286.

*National Gardening,* published bimonthly. National Gardening Association, 180 Flynn Ave., Burlington, VT 05401; phone 802-863-1308; Web site www.garden. org. $18.95. Subscriptions: P.O. Box 51106, Boulder, CO 80323-1106; phone 800-727-9097.

*Organic Gardening,* published eight times a year. Rodale Press Inc., 33 E. Minor St., Emmaus, PA 18098; phone 610-967-5171; Web site www.organicgardening.com. $19.96.

# Index

onions *(continued)*
  spacing and thinning
    seedlings, 83
  spacing and yield guide,
    25, 321
  storing, 299, 301
  successive plantings of, 264
  varieties, 77–79
open-pollinated varieties
  described, 15
  seeds from, 300
  tomatoes, 43
orach (mountain spinach), 146
oregano, 186–187, 263
organic gardening, 1, 224
*Organic Gardening* magazine
  (Rodale Press), 338
organic materials, for garden
  paths, 27, 28
organic matter as soil
  amendment, 225–227
organic mulches, 242–243
Oriental chives, 183–184
Oriental stir-fry theme
  gardens, 12
oscillating hoes, 308
overwintering, 76, 78

● *P* ●

pac choi, 12, 172
pansies, with rhubarb for
  color, 10
parsley
  as attractor of beneficial
    insects, 278
  average days to germination
    and maturity, 321
  frost tolerance, 321
  growing, 187–188
  in ornamental edible
    gardens, 10, 11
  in salad greens gardens, 11
  spacing and yield guide,
    25, 321
parsnips
  average days to germination
    and maturity, 321
  frost tolerance, 321
  growing, 172–173
  harvesting, 296
  preference for direct
    sowing, 199
  spacing and yield guide,
    25, 321
  storing, 299

paths
  suggested surface materials,
    27–28
  weeding, 258
  width considerations, 10, 27
pea aphids, 104
pea enation virus, 104
Peaceful Valley Farm
  Supply, 260
peanuts
  growing, 173–174
  harvesting, 296
  planting schedule guidelines,
    36, 38
  storing, 299
peas
  average days to germination
    and maturity, 321
  in containers, 98, 271
  as cool-season vegetable, 29
  critical watering periods, 235
  fertilizing, 99–100, 253
  field peas as cover crop, 261
  filling out, 98
  frost tolerance, 321
  harvesting, 103–104, 296
  mulching, 102
  origins and history, 92
  pest prevention
    measures, 104
  planting schedule guidelines,
    34, 35, 36, 38
  preference for cool weather,
    91, 99
  preference for direct sowing,
    199, 211
  pregerminating, 100
  in raised beds, 99
  soil preparation, 99–100
  spacing and yield guide,
    25, 26, 321
  storing, 299
  supporting sprawling
    plants, 255
  supporting vines, 101–102
  varieties, 97–99
  weeding with care, 102
  when to plant, 100
peat moss, disadvantages as
  mulch, 243
peat pots for seedlings,
  200–201, 206, 210
pelletized pulverized limestone, 225
pepper maggots, 70

peppers. *See also* green
    peppers; red peppers
  average days to germination
    and maturity, 321
  in containers, 58, 63, 271
  critical watering periods, 235
  fertilizing, 68–69, 253
  frost tolerance, 321
  harvesting, 69–70, 296
  hot, 61–64
  in Mexican salsa theme
    gardens, 11
  mulching, 68
  nutrition information, 71
  origins and history, 58
  ornamental and edible, 64
  pest prevention
    measures, 70
  in pizza toppings theme
    gardens, 12
  planting schedule guidelines,
    34, 35, 36, 38
  popularity and new
    varieties, 57
  in raised beds, 68
  recipe, 72
  in rows, 22
  spacing and yield guide,
    26, 321
  starting, 66–67
  storing, 299
  sun requirements, 19
  sweet bell varieties, 58–60
  transplanting seedlings, 68
  watering, 68
perennials
  asparagus, 158
  cover crops, 260
  onions, 79
  peppers and eggplant, 67
  rhubarb, 176–177
*Perennials For Dummies,* 10
pest prevention measures
  advantages of diversity in
    gardens, 278
  advantages of good garden-
    ing practices, 287
  avoid overhead watering, 287
  beans, 104–105
  beneficial insects for pest
    control, 16, 260, 278–279
  biological controls, 284–285
  boards for cutworms, 281
  cabbage, 137
  cauliflower, 137

# Notes

# Notes

# SAVE 33% on a one-year subscription to **National Gardening** magazine

No other magazine gets to the root of planting and growing like *National Gardening*. That's because here at *National Gardening*, we haven't forgotten what down-to-earth, practical gardening is all about. And we're talking about all kinds of gardening—fruits, vegetables, roses, perennials— you name it and *National Gardening* knows it.

We bring you hands-on growing information you can use to become a more successful gardener. Make smarter variety selections. Time your plantings more efficiently for better results. Extend your growing season. Fertilize your garden more effectively, and protect it from pests using safe, sensible, and effective methods. Harvest healthier, tastier, more beautiful crops of all kinds.

Plus: Swap tips and seeds with other avid gardeners from around the country and around the world. Choose the best, most practical gardening products for your needs. Get expert gardening advice. Let the gardening experts at NGA help you grow everything more successfully!

**Special offer to ...*For Dummies*® readers:**
For a limited time, you're entitled to receive a one-year (6 issue) subscription to *National Gardening* magazine—for just $12! That's 33% off the basic subscription price. Just fill out the coupon and mail it to the address listed below, today!

**Published by the National Gardening Association • *http://www.garden.org***

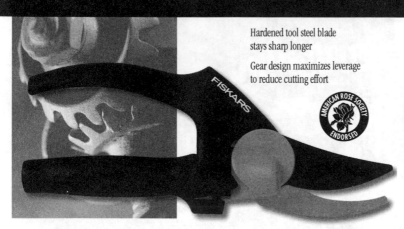

# IDG BOOKS WORLDWIDE
# BOOK REGISTRATION

## We want to hear from you!

**Register This Book and Win!**

Visit **http://my2cents.dummies.com** to register this book and tell us how you liked it!

- Get entered in our monthly prize giveaway.

- Give us feedback about this book — tell us what you like best, what you like least, or maybe what you'd like to ask the author and us to change!

- Let us know any other *...For Dummies*® topics that interest you.

Your feedback helps us determine what books to publish, tells us what coverage to add as we revise our books, and lets us know whether we're meeting your needs as a *...For Dummies* reader. You're our most valuable resource, and what you have to say is important to us!

Not on the Web yet? It's easy to get started with *Dummies 101*®: *The Internet For Windows*® *98* or *The Internet For Dummies*®, 5th Edition, at local retailers everywhere.

Or let us know what you think by sending us a letter at the following address:

*...For Dummies* Book Registration
Dummies Press
7260 Shadeland Station, Suite 100
Indianapolis, IN 46256-3945
Fax 317-596-5498

™

**BESTSELLING BOOK SERIES FROM IDG**